Barbara Frischmuth in Contemporary Context

Studies in Austrian Literature, Culture and Thought

Barbara Frischmuth in Contemporary Context

Edited by

Renate S. Posthofen

ARIADNE PRESS
Riverside, California

Library of Congress Cataloging-in-Publication Data

Barbara Frischmuth in contemporary context / edited by Renate S. Posthofen.

p. cm. -- (Studies in Austrian literature, culture, and thought.)

Includes bibliographical references and index.

ISBN 1-57241-054-X

1. Frischmuth, Barbara--Criticism and interpretation. 2. Frischmuth, Barbara--Interviews. 3. Authors, Austrian--20th century--Interviews. I. Posthofen, Renate S. II. Series.

PT2666.R558Z57 1999

833'.914--dc21

98-29033

CIP

Cover design:

Art Director & Designer: George McGinnis

by Ariadne Press

270 Goins Court

Riverside, CA 92507

Printed in the United States of America.

ISBN 1-57241-054-X

Dedicated to my children
Noah and Sohia Posthofen with much love!

Acknowledgments

I wish to thank my colleagues whose work is represented in this collection of articles. Some of them have been instrumental in assisting me to develop the profile for this volume at a very early stage in conjunction with Barbara Frischmuth's lecture tour through the U.S. and Canada in the Fall of 1996. Others joined the project at a later stage as they became aware of the volume's scope and parameters in relation to their own work and research interests. All of them have been generous with their time and efforts in contributing to the volume's rapid progress during the final editing phases.

Another person who has been central to this project is my copy editor Sabine Barcatta, who has devoted her untiring help and expertise to this book. She has gone beyond the call of duty to insure the consistency and quality of the overall manuscript in terms of style, footnoting, endnoting, and spelling. She has also insured the consistency between individual contributions and standardized the overall manuscript. She has worked overtime, on weekends, and through many nights to meet deadlines and get the book into its final form.

I am very much indebted to Diane Michelfelder, Department Head and Professor in the Department of Languages and Philosophy at Utah State University and Hans Mussler, Professor and Head of the German section in my Department for the arrangements they have helped make to see this project to completion. In addition, to the Department's financial assistance with the publication subsidy, the Research Quarter, and teaching-free time in the Winter of 1998, which they granted to me made it realistic to concentrate solely on this volume and devote all of my scholarly energies to it. Their untiring support of my academic pursuits and encouragement made it ultimately possible for me to realize this volume. Furthermore, I owe recognition and thanks to Peter Gerity, Vice President for Research at Utah State University for awarding a truly generous publication subsidy to fund the volume in its final stages.

My sincere appreciation and gratitude go to Barbara Frischmuth herself, who has been a constant source for advice, inspiration, and reliable feedback throughout the various stages of the project. She answered many inquiries and clarified many aspects during the editorial phases of this project. Her prompt and competent replies to my many inquiries via phone and FAX made it possible to solve not only complex questions but also helped clarify many aspects of her works and contributions, which she so willingly shared with me, and all of the contributors, and ultimately the readers of this volume. Donald Daviau, Jorun Johns, and Richard Lawson have been a constant source of advice, inspiration, and reliable feedback throughout the final stages of the project. I wish to thank them for their unequivocal commitment, as they provided a rigorous evaluation of the entire manuscript, helpful as well as constructive criticism, and most importantly their generous assistance to help produce a quality product in their function as the general editors of Ariadne Press.

Finally, I wish to thank my children Noah and Sophia Posthofen for their encouragement, patience, and undying love. We all sacrificed time together in order for the project to be completed. Their support, curiosity, and great sense of humor always remind me to share with them my passion for books, and critical inquiry. To Jennifer Michaels goes my deep gratitude for her continuous interest in the book as it unfolded in its various stages. She has shared with me countless insights into Frischmuth's work and nurtured this project with her commitment as a friend and mentor. Thank you!

Renate S. Posthofen
Utah State University

Barbara Frischmuth

©Jo Pesendorfer

CONTENTS

Introduction

Renate S. Posthofen

In the last decade, emerging paradigms of Austrian literature have been discussed and examined in the framework of late modern and postmodern trends. While a variety of such analyses has focused on themes and topics in the context of German-speaking literatures, this volume on the author Barbara Frischmuth contributes more specifically to the significance of her work in the larger contemporary literary sphere. It is the first work of its kind to be designed for English-speaking readers. The articles in this collection aim to provide new insights not only for scholars and students of Austrian and German literatures, but equally for those who are in the field of comparative literature and share an appreciation for world literatures. Thus, the goal to expand the current discussion and debate about Frischmuth's works and their international significance is accomplished by overcoming linguistic barriers. This volume is aimed at a global readership in order to reflect current concepts and evolving theories concerning global literature and the accompanying changing patterns of literary representation.

Working within the boundaries of German and English, with the constant need to cross and the occasional need even to merge these two languages, requires a great deal of imagination on the part of the scholar and translator. The essays in this volume reflect equally serious scholarship in conjunction with the art of translation, since all of the contributors represented in this volume have translated passages from the original German texts by Frischmuth into English in order to make their analyses and reflections accessible in their entirety. Most of the translations in the individual articles are as accurate as they are artistic and creative in their representation of the original Frischmuth texts.

With his publication of *Dossier 4: Barbara Frischmuth* in 1992,[1] Kurt Bartsch contributed to a heightened interest in Frischmuth's work by examining pertinent issues governing the reception and aesthetics of her literary œuvre. The collection of articles, essays, analyses, and book reviews in Bartsch's book provides a broad overview of her prose writings beginning with her first and acclaimed novel *Die Klosterschule* (1968; *The Convent School,* 1993).[2] The background for the critiques and book reviews in this volume is provided by including Frischmuth's biography as well as an extensive bibliography of her works. By providing an overview of her literary reception by her critics, Bartsch established a scholarly base from which further research could develop.

Prior to Bartsch's work on Frischmuth it was Donald Daviau who recognized the significance and growing importance of Frischmuth's œuvre for literary scholars and interested readers alike in the United States. Daviau wrote the first article on Frischmuth in English, introducing her to a US readership, which has a special interest in Austrian literature. In "Neuere Entwicklungen in der modernen österreichischen Prosa: Die Werke von Barbara Frischmuth" (1980, Recent Trends in Modern Austrian Prose: The Works of Barbara Frischmuth),[3] he emphasizes Frischmuth's skeptical attitude as it concerns the use of language as a medium for interpersonal communication and indoctrination. In addition, he demonstrates the development which Frischmuth as a writer has undergone since she wrote *Die Klosterschule.* Most noticeable is Frischmuth's trend away from the experimental use of language to her focus on social concerns, women's issues and the complexity of human relationships in general, while she orients herself more toward traditional literary paradigms. As early as in 1980 Daviau analyzed in this article the recurrent role of nature as an important and predominant theme in Frischmuth's texts, while simultaneously pointing to her interest in the genre of fairy tales and myths.[4] He concludes that Frischmuth's works are representative of the literary development that characterizes Austrian prose in the late 1960s and the 1970s. As the general editor for a collection of articles which focus on *Major Figures of Austrian Literature*,[5] published by Ariadne Press, Donald Daviau expanded his analysis of Frischmuth's works by including an article on Frischmuth in the first volume of this series entitled *Major Figures of Contemporary Austrian Literature*.[6] He points to her "increasing turn to reflectiveness" and stresses her "unique ability to combine her own fictional worlds, . . . with the real world.[7] As Daviau follows up on his committment to make Frischmuth's works accessible to her English-speaking readership, in his capacity as a leading literary critic in Austrian literature, he predicts her lasting reputation. As an educator he also explored the pedagogical dimension of Frischmuth's works in an article entitled "Barbara Frischmuth in the Classroom."[8] He recommends that certain texts by Frischmuth, whom he sees as "a leading spokesperson for women's emancipation,"[9] should even be included in undergraduate classes, since her topical issues are "relevant to young people today."[10] As one of "her strongest and most positive features" he sees her sensitive and balanced approach "to complex and controversial issues" in her writings.[11]

The growing scholarly interest in Frischmuth as a writer and culturally engaged intellectual led to more translations of her novels. At a time when New York publishers were reluctant to publish the translations of Frischmuth's works, Ariadne Press in California took on this task under the aegis of Donald Daviau, the general editor of the Press. These translations offer an additional opportunity for English-speaking readers to appreciate Frischmuth's writings. In addition to the 1993 translation of *Die Klosterschule*, two other translations of her prose have been published: the four stories that make up Frischmuth's *Haschen nach Wind* (1974) were translated as *Chasing after the Wind* in 1996.[12] These stories reveal Frischmuth's interest in women and women's issues, a theme which is also indirectly represented in subtle modes in her widely known novel *Das Verschwinden des Schattens in der Sonne* (1973), which has appeared recently as *The Shadow Disappears in the Sun* (1998). The multicultural dimensions of this biographical novel mix with gender specific observations relating to the narrator's position in Istanbul (Turkey). The narrator is a young female student of Oriental Studies who visits Istanbul to carry out research for her dissertation about the dervish order of the Bektashi.[13]

It is obvious that since the 1970s Frischmuth has demonstrated a growing concern for multiculturalism,[14] racial tensions, and ecological as well as political changes.[15] She addresses these issues not only in her novels for adults, but in her literary essays and prose for children as well. As mentioned above, she has become increasingly reflective about her own writing process. It was Paul Michael Lützeler who contributed to advancing the reception of her poetics by placing her lectures on poetics[16] in the larger context of contemporary aesthetics.[17] He had previously broken new ground by demonstrating how Frischmuth as a writer uses postmodern strategies to transform thematically conventional concepts into new modes of expression between tradition and innovation.[18] Subsequently Lützeler situated her reflections and essays on multiculturalism within the contemporary debate and was the first to stress the importance of Frischmuth's works in bridging the gap between late modern and postmodern concepts of thinking and writing. The primary focus of his investigation centers on the multicultural debate in contemporary German-speaking literatures that stresses the importance of consideration for multiple identities and intercultural awareness.[19]

The present collection of articles builds on Lützeler's work by combining the singular focus on one author with the correlated concept of creating a contemporary context and discourse within which the specific analyses are situated. The essays here employ comparative methods as well as intertextual models of interpretation in order to create a broad thematic spectrum within which particular aspects of Frischmuth's works are discussed. In some of the contributions Frischmuth's work is seen as one singular element and partial expression of postwar Austrian literature as a whole.

The overall discussion of Frischmuth's place in postwar Austrian literary history has yet to explore fully the creative constellation and socioliterary background within which Frischmuth functions as an author. Except for her limited involvement with the Forum Stadtpark in Graz, "the group of young, anti-establishment literary rebels" and activists influential in the 1960s,[20] Frischmuth has always refused to align herself with such literary groups as the *Wiener Gruppe* (Vienna Group). Her life and work outside most established literary centers and paradigms leads to yet other important questions regarding the critical reception of her works in Austria and the challenges they pose for their readers. An example of this discourse about Frischmuth's reception and subsequent career as an author can be found in *Bruchlinien* (1995, Fraction Lines) by Wendelin Schmidt-Dengler.[21] The book emerged out of university lectures that he gave at the University of Vienna during the years 1982 and 1994. His main intention was to provide a basis for discussion about this period of Austrian literature with a special consideration for future teachers.[22] Schmidt-Dengler readily admits that the choices of texts he discussed in his lectures and subsequently included in this volume could by their very nature not be comprehensive in the sense of a complete presentation of all the authors and texts from the period between 1945 and 1990. He is also equally aware of the fact that his mode of selection constitutes a rather exclusive concept of representation. It is ultimately problematic though that a leading scholar admits to and consciously reaffirms the exclusive value of the traditional literary canon. That he includes Austrian women writers such as Ingeborg Bachmann, Elfriede Jelinek, and Friederike Mayröcker in his volume deserves special mention, since it is important to note that Schmidt-Dengler affirms an established pattern of literary reception. Frischmuth, whose works he does not include in his book, has to some degree either been unduly overlooked or — as is the case with Schmidt-Dengler and other critics who have neglected to include her works in the traditional literary forum — has consciously not been given the importance that her fictional and nonfictional texts deserve, as will be shown in this introduction and the following contributions.

If one were to rewrite the literary history of Austrian literature with a specific focus on the contributions that women writers have made, it is likely that Frischmuth would be a central figure in such an approach. Specifically within the context of transforming and redefining the literary center and its margins,[23] this volume intends to expand the literary and scholarly discussion about Frischmuth. In terms of her literary significance Frischmuth serves as an important link between the first and second generation of postwar Austrian women writers, for she combines classical and conventional approaches to literary themes with postmodern textual strategies. As she continues to participate in the Austrian cultural and literary sphere, she will appeal to a broader readership as an advocate for children's, women's, and environmental issues alike.

The new global trend focusing on postcolonial, feminist, and postmodern discourses and modes of literary representation has as one result developed a growing interest in literature written by women in, among many other places, contemporary Austria. In an anthology entitled *Die bessere Hälfte, Österreichische Literatur von Frauen seit 1848* (1995, The Better Half, Austrian Literature by Women since 1848),[24] Christa Gürtler and Sigrid Schmid offer representative texts and poems created by seventy Austrian women authors. Frischmuth's "Vom Leben des Pierrot" (About the Life of Pierrot),[25] an excerpt from her collection of stories entitled *Vom Leben des Pierrot* (1982),[26] touches on the problematic relationship between Pierrot and Colombina, two imaginary figures who have a close personal encounter in an artistic environment resembling that of a circus on tour. The story offers an example of the fantasylike and reality-oriented atmosphere within which the two protagonists are oscillating. The short text demonstrates Frischmuth's narrative fluidity, her willingness to navigate between male and female viewpoints, between the poetic world of fairy tales, surrealism, and a reality characterized by constant movement along with change symbolized by the traveling vagrants. The goal of Gürtler and Schmid, as they declare in their introduction, is to feature texts and poems containing poetic and literary innovations in terms of their new and creative use of language. They focus on texts that enrich the literary canon by adding new dimensions partially based on formal and contextualized linguistic experiments.

Issues of change and innovation, the dichotomy between the foreign and the indigenous in light of recognizing the modes of literary expression that explore the experience of difference and alterity are becoming increasingly essential in recognizing a broader spectrum of literary trends, here with the specific focus on Austria.[27] In the anthology entitled *Out from the Shadows, Essays on Contemporary Austrian Women Writers and Filmmakers* (1997),[28] this focal shift to an interest in issues governing authorship from the margins has found one important forum besides other newly surfacing ones. With the gender-specific approach of this anthology in mind Pamela Saur contributed an article about Barbara Frischmuth's Demeter trilogy that elaborates on Frischmuth's creative ability to fuse together mythological dimensions and fantastic elements within the expanding boundaries of an evolving story line about women's lives, structured according to principles governing the realist mode of narration.[29] By placing Frischmuth's trilogy in the context of contemporary feminist issues and by analyzing her narrative strategies in terms of their multivalence and flexibility, Saur demonstrates in this and in a previous article how Frischmuth's dynamic mode of composition contributes successfully to the aesthetic complexity of these texts.[30]

With the body of essays in *Out from the Shadows, Essays on Contemporary Austrian Women Writers and Filmmakers*, it becomes increasingly evident that the literary works and films created by women authors have greatly enriched the Austrian cultural scene since 1945. Thus it is clear that sensitive scholars whose works contribute to the transformation of the traditional canon need to concern themselves continuously in every way with the literary contributions made by women writers. This focus will ultimately bring about the changes necessary to expand the traditional core of established literary works into a body of texts that includes lesser known authors and their experiences and literary expressions. Those writers who have emerged from the margins to be assigned a more visible location within the changing canon are now assuming a pivotal role as agents for change. Their reflections, values, and experiences of difference are contributing to changing the traditional paradigms of literary expressions.

With these considerations in mind, the following essays illustrate the broad range of topics and themes found in the expanding scholarship about Barbara Frischmuth. The variety of her œuvre is reflected in the range of the individual contributions, which include examinations of single fictional texts and essays, her role as an author of radio plays, her various interviews which contain her personal reflections on her theoretical literary essays, and her interest in multiculturalism.

The context of her novels and radio plays is examined in terms of the multicultural and multinational issues informing Frischmuth's thought and literature and the identities inscribed therein. Her works are positioned among similar ones by female authors of Austrian as well as German origin and examined in the context of contemporary German-speaking literature.

The aesthetics of selected prose writings are analyzed, and Frischmuth's thematic emphasis on literary traditions that cross boundaries are illustrated in several contributions. An additional focus on her most recent essays dealing with Austrian cultural politics provides further insight into her commitment as an engaged writer concerned with societal and political change and with the attempt to bridge the cultural gaps between different ethnic identities within the German-speaking locales of Europe.

This collection of essays concentrates not only on new approaches to selected prose writings and theoretical texts by Frischmuth but also on the discourse of change and transition in most of her literary works and theoretical writings. It contributes to a deeper understanding of the dynamics of her overall literary production and her essays on cultural as well as political issues by including the comparative dimension. The articles illustrate her versatility in the context of postmodern concepts of writing and thinking. Barbara Frischmuth has successfully managed to position herself on the literary horizon in Austria as a writer particularly concerned with sincere communication and a true focus on change in consciousness in order to be open to the next century and its many challenges. She represents not only past and present literary voices and themes, but also reflects a true concern for the future in its social, ecological, multicultural, and literary dimension from a woman writer's point of view.

The individual articles, grouped here by their particular thematic approach to the topic, address each of these aspects. Dagmar C. G. Lorenz elaborates on the central role that Austrian women writers have played "in shaping Austrian literature at home and abroad." She makes her observations and analyses in the context of literary history and the historical context of the Second Republic from the perspective of Ilse Aichinger, Ingeborg Bachmann, Marlen Haushofer, and Barbara Frischmuth. With the focus on Frischmuth and the women protagonists in her Sternwieser trilogy, Lorenz points out that Frischmuth "creates a discursive space to accommodate emancipated Austrian women." She concludes that Frischmuth does not write from the marginal position of an outsider. Instead, she favors a moderate point of view from within the societal margins that allows for cautious negotiation of the gender gap, offering equitable solutions for both men and women. All of these Austrian women writers — Aichinger, Bachmann, Haushofer, and Frischmuth — however different their perspectives, broadened the basis for literary expression by combining a wealth of personal experiences with innovative textual strategies and narrative approaches to keep the past and a continued critical as well as individual memory of it alive.

Gisela Roethke's article entitled "Barbara Frischmuth's Novel *Einander Kind*: Fifty Years after the Takeover of the Nazis in Austria" focuses on Frischmuth's treatment of the past in that novel. By contextualizing the historical, political, and autobiographical dimensions of the text, Roethke explains that the Waldheim scandal in 1986 and the fifty-year commemoration of Austria's annexation to Germany in 1988 provided the external impetus for Frischmuth to revisit "the topic of Austria's Nazi past." She points out that on the literary level of *Einander Kind* (1990), Frischmuth's use of the myth of Demeter and Persephone reveals her focus on the complex past and its different layers. Frischmuth's search "for a countermyth and a new literary form that would correspond to her ethos of mutual care and parenting one another" leads her to superimpose her version of the actualized myth on the novel's plot, which is centered around the ancestral hometown of the Schwarz family. Roethke shows how Frischmuth merges the myth with the novel and embeds both in Austrian history. Frischmuth constructs a true historical dimension in the text by exposing the all-pervasive patriarchal structures and the Nazi period as they relate to the fate of the Schwarz family.

Gerlinde Ulm Sanford's study, the first of its kind, focuses on a contextualized analysis of selected children's books by Frischmuth, who engages in many linguistic as well as narrative experiments and applies various poetic devices that are not only demanding, but also lead young readers to sharpen their sensitivity to the many dimensions of language. As a result children might learn to discern between literal and figurative meanings of idioms or proverbs and might delight in repeating alliterating rhymes. Ulm Sanford concludes that Frischmuth's stories are "modern" in the best sense while alerting her readers to such important issues as the endangered environment and equality among all creatures. Furthermore, Frischmuth avoids didactic tones and is able to defend women's rights without being aggressive; she subverts traditional gender roles by reversing them. Her texts for children are humorous in their many nuances and subtle in their messages, which already at this early stage for readers emphasize the overall need for tolerance and fairness in human interactions, a recurrent theme in most of Frischmuth's texts.

With her focus on crosscultural and transnational representations, Jennifer Michaels shows that Frischmuth's interest in other cultures runs throughout her œuvre. On the basis of the novel *Das Verschwinden des Schattens in der Sonne*, Michaels analyzes Frischmuth's thematic treatment of two different cultural paradigms: the different Muslim cultures in Turkey versus the Central European (Christian) traditions that have shaped her own and the narrator's viewpoint. Michaels emphasizes Frischmuth's expertise in Orientalism, including Oriental mysticism as well as traditional Oriental literatures — a source for her engagement as an informed mediator between these cultures. She has a cautiously optimistic outlook on the mutual recognition of cultural differences. Given Frischmuth's scholarly background, including her fluency in the Turkish language — contextualized in this essay as well — it is clear how her firsthand knowledge of Turkey and its Islamic traditions enables her to provide the reader with many examples which demonstrate "that different cultures can approach each other with warmth and respect."

Cultural identity and communication are also featured in Edith Toegel's article, in which she touches on the various ways in which "Frischmuth's prose reflects her Austrian heritage." Toegel points to Frischmuth's unequivocal and critical commitment and continued interest in Austria, noticeable in her writings and the autobiographical aspect of her works. She examines just how Frischmuth envisions Austrian cultural identity in her more recent literary works from the late 1980s and 1990s. Toegel concludes that the sense of home (*Heimat*) that emerges from Frischmuth's works is closely linked to that of a particular cultural identity. Both are connected to a specific place, "a place of local, anecdotal, and personal significance; a place where colloquial and vernacular speech reflect its uniqueness and singularity." These distinct geobiographical markers and the obvious linguistic specificity make it clear that Frischmuth's fiction and indeed the entire body of literary works contribute greatly to the particular distinctions not only "between postwar Austrian and German national identities," but also, as a consequence, between those national literatures.

In a pioneering effort Johannes Evelein examines Barbara Frischmuth's radio plays (*Hörspiele*) in the context of their spatial dimensions. He selects three radio plays representative of both the genre and

Frischmuth's own radio plays. He discusses their commonalities and thematic approaches. *Die unbekannte Hand* (1970, The Unknown Hand), *Binnengespräche* (1984, Inner Conversations), and *Eine Liebe in Erzurum* (1994, A Love in Erzurum) reflect Frischmuth's social as well as ethical, moral, and ecological responsibility as a writer. Despite the obvious thematic differences, as Evelein argues, the plays have in common "the problematized interaction between the characters and their surroundings, a dysfunctionality of the protagonists caused by their disharmonious, dualistic position taken against the space in which they reside." Evelein's article deepens the understanding of Barbara Frischmuth as a versatile author of radio plays in the context of modern media, crossing the bounds between genres, cultures, and countries to engage with her audience in an ongoing dialogue to share her thoughts about contemporary Europe and the emerging politics of mutual recognition.

Relegated to the aural dimension, but connected to a powerful process of distribution via public broadcast — reaching a more diverse audience than do books in general — are Frischmuth's radio interviews, a means she uses to elaborate on her strategies and her responsibilities as a writer and engaged intellectual. In a number of transcribed interviews from 1994 to January 1997 Frischmuth provides firsthand insights into her poetics, her contributions to and her understanding of the process of creative writing, and her use of myth in selected prose texts. Evelein edited and introduced the interview given by Frischmuth during her reading tour in the fall of 1996 at the local studio of KUSU — FM Utah Public Radio in Logan, Utah on October 4, 1996. The interview was conducted by Lee Austin, radio host for the program "Etcetera" on the occasion of Frischmuth's visit to the Utah State University campus. In "On Language, Writing, and Crossing Borders" Frischmuth explains her interest in people who cross borders and discusses the importance that literature "more than any other discipline" plays in helping people to overcome their limitations and to counteract their stereotyping and prejudices. Her interest in the borders of language and in crosscultural communication is reflected in her own travels throughout her life and her interest in Islam, Orientalism, and mysticism as well as in the way she uses language in her prose. Subsequently she discusses some of her works and their autobiographical dimensions, the dichotomies between "real life characters" and their literary transformations as well as her convictions and agenda as a "naturally born feminist" as they relate to her literary approach and treatment of gender issues.

A primary theme of Frischmuth's work explores the world of children, a theme which Ulm Sanford takes up among others in her interview "From a Meeting with Barbara Frischmuth" in December of 1996. In creating appropriate books for children, Frischmuth explains her use of language and illustrations. As to the autobiographical dimension of her children's books, Frischmuth explains that she writes them not so much for other children as for the child within her, the child she once was herself. In the context of her most recent children's book, *Donna & Dario* (1997, Donna & Dario)[31] — a story about different free-roaming animals who live in a city in an animal state and deal with the basic ideas of our civilization — and with regard to the integration of animals in her children's books who have "gained access to human communication," Frischmuth reflects on her thoughts as a writer on the self-emerging question of morality. Other issues raised in the interview include Frischmuth's perspective on the Turkish population in Austria and Germany and their integration into society as well as her attitude toward the European Union. She ends the interview explaining her position as an author, feminist, and creative writer in light of family issues that have proved formative for her, including her observations about children and art as well as her role as a mother.

When Gisela Roethke interviewed Barbara Frischmuth in the spring of 1994, she focused on Frischmuth's use of the Demeter and Persephone topos in her works. Frischmuth elaborates on the lasting impression that Hermann Broch's Demeter novel made on her and on the developments that led to her own transformation and adaptation of the Demeter myth. Her primary interest is the cultural connection and context within which the myth is embedded. Approaching this adaptation of an archaic myth from the experimental side, Frischmuth notes that myths vary and thus provide the possiblity of adding several new dimensions to a text. As to her own Demeter trilogy, she points to myth as a way to complement history and politics. She also sees its creative potential for her as a women writer who designs her own history/story, almost like carrying out genealogical research. For her, "it is less important that one starts prescribing something again." That is why, for instance, in her novel *Über die Verhältnisse* (1987, Beyond One's Means) she dwells on such multivalent elements as role reversals and emerging relationships. In all three interviews in this volume it becomes clear that Frischmuth does not want to be labeled as either a writer, a mother, or a feminist per se but rather sees herself not bound by special limitations in any one direction.

As a result of this individualist and nondogmatic approach to life, Frischmuth explains how her protagonists, too, are created as complex and multilayered characters in a world that allows and leaves room for constant transformations and movements.

On the occasion of her recent lecture tour through the United States and Canada as part of the commemoration of Austria's millennium, Frischmuth gave a talk at the annual German Studies Association meeting in Seattle on October 12, 1996. As one of the keynote speakers, she devoted her address to Friedrich Rückert (1788–1866), a nineteenth-century Islamicist and professor of Oriental languages who translated part of the Koran.[32] She introduced Rückert to the audience by describing his artistic imagination that enabled him to experiment with language and to create linguistic innovations which to this date remain unsurpassed in quality and originality — much like his translation of the Koran. Frischmuth then pointed to his love for literature, which truly fascinated him and led him to develop a strong interest in Islamic art and literature. She described Rückert's translations in the context of the widespread interest in Muslim literature and the Orient in German-speaking countries in the late eighteenth and early nineteenth centuries. In stark contrast to this earlier cultural exchange with the Orient is the present situation, characterized to a large degree by "the invisibility of Muslim culture in German literature." Frischmuth feels that Rückert has been unduly forgotten. Since he was a dedicated mediator of Islamic culture, he can be seen as a predecessor to contemporary border crossers between Eastern and Western cultures.[33]

The contribution of Gerald Chapple analyzes Frischmuth's most recent short prose collection *Hexenherz* (1994, Heart of a Witch), which is more structured than her previous volumes. He focuses largely on formal elements and briefly analyzes the thirteen stories that pivot around the middle one, entitled "Wild-Frau" (Witch of the Wildwood).[34] This story about a hunter and his secret lover is the central tale and main narrative axis of the collection. Chapple concludes his examination with a detailed analysis of "Wild-Frau" and the powerful finale, "Das Lachen des Dalai Lama" (The Laughter of the Dalai Lama). His analysis describes how these particular stories by Frischmuth reveal her craft in detail and show the workings of the controlling metaphor signaled by the volume's title, while she uses the principle of doubling and pairing stories as a central organizational theme for this short prose collection.

Peter Arnds also takes a comparative approach to show certain similarities between Robert Menasse's *Selige Zeiten, brüchige Welt* (1991, Blissful Times, Fragmentary World) and Barbara Frischmuth's *Über die Verhältnisse*. He investigates the ways in which both authors frequently transform their experiences of living and traveling abroad in their literary texts in order to confront their readers with a presentation of divergent cultures. Arnds demonstrates that both Frischmuth and Menasse combine their goal of a stronger multicultural presence in literature by reinscribing traditional literary constellations. The novels share a similar pattern "with regard to the role / rule of the mother in Austria and the patriarchal structure in the foreign setting" in Brazil and Turkey. Arnds observes that this two-dimensional relationship between matriarchy and patriarchy is transformed into a three-dimensional relationship as both authors also adapt Greek mythology. Both authors essentially matriarchalize the original myth of Oedipus and Demeter, by "empowering the mother figure and a matriarchal figure of the next generation" as they destabilize patriarchal structures on the fictional level. He concludes that Menasse and Frischmuth are ultimately able to bring Austria, Turkey, and Brazil closer together as they successfully transcend the boundaries of Austria in favor of expanding multicultural considerations.

Ingo Stoehr illustrates other contrasts as well as similarities in texts by Karin Struck, Christa Wolf, and Barbara Frischmuth. He establishes the commonalities among the narrative strategies of these texts and the existing patriarchal structures in our Western societies. He uses his premise of the connection between patriarchy and addiction while employing a comparative approach to *Bitteres Wasser* (1988, Bitter Water) by Karin Struck, *Kassandra* (1983, Cassandra) by Christa Wolf, and *Die Frau im Mond* (1982, The Woman in the Moon) by Barbara Frischmuth. By dethroning the patriarchs on the literary level, these writers unmask in their own ways the dual patriarchal system in society that is characterized by power on the one side and by addiction on the other side. As alternative models, these three writers offer innovative solutions to open the avenues for new concepts in the literary dialogue between men and women. With the specific focus on Frischmuth, Stoehr asserts that, contrary to Struck and Wolf, Frischmuth uses a utopian model to explore the future in her novel *Die Frau im Mond*. She shares with Wolf the belief that historically speaking the rule of "patriarchy meant the end to the female principle." Unlike Wolf, however, who focuses on a rational analysis, Frischmuth uses elements of fantasy to oppose and escape a reality void of affection and emotion. She uses the subversive power of love between the protagonists to assert the need for the necessary changes in society to render her creative version of hope for a better world.

Monika Shafi also undertakes a comparative approach. She relates the perspective of Anna Mitgutsch to Barbara Frischmuth, examining the theme of home and displacement in two of their contemporary novels. First, she refers to the biographical parallels between Frischmuth and Mitgutsch, who share similar experiences of having lived abroad at different times during their lives. By comparing Frischmuth's *Das Verschwinden des Schattens in der Sonne* and Mitgutsch's *In fremden Städten* (1992; *In Foreign Cities*, 1995), Shafi shows the plot similarity. Both novels focus on female protagonists who deal with the fear of losing their own sense of identity as they participate in and observe the other culture at the same time. Shafi concludes that both protagonists attempt to seek and find a mystical union, a true integration of self and world, which proves to be utopian to varying degrees. In addition, she comments on the examples of intercultural encounters in both texts. Frischmuth's narrator as well as her allegorical style ultimately expose "the limits of Western ways of knowledge and logic." At the same time, the protagonist is able to experience a close encounter with the other culture by synthesizing important elements of both cultural traditions and transcending this knowledge as she begins to feel at home in more universal terms. According to Shafi, Mitgutsch's protagonist is configured more along the lines of a clinical case study, feeling ultimately excluded from both cultures, her own and the foreign, as she succumbs to her ontological homelessness and commits suicide, unable to close the gap between the resident and the alien part of her displaced existence and experience.

With continued emphasis on gender issues and postcolonial discourse, Dagmar C. G. Lorenz's examination of "Orientalism and the Women's Perspective in Barbara Frischmuth's novel *Das Verschwinden des Schattens in der Sonne*" adds a different point of view to the interpretations of this text. Lorenz elaborates on the strategies that Frischmuth uses to portray the world of Islam, which she thematizes in her novel. By using Edward Said's seminal *Orientalism* study (1978) as her theoretical underpinning, Lorenz draws attention to what she claims are Frischmuth's biased ways of *representing* other cultures. Lorenz introduces a new reading in concluding that Frischmuth's text is neither innovative nor truly mediating "between German-speaking and Turkish, Christian, and Islamic" cultures. Instead, she points to examples and portrayals in the novel that confirm time-honored clichés; she asserts that the text discusses "only superficial contacts between members of Eastern and Western cultures." To her, the novel lacks the complexity that would be needed to explore promising "avenues of negotiating cultural discourses." Consequently Lorenz does not see Frischmuth's novel as a vehicle for change, but rather as an example of the established Western mode of narration, reproducing the traditional Western image of the Orient by employing a biased position from her occidental perspective.

In her article entitled "Ecological Aspects of Barbara Frischmuth's Sternwieser Trilogy," Julie Klassen points to her essentially biocentric views that invite the insights of ecological literary study. In the theoretical context of ecocriticism and ecofeminism, Frischmuth's Sternwieser trilogy is a prominent example of the literary strategies she uses to portray the interconnectedness among and between all peoples, creatures, and things. A close reading of these texts makes it evident that Frischmuth's trademark, the creative and superimposed use of myth and imagination, is the basis of her own literary identity as well as that of her oscillating protagonists. She examines the expanding ecological dimension of women in the Sternwieser trilogy and their ways to realize their true potential to give "a more inclusive grounding to the feminist venture." Subsequently Klassen represents Frischmuth "as a present-day agent to communicate insights that might help save the world" and cites as an example Frischmuth's calling for "the biocentric imperative for partnership" as a literary as well as ecological strategy for survival.

Issues regarding women's emancipation and the equality of gender are also central to Rhonda Duffaut's article. With the focus on female writing and feminine aesthetics, she shows how Frischmuth's "feminine dream" has been an integral part of her work since she made her literary debut. Using her lectures on poetics and her collection of stories *Mörderische Märchen und andere Erzählungen* (1989, Deadly Fairy Tales and Other Stories) as well as *Geschichten für Stanek* (1969, Stories for Stanek) as the basis of her investigation, Duffaut asserts that the key components of Frischmuth's dream center around three important and recurrent concepts: aspects of motherhood, women's imaginative powers, and the challenge to overcome the threat of silence. Despite this challenge, Frischmuth has been able to maintain the presence of women in literature through the very act of her own writing and the creative narrative of her female protagonists. The imaginative elements particular to this kind of feminine aesthetic close in on the discrepancy and mutual exclusiveness of motherhood and creative writing. By stressing the consistencies in Frischmuth's work, Duffaut concludes that she "continues to pursue sociocultural aspects that underscore the socialization of gender roles, especially those of women."

Robert Weigel contributes to the investigation of Frischmuth's lectures on poetics through his careful and thought-provoking examination of her ethical discourse, its grounding in her aesthetic creativity, and the dimensions of her utopian model in *Traum der Literatur — Literatur des Traums* (1991, Dream of Literature — Literature of the Dream). His study rounds out this collection of essays in that he acknowledges Frischmuth's position within the contemporary discourse as it concerns literary theory and illustrates certain affinities to postmodern thought. He points to her multilingualism and her ongoing advocacy of a peaceful coexistence of many languages and peoples. For Frischmuth, language is an important medium to explore "the other" and as a result, she sees literatures as instrumental in transporting and mediating multicultural messages. His essay emphasizes Frischmuth's originality and her refreshing look at literature, by stressing the enjoyment and playful pleasure it can provide, as well as its connection with the world of dreams and its mythological dimension.

I would like to conclude with a look toward the future by mentioning Frischmuth's latest novel, *Die Schrift des Freundes* (1998, The Writing of the Friend).[35] This text focuses on multiculturalism and on issues that are central to new ways of reevaluating peaceful coexistence and mutual recognition in a global context at the beginning of yet another century. With this new novel, dealing with the Turkish population in Austria and Germany as well as with Islamic mysticism, Frischmuth encourages us once more to bridge and overcome the gaps between traditional binary oppositions that mark off the foreign and the self. She invites her readers to cross the borders and boundaries in their own minds as they travel with her through the imaginary landscape of her text, which serves as an illustration of her sensitive and hopeful way of looking on the emerging changes in a transforming and increasingly inclusive society. Frischmuth's newest literary contribution to this discourse related to inclusive and open ways of thinking and societal changes will no doubt provide a forum for more discussion about literature as a basis for cultural changes and transformations as we approach the new millennium.[36]

Utah State University

Notes

1. Kurt Bartsch, ed., *Dossier 4: Barbara Frischmuth* (Graz: Droschl, 1992).

2. Barbara Frischmuth: *Die Klosterschule* (Frankfurt/Main: Suhrkamp, 1968); trans. as *The Convent School* by Gerald C. Chapple and James B. Lawson (Riverside, CA: Ariadne, 1993).

3. Donald G. Daviau, "Neuere Entwicklungen in der modernen österreichischen Prosa: Die Werke von Barbara Frischmuth," *Modern Austrian Literature*, special issue 13.1 (1980): 177–216.

4. Donald G. Daviau, "Neuere Entwicklungen in der modernen österreichischen Prosa: Die Werke von Barbara Frischmuth" 203–213.

5. This series includes the following titles to date: Donald G. Daviau, ed., *Major Figures of Modern Austrian Literature* (Riverside, CA: Ariadne, 1988); Donald G. Daviau, ed., *Major Figures of Turn-Of-The-Century Austriam Literature* (Riverside, CA: Ariadne, 1991); Donald G. Daviau, ed., *Major Figures of Austrian Literature : The Interwar Years 1918–1938* (Riverside, CA: Ariadne, 1995); Donald G. Daviau, ed., *Major Figures of Nineteenth-Century Austrian Literature* (Riverside, CA: Ariadne, 1998).

6. Donald G. Daviau, ed., *Major Figures of Contemporary Austrian Literature* (New York: Peter Lang, 1987), "Barbara Frischmuth" 185–206.

7. Donald G. Daviau, ed., *Major Figures of Contemporary Austrian Literature*), "Barbara Frischmuth" 202.

8. Donald G. Daviau, "Barbara Frischmuth in the Classroom," *Österreich in amerikanischer Sicht: Das Österreichbild im amerikanischen Schulunterricht* 4 (1988): 2–9.

9. Donald G. Daviau, "Barbara Frischmuth in the Classroom," *Österreich in amerikanischer Sicht: Das Österreichbild im amerikanischen Schulunterricht* 3.

10. Donald G. Daviau, "Barbara Frischmuth in the Classroom," *Österreich in amerikanischer Sicht: Das Österreichbild im amerikanischen Schulunterricht* 2.

11. Donald G. Daviau, "Barbara Frischmuth in the Classroom," *Österreich in amerikanischer Sicht: Das Österreichbild im amerikanischen Schulunterricht* 7.

12. Barbara Frischmuth, *Haschen nach Wind* (Salzburg: Residenz, 1974); trans. as *Chasing after the Wind: Four Stories* by Gerald Chapple

Chapple and James B. Lawson (Riverside, CA: Ariadne, 1996).

13. Barbara Frischmuth, *Das Verschwinden des Schattens in der Sonne* (Frankfurt/Main: Suhrkamp, 1973); trans. as *The Shadow Disappears in the Sun* by Nicholas Meyerhofer (Riverside, CA: Ariadne, 1998).

14. As an example see Barbara Frischmuth, "Der Blick über den Zaun," *Schreiben zwischen den Kulturen: Beiträge zur deutschsprachigen Gegenwartsliteratur*, ed. Paul Michael Lützeler (Frankfurt/Main: Fischer, 1996): 19–27; trans. as "Looking over the Fence" by Lisabeth Hock, *Multiculturalism in Contemporary German Literature*, special issue of *World Literature Today* 69.3 (Summer 1995): 459–62.

15. As an example see Barbara Frischmuth, "Europa, das ich meine," *Literatur und Kritik* 305/306 (Juli 1996): 46–59.

16. Barbara Frischmuth, *Traum der Literatur — Literatur des Traums: Münchner Poetik-Vorlesungen* (Salzburg: Residenz, 1991).

17. Paul Michael Lützeler, "Ethik, Traum und Lust: Barbara Frischmuth, Traum der Literatur — Literatur des Traums," *Poetik der Autoren: Beiträge zur deutschsprachigen Gegenwartsliteratur,* ed. Paul Michael Lützeler (Frankfurt/Main: Fischer, 1994): 295–310. A revised version of this article was recently published as "Traum und Ethik: Barbara Frischmuths Poetikvorlesung," *Klio oder Kalliope? Literatur und Geschichte: Sondierung, Analyse, Interpretation,* by Paul Michael Lützeler (Berlin: Erich Schmidt, 1997): 158–69.

18. With the specific focus on Frischmuth's Demeter trilogy in the context of mythological and historical concepts, he contributed an article: Paul Michael Lützeler, "Barbara Frischmuths Demeter-Trilogie: Mythologische Finde-Spiele in der postmodernen Literatur," *Dossier 4: Barbara Frischmuth* 73–97. A revised version of this article was recently published as "Mythos und Geschichte: Barbara Frischmuths 'Demeter'-Trilogie," *Klio oder Kalliope?:* 133–49.

19. Paul Michael Lützeler, "Einleitung," *Schreiben zwischen den Kulturen: Beiträge zur deutschsprachigen Gegenwartsliteratur*, ed. Paul Michael Lützeler (Frankfurt/Main: Fischer, 1996): 7–18; trans. as "Introduction," *Multiculturalism in Contemporary German Literature*, special issue of *World Literature Today* 69.3 (Summer 1995): 453–58.

20. Gerald Chapple, "Rescuing the Child Within," *Austria Kultur* 6.5 (1996): 12–13. Quote from page 12. The text is a very short and concise summary of Frischmuth's works and accomplishments for a lay readership.

21. Wendelin Schmidt-Dengler, *Bruchlinien: Vorlesungen zur österreichischen Literatur 1945 bis 1990* (Salzburg: Residenz, 1995).

22. Schmidt-Dengler, "Ein kleines Avant-propos," *Bruchlinien:* 5–7.

23. Dagmar C. G. Lorenz and Renate S. Posthofen, eds., *Transforming the Center, Eroding the Margins: Essays on Ethnic and Cultural Boundaries in German-Speaking Countries* (Columbia, SC: Camden House, 1998).

24. Christa Gürtler and Sigrid Schmid, ed., *Die bessere Hälfte: Österreichische Literatur von Frauen seit 1848* (Salzburg: Otto Müller, 1995).

25. Barbara Frischmuth, "Vom Leben des Pierrot," *Die bessere Hälfte:* 341–47.

26. Barbara Frischmuth, *Vom Leben des Pierrot: Erzählungen* (1982; repr., Pfaffenweiler: Pfaffenweiler, 1989).

27. Another recent publication focuses on literary contributions by women from a geobiographical perspective: Barbara Neuwirth, ed., *Schriftstellerinnnen sehen ihr Land: Österreich aus dem Blick seiner Autorinnen* (Vienna: Wiener Frauenverlag, 1995).

28. Margarete Lamb-Faffelberger, ed., *Out from the Shadows: Essays on Contemporary Austrian Women Writers and Filmmakers* (Riverside, CA: Ariadne, 1997).

29. Pamela S. Saur, "Barbara Frischmuth's Use of Mythology in her Demeter Trilogy," *Out from the Shadows:* 101–10.

30. Pamela S. Saur, "A Feminist Reading of Barbara Frischmuth's Trilogy," *Modern Austrian Literature* 23.3/4 (1990): 167–78.

31. Barbara Frischmuth, *Donna & Dario* (Frankfurt/Main: Sauerländer, 1997).

32. Barbara Frischmuth, "Verrückt wie Rückert," *Neue deutsche Literatur: Monatsschrift für Literatur und Kritik* 45.513 (May-June 1997): 195–200.

33. The original German lecture was translated into English by Gerald Chapple and James B. Lawson, two experts on Frischmuth's œuvre. Having translated two of Frischmuth's books and published three of her stories in English, they have both been instrumental in introducing Frischmuth to her English-speaking audience. (The three published stories include Barbara Frischmuth, "Auf mich kannst du dich verlassen," *Protokolle* 1 (1981): 77–79; repr. in *Traumgrenze: Erzählungen* [Salzburg: Residenz, 1983]: 71–77; trans. as "I Am Somebody You Can Count On" by Gerald Chapple and James B. Lawson and published in *Southern*

Humanities Review 29.3 [Summer 1995]: 267–70; Barbara Frischmuth, "Wild-Frau," *Hexenherz: Erzählungen* [Salzburg: Residenz, 1994]: 96–104; trans. by Gerald Chapple and James B. Lawson as "Witch of the Wildwood" and published in *The Malahat Review* 118 [Spring 1997]: 16–22; Barbara Frischmuth, "Das Wasser der Liebe," *Mörderische Märchen* [Salzburg: Residenz, 1989]: 7–12; repr. as paperback: *Mörderische Märchen* [Munich: dtv, 1992]: 9–13; trans. as "The Waters of Love" by Gerald Chapple and James B. Lawson and published in *Dimension²* 4.2 [May 1997]: 244–51.)

34. Barbara Frischmuth, "Wild-Frau," *Hexenherz: Erzählungen* 96–104.

35. Barbara Frischmuth, *Die Schrift des Freundes* (Salzburg: Residenz, 1998).

36. See also Paul Michael Lützeler's favorable review of this novel: "Ein Derwisch verschwindet," *Die Zeit*, 27. August 1998: 48.

Alien Homeland: The Second Republic from the Perspective of Austrian Women Authors Aichinger, Bachmann, Haushofer, and Frischmuth

Dagmar C. G. Lorenz

Among the most frequently noted differences between the postwar Federal Republic of Germany and Austria are the attitudes toward the Nazi past, evident from official policies and critical discussions. The apocalyptic stance taken by German writers vis-à-vis the end of World War II, the so-called Point Zero, was virtually absent from Austrian discourses. In "Rede unter dem Galgen" (1949, Speech under the Gallows), Ilse Aichinger, herself a victim of Nazi persecution, cautioned, among other things, against the *Kahlschlag* (clear-cutting) advocated by the (predominantly West German) postwar critics and authors proclaiming the so-called Point Zero, the *Stunde Null.* To her, the concept of a radically new beginning after 1945, programmatically proclaimed by West German authors of the postwar era, required an attitude of greater certainty than the survivors of a cataclysmic war were able to muster.[1] Many of the German postwar authors were veterans, including Hans-Werner Richter, Wolfgang Borchert, and Heinrich Böll. In contrast to their either deliberately bombastic or heroic end-time rhetoric, Aichinger's emotional early prose texts suggest that the task at hand was returning to normal life. To Aichinger, the return to normalcy is by far a greater challenge than the experience of existential *Grenzsituationen*, extreme situations.[2]

Ruth Beckermann maintains in her retrospective assessment of Jewish life in postwar Vienna in *Unzugehörig* (1989, Not Belonging) that Austria's dealing with the Nazi past leaves much to be desired. "The Austrians distanced themselves extremely fast from National Socialism. In order to live with their experiences of that time, they successfully used a powerful psychological trick," she comments. She argues that the majority of Austrians mythologized and irrationalized Nazism.[3] Like Beckermann, Helmut Müssener also claims that today's image of Austria is one of a country that suffered foreign bondage and tried its best to shake off its shackles. This impression confirmed the "un-Austrian character of National Socialist oppression."[4]

Austrian cultural politics after 1945 aimed at redefining an Austrian identity distinctly different from Germany and untainted by the Nazi past. Even the term *Deutsch* (German) was replaced in school by the generic *Unterrichtssprache* (language of instruction). Instead, Austria's imperial past and its historical bond with the nations of the former Habsburg Empire were emphasized, although in actuality the Second Austrian Republic affiliated itself with the Western democracies economically and politically. To this day, the imperial legacy, defined by Claudio Magris as the Habsburg Myth,[5] continues to be invoked to cast the Second Republic as the heir of the multination-state. This device, among other things, serves to blot out the memory of the Austrian Nazi era, 1938–1945.

The journals of the 1950s and 1960s supported the strategy of Austrian self-definition and self-renewal. The editors of *Wort in der Zeit* (1955–1965, Word in Time) and *Literatur und Kritik* (Literature and Criticism) conducted frequent polls concerning Austrian literature and identity to bolster Austrian national self-confidence and pride. Particularly self-serving polemics were staged under the editorship of Rudolf Henz and Gerhard Fritsch.[6] Nowhere, however, did the tenuousness of post-1955 Austrian identity become more obvious than in 1986, during Kurt Waldheim's campaign for the presidency. Stating that serving as a Nazi officer during World War II he had served his country and performed his duty as an Austrian, the presidential candidate de facto denied Austria's nation status. Yet, he was acclaimed by millions and elected *after* his involvement in war crimes on the Balkans had become public.[7]

Some of the identity problems that came to the fore during the Waldheim debates are already present in the postwar literature by Austrian women authors, most notably Aichinger and Ingeborg Bachmann. Critical of the attempt to rebuild Austria under the auspices of patriarchy, nationalism, and capitalism, these writers confronted National Socialism historically as well as in terms of its legacy, the so-called everyday fascism: Aichinger in *Die größere Hoffnung* (1948, The Greater Hope),[8] Bachmann most notably in the novel fragment *Der Fall Franza* (1972, The Case of Franza) and the narrative "Drei Wege zum See" (1972, Three Paths to the Lake).[9] Wary, ambivalent, and anything but detached from their native country, both writers articulated the conflict arising from their continued emotional attachment and association with Austria, including their Austrian origins, with their native country's anti-Semitic and National Socialist past. Without using the terms "Nazi" or "Jew," even without naming the city in which her novel is set (clearly it is Vienna), Aichinger reveals the identity crisis of a girl of Austrian Jewish and Gentile ancestry. Her protagonist reflects, in part, her own predicament. This work, as well as Aichinger's later writings, reveals a profound loyalty to the victims of the Holocaust and Austrian culture before the emergence of Nazism. Bachmann, although not of Jewish background, positions her narrative voice in such a way as to create a distance from the Austrian mainstream and the perpetrators. She exposes the mind-set of former Nazis and Nazi supporters in the Second Republic, immune to re-education of any kind, and the presence of racist and misogynist attitudes in Austrian society. By establishing, in "Drei Wege zum See" (159), an intertextuality with Shoah survivors such as Jean Améry, whose works had a significant impact on the Jewish post-Shoah intelligentsia in Austria, Bachmann sets herself apart from the discourses and practices of the dominant Gentile culture. Her texts contain critical voices that sensitize her readers to the brutality of the public sphere of the 1950s and 1960s : "Do you truly believe that it is necessary to photograph the destroyed villages and the dead bodies for me to be able to imagine war or to photograph the Indian children so that I know what hunger is like? What a stupendous arrogance" (154–55), says one of Bachmann's characters, a dissenter and a representative of Habsburg Jewish culture, and, more specifically, a reflection of the poet Paul Celan.[10]

By assuming a victim status, Austria, similar to the German Democratic Republic (GDR) (Beckermann 65), avoided facing up to the Nazi past and recognizing its legacy. Early on, critics affirming the link with Germany made their voices heard in opposition to the advocates of a non-German Austrian identity. Among the latter were several Austrian Jews who had returned from exile, among them Hans Weigel. He was critical of the attempts to define Austrian identity in isolation from the larger German heritage, for example in his essay "Das verhängte Fenster" (1946, The Draped Window).[11] Contrary to his regionalist contemporaries, he acknowledged the canon of eighteenth-and nineteenth-century German literature. At the same time, he did not oppose those who emphasized Austria's unique identity within this larger canon. The antimodernist images of a quaint picture-book Austria that haunt the videos and brochures of tourist agencies are more than a gimmick. They project to the world an image of Austria endorsed by many Austrians. "The German landscapes of Austria have a different life rhythm. The poetry is germane to the people, open to their community, and shaped by a strong tradition whose characteristic is subordination to a universal idea rooted in the Baroque,"[12] Kurt Adel wrote in 1964, echoing the views of literary historians who had found favor with the Nazis, such as Herbert Cysarz and Josef Nadler.

Inside Austria, regionalism, Habsburg nostalgia, and literary conservatism reigned supreme. The journals *Wort in der Zeit* and *Literatur und Kritik* supported the ostentatiously apolitical orientation of the majority of Austrian writers. Nonetheless, Austria was unable to maintain an insular existence. International aesthetic and social developments had an impact on the literary production within Austria as well. In the works of some younger writers, although written under the mentorship of conservative senior writers and critics, innovative ideas clashed with conservative forms. Marlen Haushofer is a case in point. Inspired by Simone de Beauvoir's feminist writings, she critically examined postwar Austria's patriarchal structures.[13]

Austrian authors who dealt forthrightly with the Nazi past or did not conform to the prevalent conservative aesthetic programs ended up publishing outside of Austria, most of them in the Federal Republic, or they did not publish at all. The ensuing discrepancy between internally and externally produced and directed literature by Austrian authors engendered different literary styles. Many writers turned to traditional and apolitical themes and favored regional settings and interpersonal and psychological plots, while others connected with international philosophical and aesthetic movements. Often berated by the Austrian media, the political and artistic Austrian avant-garde became internationally known, while the more internally directed literature enjoyed a positive reception within Austria, where some of the leading critics objected to even the smallest departure from traditional literary norms and considered achronological texts anathema. The conservatism of the most recognized writers and critics in postwar Austria, including Heimito von Doderer, Alexander von Lernet-Holenia, Hans Weigel, Rudolf Henz, Gerhard Fritsch, Wolfgang Kraus and, in *Germanistik* (German literary studies), figures such as the notorious Heinz Kindermann,[14] prevented interwar Austrian Socialist, Communist, and experimental authors from receiving their due recognition. Likewise, the heritage of pre-Anschluß (pre-annexation) women's literature was lost to the following generations and still awaits rediscovery. These impediments notwithstanding, some of the critical and experimental trends characteristic of women's literature of the interwar period ultimately did resurface. So did elements of Austria's, particularly Vienna's, Jewish literary tradition. Numerous postwar writers connected to both or either one of these critical traditions, thereby setting themselves apart from the dominant discourse.

The politically emancipated women intellectuals of the pre-Nazi era had laid the foundation for the rich production of the following generations of women authors. Among those who played a significant role in the First Republic were Adelheid Popp (1869–1939), the editor of the *Arbeiterinnenzeitung* (Women Workers Newspaper), the women's paper of the Social Democratic Party, the journalist Alice Schalek (1874–1939), and Rosa Mayreder (1858–1938), a member of the radical wing of the feminist movement and cofounder of the journal *Dokumente der Frauen* (Women's Documents), together with Auguste Fickert (1855–1910) and Marie Lang (1855–1934). In the interwar period, women were represented in all styles and genres, in the avant-garde or, like the novelist, dramatist, and film author Vicki Baum (1888–1960), in popular literature. Non-Jewish women writers who adhered to traditional forms and themes were able to extend their careers beyond 1938 and 1945: Enrica von Handel-Mazzetti (1871–1955), Imma von Bodmershof (1895–1982), Martina Wied (1882–1957), and Erika Mitterer (1906–). Expressing discomfort with modernity, big city culture, and ethnic diversity, the works of the latter authors did not clash with Nazi ideology.

On the other hand, writers who took issue with androcentric discourses, including fascism, were persecuted. Mela Hartwig (1895–1963), for example, rejected the assumption that women were defined by their biology (e.g., in her novellas *Ekstasen* [1928, Ecstasies]) and criticized the persecution of the Jews in *Das Wunder von Ulm* (1936, The Miracle of Ulm). Jewish authors, regardless of their outlook and literary practice, were forced into exile, imprisoned, or murdered, and their works were outlawed. For most of them, their career in Austria ended in 1938. Postwar intellectuals searching for the prefascist tradition of culture-critical, leftist, feminist, and antifascist women's literature of the 1920s and 1930s had to make special research efforts by reviewing the archives of leftist papers such as the *Arbeiter-Zeitung* (Workers Newspaper), or of international German-speaking papers such as the New York *Vorwärts* (Forward).

Generally speaking, the authors who became ambassadors for the Second Republic almost despite themselves had found favor neither with the Austrian literary establishment nor the Austrian publishers—the Residenz Verlag did not yet exist. Thus the works of many Austrian insiders, regardless of their quality, remained little known to readers outside Austria: Jeannie Ebner, Elfriede Mayröcker, Marlen Haushofer, Christine Busta, Christine Lavant, Doris Mühringer, Jutta, now Julian, Schutting, and Brigitte Schwaiger. Conversely, some of the authors who had been marginalized at home because of their experimental forms and critical subject matter achieved international acclaim, which, in turn, improved their status in Austria. This was undoubtedly the case with Elfriede Jelinek, who was initially considered little more than an *enfant terrible*. The most precarious situation was that of avant-garde writers who tried to stake out their territory inside Austria. Except among experts, Elfriede Gerstl and Dorothea Zeemann remained virtually unknown at home and abroad, and the Vienna Group, still in the process of being discovered, gained a measure of fame and notoriety only after it had disbanded.

Notably, there are several women among the Austrian authors with the greatest international name recognition: Aichinger, Bachmann, and Jelinek. Among *Germanisten* (Germanists) and audiences with more specialized interests, Marlen Haushofer, Marie-Thérèse Kerschbaumer, and Barbara Frischmuth have also been well received. Known for their critical attitude toward postwar German-speaking society, especially their scrutiny of the continuing Nazi legacy, it is not uncommon for Aichinger, Bachmann, and Jelinek to be identified as German rather than Austrian authors, all the more so since they published extensively in the Federal Republic. Aichinger and Bachmann were associated with the Group 47. Like their prewar predecessors, these authors maintained close ties to other German-speaking countries and worldwide, which made their work part of the global intellectual community. In spite of their international flair and appeal, however, key elements in their works connect them to Austria in historical, biographical, and intellectual terms. Clearly, their internal geography is Austrian, as is apparent from their settings, their reference points, and the perspective from which they construct problems and plots.

As mentioned earlier, Aichinger and Bachmann, the most distinguished postwar women authors, confronted Austria's Nazi past and its continued impact directly. They did so from a perspective of alienation and distrust, and they continued to discuss their ties to Austria in problematic and troubling terms. Deeply affected by the Shoah, they used their wartime experience as a touchstone to examine postwar society from the margins; as radical individualists and women with a declared affinity for the victims of Nazism, they expressed solidarity with individuals and groups suffering cultural and ethnic oppression in the postwar era. They were painfully aware of their native country's isolation during the Nazi era and beyond. Aichinger and Bachmann, who had grown up in fascist Austria, compensated for their cultural deficit by connecting to the international trends of the postwar era. Existentialism as well as abstract and absurdist literature strongly influenced their works, and both of them supported anti-nuclear and anti-imperialist initiatives. Rather than considering 1945 a *tabula rasa,* they emphasized their indebtedness to the legitimate, nonfascist, tradition of German literature repressed by the Nazis, most notably German-Jewish literature. The repressed and destroyed literature by Jewish authors, the German and Austrian classics, biblical tradition, motifs from Austrian and German legends and fairy tales, as well as historical motifs emerge in the works of Aichinger and Bachmann. The major works of both authors are set in or written in reference to Austria, including Aichinger's novel *Die größere Hoffnung,* several of her radio plays, short texts, and poems all of which contain references to the situation of Jews, women, and other marginalized groups. Many of these texts depict the search for alternatives to the ethnocentric and authoritarian patterns of the past only to suggest that the political and social pressures of their era can only be eluded individually, by complete and radical withdrawal. This path is traced in Bachmann's *Malina* (1971; *Malina,* 1990) and it is clearly articulated in some of Aichinger's poems, for example "Neuer Bund" (New Alliance).[15] Bachmann thematized gender-related oppression, genocide, and the suicidal path of Western civilization throughout her work, e.g., in one of her most widely read early poems "Anrufung des großen Bären" (1956, Invocation of Ursa Major) and in her posthumously published novel fragment *Der Fall Franza.*[16]

In contrast to Aichinger and Bachmann, Marlen Haushofer (1920–1970), who began publishing in the same era and in the same environment, adhered to traditional narrative structures and did not engage in formal experiments. She did, however, engage in cultural criticism, although from a different vantage point than her prominent fellow authors, some of whose works were informed by leftist theory, in particular the Frankfurt School. Haushofer focuses on gender difference, which she discusses in a conceptual framework based on Simone de Beauvoir. Nonetheless, Haushofer's awareness of the Nazi crimes becomes apparent in the short story "Die Willows" (1968, The Willows) a narrative about the deportation of an elderly Jewish couple, who try to pass as non-Jews by posing as Englishmen, to Theresienstadt.[17]

Haushofer's opposition to patriarchal structures, evident throughout her entire œuvre, caught the attention of feminist critics during the women's movement. In *Wir töten Stella* (1958, We Kill Stella), *Die Wand* (1968, The Wall), and *Die Mansarde* (1969, The Attic), Haushofer designs women's psychology and experiences so as to reveal the legalized oppression and destruction of women in average Austrian homes. Ascribing to men and women fundamentally and irreconcilably different mentalities and interests, and analyzing the structures that give the former control over the latter, Haushofer shows everyday fascism in postwar Austria no less distinctly than Bachmann in *Der Fall Franza.* Moreover, in her novel *Die Wand*, she establishes a direct link between ecological and feminist concerns. The latter is most clearly expressed in her protagonist's decision to kill whom she presumes to be last man on earth because he has killed two of her animals and threatened her independence by intruding into her space which she considers a safe haven.[18] "Still today I ask myself, why this stranger killed Bull and Luchs. After all, I had called Luchs back, and he had to wait defenselessly to have his skull crushed. I would like to know why the stranger killed my animals. . . . When in November winter came crashing in, I decided to write this account. It was a last attempt. I could not bear to sit all winter at the table with this question going round and round in my head, a question that no one, no one in the world, can answer."[19]

Haushofer's direct, realistic approach foreshadows the integrated way in which Marie Thérèse Kerschbaumer discussed environmental issues at the 1995 convention *Frauen im Exil* (Women in Exile) in Vienna. In a certain respect Kerschbaumer can be viewed as the missing link between Haushofer and Aichinger and Bachmann: Like the latter two authors, she is concerned with the dilemma of the post-Holocaust, postnuclear world, and her experimental texts challenge genre definitions and the concept of the subject and subjectivity. Kerschbaumer holds Eurocentric attitudes, capitalism, and the narrow definitions of freedom and democracy up to criticism. She does so from a distinctly feminist point of view. In fact, Kerschbaumer's work combines a local perspective with a global outlook. This is the case in "Das Verhältnis der österreichischen Autoren zur österreichischen Geschichte" (1989, Austrian Women Authors' Relationship to Austrian History), an essay about the interaction of the Austrian public and Austrian intellectuals, which argues that the literary formalism and the suppression of antifascist literature in the postwar era were motivated by the general reluctance to face and stamp out Austro-fascism.

Even for the women writers who left Austria intellectually and physically Austrian settings remain important. Aichinger, for example, continued to write about specific Vienna neighborhoods and used the Alpine landscape as a poetic reference point. So does Bachmann. *Malina, Der Fall Franza,* "Drei Wege zum See," and many other of her narratives derive their inner consistency from associations evoked by specific Austrian settings. The same is true for authors as diverse as Haushofer and Jelinek, and filmmakers such as Ruth Beckermann and Nadja Seelich. Haushofer, for example, uses the familiar setting of the Austrian landscape in *Die Wand* to establish a discrepancy between the relative harmony of nature and its creatures, including her woman protagonist, and the violence inherent in civilization and the relationships between men and women. Whether in an affirmative or in a distancing mode, more so than in German literature, Austrian geography with Vienna as its central location, is a recurring element in the works of Austrian writers, male and female.

The works of Barbara Frischmuth, a native of Altaussee, are no exception. Her continued emotional and intellectual ties to her native region are expressed in many of her works, while the setting of others is urban Austria, namely, Vienna. Early in her career already, Frischmuth appropriated Austria in cultural, social, and personal terms as sphere for women and women's culture. In *Die Mystifikationen der Sophie Silber* (1976, The Mystifications of Sophie Silber) and its sequels, *Amy oder Die Metamorphose* (1978, Amy, or The Metamorphosis), and *Kai und die Liebe zu Modellen* (1979, Kai and the Love of Models), Frischmuth portrays women's lives as integrated into Austrian regional and urban society, rewriting and reinterpreting folklore, fairy tales, thereby shaping everyday reality and superimposing on it feminine perspectives.[20] She describes an Alpine scenery populated with supernatural beings, fairies and sprites, whom she positions into a matriarchal network. The names, most of which carry associations to minerals, regionally distinct plants, and animals suggest a strong bond between human beings, legendary figures, plants, and animals:

> On one of their nocturnal walks, or better, their nocturnal flights, they arrived at a meadow full of daffodils located higher up. Everything was in full

> bloom. The view and the scent emanating from the white stars intoxicated the clan so much that they had a huge dance. . . . But when the elves had grown tired of dancing in the early morning hours, and wanted to slip into the blossoms to lie down and rest, they were unable to do so.[21]
>
> She had noticed him during the night walking through the creek in the nude (his body was so sun-tanned that even her experienced eye had difficulty perceiving him). With his hand he pulled the trout from under the stones. Since his fingers were clammy from the night cold the fish slipped through his fingers, and he laughed triumphantly as if he himself and not his prey had escaped death. . . . Amaryllis Sternwieser secretly doubted that the rumors about a conventional love relationship between him and Rosalia, the Wild Woman, were true at all.[22]

Although there are conflicts and violent disruptions in Frischmuth's poetic universe, there could be no greater difference between her vision of nature and the relationship between men and women than the portrayal of either one by Jelinek. Similar to Haushofer's portrayal of heterosexual relationships, albeit with the hope that reconciliation and coexistence can be achieved, Frischmuth describes violent encounters, especially in the metropolitan setting of Vienna:

> My neighbor lady's situation is truly terrible. The man is so bad that the doctor has to prescribe pills against his constant sexual urges. When he took them he was halfway normal. . . . Anyway, he went completely wild and I heard the woman's screams all the way to my place. . . . I placed my ear against the wall again, listening to her sobbing and her yelling stop. And then she must have escaped him . . . but then it started up again and the people were standing around. Not only that he drove his prick into her like a power drill, following the same rhythm he took her head and threw it back and forth on the tile floor. The poor woman could no longer scream; blood was streaming from

> both sides of her body. . . . And the men who have never seen such virility stand and stare.[23]

Frischmuth's earlier texts leave traditional paradigms such as that of the countryside as a site of wholeness and the city as the site of alienation intact.

> The panther's green eyes were glowing into thousands of windows. Happiness for all those who had moved here from basements and humid studio apartments, from dusty attics and mildewed flats with a community toilet in the hallway. One's own warm four walls with big windows, a bath, and a loggia, which sounds like Italy and where oleander might grow. Perhaps happiness is sometimes shaped like a cubicle, uniform and with thin walls? A happiness for which one has made savings, which for a long time has been held out like a promise, a happiness administered by the city.[24]

In contrast to Haushofer and Frischmuth, Jelinek undermines binary models. In her texts informed by Marxist and feminist theory as well as by Austrian Jewish satire and interwar women authors, e.g., Veza Canetti's literature, she attacks the notion that there are places of refuge and integrity in her society. This is already the case in her novel *die liebhaberinnen* (1975, Female Lovers),[25] which deals with the oppression of women under capitalism in a rural Austrian setting. The chaotic mountainscape in Jelinek's *Die Kinder der Toten* (1995, The Children of the Dead) with its ghostly fragmentary characters is fundamentally different from the mountains in Frischmuth's novel *Die Mystifikationen der Sophie Silber,* a site of female bonding and of the interchange between humans and extrahumans. Indeed, Jelinek's narrative, preceded by the Hebrew invocation ("Let them come, the Spirits of the Dead that were not seen for years, and bless their children")[26] to establish a link to the past, associates the Austrian countryside with guilt and destruction: "So much nature has been applied to this country. In turn, it has always generously spent its human inhabitants, perhaps in order to pay back its debt to nature (7). . . . In the mountains where introspection can easily be torn to pieces by flashes of lightning, these transitory horrors, which create only little but destroy a lot, in the mountains a few people have disappeared. In return others whom we did not even miss have come back" (14).[27]

Frischmuth registers the problems involving gender, ethnicity, and power that are thematized by other women writers from a critical distance, a detachment she achieves through her use of humor. She uses her writing to conquer her homeland, be it the Alpine regions, be it Vienna. Aware of the abuses of male power in a patriarchal system, she nonetheless configures Austria as a country of mothers and fathers, women and men, who try to come to terms with their complex modern society.[28] She reinterprets Austrian traditions and lore in an attempt to make a contribution to the changing discourses on Austria. From an insider's position, Frischmuth creates a discursive space to accommodate emancipated Austrian women.

Frischmuth's literature and views stand in contrast to the works of authors who approach Austrian mainstream culture from the outside for historical and autobiographical reasons and who distance themselves from Austrian society by defining themselves as outsiders. Aichinger, Bachmann, and Jelinek embraced a position of marginality that is distinctly different from Frischmuth's chosen position. Frischmuth's outlook also differs from the fundamental pessimism of Haushofer, who painted a bleak picture of the conditions under which Austrian women live, and who suggests a profound incompatibility between men and women. Frischmuth in contrast tries to come to terms with the gender gap by defining and examining the differences and by seeking equitable solutions for both genders.

Since the end of World War II, women writers have played a central role in shaping Austrian literature at home and abroad. Austrian authors, male and female, had to overcome significant initial philosophical and economic political difficulties. In addition, women writers faced the misogyny of publishers and the literary establishment. With its greater openness to literary and conceptual innovation, West Germany attracted the most notable Austrian women authors. The latter's change of residence and place of publication did not signify, however, a disinterest in things Austrian. Quite the contrary, they continued to thematize their country of origin. The geographic distance contributed to their ability to formulate distinct antipatriarchal and antiauthoritarian positions.

The impact of avant-garde Austrian women's literature reflected back on the Austrian scene in general, where increased publication possibilities allowed for the development of a broader basis for literary expression, combining, in particular, local and international, regional and urban perspectives as, for instance, in the works of Barbara Frischmuth, Anna

Mitgutsch, and in the films of Ruth Beckermann. Since the postwar years Austrian women authors have introduced significant impulses for change into Austrian literature and German-speaking literature in general, including an unyielding integrity with which many of them confronted fascism and the Nazi legacy and questioned authoritarian, ethnocentric, and misogynist structures. Without identifying themselves explicitly as adherents of the feminist movement of the 1970s, they wrote from the perspective of women and feminists, expanding the scope of the reality conveyed in literary discourse, thereby expanding the boundaries of literary discourse. They did so in a variety of ways: by establishing alternatives to traditional narrative patterns, by undermining patriarchal discourse by way of satire, humor, overt criticism, and/or by redefining and reconfiguring literary language. The works of Austrian women authors, sensitive to their own marginality in postwar society, and some of them marginalized as Jews and members of other minorities, contested claims of universality and homogeneity in linguistic and philosophical terms and, through their openness to cultural and linguistic multivalence and diversity, reestablished the ties between Austrian and world literature, severed during the Nazi era. At the same time, they transformed the Austrian literary scene internally, bridging the gap between seemingly mutually exclusive approaches.

Even if Austria and Austrian identity remain to be important issues in the works of Austrian women authors, good Austrian women's literature is not provincial. Although the renown of Austrian literature has been established to a large extent by women authors, these authors are far from being uncritical advocates for Austria. Their cautious or vehement criticism of Austria, their representation of the familiar and the uncanny as residing side by side in, as Jelinek sarcastically calls it, "this beautiful country with its valleys and hills"[29] is evidence of their tentative and conditional acceptance of their native country.

University of Illinois at Chicago

Notes

1. Ilse Aichinger, "Aufruf zum Mißtrauen," *Aufforderung zum Mißtrauen. Literatur, bildende Kunst, Musik in Österreich seit 1945,* ed. Otto Breicha and Gerhard Fritsch (Salzburg: Residenz, 1967) 10.

2. Ilse Aichinger, *Rede unter dem Galgen. Erzählungen. Junge österreichische Autoren VI,* ed. Hans Weigel (1949; Vienna: Jungbrunnen, 1952).

3. Ruth Beckermann, *Unzugehörig. Österreicher und Juden nach 1945* (Vienna: Löcker, 1989) 27–29. Original quote: "Die Österreicher setzten sich äußerlich in großer Eile vom Nationalsozialismus ab. Um jedoch mit ihren Erfahrungen aus dieser Zeit weiterleben zu können, bedienten sie sich eines wirkungsvollen psychischen Tricks."

4. Helmut Müssener, "Ein großes Tabu? Zum Umgang mit der Vergangenheit im Österreichischen Exil im Exilland Schweden," *Austrian Writers and the Anschluss* (Riverside, CA: Ariadne Press, 1991) 349. Original quote: "In der Rückschau [dominiert] erneut das Bild eines in fremden Ketten schmachtenden Österreich, das sich mit aller Gewalt . . . darum bemüht hatte, diese Ketten zu sprengen. Somit wurde der 'nichtösterreichische Charakter der nationalsozialistischen Gewaltherrschaft' (Pelinka, s.o.) bestätigt."

5. Claudio Magris, *Der habsburgische Mythos in der Österreichischen Literatur* (Salzburg: Müller, 1966).

6. Dagmar C. Lorenz, "Ein Definitionsproblem: Österreichische Literatur," *Modern Austrian Literature* 12.2 (1979): 14.

7. Josef Haslinger, *Politik der Gefühle. Ein Essay über Österreich* (Frankfurt/Main: Luchterhand, 1987) 27.

8. Ilse Aichinger, *Die größere Hoffnung* (Frankfurt/Main: Fischer, 1974).

9. Ingeborg Bachmann, *Der Fall Franza—Requiem für Fanny Goldmann* (Munich: Piper, 1979) and "Drei Wege zum See," in *Simultan. Erzählungen* (Munich: dtv, 1978) 129–232.

10. Original quote: "Glaubst du, daß du mir die zerstörten Dörfer und Leichen abfotografieren mußt, damit ich mir den Krieg vorstelle, oder diese indischen Kinder, damit ich weiß, was Hunger ist? Was ist denn das für eine dumme Anmaßung."

11. Hans Weigel, "Das verhängte Fenster," *Plan* 5 (1946): 397–398. Ruth Gross, *Plan and the Austrian Rebirth* (Columbia, SC: Camden House, 1982) 94–95.

12. Kurt Adel, *Vom Wesen der Österreichischen Dichtung* (Vienna: Bergland, 1964) 24–26. Original quote: "Die deutschen Landschaften Österreichs haben einen anderen Lebensrhythmus. Die Dichtung ist volkstümlich, gemeinschaftsoffen, getragen von starker Überlieferung, gekennzeichnet durch die Einordnung in eine überzeitliche Idee auf deutlich barocker Grundlage."

13. Dagmar C. G. Lorenz, "Marlen Haushofer. Eine Feministin aus Österreich," *Modern Austrian Literature* 13 (1980): 171–191.

14. Cf. Hans H. Hiebel, "Der 'Anschluß der Ostmark an das Reich.' Zur präfaschistischen Germanistik in Österreich," *Austrian Writers and the Anschluss,* ed. Donald Daviau (Riverside, CA: Ariadne, 1991) 71. "Heinz Kindermann declared in 1938: 'It was no coincidence that the National Socialist renewal of the Empire was undertaken by a German-Austrian man." Hiebel also discusses Franz Koch, Josef Nadler, and Herbert Cysarz. Especially Kindermann, Nadler, and Cysarz continued to play a role in Austrian *Germanistik* (German studies) after 1945, and their works continue to be read and thus influence younger scholars.

15. Ingeborg Bachmann, *Malina. Roman* (Frankfurt/Main: Suhrkamp, 1971). [English edition: Ingeborg Bachmann, *Malina. A Novel,* trans. Philip Boehm (New York: Holmes and Meier, 1990).] Ilse Aichinger, *Verschenkter Rat* (Frankfurt/Main: Fischer, 1978) 77.

16. Ingeborg Bachmann, "Anrufung des Großen Bären," *Anrufung des Großen Bären* (Munich: Piper, 1956) 132–33. Helgard Mahrdt points out that *Der Fall Franza* "picks up the scientific discourse of the 1960s, in which the focus was not on the economy or politics as causes for fascism, but on what kind of human being it was that had tortured and murdered." In "'Society Is the Biggest Murder Scene of All': On the Private and Public Spheres in Ingeborg Bachmann's Prose," *Women in German Yearbook* 12 (1997): 176.

17. Marlen Haushofer, *Schreckliche Treue* (Hamburg: Claassen, 1968) 133–146.

18. Marlen Haushofer, *Die Wand* (1968; repr., Munich: dtv, 1991) 224.

19. Original quote: "Noch heute frage ich mich, warum der fremde Mann Stier und Luchs getötet hat. Ich hatte doch Luchs zurückgepfiffen, und er mußte wehrlos darauf warten, daß ihm der Schädel eingeschlagen wurde. Ich möchte wissen, weshalb der fremde Mann meine Tiere getötet hat. . . . Als im November der Winter hereinbrach, beschloß ich, diesen

Bericht zu schreiben. Es war ein letzter Versuch. Ich konnte doch nicht den ganzen Winter am Tisch sitzen mit dieser einen Frage im Kopf, die mir kein Mensch, überhaupt niemand auf der Welt, beantworten kann" (*Wand* 226).

20. Barbara Frischmuth, *Die Mystifikationen der Sophie Silber* (Salzburg: Residenz, 1976); *Amy oder Die Metamorphose* (Salzburg: Residenz, 1980); *Kai oder die Liebe zu Modellen* (Salzburg: Residenz, 1979).

21. Original quote: "Aus einer ihrer nächtlichen Wanderungen, besser gesagt auf einem ihrer nocturnen Umflüge, kamen sie auch zu der höher gelegenen Narzissenwiese, die voller Blüten stand. Der Anblick und der Duft, der von den weißen Sternen ausging, berauschte den Stamm so sehr, daß er ein großes Tanzgelage abhielt. . . . Doch als die Elfen gegen Morgen, vom Tanzen müde geworden, in die Blüten kriechen und sich zur Ruhe legen wollten, gelang ihnen das nicht" (*Mystifikationen* 73).

22. Original quote: "Sie hatte ihn nachts bemerkt, wie er nackt (dabei war sein Körper so braun von der Sonne, daß selbst ihr kundiger Blick ihn kaum ausnehmen konnte) durch den Bach schritt und die Forellen mit der Hand unter den Steinen hervorzog, wobei seine Finger manchmal der Nachtkühle wegen schon so klamm waren, daß der Fisch ihnen wieder entschlüpfte, was ihm ein triumphierendes Auflachen entlockte, als sei er selbst und nicht seine Beute dem Tod entronnen. . . . Amaryllis Sternwieser zweifelt insgeheim daran, daß die Geschichten, die diesen Mann zusammen mit Rosalia, der Saligen, in das übliche Liebesverhältnis zwängte, überhaupt stimmte" (*Mystifikationen* 123–125).

23. Original quote: "Bei meiner Nachbarin ist es wirklich ein Kreuz. Der Kerl ist so, daß der Arzt ihm Tabletten verschreiben muß gegen den ständigen Trieb. Und wenn er die genommen hat, dann war's halbwegs normal. . . . Jedenfalls ist er ganz wild geworden, und ich hab' die Frau schon bis zu mir herüber schreien gehört. . . . Ich wieder mit dem Ohr an die Wand, hör', wie sie schluchzt, wie sie aufhören schreit. Und dann muß sie ihm entwischt sein . . . aber da ist schon alles in vollem Gang und die Leute stehen herum. Nicht nur, daß er ihr seinen Schwanz hineintreibt wie einen Preßluftbohrer, er nimmt auch noch im selben Rhythmus ihren Kopf und wirft ihn wieder zurück auf den Steinboden. Die arme Frau kann schon nicht einmal mehr schrein, und das Blut rinnt ihr oben und unten heraus. . . . Da stehn die Mannsbilder und glotzen, weil sie sowas von Potenz halt noch nicht gesehen haben" (*Amy* 136).

24. Barbara Frischmuth, *Die Frau im Mond* (Salzburg: Residenz,

1982) 10. Original quote: "Der Panther leuchtete mit den grünen Augen in tausende Fenster hinein. Glück, für all die, die aus Kellern und feuchten Kabinetten kamen, von staubigen Dachböden und Schimmelwohnungen mit Gangklo. Die warmen eigenen vier Wände mit großen Fenstern, Bad und nach Italien klingender Loggia, in der Oleander gedeihen würde. Ob das Glück manchmal würfelförmig ist? Und hellhörig und einheitlich? Ein erspartes, lang versprochenes, von der Stadt verwaltetes Glück."

25. Elfriede Jelinek, *die liebhaberinnen* (Reinbek: Rowohlt, 1975).

26. Hebrew quote translated by Neil Jacobs.

27. Elfriede Jelinek, *Die Kinder der Toten* (Reinbek: Rowohlt, 1995). Original quote: "So viel Natur ist auf dieses Land verwendet worden, daß es seinerseits, vielleicht um seine Schuld an die Natur zurückzuzahlen, mit seinen Menschen immer recht freigiebig umgegangen ist" (7). . . . "Im Gebirge, wo die Beschaulichkeit leicht von Blitzen zerrissen werden kann, diesen vorübergehenden Schrecken, die im Grunde wenig hervorbringen, aber viel kaputtmachen, im Gebirge sind ein paar Menschen verschwunden. Dafür sind andere wiedergekommen, die wir gar nicht vermißt hatten" (14).

28. Barbara Frischmuth, *Traumgrenze* (Salzburg: Residenz, 1983) 89–105. For example, the story "O du lieber Augustin" (Oh, you, my dear Augustine), which exposes the sexism, the arrogance, the complacency, and the bigotry of a composite character symbolic of contemporary Viennese culture.

29. Jelinek, *liebhaberinnen* 3. Original quote: "dieses schöne land mit seinen tälern und hügeln."

Barbara Frischmuth's Novel *Einander Kind*: Fifty Years after the Takeover of the Nazis in Austria[1]

Gisela M. Roethke

The topic of the time of the takeover by the Nazis in 1938 and the way in which Austrians have dealt with this part of their history has drawn a lot of public and academic attention during the past ten years. Austrian authors such as Thomas Bernhard, Peter Henisch, Elfriede Jelinek, Marie-Thérèse Kerschbaumer, Elisabeth Reichart, Brigitte Schwaiger, and Gerald Szyszkowitz, to name just a few, have taken up this topic. A whole series of symposia worldwide have focused on it, and a number of collective volumes and numerous monographs dealing with it have appeared since 1988.[2]

Frischmuth's public grappling with this topic came relatively late, at a time when discussion of the Nazi past of Austria was not a taboo any longer, but rather a focus of attention, even though still rejected by large parts of the Austrian public. However, as Frischmuth publicly explained,[3] she had actually worked with materials from the Holocaust many years earlier when she translated from Hungarian into German the diary of a Hungarian Jewish woman in which this woman described her Auschwitz experiences.[4] According to Frischmuth, the identification process that Frischmuth underwent as a literary translator proved to be a truly traumatic experience, so that for years afterward she was not able to speak or write on the subject.

Probably the external impetus for revisiting the topic of Austria's Nazi past in her novel *Einander Kind* (1990, One Another's Child)[5] was provided by the Waldheim scandal from 1986 on, the many commemorative events of the year 1988, which marked fifty years after the *Anschluss* (annexation), and the mixed reactions of the population to these. Frischmuth herself had been invited to give a speech for such an occasion at the *Ensemble* Theater in Vienna, which she entitled "Vieles ist ein Schwindel, aber nichts ist Zufall" (1988, Much Consists of Lies, But Nothing Is an Accident).[6] Back to *Einander Kind* and its grounding in the historical past: one of the three narrative strands of the novel deals with a performance tour of the actress Vevi Schwarz and her companion Sigune Pröbstl through the Austrian provinces in the significant year 1988. In these reading performances, Vevi Schwarz presents texts by those authors whose works were burned by the Nazis and who themselves were either driven into exile, survived the concentration camps, or perished in the death camps. The reactions of the public as well as the organizers of these readings portray the spread of the different opinions and attitudes of Austria's contemporary population to these texts, their authors, and the history that shaped the texts.

A further external impetus for writing this novel may have been of autobiographical nature: In 1988, after getting married for the second time, Frischmuth and her husband built a house in Frischmuth's old home town, Altaussee, a place where the Frischmuth family had lived for generations, and which had attracted Barbara Frischmuth again and again for vacations and retreats to work. The stronger reminder of her family's history, evoked by this new domicile, and the critical distancing required due to this greater proximity entered into the novel in at least two of the narrative strands. One strand is called "Die andere Welt" (The Other World), the other one "Tag- und Nachtstücke in Schwarz'scher Manier" (Day and Night Pieces in Schwarzian Manner).

"Die andere Welt" plays predominantly in the memories of Trude Schwarz, an old retired woman suffering from cancer. Trude had married into the Schwarz family and because of the war, she was prematurely widowed as a young woman, yet without children from this brief marriage. In her memories, she returns again and again to the ancestral village of the Schwarz family, as she remembers it from the war years and shortly thereafter. The village is easily recognizable as Altaussee, just as the family constellation is recognizable as that of Barbara Frischmuth's extended family.[7] The other narrative strand, "Tag- und Nachtstücke," consists of excerpts from the autobiography of Vevi Schwarz, which she is writing in 1988. These excerpts go back mostly to the 1950s, the time after World War II, when the practically universal conventions of silence and silencing about the past took shape. Vevi Schwarz could be taken as one of Barbara Frischmuth's *alter egos*, although certainly she is a fictitious character.

Beyond the historico-political and autobiographical dimensions, a literary level of the novel also plays an important role with regard to the past, namely, the use of the myth of Demeter and Persephone. Frischmuth's trilogy has been analyzed repeatedly for its aspects of the Demeter/Persephone myth by a number of critics.[8] This novel was the third one in Frischmuth's Demeter and Persephone trilogy project. The story *Herrin der Tiere* (1986, Mistress of the Animals) and the novel *Über die Verhältnisse* (1987; as a play on words, this can mean both "About the Conditions" and also "Beyond One's Means") are the two first parts of the trilogy. Frischmuth herself gave extensive explanations about this mythic frame in her Munich poetics lectures of 1990 entitled *Traum der Literatur — Literatur des Traums* (Dream of Literature — Literature of the Dream):[9]

> The wonderful thing about dealing with a myth is that there is no strictly prescribed, canonized original text. The myth has been there always and whichever version we hear or consider original, the next mythographer will tell the story quite differently, will connect it to different traditions, will associate it in another direction, will relate the names in it (what Ranke-Graves calls the realistic element of myth) to other names, will maybe even give them to other persons, will form other etymologies. . . . This imagining on a never secured ground is the most enticing invitation to a female author to become part of this hide-and-go-seek game, to continue playing with it, and to newly write the story of Demeter and Kore for herself. (*Traum* 65)[10]

As Frischmuth said, "Above all I attempted to translate three aspects into contemporary life: the archaic, the classical, and the mystical aspect" ("Von all den Möglichkeiten . . . versuchte ich vor allem drei Aspekte ins Heutige zu übersetzen: den archaischen, den klassischen und den mystischen," *Traum* 68).

In his article "Barbara Frischmuths Demeter-Trilogie: Mythologische Finde-Spiele in der postmodernen Literatur" (1992, Barbara Frischmuth's Demeter Trilogy: Mythological Hide-and-Go-Seek Games in Postmodern Literature"), Paul Michael Lützeler understands Frischmuth's trilogy as a postmodern playing-through of different possibilities for this myth. Coming from postmodern theories, Lützeler states: "Nothing is further from the self-reflexive, self-critical, skeptical, ironic-parodistic literature of postmodernism than to collaborate in founding new myths or helping old myths to new significance."[11] Thus, Lützeler emphasizes mainly the playfulness of this undertaking, and thus he himself engages in a hide-and-go-seek game with the three texts in which he discovers as many allusions as possible to the old myth in its various versions within these texts.

I want to raise the question whether Frischmuth did not intend to address a more serious purpose with these literary "games." Lützeler already hinted at that when he saw attempts at a new social ethics in *Einander Kind*.[12] He quotes Frischmuth: "'Kindschaft' in contrast to domination. Eleusis is also the mystery of continuously renewing 'Kindschaft,' the return to the womb, of being reborn."[13] The term *Kindschaft* is exceedingly difficult to translate into English, since there is no abstract noun that exactly captures the German meaning. An attempt at such a translation might be "the state of being a child."

Foregrounding the historical dimensions, the Eleusinian mysteries around the Demeter/Persephone myth offered a mystery/religion whose most important components were belief in metamorphoses, death, and rebirth.[14] In the trinity of Demeter-Kore-Hekate, the major stages of women's lives are reflected: young girl/virgin, the metamorphosis to wife and mother, and the metamorphosis to the old, wise woman/crone after menopause. Connected to these are the acceptance of birth and death as parts of the natural, biological, but also mystical cycle. Because of these contents, the Eleusinian mysteries were above all, although not exclusively, a religion for women, a religion in which death of the old self and rebirth played a predominant role.

The myth of Demeter-Persephone-Hekate formed a countermyth to a hierarchical, patriarchal order, even though in its most famous, Homeric form, in which it has come down to us, it has already been subsumed by Olympic patriarchy. But traces of the older order remain: While the Olympians were continuously struggling with each other for the best places, Demeter, Persephone, and Hekate stand out through their love, mutual caring, and mourning for each other. With the rape of Persephone and her abduction into the underworld, patriarchy had raped matriarchy and victimized it. Demeter's power did not suffice to free Persephone from the underworld, but only in the cycle of the seasons was she able to return to Earth and to her mother. This cycle is obviously connected to ancient rites of fertility.[15]

It is well known that the Nazis used ancient heroic myths for their own purposes. This only demonstrates the hypertrophic extension of the ethos inherent in these myths to their limits. In her essays accompanying her novel *Kassandra* (1983, Cassandra), Christa Wolf lucidly analyzed the connections between ancient myths, heroic epics, and the historical development of patriarchy down to our days.[16] According to her, there was a direct developmental line from the heroic epics to the violence of the Nazis and the violence of the arms race between NATO and the Warsaw Pact. The consolidation of the ethos of victor and victim permeates the relations between the sexes, classes, races, and those between the developed to the developing countries. In this context, aesthetics and ethics are seen by Wolf as insolubly intertwined. Just as Wolf was searching for a new aesthetic in order to demonstrate other modes of behavior and a new ethos, so Frischmuth searched for a counter-myth and a new literary form that would correspond to her ethos of mutual care and parenting one another in turn just like a mother takes care of her child. Wolf speaks of her texts as *Muster* (patterns) and *Gewebe* (weavings), whereas Frischmuth speaks of *Modelle* (models), as for instance in the title of her novel *Kai und die Liebe zu den Modellen* (1979, Kai and the Love of Models). In Frischmuth's literary works, the mother-child relationship plays a significant role from early on.

In *Einander Kind*, she invents a new form that in a supple way expresses the metamorphoses and at the same time the equality of the main figures. In the form of this novel, we do not just find three parallel strands, since the strands are not just placed next to each other, but rather they are literally intertwined. The form of the text can be described with the metaphor of a braid of three strands that are joined at the root, the ancestral hometown of the Schwarz family. As in a braid, first one, then the other, then the third perspective is foregrounded. And as in a braid, beauty is produced through the evenness, that is, the equality of the perspectives. Braiding has always been a women's art in Europe, and it was mostly an activity between mother and daughter, since it was too difficult for a daughter to braid an even braid by herself. In this novel, in the end all the strands come from the same root. And this root is the familial place of birth and death, as the novel makes clear in its final chapter entitled "Eleusis." In the ancestral town of the Schwarz family, all three main figures and the extended family come together to bury Regula, Vevi Schwarz's mother, and to baptize the new child of the family, who, as a sign of rebirth, shall even bear the name of the deceased. Here, the cycle closes and begins again.

What does this ethos, centered around death and rebirth, of the cycle of mother and child have to do with Austrian history? Do we not have an ahistorical, natural cycle here? Frischmuth does indeed not treat the myth this way, but rather she gives it a historical dimension of a depth of fifty years through the different women figures of various generations and through their work of memory and their historically anchored fates, which reflect Austrian events and attitudes of those fifty years.

The narrative strand of Trude Schwarz, the oldest of the three women, is told throughout as an interior monologue in the third person except for when she is directly conversing with the dead, who appear to her in her bits of memories and feverish hallucinations. Mostly, Trude moves in a "shadow world" and more and more loses touch with present reality. As a young widow, she lived with the family of her husband, who died as a soldier on the eastern front. As the daughter-in-law, she became a critical witness to the opportunistic and ideological blindness of the family patriarch and his wife, who saw their "heroic" sons perish as soldiers one by one. Trude is criticized by the patriarch for her interest in politics: "No matter how much leeway I grant you, politics is men's business, after all" ("Bei allem, was ich dir zugestehe, Politik ist nun einmal Männersache," 55).

That politics is not women's business is clearly contradicted by Frischmuth in her showing how each one of the women takes a different political position: Mother and daughter in the Schwarz family are Nazis. The daughter-in-law, Regula, whose husband returns from the war with a wound that has made him impotent, is an illegitimate child of potentially noble lineage; the family even rumors that she might be of Habsburg blood. Correspondingly, she coolly distances herself from Nazi doings. She calls Hitler "that Mr. Schickelgruber,"[17] "that 'Parvenü'" (upstart, 41). This expression is usually attributed to Paul von Hindenburg, the tottering old aristocratic last president of the Weimar Republic. Regula withdraws into an impotent aestheticism, which makes her into an icon. In this figure, Frischmuth expresses the nostalgia of many Austrians during the war and postwar period for the old Habsburg monarchy, which had frozen in aestheticism toward its end. Trude herself joins the resistance to the Nazis by hiding partisan fighters and stealing food supplies for them from the hotel business of her in-laws.

The consequences of the war cast shadows over the lives of all the women who have lost their husbands, sons, or brothers. Toward the end of the war, Trude meets the head of the Austrian resistance, who, however, has fallen prey to the same heroicism as the Nazis, just at the opposite end of the political spectrum. He tells her: "No good times when women have to get mixed up in men's business. But that will change" ("Keine gute Zeit, wenn Frauen sich in Männerdinge mischen müssen. Aber das wird sich ändern," 99). It dawns on Trude that the patriarchal order will not change after the war in spite of all the bloodshed and losses.

Even the victors prove to be no better than the vanquished. Trude is ultimately put in her place as an object when she becomes the victim of a particularly gruesome rape by an American soldier. This soldier finds himself impotent when faced with this *Flintenweib* (gun-toting Annie), and to get back at her, he plays Russian roulette with his pistol in her vagina. This is the moment of the rape of Persephone, her abduction into the underworld. Trude withdraws from nearly all human contact and for forty years lives in another world, a world of numbers, doing her job as an accountant in a sterile, inhuman environment. At her home — built cavelike into a mountain — she receives visits from the dead. Her opinion, which only gets reinforced again and again, is "that in this world, murder and manslaughter prevail at all levels" ("daß in dieser Welt Mord und Totschlag auf allen Ebenen vorherrschen," 11).

Contrary to Lützeler and Chapple, I take Trude Schwarz to represent the quintessential Persephone figure in this novel, not a Demeter figure.[18] The "other world" in which she lives is not the world of the older generation, but rather in my estimation the realm of Hades.[19] If one takes Trude to represent a Persephone figure, the rape scene, her retreat into an accounting office located in a cellar, her apartment half hidden in a mountain cave across from a cemetery, the multiple deaths that surround her, her conversations with the dead, and the grotesque scene in the "Eleusis" chapter at the end all make sense. Her life ends when she falls or drops herself — it does not become clear which — into Regula's open grave. Thus, she reveals herself mysteriously as the one who will accompany Regula in death, as Persephone, the Queen of the Dead. The pomegranate tree on her porch evokes the symbol with which Persephone was always associated in ancient iconography. Trude's interest in vegetation does not necessarily make her a Demeter figure, since Persephone's cyclical disappearances and returns are also intimately associated with the changes of the seasons and vegetative life.

Sigune Pröbstl is also a woman damaged by patriarchy and the Nazi period. Her connection to the Schwarz family and their hometown happened through her own family's evacuation to that town. In 1988, Vevi Schwarz appears at the right moment to save Pröbstl from unemployment and alcoholism after she has just been fired. Frischmuth affords this severely inhibited woman her own perspective. She deals with Pröbstl's original speechlessness by assigning to this character the task to function not only as Vevi Schwarz's secretary and travel companion, but also as the observer of the audiences' reactions to Vevi's political readings. Even though this narrative strand is told from Pröbstl's perspective, it is told in the third person, since Pröbstl herself is speechless in the beginning. With time, Vevi succeeds in slowly helping to free the inhibited Pröbstl from her cocoon. This is accomplished through working on her memories, which Vevi helps her to retrieve and confront through insistent questioning. Nobody ever before was as intensely interested in Pröbstl's life. Through her family background as the daughter of an officer, through her war experiences, and through her marriage, Pröbstl had become totally inhibited and closed off, and she had lost all self-confidence. She undergoes a metamorphosis in which she finds her own language and self-confidence. At the time of her metamorphosis, which is portrayed as quite a pointed breakthrough out of her cocoon, she is described in the following manner: "She wears her hair pinned up and looks as if modeled after an antique cameo" ("Sie trägt das Haar hochgesteckt und sieht aus wie einer antiken Gemme nachmodelliert," 209). The metamorphosis portrayed with Pröbstl serves as a model for Austrian society, which needed yet to learn such insistent questioning that had brought forth Pröbstl's release. The cocoonlike state in which Pröbstl found herself has been rightly interpreted by Chapple as another Kore figure.[20] By shedding her cocoon in the end and by starting to speak for herself, she undergoes a metamorphosis from a Kore to a Demeter figure. This is stressed through her likeness with the beautiful Regula, Vevi's mother, who in her beauty and loftiness embodied certain aspects of Demeter.

Vevi Schwarz writes her autobiography in the first person, as someone fully self-confident. Having been marginalized at an early age as an ugly duckling, she developed into a young rebel. Because of her "gypsy-likeness," she seemed unsuited for the traditional female role. In Vevi Schwarz's autobiography, Frischmuth can let loose some of the hilarious humor that she is capable of. This type of humor Vevi could never have developed from the model of her regal, sedate mother, Regula. Rather, it is the example of her nanny, the maid Seraf, who serves as her model.[21] Vevi calls her "the true chronicler of the family history" ("die wahre Chronistin der Familiengeschichte," 42), since Seraf is the only one who will come out with the truth in front of the child, although even she sees a limit in not telling the eleven-year-old child about the Nazi death camps. Seraf is a Baubo figure whose humor works especially at the sexual level, just as the Baubo in *The Homeric "Hymn to Demeter."*[22] Vevi learns her humor from Seraf: "Even if I told a joke — and I tried this genre at an early age — she tried to teach me how the comic twist functioned and that one shouldn't divulge it for as long as possible so that the comic tension wouldn't give out at the same time" (127).[23] And it is Seraf who makes sure that Vevi has a wonderful first sexual encounter full of surprises.

As a talented actress, Vevi finds her way, appears strong and completely independent. Thus, she can function as a Demeter-like figure for Pröbstl, to bring her out of her cocoon. She even finds a late, but successful love relationship to a man who is truly capable of an egalitarian partnership. In this love relationship, each partner is capable of cushioning the moments of weakness for the other one in turn, which Frischmuth compares to the relationship of a mother to her child. Still, in her rebellion against the traditional female role, Vevi has also rebelled against her family and has excluded the possibility of creating a family of her own. In that sense, she is a Persephone figure. The death of her mother, Regula, with whom she had had hardly any contact at all anymore, plunges her into deep mourning, akin to a depression. She has to learn to accept her own vulnerability as a child and to mourn her being orphaned. Her partner helps her in a motherly way to accomplish this task of mourning and to restore her relationship to her extended family by attending the baptism of the newborn child.

The political dimension of this lesson for the people of Austria is not lost: It is necessary to accomplish this work of mourning before one can proceed with one's work for shaping the future with a freed and renewed consciousness. Only thus will the future not be poisoned by the past. This is to be understood in the sense of Margarete Mitscherlich's concept of *Erinnerungsarbeit* (work of remembering).[24]

Frischmuth thus embeds the myth of Demeter and Persephone in this novel into a historical dimension. She shows that the victimization of women by their Nazi past on the family level is a victimization of women by the larger, all-pervasive patriarchal myth. The mystery of healing through death of the old self and rebirth to a new self, through the constant metamorphoses of relationships from motherliness to childlike vulnerability and back, form a model for a new ethos through which Austrian society — but not only Austrian society alone — could transform itself.

Dickinson College

Notes

1. This article was first given as a conference paper at the twentieth annual meeting of the German Studies Association in Seattle on October 12, 1996, and it appears here in revised form. I would like to thank Barbara Frischmuth, who was in the audience. Her comments on my paper caused some of my revisions.

2. Donald Daviau, ed., *Austrian Writers and the Anschluss: Understanding the Past — Overcoming the Past* (Riverside, CA: Ariadne, 1991); William E. Wright, ed., *Austria 1938–1988: Anschluss and Fifty Years* (Riverside, CA: Ariadne, 1995).

3. This was at the same German Studies Association meeting as mentioned in note 1.

4. Ana Novac, *Die schönen Tage meiner Jugend* (Reinbek: Rowohlt, 1967).

5. Barbara Frischmuth, *Einander Kind* (Salzburg: Residenz, 1990).

6. "Vieles ist ein Schwindel, aber nichts ein Zufall. Wovon hierzulande die Rede ist," *Reden an Österreich: Schriftsteller ergreifen das Wort*, ed. Jochen Jung (Salzburg: Residenz, 1988) 38–56.

7. Biographical data can be found in Hans Haider, "Barbara Frischmuth, eine Biographie," *Dossier 4: Barbara Frischmuth,* ed. Kurt Bartsch (Graz: Droschl, 1992) 151–162.

8. P. M. Lützeler, "Barbara Frischmuths Demeter-Trilogie: Mythologische Finde-Spiele in der postmodernen Literatur," *Dossier 4: Barbara Frischmuth* 73–97; Gerald Chapple, "Demeter in Altaussee: Frischmuth's Response to Broch's *Die Verzauberung,*" *Geschichte der österreichischen Literatur — Teil 2,* ed. Donald Daviau and Herbert Arlt (St. Ingbert: Röhrig Universitätsverlag, 1996) 544–558; Pamela S. Saur, "Barbara Frischmuth's Use of Mythology in Her 'Demeter Trilogy,'" *Out of the Shadows: Essays on Contemporary Austrian Women Writers and Filmmakers,* ed. Margarete Lamb-Faffelberger (Riverside, CA: Ariadne, 1997) 101–110.

9. Barbara Frischmuth, *Herrin der Tiere: Erzählung* (1986; repr., Munich: dtv, 1990); *Über die Verhältnisse* (Salzburg: Residenz, 1987); *Traum der Literatur — Literatur des Traums: Münchner Poetik-Vorlesungen* (Salzburg: Residenz, 1991).

10. Original quote: "Das Wunderbare an der Beschäftigung mit einem Mythos ist, daß es keinen streng vorgegebenen, kanonisierten Originaltext gibt. Der Mythos war immmer schon da, und welche Version wir auch

hören oder für ursprünglich halten, schon der nächste Mythograph wird die Geschichte anders erzählen, sie mit anderen Traditionen verknüpfen, in eine andere Richtung assoziieren, die in ihr vorkommenden Namen (das, was Ranke-Graves das Realistische am Mythos nennt) mit anderen Namen in Verbindung bringen, sie vielleicht sogar auf andere Personen beziehen, andere Etymologien bilden. . . . Dieses Sich-Vortasten auf nie ganz gesichertem Grund ist die verführerischste Einladung an eine Autorin, sich an dem Finde-Spiel zu beteiligen, es weiterzuspielen und die Geschichte von Demeter und Kore für sich neu zu schreiben."

11. Original quote: "Nichts liegt der selbstreflexiven, selbstkritischen, skeptischen, ironisch-parodistischen Literatur der Postmoderne ferner, als daran mitzuarbeiten, neue Mythen zu stiften oder alten wieder zur Geltung zu verhelfen" (Lützeler 76).

12. Lützeler 91.

13. "Kindschaft im Gegensatz zu Herrschaft. Eleusis ist auch das Mysterium der ständig sich erneuernden Kindschaft, des Zurückkehrens in den Schoß, des Wiedergeborenwerdens" (Lützeler 76).

14. During the last fifteen years, various meanings of the Demeter/Persephone myth have been researched intensively by feminist literary scholars, psychologists, and theologians. To name just a few: Heide Göttner-Abendroth, *Die tanzende Göttin: Prinzipien einer matriarchalen Ästhetik,* 4th exp. ed. (Munich: Frauenoffensive, 1988); Susanne Heine, *Wiederbelebung der Göttinnen?* 2d ed. (Göttingen: Vandenhoeck & Ruprecht, 1989); Heide Göttner-Abendroth, *Das Matriarchat I: Geschichte seiner Erforschung,* 2d ed. (Stuttgart: Kohlhammer, 1989); Marianne Hirsch, *The Mother/Daughter Plot: Narrative, Psychoanalysis, Feminism* (Bloomington: Indiana UP, 1989); Gerda Weiler, *Der enteignete Mythos: Eine feministische Revision der Archetypenlehre C. G. Jungs und Erich Neumanns* (Frankfurt/Main: Campus, 1991).

15. Saur in her "Use of Mythology" is particularly interested in the feminist aspects of this myth, although I think that she expands it too far to be useful when she states: "If Oedipus is the model for the life span of a man, then Demeter functions as the model for a modern woman" or "While any story of a daughter's maturation and independence fits the Demeter structure" (102).

16. Christa Wolf, *Voraussetzungen einer Erzählung: Kassandra — Frankfurter Vorlesungen* (1983; repr., Hamburg: Luchterhand, 1990).

17. Schickelgruber was the name of Adolf Hitler's father, who was

born as an illegitimate child to Maria Anna Schickelgruber. Thus, this would have been Hitler's real name.

18. Lützeler 92; Chapple 549.

19. Some of the interpretive difficulties that Lützeler encounters have to do with his interpreting Trude as a Demeter figure. Then the persistent symbolism of death doesn't make sense to him, and he finds it exaggerated ("Mythologische Finde-Spiele" 93).

20. Chapple 553–554.

21. Lützeler mistakenly attributes angelic qualities as well as Demeter qualities to this figure because of her name and because of her maternal behavior with Vevi ("Mythologische Findespiele" 95).

22. The Baubo figure is featured in *The Homeric "Hymn to Demeter": Translation, Commentary, and Interpretive Essays*, ed. Helene P. Foley (Princeton, NJ: Princeton UP, 1994).

23. Original quote: "Selbst wenn ich einen Witz erzählte — und ich versuchte mich sehr früh in diesem Genre — versuchte sie mir beizubringen, wie das mit der Pointe funktionierte und daß man sie so lange wie möglich nicht verraten durfte, ohne daß gleichzeitig die Spannung nachließ."

24. Margarete Mitscherlich, *Erinnerungsarbeit: Zur Psychoanalyse der Unfähigkeit zu trauern* (Frankfurt/Main: Fischer, 1987).

The Child within Us: On Barbara Frischmuth's Books for Young Readers

Gerlinde Ulm Sanford

Perusing a bibliography of Barbara Frischmuth's works, it becomes obvious that she has been writing children's books during most of her writing career.[1] Indeed, children's books represent an important part of her impressive œuvre. This study[2] tries to determine some of the outstanding characteristics of her books in that genre and, furthermore, to ponder with some concrete examples the relationship between written texts and illustrations in her books for children.

When I interviewed her in Altaussee in December 1996, Barbara Frischmuth touched on a number of subjects, including her children's books. She said that she had discovered the magic of children's books when she was about twenty-six or twenty-seven years old. For her, this did not only mean reading German fairy tales, however. Moreover, she read and enjoyed especially Lewis Carroll (1832–1898), George MacDonald (1824–1905), J. R. R. Tolkien (1892–1973). Barbara Frischmuth was an enthusiastic reader from childhood on and later read her English favorites in the original language. During her childhood, she felt a lack of variety in children's books, as only a few classics were available during the years after World War II. Later, when she started writing children's books, she attempted to write the kinds of books she would have liked to read as a child.

Sometimes Barbara Frischmuth tells her stories slightly "against the grain" by correcting clichés as we might have inherited them from classical children's books.[3] For instance, in contrast to the situation in the fairy tale of "Der Froschkönig" (1812, The Frog Prince), the toad in *Gutenachtgeschichte für Maria Carolina* (1994, Bedtime Story for Maria Carolina)[4] is neither disgusting to little Maria Carolina, nor does she want to throw it against the wall, nor does she even want it to turn into a prince. In the story "Die Prinzessin in der Zwirnspule" (1972, The Princess in the Twisting Spool),[5] the magician is outwitted by princess Garlieb,[6] who is being helped by the Bücherwurm (the Bookworm). From *Der Struwwelpeter* (1847, The Sloppy Head),[7] we might have adopted the idea that sloppiness is a very bad vice. In Barbara Frischmuth's *Gutenachtgeschichte für Maria Carolina*, sloppiness is not exactly promoted to being a virtue. Yet, it is at least "fun" in Maria Carolina's dream, and neither the mother of the Sloppies, nor her own mother get very angry with their sloppy children. With these and many other examples that go against the grain, Barbara Frischmuth perhaps wishes to invite us, the adults, to reevaluate certain outdated concepts for their appropriateness in our modern times.

Other concepts are upheld. Cruelty, for instance, is a vice in old children's books and remains one in Barbara Frischmuth's, as we can learn in the story of the "Der grasgrüne Steinfresser" (1972, Grass-Green Stone Gobbler),[8] in *Vom Mädchen, das übers Wasser ging* (1996, Of the Girl Who Walked across the Water),[9] in *Donna & Dario* (1997, Donna & Dario).[10] Frightening others is considered dangerous as well as cruel in the story "Der Mäuseschreck" (1972, The Mouse Scare).[11] Here, a hidden lesson is directed foremost toward adult and adolescent males. First, the mouse father frightens the mouse mother by grabbing her around the waist and meowing. Later, the mouse brother, Franz, and his little sister, Sieglinde, play the "frightening game." Franz dons a cat mask and frightens Sieglinde in the same way as his father had frightened his mother. When Franz then mistakes a real cat for his father he almost gets killed.

One might assume that one's children would play a fairly big role in writing children's books, but Barbara Frischmuth contradicts that thought. For her, the process involves writing for the child within each of us.[12] Consequently, throughout all of her children's books, Barbara Frischmuth avoids a didactic tone. Nonetheless, children learn many things from her books. She applies various poetic devices, some of which are rather demanding. Without being fully aware of these devices, the children probably sharpen their sensitivity for the many dimensions of language in Barbara Frischmuth's texts. They might learn to discern between literal and figurative meanings of idioms or proverbs. They might delight in repeating alliterating rhymes or find out that someone who cannot or does not distinguish between certain sounds might produce a very funny effect.

Of course, the language in a children's book has to be somewhat simpler than in books for grown-ups. Barbara Frischmuth maintains that writing in a simpler language is for her not a conscious effort. She says that when talking to the child within her, or when imagining to speak with other children, the language automatically becomes simpler. Furthermore, she does not consider herself an author who specifically writes for children.[13]

Barbara Frischmuth wishes to communicate information and cultural as well as moral values to children, yet she objects adamantly to apparent pedagogical strategies in children's books. Perhaps she takes to heart the wisdom of the following quote by Johann Carl August Musäus:

"Excellent morals, however, are for youth zeros without numbers" ("Jedoch die trefflichen Moralen sind bey die Jugend Nullen ohne Zahlen").[14] Nonetheless, she is very careful to distinguish clearly between good and evil. She emphasizes that this is an absolute must when writing children's books, because children tend to follow the models presented in a book. The author of a children's book, therefore, has to take a clear position. Consequently, the writer has to express the distinction between good and evil in a more straightforward manner than when writing for grown-ups. That also affects the technique of storytelling. The simpler language required in a story for children enforces narrative explicitness in general and clarity in the distinction between good and evil in particular. Writing for adults, the author may and perhaps should play with the language. Multiple layers of meaning produced by ironic play with the language are attractive to grown-ups. Writing for children, the alternatives of play with language are reduced. The place for "play" is the action of a story rather than the language. With simpler sentences, attitudes, and viewpoints, opinions inevitably become more closely determined.

While the above represents Barbara Frischmuth's own assessment and might, furthermore, be a general characteristic for children's books, I dare observe that Barbara Frischmuth plays relatively much with language, even in her children's books. The children, however, might not always comprehend the full scope of her play. The pleasure in playing with language can even become the main object of a poetic task. This is, for example, the case in her book *Amoralische Kinderklapper* (1969, Amoral Children's Rattle).[15] The title of the book might make one believe that it is a book for children. In reality, this is not a children's book at all. Instead, it is a book for grown-ups. It is a play with the *sujet* children's book, a play with language: exploring the mimicry of language, experimenting with jargons, with special languages, and so forth.

Many children's stories involve animals. The author, therefore, has to take into consideration the natural characteristics of the animals. At least, this is what Barbara Frischmuth attempts to do. She has undertaken thorough studies in animal behavior and carefully tries to maintain an animal's typical attributes in her stories.

Der Pluderich (1969, Mister Puffy)[16] is one of her earliest works. This name arouses several associations: *Pluderhosen* are wide breeches; *pludern* means to puff or swell out; *sich aufplustern* can refer to a bird's ruffling up its feathers, but it can also mean to give oneself airs, to puff oneself up; *plodern* means to flutter and wave in respect to loose clothes.

The wonderful illustrations for this book are by Walter Schmögner. Text and illustrations complement and enhance each other. On the title page, we see Pluderich in all his splendor. He is round as a ball and seems ready to burst. The text says: "On his body, Pluderich wore wide breeches and a wide jacket, all blown up and tight. If chance would have it that he was not puffing himself up, then his clothes were fluttering and waving, and kept fluttering and waving until Pluderich hurried to puff himself up again in order to fill his clothes."[17] The second illustration shows Pluderich in a sad state of deflation: "Pluderich was what one calls a babbler, a prattler, a chatterbox." To describe Pluderich with the corresponding German descriptive nouns *Plaudertasche* (babbler), *Dampfplauderer* (prattler), *Plapperkasten* (chatterbox) is of course funnier because of the alliterations. We are further told in metaphoric idioms that he "could not tame his tongue," that he "did not mince matters," and that he "picked everybody to pieces" ("Er konnte seine Zunge nicht im Zaum halten, sich kein Blatt vor den Mund nehmen und an anderen kein gutes Wort lassen"). Nonetheless, Pluderich had followers. Some people, though, were so shocked at his stories that they opened their mouths in amazement and could not close them anymore. No physician was able to help them.

The paragraph I just paraphrased is only four lines long, yet Barbara Frischmuth acquaints her young readers in these lines with six or seven idioms, and she sharpens their artistic sense with alliterations. A common pitfall for authors of children's books "is the temptation to 'talk down' to their readers."[18] This never happens to Barbara Frischmuth. The opposite might be the case. Her playing with actual and figurative meaning of idioms, with alliteration and other aspects of language might sometimes be fully appreciated only by observant adults while children might grasp a number — yet not all — of these artistic devices.

Without Walter Schmögner's illustrations, of course, her words would be only half as effective. We see Pluderich first in his suit that is so tight that the buttons might slip out of the buttonholes any second. In the second illustration, we see him with his clothes infinitely sadly hanging down. Two onlookers stand by, with mouths agape. The next picture shows the office of Dr. Simsalabim, who tries in vain to help four patients with their affliction of abiding mouth agape. When Pluderich has done the rounds of the entire world, he positions himself in the middle of the market square and waits until enough people have gathered. Then he puffs himself up more and more while his listeners become more and more flabbergasted. The German word for flabbergasted is *platt. Platt*, however, has several meanings. It can mean flat, flabbergasted, and also shallow. As could be expected, Pluderich finally explodes. We see in Walter Schmögner's illustrations a police officer recording the outcome of that explosion. At the end of the story, the city has a monument erected for Pluderich because, after all, he was a well-known and well-traveled personality. An adult might get an ironic message from this story. Whereas bragging might lead to a catastrophe, it might also bring temporary fame. People are the more impressed or even mesmerized (mouth agape) the more scandalous and uncanny a story is. A child who does not yet know the world and the weaknesses of the people might beware of acting like Pluderich because of the explosion and learn only much later that there are many Pluderichs among us and as many who admire them, mouth agape.

Polsterer (1970, Mr. Plumy)[19] is another one of Barbara Frischmuth's books that features relatively little text and relies all the more on illustrations. The meaning of the German name *Polsterer* respresents here the synopsis of the story, as it were: Polsterer is the one who makes everyone feel as if lying on a soporific cushion. It is the story about a man who makes people sleep well — his presence has the effect of a cushion. Polsterer becomes the intimate friend of the king, who suffers from insomnia. Not only the king falls fast asleep whenever he is in Polsterer's presence. But Polsterer also strokes the police and safety officers' pillows in such a perfect way that they are overcome by heavy sleep. For the young readers, this might be a calming bedtime story, while the adult reader cannot miss the implied political satire on Austria's sleepy government.

The natural environment is a very important topic to Barbara Frischmuth. Several of her stories clearly portray the human beings as the "evil" ones, because they endanger or ruin various natural habitats. In *Biberzahn und der Khan der Winde* (1991, Beaver Tooth and the Khan of the Winds),[20] for instance, two men from the surveyor's office are charged with surveying a river basin for its suitability as location of a future dam. Windis Khan, the chief of the winds, named in analogy to the famous Mongol ruler Genghis Khan, who brought all the nomadic tribes of Mongolia under his rule, produces such devastating storms during the time of the survey that the plan to build a dam is dropped for the time being. With this action, Windis Khan tries to please his beloved princess Beaver Tooth, as he fears the destruction of the beavers' lodge from the effects of such a dam. The German word for beavers' lodge, or beavery, is *Biberburg*, meaning beavers' fortress, a word that is of course much more suitable for the romantic love story between the beaver princess, Beaver Tooth, and the wind chief, Windis Khan.

Another example of Barbara Frischmuth's concern for healthy natural habitats is her story *Vom Mädchen, das übers Wasser ging.* The story takes place in and along a river that once had become so polluted by human beings that the fish were floating in the river with their bellies up. Fortunately, at the time of the story, matters have slightly improved so that an otter who escaped from the preserve dares to remain in freedom in that river basin.

Biberzahn und der Khan der Winde also illustrates another of the recurring subtle lessons in Barbara Frischmuth's books for children: a lesson in kindness. This story portrays three types of relationships: Chubby Max and Gussi as well as the other friends; Max and the Storyteller; Beaver Tooth and Windis Khan. In all three relationships, kindness and consideration are of great importance. When Max and his friends are playing ball, Gussi, one of the boys, unintentionally hits Max on the head with a ball. Max was hit so hard that he has to lie down under a tree. The friends, especially Gussi, express kindness and consideration with their concern about Max's health. Max, on the other hand, does not blame the more athletic Gussi for this accident.

While Max is lying down under a big tree, his drowsy head imagines perceiving a storyteller sitting in the branches. It is a very experienced storyteller who can remember the times when people were not yet able to write. He and Max together set out inventing a story: the storyteller in more solemn terms, Max in his blunt boyish language. Through the contrast in their way of expression and by having them argue with each other how the story should go on, Barbara Frischmuth achieves many comical effects. This notwithstanding, she shows how both, the old storyteller and the boy, politely defer to each other. The storyteller cringes a number of times at Max's casual narrating style, and Max accepts his critique. Yet, in several instances it is the storyteller who learns from Max's realistic and unsentimental viewpoint.

The third relationship demonstrating such a subtle lesson in kindness is that of Beaver Tooth and Windis Khan. Their love story constitutes the main action of the book. They are the most unlikely lovers one could imagine. The stormy chief of the winds, who enjoys wild flights around the world, falls in love with a "democratic" beaver princess, who cherishes water, gnawing on trees, and wants to live up to her responsibilities within the democratic beaver society. After most of Windis Kahn's visits to the beaver fortress, the fortress needs repair, even if he is as gentle as possible. Meeting each other on a meadow instead makes their rendezvous very uncomfortable, especially in the winter. One day, therefore, Windis Khan persuades Beaver Tooth to come along on a flight around the world. The first attempt fails right away as Beaver Tooth falls through a hole she gnaws into Windis Khan's cloak. Fortunately, she falls into a lake. Windis Khan tries to find her and thereby blows so hard into his panpipe that it bursts. Of course, he finds her, and she assembles another panpipe for him out of reed that she chews off to the right size. In a boat chewed by Beaver Tooth and equipped with Windis Khan's coat as a sail, they enjoy a brief idyllic time. Nevertheless, Beaver Tooth soon realizes that Windis Khan misses aviation. Very kindly, albeit with great fear, she agrees therefore to another flying enterprise around the world with him. He holds her tightly this time, and Beaver Tooth bravely tries to enjoy the flight. Nonetheless, she becomes so frightened that her face turns all green. Windis Khan finally brings her to one of his cloud castles. Needless to say that Beaver Tooth, despite her love, cannot be happy there in the long run. One day, when they focus the "earth observatory" onto the beaver fortress to alleviate her homesickness, they observe two human surveyors. Windis Khan understands very well that the presence of these men means danger to the beaver habitat. He summons the North Wind, and they produce such a powerful storm that the surveyors intend to report to their superiors that the river basin area would be completely unsuitable for a dam. The beavers are happy and thank Windis Khan and their princess. Windis Khan accepts that Beaver Tooth cannot live with him up in the clouds; she accepts that he cannot sit still and live in a boat. Yet, she promises to come along on some flight in late fall, and he promises to visit her as often as possible up on a little bluff in the meadow. They love each other and are forgiving and understanding of each other's limitations.

Children have a hard time understanding why grown-ups always insist on orderliness and cleanliness. Barbara Frischmuth's book *Gute-nachtgeschichte für Maria Carolina* tells the adventures of Maria Carolina in the mysterious land of the Sloppies. This is how the story goes:

One day, a huge toad[21] with golden eyes appears in Maria Carolina's room on top of her former nursery table. Unlike the princess in the fairy tale "The Frog Prince," Maria Carolina is afraid that the toad might fall down, crash into the wall and change into a prince who then perhaps would want her to pay more attention to clean dresses. In Barbara Frischmuth's tale, it is not a princess who gives a promise to a toad for retrieving her golden ball from the water. Instead, it is the toad who promises Maria Carolina an adventure. They set out in a boat and finally arrive in the land of the Sloppies.[22] Its inhabitants speak in a strange hissing language that is produced by not distinguishing between the German sounds for *z, sch,* and *s.*[23] It is hard to convey in English an impression comparable to the one produced in German. To Maria Carolina, this strange-sounding language is so intriguing that she remembers and hums the little stanza she heard from *Sudel-Sors* (Sloppy-Sors) in the morning, when her dream adventure is over and when reality sets in. His language reminds her probably of her own language, perhaps at a time when she was having trouble with her pronunciation because of a missing tooth.

The prerequisite for being able to see the Sloppies and for entering their country is admitting to be a Sloppy. Therefore, the Toad and Maria Carolina admit to being sloppy, the Toad adds with a philosophical sigh: "In one way or another, we all are Sloppies" ("Auf die eine oder andere Weise sind wir alle Sudel").

In the land of the Sloppies, Maria Carolina enjoys doing all those things she is not permitted at home. She rolls in the mud, just as the Sloppies do in order to groom their fur; she eats with her hands; she messes up her dress with pretty patterns of blueberry stains. In other words, she enjoys a feast of sloppiness.

After the Sloppies roll in the mud, wait for seven hundred seconds, and finally shake themselves, their fur shines and looks as if it had been brushed. Of course, that method works on furs only, and when Maria Carolina tries it on her messy dress, it does not have the same effect. The dress continues to look messy and stained. At her sight, the Toad reiterates with composure: "In a certain way, we all are Sloppies" ("In gewisser Weise sind wir alle Sudel"), and he adds: "Except that it's not equally suiting for everyone" ("Es steht nur nicht jedem gleich gut").

The book *Vom Mädchen, das übers Wasser ging* is about being kind to each other and about the danger our environment is in. It is the story of a little otter who escaped from the nature preserve through a hole in the fence. Once again, Barbara Frischmuth shows that she is well acquainted with the looks and behavior of the animals that play a role in her story. That is especially true for the otter who dons in this story an impressive array of a real otter's typical characteristics.[24]

Little Otter finds it somewhat cumbersome to find enough food for himself[25] in the river. In the preserve, the food had been laid out for him at a certain place. That was much easier. Furthermore, he feels lonely without his siblings. Nonetheless, he enjoys his freedom and, therefore, does not wish to return to the preserve. He tries to make friends with a Water Vole, a Ring-Snake, and a Cormorant. This does not work out too well though, because of these animals' different lifestyles. When Otter wants to play hide-and-seek, the Water Vole disappears in narrow crevices. The Ring-Snake swims much too slowly and is not able to dive, so playing catch is not much fun. Practicing target with the Cormorant proves likewise a failure because the Cormorant catches and devours immediately all the fish that Otter throws. Or else the Cormorant throws his own fish so high that the other Cormorants catch them in flight long before Otter can catch them. Among the animals on the river there is also a big, old Toad. She has golden eyes and is covered with warts that glimmer like amber. When Otter cannot find quite enough food to feel satisfied, her constant advice for Otter is: "You must have patience!" She remembers the times when the dead fish were floating belly-up on the river's surface.

Fish, mussels, and snails seem to function in this Frischmuth story as creatures who do not deserve the same empathy as more developed animals. As mentioned above, little fish serve not only as food, but in addition as toys for Otter and the Cormorants. If Otter cannot get enough fish or mussels, he resorts to eating slugs. Likewise, we are told of the Toad's catching a fat black fly without qualms. This is the situation in and along the river. Then one day something interesting happens.

Otter usually enjoys sleeping late. On this particular day, the Ring-Snake comes to Otter's cave and almost frightens Otter out of his sleep. She has caught sight of a very strange thing: a little girl sitting on a fallen tree trunk, crying — crying so intensely that her tears make the river salty. "She had her arms wrapped around her legs, her head on her knees. / Her slender body shaking and all sobs, / she wept as if her heart would break, causing her dress's gay colors / and her scarf's even gayer ones to fade, as it were, / and her brown curls to uncurl from grief."[26] When Otter comes to the exit of the cave, all kinds of animals are already assembled and wonder about the meaning of the girl's sobbing. Concluding from his own situation, Otter volunteers the opinion that the girl might be weeping because she feels lonely. The wise Toad considers that possibility unlikely, as — from his perspective — there are more than enough human beings everywhere.

A little Fire-Bellied Toad suspects that one of the girl's relatives might have become flattened down on the road that leads to the river, as happens so often to toads. In order to command respect, the Fire-Bellied Toad raises her legs so that the Ring-Snake might be shocked when perceiving the red and black warning coloration of her belly. Each animal comes up with a different explanation reflecting the different dangers threatening their lives. A migratory Tippet Grebe suspects that the girl's parents might have gotten lost on their travel route. A Black-Tailed Godwit fears that the girl's parents might have been hunted. A Field Adder who is said to be extinct yet has secretly survived proposes that the girl might cry because people always shriek when they see her, just as happens to the poor Field Adder.

A big Purple Emperor who tries to sip from the flowers of the girl's dress is not able either to comfort the girl. She keeps weeping and weeping. The old wise Toad finally suggests that Otter should caress her with his beautiful fur. Otter is a little bit afraid at first, as the girl is so much bigger than he is. Yet, he moves closer and closer and finally touches her back with his fur. Her tears slowly begin to cease flowing, and she looks at her surroundings. The first creature she sees is a kingfisher rocking himself on a twig, pensively slanting his head. That makes her smile. When she discovers that Otter has already ventured to place his head onto her knees, she laughs out loud and begins to caress him cautiously. The animals feel attracted to her smiles and her silvery laughter. Now they all come closer and closer, yet the girl does not show any fear. "The old Toad whispered: 'She seems to be of the ancient kind [of human beings] / of the kind who maintained good neighborly relations with the animals'" ("Sie scheint von der alten Art zu sein," flüsterte die Kröte, / "von der Art, die in guter Nachbarschaft mit den Tieren lebten"). The little girl does not even seem afraid of snakes, she even caresses with one of her fingers the back of the Ring-Snake as if it were "a precious bracelet that she had just received as a gift" ("wie ein kostbares Armband, / das es soeben geschenkt / bekommen hatte").

What do the children learn here? To be sure, Barbara Frischmuth does not teach anything in boring sermon form, nor with raised finger. Yet indirectly, as the story progresses, the young readers learn many things that are important for any group of creatures living together: tolerance toward each other, consideration for other creatures' peculiarities, appreciation of different expressions of beauty, and much more.

Barbara Frischmuth corrects stereotypical clichés such as snakes being dangerous or toads being ugly and poisonous.

It is again the wise old Toad who draws the conclusion from this unusually peaceful scene. “Life can be like that too,” croaks the Toad, “remember that!” (“So kann das Leben auch sein,” quäkte die Kröte, “merkt euch das!”) Then, in order to demonstrate this possible peacefulness of life, she refrains from snapping at the Damsel Fly that hovers with curiosity above the girl’s toes.

The idyll is interrupted by a group of boys and girls who approach, shouting loudly and with sticks in their hands. They obviously want to hurt the little girl. In panic, the little girl goes into the water. Otter, the clever fellow, immediately senses the danger and places himself under the feet of the little girl. Then he swims out into the river, with her standing on top of him.

> It was an overwhelming sight,
> as the girl moved over the water.
> A snake in her hand, little animals on her shoulders
> and a halo of orange speckled butterflies
> around her head.[27]

The wild horde of children is silenced as they fall down on their knees before this miracle. Arrived on the other shore, the little girl hugs Otter and says good-bye to all the different friendly animals, while the other children return home, ashamed and perhaps a little pensive.

Solidarity is one of the important basic ideas of our civilization. Despite this, it almost seems to have been forgotten in our times, as Barbara Frischmuth observes. In her book *Donna & Dario* (1997, Donna & Dario), she refreshes our consciousness about the significance of solidarity by discussing it in the framework of an animal state.

Donna and Dario are spoiled cats. They live luxurious lives because their master brings home delicious lox or caviar leftovers from his business. They are well nourished, well groomed, and can sleep as long as they like. Donna is the mother, Dario her son. They are perfectly happy until one day little Dario jumps after his favorite toy, a black bathtub plug. The bathtub plug flying through the air this time is not really the bathtub plug, however. Instead, when the unsuspecting little Dario jumps after it out of a window on the sixth floor, he lands on the back of a crow! With that, a kind of Odyssey starts for the young tomcat, Dario, as well as for his mother, Donna, who sets out to find her son in the bewildering jungle of a metropolis resembling Vienna. Donna learns that a so-called canal-bank society tries to induce law and order among all kinds of animals living in the city. Stray cats and dogs, mice, rats, crows, seagulls, and even a few animals that belong to a human being have become members of this canal-bank society and strive to introduce the principles of democracy among all animals. Killing is forbidden; edible waste is to be collected in communal efforts and is to be divided justly. So far, however, this democratic canal-bank society has been effective only on the city side of the canal. On the opposite side of the canal where there is still some open land, cats and other animals live in anarchistic chaos and even rob from the peacefully organized side. However, they kill and rob not for pleasure, but only for their survival. The martens, however, who for unknown reasons have invaded both sides of the canal-bank, pose the greatest danger. They nip off little cats' and little birds' heads, not in order to survive, but rather because of pure bloodthirstiness.[28] They are the "evil" creatures within this animal democracy, much like the human beings in *Biberzahn und der Khan der Winde* and in *Vom Mädchen, das übers Wasser ging.* Dario gets first into the companionship of the uncivilized animals on the opposite canal-bank while Donna keeps looking for him on the city side, where the canal-bank society is effective.

These are elements for a detective story. Barbara Frischmuth exploits them to the limit, keeping our attention to the very end. Two juvenile martens are taken hostage, and later the headquarters of the martens is besieged. The evil martens are finally forced to capitulate, because the members of the canal-bank society, as well as the free animal gangs from the other side of the canal join forces against them. Spies shadow the martens to ensure that they finally stick to a truce. At the end of the book, finally, Donna and Dario find each other again. Furthermore, they find their way back to their human caretaker and are again spoiled with lox and caviar. They have learned a lesson in solidarity and kindness and insist, therefore, on bringing less fortunate friends to their luxurious home. Their human caretaker likewise proves capable of learning: He shows increased magnanimity by installing a cat door. Now Donna and Dario can enjoy the utopian state of having freedom while nonetheless being protected.

Whereas George Orwell in his *Animal Farm*[29] criticizes a totalitarian state in animal disguise, Barbara Frischmuth projects an almost-utopia into the animal world. In *Donna & Dario*, written for young readers yet interesting to adult readers, as well, the author once more speaks up for an enlightened and considerate society, as she has done in many of her books. As in all of her books portraying animals, she proves that she is well acquainted with the natural behavior of the animals, a prerequisite for writing a convincing and engaging animal story.

Selecting good books for young readers might be a dilemma. What should one look for? Children's books can be a valuable resource, enriching other educational resources we provide young children and facilitating their growth and development. In reviewing the literature, most early childhood experts agree that young children learn by doing. Through activities, children assimilate knowledge and broaden their experiences. For this reason, the focus of early education is encouragement to do things, ask questions, and explore. A good children's book should have the potential to stimulate young readers in the mental actions of transforming, comparing, organizing, and symbolizing. In this sense, then, learning through reading books can become active learning. I think that Barbara Frischmuth's books further exactly that. Her readers learn and are stimulated to observe animals and their surroundings, to interact with each other, or to learn to appreciate different dimensions of language. Barbara Frischmuth's stories are "modern" in the best sense. She does, however, offer interesting scenarios and descriptions and utopian models of the world to children in which the traditional binary oppositions between nature and culture, people and animals, male and female are frequently negotiated and restructured in favor of a more open and inclusive approach to and view of the world. Thus, her world for children does appear to be a magically transformed place that is equally hospitable to all creatures alike without erecting new and artificial hierarchies. She alerts her young readers to our endangered environment as she stands for tolerance and fairness in human interactions. Even though children's books might not be the ideal forum to defend women's rights, Barbara Frischmuth finds ways to do so occasionally. Without being aggressive, she assigns typical "boy's roles" to girls and vice versa. These and many other lofty principles are, however, not spelled out in boring didactic treatises. Instead, laughing is permitted and lessons are given only ever so subtly in her stories.

Syracuse University

Notes

1. Here, in chronological order, Barbara Frischmuth's best-known children's books: *Der Pluderich* (Frankfurt/Main: Insel, 1969), with illustr. by Walter Schmögner; *Philomena Mückenschnabel* (Frankfurt/ Main: Insel, 1970), with illustr. by Robert Doxat; *Polsterer* (Frankfurt/ Main: Insel, 1970), with illustr. by Robert Zeppel Sperl; *Die Prinzessin in der Zwirnspule und andere Puppenspiele für Kinder* (Munich: Ellermann, 1972), with illustr. by Ulrike Enders; *Ida und Ob* (Vienna: Jugend & Volk, 1972), with illustr. by Karlheinz Gross; *Grizzly Dickbauch und Frau Nuffl* (Pfaffenweiler: Pfaffenweiler, 1975), with block prints by Axel Hertenstein; *Die Ferienfamilie* (Salzburg: Residenz, 1981); *Der liebe Augustin* (Lucern: Reich, 1981), with illustr. by Inge Morath; *Biberzahn und der Khan der Winde* (Vienna: Jugend & Volk, 1990), with illustr. by Angelika Kaufmann; *Sommersee* (Vienna: Jugend & Volk, 1991); Barbara Frischmuth and Jutta Treiber, *Ida, Bine und die Pferde* (Munich: Schneider, 1991); *Machtnix: oder Der Lauf, den die Welt nahm. Eine Bildergeschichte* (Salzburg: Residenz, 1993); *Gutenacht-geschichte für Maria Carolina* (Vienna: Jugend & Volk, 1994), with illustr. by Dusan Kállay; *Vom Mädchen, das übers Wasser ging* (Vienna: Dachs, 1996), with illustr. by Dusan Kállay; *Donna & Dario* (Frankfurt/Main: Sauerländer, 1997).

2. A study of this small scope can, of course, not be complete. I restricted myself to a number of Barbara Frischmuth's books for readers of approximately age six to twelve, *Donna & Dario* perhaps being the exception, as it might be suited for more mature adolescents as well.

3. The following books proved to be valuable background materials in regard to this essay and might be of general interest to anyone involved with children's literature. The books listed are in random order: Bettina Hurlimann, *Europäische Kinderbücher in drei Jahrhunderten* (1963); Florence V. Barry, *A Century of Children's Books* (1922; repr. 1968); Irene Dyhrenfurth-Graebsch, *Geschichte des deutschen Jugendbuches* (1967); H. L. Koster, *Geschichte der deutschen Jugendliteratur* (1968); Marie-Therese Latzarus, *La Littérature enfantine en France dans la seconde moitié du XIXe siècle* (1923); Richard Bamberger, *Jugendlektüre* (1965); Eleanor Cameron, *The Green and Burning Tree: On the Writing and Enjoyment of Children's Books* (1969); Hans Cornioley, *Beiträge zur Jugendbuchkunde* (1966); Margery Fisher, *Intent upon Reading: A Critical Appraisal of Modern Fiction for Children* (1961); Lillian H.

Smith, *The Unreluctant Years: A Critical Approach to Children's Literature* (1953); Anne Pellowski, *The World of Children's Literature* (1968); Brian Doyle (ed.), *The Who's Who of Children's Literature* (1968); Bettina Hurlimann, *Die Welt im Bilderbuch* (1965).

4. Barbara Frischmuth, *Gutenachtgeschichte für Maria Carolina* (Vienna: Dachs, 1994).

5. Barbara Frischmuth, *Die Prinzessin in der Zwirnspule und andere Puppenspiele für Kinder* (Munich: Ellermann, 1972).

6. The invented German name *Garlieb* means "completely lovely." It is probably in contrast to the expression *jemandem den Garaus machen* (to kill someone).

7. Heinrich Hoffmann, *Der Struwwelpeter* (1847).

8. Barbara Frischmuth, "Der grasgrüne Steinfresser," in *Die Prinzessin in der Zwirnspule.*

9. Barbara Frischmuth, *Vom Mädchen, das übers Wasser ging* (Vienna: Dachs, 1996).

10. Barbara Frischmuth, *Donna & Dario* (Frankfurt/Main: Sauerländer, 1997).

11. Barbara Frischmuth, "Der Mäuseschreck," in *Die Prinzessin in der Zwirnspule.*

12. See my interview with Barbara Frischmuth as contained in this volume.

13. See my interview with Barbara Frischmuth as contained in this volume.

14. Johann Carl August Musäus, *Moralische Kinderklapper* (Gotha: Carl Wilhelm Ettinger, 1794) 78. Barbara Frischmuth uses this quote as a motto for her *Amoralische Kinderklapper* (1969, Amoral Children's Rattle).

15. Barbara Frischmuth, *Amoralische Kinderklapper* (Frankfurt/Main: Suhrkamp, 1969).

16. Barbara Frischmuth, *Der Pluderich* (Darmstadt: Insel, 1969).

17. Original quote: "Auf dem Leib trug Pluderich eine Pluderhose und eine Pluderjacke. Wollte es der Zufall, daß Pluderich sich gerade nicht aufpluderte, dann ploderten seine Kleider, und ploderten, und ploderten. Bis Pluderich sich schleunigst wieder aufpluderte, um sein Gewand auszufüllen." Here, and with several others of Barbara Frischmuth's childrens' books, it is not possible to indicate a page number, as some books contain no pagination.

18. Lisa Carpenter, ed., *Children's Writer's & Illustrator's Market*

(Cincinnati: F&W Publications, 1993) 17.

19. Barbara Frischmuth, *Polsterer* (Frankfurt/Main: Insel, 1970).

20. Barbara Frischmuth, *Biberzahn und der Khan der Winde* (Reinbek: Rowohlt, 1991).

21. Barbara Frischmuth uses the German word *Kröte,* which is feminine and usually translates as "toad." The association with the frog from the fairy tale "The Frog Prince" would go more smoothly with *Frosch,* which is masculine. Throughout the story, *die Kröte* and the feminine pronoun *sie* are used. The illustrations show "her" with male clothes, however.

22. In German, *die Sudel* (plural) is derived from *sudeln* (to make a mess, to be sloppy).

23. It might be difficult to produce a translation without losing the acoustic effect of the stanza: "Sön und saurig ist die Seit / Sonne seint und Snee, der sneit. / Sieben Swerge, sieben Sachen / lassen keine Seit zum Snarchen."

24. This rare animal appears in nature with a lithe, slender body, a long neck, small ears, and short legs. Its head is flattened, and the base of the tail is almost as thick as the body. It has a fur that is highly valued by man, webbed feet permit it to be an excellent swimmer, it can travel long underwater without surfacing for air. It prefers to travel by water but, its short legs notwithstanding, it can travel on land faster than a man can run. Its food consists of all manner of small aquatic animals, including fish, which are caught sometimes by teamwork. Unlike almost all other wild animals, otters are playful as adults. A favorite sport is sliding down a steep bank of mud or snow and plunging into water or a snowdrift. Otters are intelligent, friendly, and inquisitive. Shortened from an article under keyword "otter" in Britannica Online. <http://www.eb.com:180/cgibin/g?DocF=micro/444/18.html>.

25. Here, and all through this essay, I assign to the animals male or female gender, corresponding to the gender an animal has in German. With this, I try to express in my English renderings that the animals are a family, with male and female members, just as Barbara Frischmuth tries to convey it to her readers in German. Furthermore, I capitalize the animals' names in order to indicate that often they are not just animals, but personalities in a story.

26. Original quote: "Es hatte die Arme um die Beine geschlungen, den Kopf auf den Knien, / und ein einziges Schluchzen schüttelte seinen dünnen Körper. / Es weinte so herzzerreißend, daß die bunten Farben

seines Kleides / und die noch bunteren seines Tuches zu verblassen schienen, / und seine braunen Locken sich vor Kummer entkringelten."

27. Original quote: "Es war ein überwältigender Anblick, / wie das Mädchen so übers Wasser ging. / Eine Schlange in der Hand, kleine Tiere auf den Schultern / und eine Gloriole aus orange gesprenkelten Schmetterlingen / um den Kopf."

28. See Barbara Frischmuth's explanation for choosing the martens to represent the "evil" ones among the animals in my interview with Barbara Frischmuth as contained in this volume.

29. George Orwell, pseudonym of Eric Arthur Blair (1903–1950), *Animal Farm* (New York: Harcourt, Brace, 1946). Orwell finished *Animal Farm* in 1944. It is a political fable built on the story of the Russian Revolution and its betrayal by Joseph Stalin. A group of barnyard animals overthrow and drive off their exploitative human masters and set up an egalitarian society of their own. Eventually, the animals' intelligent and power-loving leaders, the pigs, subvert the revolution and form a dictatorship whose bondage is even more oppressive and heartless than that of their former human masters ("All animals are equal, but some animals are more equal than others"). When *Animal Farm* appeared in 1945, it made Orwell famous.

Multiculturalism in Barbara Frischmuth's Works: The Representation and Mediation of Turkish and Other Islamic Cultures in *Das Verschwinden des Schattens in der Sonne* and in Various Short Pieces

Jennifer E. Michaels

The Shadow Disappears in the Sun, Ariadne, 1998

In "Ex Oriente 1," the first of a series of ten short articles Barbara Frischmuth published in *Die Presse* (The Press) from February 1 to April 4, 1996, she observes that according to recent estimates around twenty million Muslims live in Europe. Of these some twelve million live in the European Union and eight million in the Balkans. The over two million Muslims, predominantly Turks, Persians, and Arabs, who now live in Germany and Austria, came not only as guest workers but also as refugees, business people, or students. Some of them have become immigrants and have been granted Austrian or German citizenship, and they have raised families in their new countries. Their children, who have gone to local schools, no longer speak a German colored by Turkish, Persian, or Arabic accents but by those of the areas where they now live.[1] Despite what some Europeans think, she remarks, they are no longer foreigners but they are, nevertheless, still treated as outsiders in their adopted countries. Because Germany and Austria, like Western Europe as a whole, have evolved into multicultural societies, it is essential "to initiate a dialogue about the new circumstances, to urge the majority to promote the acculturation and assimilation of the minority, to practice tolerance toward the culturally different, the stranger,"[2] but many Europeans have been reluctant to do this. Initiating such a dialogue that she hopes will foster cross-cultural understanding and tolerance is central to several of Frischmuth's works. Through such literary works as the novel *Das Verschwinden des Schattens in der Sonne* (1973; *The Shadow Disappears in the Sun,* 1998), which was first published in 1973 and reissued in 1996, her translations from Turkish, and her essays about Turkish and other Islamic writers, she has sought to nurture a "genuine interest and a readiness to become spiritually and emotionally involved with the other."[3] In this essay, I will examine Frischmuth's exploration of the other as well as her depiction of Islamic, especially Turkish, culture and discuss the important role she has played — and continues to play —

in promoting among her German-speaking readers a deeper understanding and appreciation for the different Muslim cultures and their people.

Frischmuth has long been fascinated by other cultures. In "Looking over the Fence" (1995), she notes that her "interest in the other" began when she was quite young. Although she grew up in an isolated mountain village in Austria, she lived in a hotel that was filled in summer with many people from abroad. These guests stimulated her curiosity, and she longed to travel to see their countries (459). She also points out that *A Thousand and One Nights* helped arouse her interest in Muslim culture because through this text, which she still values highly, she was introduced to the narrative riches of the Orient.[4] Frischmuth's receptivity to other cultures led her to study Turkish and English at the University of Graz in the fall of 1959. In May 1960, she received a grant to study at the University of Erzurum in Anatolia, where she stayed for nine months, the first of several visits to Turkey.[5] On her return to Graz she gave up English and began to study Hungarian. She graduated from the University of Graz with diplomas that qualified her to translate Turkish and Hungarian. In 1964, she enrolled at the University of Vienna to pursue her interests in Turkology and Iranian and Islamic studies, but she did not write her dissertation and instead left the university to work as a writer and translator. Frischmuth's fluency in Turkish, her familiarity with Arabic and Persian, and her broad knowledge of Turkish and other Islamic cultures have given her the background to become an important and informed mediator of these cultures.

The ability to understand and communicate in a foreign language is an essential first step in bridging the gulf between the self and the other. Although language is not the only factor shaping those who speak it, in Frischmuth's opinion it is a contributing one because the "images that are fixed in a language's idioms have evolved out of daily life and the performance of its tasks."[6] These idioms give non-native speakers insights into the culture, and when they begin to use them, they no longer seem surprising or alien. Once Frischmuth felt comfortable in Turkish, for example, it no longer seemed foreign to her. Translating from Turkish and Hungarian has been an important part of her work as mediator because she has made literary texts of these cultures accessible to German-speaking readers. This work has helped her become sensitive to language and aware of the difficulty of translating from one language into another and keeping the same meaning, a problem inherent in any attempt to communicate in a foreign language. Those who deal with foreign languages know, she observes, that the range of meanings of a word in the mother tongue may overlap in part with that of the word in the foreign language but scarcely ever completely.[7] For her, exposure to such a differently structured language as Turkish — Turkish belongs to the agglutinative languages — was a liberating experience that broadened the horizons of her soul.[8]

Besides helping her gain fluency in the language Frischmuth's visits as a student to Turkey exposed her to living in an already existing multicultural society, although, as she notes in "Looking over the Fence," she experienced Turkish culture most intensively in Erzurum, not in cosmopolitan Istanbul. In Turkey she found a society composed of many different ethnic groups — Greeks, Armenians, Sephardim, Circassians, Laz, returned emigrants from the Balkans, Albanians, Kurds, and Turks — living together under one government. At the beginning of her stay, however, everything seemed to her Turkish and specifically Muslim, and she did not notice the many ethnic differences in the society. She was also not aware of the tensions in the modern republic, whose founding had dashed the hopes of various ethnic groups for their own separate states (459). As a border country where many different cultures have mixed, Turkey provides her with an ideal setting for her later exploration of multiculturalism and the other. Not only is Turkey itself a multicultural society but also, because of its geographical location at the crossroads of Europe and the Orient, it is a place where Western and Eastern cultures interact and collide. In "Ex Oriente 3," Frischmuth points out how much the Occident and the Orient have influenced each other, and this is particularly obvious, in her view, in the history of Turkey, where for two hundred years there has been not only an Eastern but also a Western tradition. Istanbul, for example, has been shaped by many different civilizations and cultures, all of which have left their traces, and in this city one can see not only various different traditions existing side by side but also their interpenetration.

Frischmuth's close contacts with Turkey led her to reflect on the difficulties involved in writing about and appropriating another culture. Looking over the fence of one's own culture at another can be both harmful and enriching since it "can result in identity crises but also in the fortunate expansion of a constricted horizon."[9] As Frischmuth puts it, the other culture looks back, and "this gaze can challenge one's sense of security within one's own culture."[10] In her view, it is impossible to appropriate another culture if one either clings to one's own identity or if one goes to the other extreme and gives it up. Frischmuth points out that without her identity, which makes her narrative stance possible, she would not be able to write. A solution to this dilemma is to become an expert because this allows one to be open to the other while still keeping one's own identity. By creating a "point of return," a course of study or a research project can shield one from completely identifying with the other. Through her research in Turkey, Frischmuth could maintain a reporter's stance, and this enabled her to come as close as possible to the other without losing her own identity and a sense of her own culture. Her identity became the site, she notes, to which she brought back her findings.[11]

Turkish culture is central to several of Frischmuth's literary works. In some of the stories in *Rückkehr zum vorläufigen Ausgangspunkt* (1973, Return to the Preliminary Starting Point), she uses Turkey as a setting to explore otherness. Such stories in this collection as "Das bessere Leben" (The Better Life) and "Istanbul," in which she shows the narrator's reaction to the state of martial law, give insights into the political tensions within Turkish society. An aspect of Turkish culture that continues to fascinate Frischmuth is the fairy tale, and in several works she includes parts of Turkish fairy tales; for example, in the radio play *Löffelweise Mond* (1972, Moon by Spoonfuls).[12] She also wrote an experimental text called "Turf-Turkey," in which she mixes dreams, racing jargon, and Turkish. Frischmuth explains why she integrated Turkish words into her German text. She wrote it when the first Turkish guest workers were being hired and the first Turkish grooms were appearing on the race tracks. The old confrontation between East and West, between Islam and Christianity, she says, was a further stimulus. Looking back later at this experiment she notes that, although she still finds the text interesting, it was not successful since those who knew racing jargon did not read and the few people who knew Turkish were not necessarily interested in a text that employed dreams.[13]

Frischmuth's most important literary work about Turkey and the longest text in which she explores the confrontation of the self with the other is the novel *Das Verschwinden des Schattens in der Sonne*. This work appeared ten years after she had studied in Turkey, a time she needed to gain a perspective on her experiences there. Like Frischmuth, the first-person narrator is a student living in Turkey who is researching the dervish order of the Bektashi for her dissertation. Although the novel contains many autobiographical references, Frischmuth stresses that this is not her story.[14] Rather it deals with the narrator's attempts to adapt to and understand another culture and the difficulties involved in this process.

Frischmuth writes in "Looking over the Fence" that her novel has two narrative levels (460). One level is the narrator's exploration of Turkey's past through her research on the Bektashi, and through this Frischmuth gives her readers insights into what for most of them is an unfamiliar aspect of Turkish history. This project provides the narrator with the expert's "point of return" that prevents her from merging completely with the other. When she first arrives in Turkey, she knows little about the Bektashi, and she struggles to find a point of view. She has not yet found the questions she wants to ask and is not sure what she wants to prove.[15] Since the Bektashi order was shrouded in secrecy, a necessity because of the frequent persecution it suffered, it is hard for her to find much reliable information. She learns about this mystical order in fragments — from reading, from legends she is told about the founder of the order, Haci Bektas Veli, and from talking to people — and she struggles to put the disparate pieces of the puzzle together. Through her narrator, Frischmuth gradually sketches the history of this order from its beginnings in the thirteenth century to its dissolution by the government in the twenties. The narrator discovers that its mysticism was closely tied to a concern for social justice, a reason why it was accused not only of sacrilege but also of subversion. So many people were, however, attracted to the Bektashi that at the beginning of the republic, one in ten Turks was either a member or was influenced by this order. This causes her to ask how mysticism could become so popular that it was like a folk religion. Because so many belonged, she cannot believe that the order could suddenly disappear when it was dissolved and is convinced that groups still exist secretly. Her research suggests to her, in fact, that virtually all revolutionary movements in Turkey have stemmed from the mystics. Although the narrator gains insights into this order, it remains foreign to her and full of contradictions.

The narrator's attempt to understand the history of this dervish order and its linguistic and political impact forms an important part of her struggle to understand the other. Studying this order gives her insights into the development of the Turkish language and makes her realize how different cultures can enrich one another. As Frischmuth observes elsewhere, Turkish presents particular problems for the translator, not only because of its different grammatical structure but also because of the history of the language. She explains why anyone who is only familiar with present-day Turkish would have difficulties understanding a text that is more than forty years old. In the process of becoming Islamic and their migration west, the Turks assimilated many aspects of the cultures they conquered, including religion, customs, and language. Although the Turks were the conquerors, they were in fact conquered by their subjects in the cultural area, she notes. For a while in the thirteenth century, for example, Persian became the language of poetry and the court, Arabic that of the law and the government, while Turkish was relegated to being spoken at home. So many Arabic and Persian words were adopted that Turkish became a hybrid language. After the collapse of the Ottoman Empire, however, the language was reformed.[16] The professor Engin Bey explains to the narrator the radical changes that have taken place in Turkish, changes which Bektashi literature helped to shape. Because this literature was secret, it was not overrun by Persian and Arabic. It is ironic, Frischmuth notes, that although the Turkish government banned the order in the twenties, its literature was regarded as a source for pure Turkish and could be published.[17]

In his analysis of the sources Frischmuth consulted for the novel, Muhammed Abu Hattab Khaled praises her solid scholarship and her thorough knowledge of Oriental mysticism. He observes that it is not only a literary work but also one that Orientalists can take seriously.[18] Mysticism plays an important role in the novel because it gives insights into how Frischmuth perceives cross-cultural understanding. She believes that it is important not to stress the differences that separate people but rather the shared aspects of humanity, and she sees the mysticism of the Bektashi and other similar orders as a unifying force. According to Frischmuth, the unity of all being is the main idea of mysticism — a spiritual outlook common to all cultures, although how different cultures conceive of this unity may vary. She argues that this idea of the unity of all being best suggests the direction that the blurring of individual boundaries can and should take: "This blurring should lead to an unio mystica that subsumes the individual into the sublime."[19] In the *Book of the Birds* (ca. 1200 A.D.) by Farudeddin Attar, Frischmuth found not only the title for her novel but also the story that she believes powerfully expresses this concept of unity. This story, which she includes in her novel, tells of the birds, led by the hoopoe, who set out to search for the Simurgh, the divine bird. Along the way, they are faced with many travails but finally thirty of them reach the "den of nearness." Here it is revealed that they themselves are the Simurgh. In Persian, *si murgh* means thirty birds. At the end, the "unity of all being establishes itself, and the shadow disappears in the sun."[20]

The narrator not only struggles to understand the past as a key to the present but also to adapt to the foreign culture, and this forms the second narrative level in the novel. She approaches this different culture with respect and empathy, qualities that are essential for coming close to the other, and she tries to be receptive and to accept this culture uncritically. Throughout her stay, she seeks to adapt to the conventions, make as few mistakes as possible, and follow the rules defining daily social intercourse. She sees these rules as a kind of language that she tries to learn. She is not content with the role of observer but wants to be part of the culture and be accepted, and at first it appears that she can accomplish this goal. By living with the student Turgut and the teacher Sevim, eating with them, and sharing their daily lives, she tries to immerse herself fully in this culture. In her opinion, she, Sevim, and Turgut are like a family, and this belief, the warm friendships she enjoys with Ayten and Engin Bey and others, and her love relationships with Turgut and Aksu mislead her into thinking that her friends no longer regard her as a foreigner but as an equal, as one of them.

Besides telling the reader that her narrator is a student and comes from a German-speaking country — she gives Sevim German lessons — Frischmuth provides virtually no information about her narrator's background. She does not even have a name. Because the narrator does not reflect on her own culture during the novel, the focus is placed sharply on her attempts to assimilate into the foreign culture. The narrator opens herself to the culture and people surrounding her, but she cannot separate herself entirely from her own culture. At the beginning of the novel, she wishes that she was already so far away that she could dream again in her own language, and she anticipates that one day she will feel distanced from her experiences in Turkey. Although she prefers to think she is different from the tourists she sees, she realizes with dismay that in her thirst to see everything, she is like them. In part, her perceptions of the city are those of a tourist. As she wanders through Istanbul, she sees its exotic aspects, its tea houses, bazaars, and mosques, and its colorful inhabitants such as the yogurt sellers and the coppersmiths in the bazaars, and does not notice its dirt and misery.

Although she tries to integrate herself into the foreign culture, she remains an observer, an outsider, in a certain sense a voyeur.[21] That she is perceived as the other is brought home forcefully to her when she visits the Süleymaniye, the famous mosque in Istanbul, where two women offer her tea and treat her as a stranger who cannot understand their language. Other experiences give her an inkling that, despite her efforts, a gulf still separates her from the other, even from her Turkish friends, because their perceptions of the society around them differ radically from hers. She cannot understand, for example, Sevim's reaction when she learns that her house is to be torn down to make way for a new clinic. Sevim tells her that when she went to the city government to protest, she was asked how she could be against progress in health care: She is one person, but the clinic will care for hundreds of people. She feels ashamed that she protested and thinks of herself as a bad patriot. In contrast, the narrator regrets that this quaint old house is to be replaced by a modern building. The narrator's reaction to the violence of the blood feud she witnesses also shows her otherness. Most shocking to her is the indifference with which the witnesses react and their unwillingness to help the victim, behavior she views as callous. When she mentions this incident to Ayten, her friend tells her these must have been people from Anatolia who came not only with their families but also with their hostilities. Ayten stresses that those involved do not want bystanders to interfere.

A central scene in the novel, a discussion between the narrator and her friend Sevim, underscores how hard it is to come close to the other. Sevim tells the narrator that although she knows them and their history, lives with them, speaks their language, and is interested in everything that concerns them, she is oblivious to what takes place around her. Sevim tells her, in fact, that she is going around in a dream. She has an understanding of the past but is not interested in what is new for them in the present. The narrator's lack of a long-term commitment to Turkey is one reason why she remains a stranger. As Sevim remarks, the narrator will go home and forget them. She will put their photos in a box or album and remember them only when she takes the photos out. She will sit quietly in her own country and think about how to interpret this or that sign while in Turkey there might be epidemics, war, or revolution. Sevim ends by saying they love her, and she loves them, and for a while, they are living together (119), a comment that underscores not only their warm friendship but also that this relationship remains transitory because the narrator is one who is just traveling through.

The narrator's failure to understand fully is not entirely the result of her obliviousness to what takes place around her, although this is the main cause, but also of her friends' reluctance to help her see what is happening beneath the surface. When Turgut is injured during his antigovernment activities, for example, he avoids telling her how it occurred. When she is in bed, she hears Turgut and Sevim quietly whispering about what happened, but they exclude her, and she cannot understand what they are saying. When Sevim reproaches her later for her blindness, the narrator senses that Sevim wants to prod her into becoming aware of something she has not seen. But when she tries to understand — by asking where Turgut is, for example — she receives no answer. She complains that because her friends make no effort to explain things to her, she is trapped in the details. They expect her to ask, she tells Sevim, but she wants her friends to volunteer information because she feels uncomfortable always asking questions.

Sevim's comments encourage the narrator to look critically at her attempts to appropriate the other. It was, she realizes, a mistake to think she could find the key to the present in the past. By searching for the past she hoped to overcome her sense of otherness, but she recognizes that what was intended to be a tool to help her understand has turned into a pretext to distance herself from the life around her. She sees the justness of Sevim's reproach that one day everything she has experienced here will no longer concern her directly. She reflects, for example, that she will tell herself that she needs to go back to visit, especially if she is not to forget the language. But perhaps she will not be able to return because the borders will be closed by civil war. When she considers what has come out of her stay, she sees clearly the mistakes she has made. She has read a lot of books, learned the language, looked at monuments, wandered through the city, and was together with people, but she has only looked around and has not resisted. Adapting to this culture was a higher priority for her than being critical. She failed to inform herself and thought only about appearances, not about necessities. That she is only traveling through is symbolized by her return ticket that protects her from dismantling the boundaries between herself and the other. If she were to stay longer, she fears that she would lose her sense of self (165).

During her stay, the narrator does become aware of some of the problems beneath Turkey's exotic surface. Through her lover, the doctor Aksu, she learns about the poor state of medicine outside of Istanbul, where most villages have no doctors. Aksu, who tried to work in such a village, tells her he could get used to the dirt, but the misery paralyzed him. She gains another insight when she visits the writer Ersever, who is distraught because two of his friends, a poet and an essayist, have been arrested for writing material critical of the government. He tells her that it is not unusual in Turkey for people to be arrested for their ideas.

The narrator's research into history has been an intellectual experience, but it has not helped her understand the complexity of present-day reality in Turkey. She realizes that she knows nothing, for example, about the legal and executive traditions of the country and is ashamed about her lack of knowledge. Although through her research she believes that she has discovered a link between the revolutionary attitude of the dervish order and the present-day disturbances, she does not pursue this connection. When martial law is declared, Turgut tells her about the protests and the acts of violence in the city, but she scarcely asks him about the reasons for the demonstrations. When she realizes that her friends are involved in anti-government activities that lead to Turgut's death, she is hurt that she was excluded, but she tells herself that her lack of knowledge was a kind of protection for them because she could have inadvertently betrayed them. She unwittingly played her assigned role perfectly, asked no questions, and adapted. The reason she did not ask questions was not only because she did not notice what was happening or was not interested, but also because she felt that as a foreigner she should not concern herself with such things. She thought that people were thankful that she did not mix in and that they would perceive any attempt on her part to criticize or to show her anger as an attack on their way of life. In her attempt to adapt, she reflects, she made the mistake of only getting to know the things as they were without looking for their ability to change.

The novel's title, *Das Verschwinden des Schattens in der Sonne,* the words that end the story of the Simurgh, suggests a merging of the self with the other, but this merging remains unrealized.[22] The narrator recognizes that she will remain a stranger because she cannot overcome the barrier between herself and the other world. Despite this failure, she returns home with a new understanding of both Turkish culture and of herself. Because the narrator grows and matures, this work, which the writer Franz Fühmann from the former German Democratic Republic calls one of the most important and beautiful novels in German that he has read in the last few years,[23] is, like the tradition of the *Bildungsroman*, to which it belongs,[24] essentially optimistic. Even though the narrator fails in her hopes of appropriating the other, Frischmuth shows that different cultures can approach each other with warmth and respect.

Muhammed Abu Hattab Khaled, who has not only published several articles on the novel but also translated it into Arabic, praises it for its contribution to cross-cultural understanding. He finds the novel fascinating because of its Islamic-Oriental and mystical background. In an interesting article he gives insights into the problems he encountered in translating the work into Arabic. He had to translate concepts that were taken from the Orient back into Arabic, and he wonders whether his translation captures Frischmuth's imaginative world.[25] Besides praising Frischmuth's informed knowledge of the Orient in the novel, he comments that a work like this can play a significant role in familiarizing a broad public with previously unknown Oriental themes and concerns. In his view, this is a great achievement since this work exposes readers, most of whom would be unlikely to inform themselves by consulting scholarly publications, to the Orient.[26] He views the novel as a valuable contribution to the deepening of cultural relationships between the Orient and the Occident, and this is a reason why its literary and artistic achievement should be highly valued.[27]

Frischmuth not only explores the difficulties that Europeans like her narrator face in adapting to the other, but also those that Turkish workers experience in adapting to European societies. Unlike the narrator in *Das Verschwinden des Schattens in der Sonne,* who enjoys warm friendships and hospitality in Turkey, the Turkish workers encounter a society filled with prejudices where they are treated coldly. In her novel *Kai und die Liebe zu den Modellen* (1979, Kai and the Love of Models), the last part of her trilogy that includes *Die Mystifikationen der Sophie Silber* (1976, The Mystifications of Sophie Silber) and *Amy oder Die Metamorphose* (1978, Amy, or The Metamorphosis), Frischmuth addresses this problem clearly. Kai, the young son of the protagonist Amy, has a baby-sitter called Rosa. Rosa has a friend, the Turkish girl Pembe, who looks after her twin brothers Oktay and Erol, and they all spend a lot of time together. Although the society surrounding them is often cold and uncaring, this group forms a tiny community that is based on friendship and respect for each other.

Frischmuth focuses in particular on the problems faced by the guest workers' children who are torn between two cultures, and the language they speak expresses their feeling that they belong nowhere. Pembe tells Rosa that they have their own language at home, where they speak a mixture of German and Turkish. Her parents have not learned much German, and she and her brothers only know the small amount of Turkish their parents have taught them.[28] Because she is a girl, Pembe experiences the clash of cultures more intensely than her twin brothers. Unlike Rosa, who enjoys the freedom to come and go as she wants, Pembe's life is constrained. As soon as her father comes home from work, she is not allowed to go out, even for something at school. When there is no school, she has to look after the twins or help in the house and cook. Actually, she remarks, her twin brothers look after her because if a man talks to her, they act as a kind of bodyguard.

Through Pembe, Rosa learns about the role women are expected to play in Turkey. Pembe explains that her father hopes to save enough money one day to return to Anatolia, and there she will be married to the son of a rich man to ensure the future success of her family. If, however, she has already had a relationship with another man, she could not be married. In Turkey, she tells Rosa, men want women to be like vegetables: young, juicy, and without blemishes (78). If a woman has no experiences with other men, so the thinking goes, she will be content with her husband and will want to please him, and the more she pleases him, the more he will try to please her. When Rosa protests about such marriages and the treatment of women, Pembe draws parallels with marriages in Europe. In Europe, she believes, people also marry for practical reasons, perhaps because they want an apartment or to leave home or because the woman is pregnant. Pembe defends Turkish marriages and stresses that the wife is secure because the husband is responsible for her and the children.

Later in the novel, Pembe tells Amy about her life in Turkey before her family moved to Vienna and her reactions to her new home, and through this Frischmuth underscores both the harshness of life in the small village in Anatolia where Pembe was born and in Vienna. In Turkey, Pembe's family was very poor. Because there were many sons in her father's family, each received only a couple of fields, and her father, unable to make a living from the land, had to leave to find work elsewhere in Turkey and finally in Austria. He writes to her mother to say he will send for them as soon as he has saved enough money. Her mother cries when she hears this, and it is not clear whether she does this out of happiness at the prospect of being reunited with her husband or out of sadness at the thought of leaving the world in which she feels secure. People in the village say she should be happy since the men who have become guest workers do not always send for their families. Some in the village tell Pembe's mother how terrible Europe is for practicing Muslims, for not only do people there eat pork and drink alcohol, forbidden to Muslims, but they also eat snails and frogs. In Vienna, Pembe's mother will have to work outside the home, something unheard of in her village, where the woman would only work for her husband. Despite the uncertainties, the family thinks itself blessed with good fortune to be moving to Europe, and Pembe dreams of the clothes she will have. When Pembe's father returns after more than a year to take them away, Frischmuth suggests the difficulties that Pembe's mother in particular will face in her encounter with a new culture. Not only is she illiterate — she had to ask her brother-in-law, who like her husband had learned to read in the military, to read her the letter from her husband — but she is even fearful of getting into the car because she has never been in such a vehicle before. When they leave the village, her mother cries. Pembe senses that her father does not like Austria. His construction job is hard, and the people are unfriendly. In this story, Frischmuth contrasts the close-knit extended family in Turkey with the isolation Pembe's family, especially her mother, experiences in the basement apartment where they now live. Pembe's mother fears to go out alone for the first several weeks. The relationship between mother and daughter changes radically in their new country. Their roles are reversed since now that Pembe can speak German, her mother is dependent on her.

After seven years in Vienna, Pembe no longer knows where she belongs. She does not want to return to her village, but she also does not like living in Vienna. She tells Amy that she could imagine living in Austria, but her parents want to go home. Pembe does not want to live apart from her parents. If she raised a family in Austria while her parents lived in Turkey, her children would not have grandparents, she says. If she lives close to her parents, she will not have to raise her children alone because her mother will help. Pembe tells Amy that her parents, who are still homesick, always planned to return to Turkey, and therefore they did not bother to learn German. She and her brothers, however, are no longer homesick. By showing how this one family struggles to adapt, Frischmuth hopes to give her readers a sympathetic understanding of the difficulties guest workers experience in their encounter with the other.

Frischmuth's "Ex Oriente" articles are another important part of her work as a mediator. In them, she attempts to make her readers appreciate the great variety of Muslim literature and culture and, by publishing them in *Die Presse*, she hopes to reach a wide audience. To make her fellow citizens aware of the contributions Muslim authors have made to German-speaking culture is critical, she believes, since their works are not well known. Austrian Germanists, for example, have taken little notice of them. In contrast to their Austrian counterparts, the French appreciate Muslim authors who have published or written in French for their sharp insights and for their poetic language, and they value these works because they enrich French literature.[29]

All the writers she discusses in these articles are border crossers, and this gives them a unique perspective on their own and on European culture. In *Kai und die Liebe zu den Modellen*, the twins Oktay and Erol express this point of view when they tell the old man Diomioni that they were born in another country and their parents are foreigners. They can thus tell him about the differences between this country and their own (37). The writers Frischmuth chooses here are shaped both by their Muslim heritage and by their adopted countries. They have cast their gaze over the fence and have become active participants in an intercultural dialogue. Frischmuth remarks that it is fortunate that there have always been mediators and border crossers, individuals who have been driven into another culture and have managed to create a dialogue out of what can sometimes be a hostile confrontation.[30] In her view, it is essential to find out how these border crossers view Europe since Islamic culture is no longer outside of Europe but within its borders. From the various Muslim authors she has read, Frischmuth observes, she has gained many different insights and these can lead to a much-needed dialogue.

Three of the authors she discusses are Turkish. One, Zafer Senocak, who was born in Ankara and has lived in Germany since 1970, writes poetry and essays in German. Frischmuth views him as an experienced border crosser, but also as one, like Pembe and her brothers, who does not feel at home anywhere and who senses his "double-tongued" identity. Today, Senocak observes, a feeling of otherness is the birth certificate of the poet. In his essays he analyzes the relationship of Germans to their largest minority and also that of this minority to their own native countries to which they are still tied, and he shows that these immigrants are neither politically nor culturally integrated into German society. Frischmuth writes that it is sometimes painful when reading his works to see all the misunderstandings, prejudices, and bad intentions he points to on both sides. In his works, Senocak performs a valuable service in undermining current stereotypes of Islam in Germany. Frischmuth notes also that in Islam, there have always been heretics, dissidents, and free thinkers, and Senocak, in her view, belongs to this tradition. He is critical of fundamentalism as well as of the kind of nationalism that tries to deny heterogeneity and that always leads, as Frischmuth remarks, to the same result, murder.[31] Another writer, the novelist Orhan Pamuk, who was born in Istanbul in 1952, exemplifies in his works the mixing of Western and Eastern traditions in Turkey. Like Frischmuth, he believes that people all over the world are basically the same.[32] In the Turkish author Sevgi Emine Özdamar Frischmuth sees a writer who tries to come to terms with her "double-tongued" identity. In her short book *Mutterzunge* (1990, Mother Tongue), she mixes German and Turkish, ignoring the conventions of "good" language usage. She does this because neither Turkish, her mother tongue, nor German alone can capture the reality of her existence. Frischmuth finds this approach fascinating, particularly since it is one she experimented with in "Turf-Turkey." Through her style of writing in this and in other works, Özdamar shows how similar people are under the surface of their different cultures, despite their efforts to make themselves distinct from each other, and how grotesque all attempts at disguising this are.[33]

In addition to Turkish authors, Frischmuth includes writers from a variety of other Muslim countries. The Tunisian writer Abdelwahab Meddeb, who has lived in Paris since 1967, is in her view typical of many Arabic authors who have drawn recently on the heritage of their mystics, of the Sufis, whom Frischmuth terms the dissidents and the creative thinkers in Islam.[34] Another writer who draws on these great mystics is Dzevad Karahasan, who was driven from his home in Sarajevo by the war in Bosnia and now lives in Germany and Austria. Through his works, he succeeds in transporting questions, confrontations, and thinkers of early Islamic mysticism into our time.[35] The Algerian Assja Djebar focuses on exploring the history and the fate of her country and gives voice especially to its women whose language had deteriorated to a whisper and whose gestures were hidden behind the veil. She comes from a country that only freed itself from colonialism in 1962, but she is also an Arab woman in a country where religious fundamentalism is increasing, a particularly discouraging direction for women who had just begun to liberate themselves.[36]

Frischmuth includes works by those in self-chosen exile, such as Abdelwahab Meddeb, as well as those by refugees from the political situation in their countries. One refugee, Said, fled from the Shah of Iran, whose regime he had opposed, to Germany in 1965 and now writes poetry in German. After the fall of the Shah, Said returned to Iran, but after seven weeks he discovered that the new government would not let him live as he wanted and he returned to Germany. Despite his long years in exile, Said still has close emotional ties to his native country. In *Der lange Arm der Mullahs* (1995, The Long Arm of the Mullahs), a kind of literary diary spanning the years 1978 to 1994, he shows both the brutality of the various regimes in Iran and also the humanity of the Iranian people that refused to be suppressed. Through this work, Said helps his German-speaking readers understand the tumultuous events taking place in Iran during these years.[37] Like Said, other Arab poets were forced to flee from the political situations in their countries. Adonis fled from the civil war in Lebanon to Paris. Badr Shakir as-Sayyab fled in the fifties from Iraq to Kuwait and Lebanon, and another Iraqi, Khalid al-Maaly, left his country during the first Gulf war in 1979 for Paris and Cologne. Frischmuth notes that it is not only the political situation in their various countries that makes life dangerous for Muslim poets, but also their relentless efforts to renew language, form, and ideas, and their persistence in this endeavor makes them the target of both religious and nationalist fundamentalists, proof for Frischmuth of the importance assigned to their poetry in Muslim countries. One of these poets, Khalid al-Maaly, summarizes for Frischmuth the significant role non-Europeans have played in creating an intercultural dialogue. Al-Maaly writes: "We were there and we made comparisons."[38]

These articles are important for several reasons. By showing the rich variety of Muslim culture in the present and by stressing the different political and social experiences of these authors in their various countries, Frischmuth tries to dispel the commonly held stereotypes in Europe of Muslim culture. She hopes that the articles will help to fill in the blank spaces in our perception before these become a disgrace. By discussing these specific authors she wants to promote the tolerant traditions of Islam that "many present-day Muslims and fundamentalists seem to have forgotten."[39] For this reason she decided in 1995 to translate Salman Rushdie's *Haroun and the Sea of Stories* (1990) into German and to transcribe it into a six-part radio play. It was not her intention, she emphasizes, "to provoke devout Muslims, but rather to introduce this treasure of fairy tales and legends, with its origins in Islamic mysticism, to a wider public."[40] Through these articles she reiterates her often-expressed conviction that there are more commonalities between the world of Islam and that of the West than would appear from superficial observations.

Frischmuth devotes her final article in this series and also "Verrückt wie Rückert" (Crazy like Rückert),[41] the talk she gave as one of the keynote speakers at the German Studies Association meeting in Seattle in October 1996, to a nineteenth-century German border crosser, Friedrich Rückert, who, in her view, has been unjustly forgotten. Rückert dedicated a large part of his life to mediating Islamic culture. Although he never visited an Islamic country or even heard Arabic spoken, he dared to translate some of the greatest literary works written in Arabic, including the Koran. His translation of parts of the Koran is the only one in German, in her view, that captures the poetic language of the original, a conclusion that Muhammed Abu Hattab Khaled shares when he calls Rückert's translations unsurpassed.[42] Rückert's great accomplishment as a mediator of Islamic culture is his ability to make his readers experience the other. Frischmuth remarks that from the late eighteenth to the beginning of the twentieth century Islamic art and literature were subjects of curiosity and artistic interest in Germany. Nowadays, however, despite the presence of large numbers of Muslims in Europe, interest in Muslim culture has scarcely left any traces in recent German literature. From the perspective of cultural exchange and literary awareness, she writes, we have fallen far behind the standards of the nineteenth century that Rückert helped set.

In "Looking over the Fence," Frischmuth observes that the term multicultural suggests the ideal of a relatively trouble-free and peaceful union of many groups with different languages and cultures. Although she recognizes that reality has not always coincided with this picture — she points out that the Ottoman, Austro-Hungarian, and British Empires, as well as the former Soviet Union, for example, all have bloody histories — there have been many times in which numerous peoples lived together peacefully and realized how much they owed each other, especially in the realm of culture. By casting one's gaze over the fence, which is what multicultural writing means to her, one may discover "a strategy for viewing and dealing with the world that is just as viable and productive as one's own" (462). By being prepared to try to understand each other and develop respect for other cultures, people can encourage peaceful coexistence. This respect, she notes, does not imply unconditional acceptance or approval but rather a willingness to reckon with the other. Frischmuth believes that because of the tendency toward dominance and influence today, it is more urgent than ever to look over the fence, and, in her view, literature can play an important role here. Through her works, Frischmuth has demonstrated that she has looked over the fence, that she, too, is a border crosser who has made a significant contribution to this intercultural dialogue.

Grinnell College

Notes

1. Barbara Frischmuth, "Ex Oriente 1: Zur Literatur von Einwanderern, Auswanderern und Gratwanderern." This series, "Ex Oriente 1" to "Ex Oriente 10," appeared weekly in *Die Presse* from February 1 to April 4, 1996. I am working from the slightly longer manuscript versions of these articles that Barbara Frischmuth kindly made available to me. Since the manuscript does not contain page numbers, further references will be to the series number only.

2. Paul Michael Lützeler, "Introduction," *Multiculturalism in Contemporary German Literature*, special issue of *World Literature Today* 69.3 (Summer 1995): 453.

3. Barbara Frischmuth, "Looking over the Fence," trans. Lisabeth Hock, *Multiculturalism in Contemporary German Literature*, special issue of *World Literature Today* 69.3 (Summer 1995): 459.

4. Barbara Frischmuth, *Traum der Literatur — Literatur des Traums: Münchner Poetik-Vorlesungen* (Salzburg: Residenz, 1991) 11. See also "Looking over the Fence" 459.

5. Hans Haider, "Barbara Frischmuth, eine Biographie," *Dossier 4: Barbara Frischmuth*, ed. Kurt Bartsch (Graz: Droschl, 1992) 154.

6. Frischmuth, "Looking over the Fence" 460.

7. Barbara Frischmuth, "Ihr Gekommensein geht zu meinem Angenehmen . . . oder über die Schwierigkeiten beim Übersetzen aus dem Türkischen und aus dem Ungarischen," *Sprache im technischen Zeitalter* 21 (1967): 65.

8. Frischmuth, "Looking over the Fence" 459.

9. Lützeler 455.

10. Frischmuth, "Looking over the Fence" 462.

11. Frischmuth, "Looking over the Fence" 460.

12. Barbara Frischmuth, "Hörspielerfahrungen: Ein persönlicher Bericht," *Schriftstellerinnen im Gespräch: Eine Dokumentation*, ed. Elisabeth Roters-Ullrich and Ursula Theißen (Dülmen-Hiddingsel: tende,

1995) 203.

13. Frischmuth, *Traum der Literatur* 51.

14. Frischmuth, "Looking over the Fence" 460.

15. Barbara Frischmuth, *Das Verschwinden des Schattens in der Sonne* (Salzburg: Residenz, 1996) 12. Future references are from this edition and are given in the text. The translation, *The Shadow Disappears in the Sun,* trans. Nicholas Meyerhofer (Riverside, CA: Ariadne, 1998).

16. Frischmuth, "Ihr Gekommensein" 67–68.

17. Frischmuth, "Looking over the Fence" 460.

18. Muhammed Abu Hattab Khaled, "Islamische Mystik in der deutschsprachigen Belletristik: Der Roman *Das Verschwinden des Schattens in der Sonne* von Barbara Frischmuth," *Gottes ist der Orient, Gottes ist der Okzident*, ed. Udo Tworuschka (Cologne: Böhlau, 1991) 306. The spelling of the author's name varies on his different publications.

19. Frischmuth, "Looking over the Fence," 460.

20. Frischmuth, "Looking over the Fence," 460.

21. Georg Pichler, "'Seltsam, daß es mir so wenig ausmacht, nicht anzukommen': Heimat und Fremde bei Barbara Frischmuth," *Dossier 4: Barbara Frischmuth* 58.

22. Muhammed Abu Hattab Khaled observes that the topos of the shadow is a common one in Islamic mysticism, see "Islamische Mystik in der deutschsprachigen Belletristik" 302.

23. Dietrich Simon, Franz Fühmann, and Joachim Schreck, "Gespräch über Barbara Frischmuth," *Sinn und Form* 28.2 (March-April 1976): 434.

24. Donald G. Daviau, "Neuere Entwicklungen in der modernen österreichischen Prosa: Die Werke von Barbara Frischmuth," *Modern Austrian Literature* 13.1 (1980): 190.

25. Muhammad Abu-Hattab, "Semantische Übersetzungsprobleme am Beispiel von Barbara Frischmuths Roman *Das Verschwinden des Schattens in der Sonne*," *Sprache im technischen Zeitalter* 96 (1985): 287.

26. Muhammed Abu Hattab Khaled, "Islamische Mystik in der deutschsprachigen Belletristik" 306.

27. Muhammed Abu Hattab Khaled, "Das Orientbild in Barbara Frischmuths Roman *Das Verschwinden des Schattens in der Sonne*," *Österreichische Literatur in Ägypten* (Cairo: Veröffentlichungen der Deutschabteilung der Al-Azhar Universität, 1978) 34, cited in Daviau 196.

28. Barbara Frischmuth, *Kai und die Liebe zu den Modellen* (Salzburg: Residenz, 1979) 43. Future references are given in the text.

29. See "Ex Oriente 2."

30. Frischmuth, "Looking over the Fence" 462.

31. See "Ex Oriente 2."

32. See "Ex Oriente 3."

33. See "Ex Oriente 6."

34. See "Ex Oriente 4."

35. See "Ex Oriente 9."

36. See "Ex Oriente 8."

37. See "Ex Oriente 5."

38. See "Ex Oriente 7."

39. Frischmuth, "Looking over the Fence" 462.

40. Frischmuth, "Looking over the Fence" 462. See also Frischmuth, "Hörspielerfahrungen" 222–224.

41. The speech was then published in German in *neue deutsche literatur* 45.513 (May-June 1997): 195–200. For the English translation, see "Barbara Frischmuth, Rocking with Rückert, or Crazy like a Fox" in this volume.

42. Muhammed Abu Hattab Khaled, "Islamische Mystik in der deutschsprachigen Belletristik" 300.

The Spirit of Place: Cultural Identity and the Concept of *Heimat* in the Recent Works of Barbara Frischmuth

Edith Toegel

In memory of Laurence Romero, Jr.

There is little doubt that Barbara Frischmuth's prose reflects her Austrian heritage. Today she is also one of that country's foremost literary figures. That Frischmuth sees herself as a committed Austrian is documented in numerous interviews and public presentations she has given over her thirty-year career. Frischmuth's opening literary gambit was *Die Klosterschule* (1968; *The Convent School,* 1993), a quasi-autobiographical account of her school days in the small upper-Austrian town of Gmunden. This delightful first book dazzled readers with its display of honesty, courage, and a remarkable talent for serious and playful language. All her major works are set in Austria and deal with topics very specific to Austrian culture and history, past and present. In the early 1980s, Frischmuth comments: "I'm quite comfortable as an Austrian, in contrast to the German citizen. That also affects my writing" ("Als Mensch fühle ich mich sehr wohl als Österreicherin im Gegensatz zu deutschen Staatsbürgern. Das trifft auch auf meine Literatur zu"). And, she adds, "much of it is Austrian although it's more difficult to draw boundaries here than on a map" ("vieles an ihr ist österreichisch, obwohl es schwerer abzugrenzen ist, als wenn man Grenzen auf einer Landkarte zieht").[1]

This statement touches on two salient aspects of this writer: her commitment and abiding interest in Austria, both in her life and in her writings. Born in 1941 in the village of Altaussee in the western part of Styria, adjacent to the famed Salzkammergut, Frischmuth returned to her home-town as a permanent summer-resident in 1974, dividing her time between there and Vienna. Her second marriage to a German psychiatrist in 1988 took place in Altaussee. In the second part of her comments above, Frischmuth alludes to the difficulty of differentiating between Austrian and German literature, and by extension, of defining a cultural heritage and a literary identity specific to Austria. This question has been much discussed in the past and is of continued interest to literary historians, academics, and writers today.[2] In a recent anthology, contributions by Hans Weigel, Julian Schutting, and Wendelin Schmidt-

Dengler, among others, address the question directly, while others review earlier positions taken in that ongoing debate.[3]

For her part, it appears that Frischmuth has always believed in a specific Austrian cultural and literary identity to which she has contributed. The decision to live and to remain in a given country is, as she once stated, often one of practicality and circumstance, "it is for the most part not based on principle or abstraction, but rather on private and concrete reasons" ("Die Entscheidung, in einem Land zu leben, ist meist keine prinzipielle, abstrakte, sondern eine von vielerlei privaten und konkreten Gründen bewirkte").[4] What interests us here is how Frischmuth envisions Austrian cultural identity, and what is the sense of *Heimat* (home) that emerges from her works. Since most of the critical discussion over the past years has concentrated on her works of the 1970s and 1980s, especially her widely acclaimed "Sternwieser trilogy" (*Die Mystifikationen der Sophie Silber* [1976, The Mystifications of Sophie Silber]; *Amy oder Die Metamorphose* [1978, Amy, or The Metamorphosis]; and *Kai und die Liebe zu den Modellen* [1979, Kai and the Love of Models]), the focus will be on Frischmuth's more recent works from the late 1980s and 1990s, very specifically the novels *Über die Verhältnisse* (1987, Beyond One's Means) and *Einander Kind* (1990, One Another's Child), and her latest collection of short stories, *Hexenherz* (1994, Heart of the Witch).

Frischmuth views her literary involvement with her homeland as part of her birthright and is convinced that being Austrian impacts one's existence, even as a writer: "But since literature does not emerge from a void but from a concrete place whether one actually lives there or, in exile, conjures it up daily in the heart, whether one allows — or consciously does not — some of the color of the vernacular to infuse the written language, whether one has a more or less tenuous relationship to Austrian literary traditions or prefers another, I am convinced that if one looks long enough, there are a lot of Austrian qualities in all of us."[5] To her mind, the ongoing polemics on an Austrian literary identity are overly academic and "rather overused" ("ziemlich strapaziert").[6] Beyond her intuitive feelings of belonging to a national entity, however, the concrete "place" to which Frischmuth has the deepest existential and literary connections is the village of Altaussee and the surrounding Salzkammergut, with its mountains, lakes, and meadows. It is here that she is truly at home, not only geographically, but emotionally and spiritually as well. This is the spirit of place, in D. H. Lawrence's words, which for

Frischmuth is a “great reality.”[7] Here, she not only knows and enjoys the breathtaking countryside, but is intimately familiar and connected to its people and the continuity of their lives there. It is here “that nothing irritates me” (“daß es nichts gibt . . . was mich irritiert”). Furthermore, “Here is a place where I've come to have a sense of six generations. It's a tempting moment to be able to read the passing and return of time on faces of people, faces manifesting generational traces but also behavioral idiosyncrasies and ways of speaking.”[8] The heroine of one of Frischmuth's earlier novels expresses a similar sentiment: “She had always avoided any notion of homeland or even hometown and at most spoke simply of birthplace. Had she been obliged at any given moment to define homeland, she would have said that it has to do with people knowing one another.”[9] Consequently, Frischmuth's hometown, or an imaginary place like it, runs through her œuvre like a red thread, at once a point of reference, a focus, and an inspiration. “My favorite place is the place of my dreams. Not always the place where my dreams occur, but much more the place that, in the form of a picture, throws light into almost all my dreams, like a citation from an unmistakable, long association.”[10]

Most of the events in her recent novel *Einander Kind* (1990), the third part of her Demeter trilogy (the others are *Herrin der Tiere* [1986, Mistress of the Animals]; and *Über die Verhältnisse* [1987]), take place in a village reminiscent of Altaussee. While Frischmuth's earlier trilogy portrayed the mysterious “world of fairies” *(Feenwelt)* and highlighted the folkloristic and magical elements of that region, this cycle is set in modern times and depicts the archaic, the classic, and the mystical aspects of the Demeter myth.[11] *Einander Kind* focuses on three women, Trude, Pröbstl, and Vevi, whose parallel lives are interwoven despite differences in ages and life-experience. Divided into four equal sections with three chapters each, covering the protagonists' lives, the story suggests a cyclical movement. Trude's life is narrated in “Die andere Welt” (The Other World) and tells of that “other” generation that witnessed the ascendancy of Hitler, the war, and Austria's occupation by the Nazis. Trude is an observer of Austria's problematic past with its inhumaneness and suffering, a painful but important memory for Frischmuth herself whose father disappeared near Kiev in December 1943 when she was only two years old. Now a sickly retired accountant of a publishing house, Trude lives a quiet, isolated existence in the city, trying to come to terms with her life, the early loss of her husband, Werner, during the war, and her subsequent participation in the Austrian partisan movement. She also reflects on her relationship with Werner's large family which owns a hotel and a pension in a small village where she worked for many years. Yearning for the past, and for the familiar mountains and lakes of her youth, Trude has transformed the patio on her roof *(Dachterrasse)* into a small nature paradise, reminiscent of earlier, happier times, and which shields her from the thicket and stench of the big city:

> Her dwarf pomegranate trees had become so domesticated there on the patio that they bloomed from June well into autumn. Lost in thought, she plucked a few rosemary needles and rubbed them between her fingers, which she then brought to her nose. Smells, noises, bird songs . . . and stretching in front of and below her, this yellow-green Mediterranean-like city of radiant haze, a city that expelled fumes such that the rising noxious vapors were visible from across the river which, flowing from the mountains, wended its way forcefully through all the gnarled façades. Most of the stench did not reach her and what did was softened by her plants, which she had put there for their scent. A garden . . . on a roof, growing out of rock. Shrubs, small trees, bushes, flowers, herbs, grass. And with the slightest breeze, fragrant smells and buzzing.[12]

Trude's decision to return to the village of her youth for the funeral of her favorite sister-in-law, Regula Schwarz, assumes existential proportions. It becomes a journey into the past: "The way would be the same. From the hotel to the church, from the church to the cemetery. Along the way the stables with the coach horses. She still had clear in her mind the schedule of the rural bus from the time" (139).[13] Her return reconnects her with her husband's family and thereby also with Vevi Schwarz's and Pröbstl's lives. Her sudden death at the funeral — by falling into Regula's open grave! — is simultaneously a dramatic connection and a closure to a difficult period in Austrian history.

The second section of the novel, "Begleitumstände" (Accompanying Circumstances), describes the life of Sigune Pröbstl, always referred to by her family name, and takes place in 1988. As a child, Pröbstl lived in the same village as the other two women. When she happens to meet her childhood friend Vevi Schwarz again, she is immediately reconnected to familiar and beloved surroundings: "The haze in her head began to clear, bringing into view a lake, mountains, meadows, and forests" ("Der Nebel in ihrem Kopf begann sich zu lichten und ließ einen See, Berge, Wiesen und viel Wald erkennen," 21). When Pröbstl becomes the personal assistant to the successful writer and "all-around genius" *(Allround-Genie)* Vevi Schwarz, the reconnection brings with it *Begleitumstände,* four stages of confrontation with the past, marked by the subtitles of the four parts of her story: "Die Fackel der Erinnerung" (The Torch of Memory), "Die Namen der Sigune Pröbstl" (The Names of Sigune Pröbstl), "Hundeleben" (A Dog's Life), and "Was heißt Liebe" (What Is Love). Pröbstl's recollections include memories of her parents and her humble upbringing, the deep attachment to her dog Zottel, her unresolved dream of becoming a veterinarian, and her problematic marriage to a Hungarian refugee, Botond, the father of her son, Aaron. These reminiscences are couched in the fairy-tale-like reflections of her childhood with Vevi Schwarz, because "for two years as kids in school they sat next to each other: Snow White and Raven Black" ("Als Kinder sind sie zwei Jahre nebeneinander in der Schulbank gesessen. Schneewittchen und Rabenschwarz," 32). These thoughts become further entwined with her friend's life and career, because "Vevi Schwarz mused over the idea of writing a book of her earlier life with special emphasis on her childhood and youth" ("Vevi Schwarz trug sich mit dem Gedanken, ein Buch über ihr bisheriges Leben unter besonderer Betonung von Kindheit und Jugend zu schreiben," 21). The chance meeting between the two women leads into the third section of the novel.

The central point of reference for Vevi's literary project was the painful fiftieth anniversary of the "annexation" *(Anschluß):* "It had of course to do with this year, with 1988, in which everything was to be finally and officially cleared up" ("Es hat natürlich mit diesem Jahr zu tun, mit dem Jahr 1988, in dem endgültig und von Amts wegen aufgeklärt werden soll," 23). Vevi Schwarz carries her message, the *Fackel der Erinnerung,* courageously and passionately from town to town: "To make people reflect on what happened then. To make them finally admit how it was. Even if no one could answer why it had come to that. To admit it. To remember, to deplore" (134).[14] The courage of confronting a difficult past distresses her immediate superior, a compromising man whose advice to Vevi smacks of dishonesty and political opportunism:

> Fifty years — enough time to forget a lot. Nevertheless beware of assigning guilt one-sidedly. What would you do with so many current relations in the provinces? Well then — you see. I think we indeed agree on what we want to accomplish. Show what happened to all those poor people. In that regard, even here in the provinces the different sides are approachable. You clearly have a completely free hand but I think it's best to emphasize general humanity. Enlightenment, enlightenment, and once again enlightenment! A little Kraus, a little Canetti, a little Horvath, and a little Grünbaum, a few witnesses from within and without the Resistance, a little MEIN KAMPF and a little NEVER AGAIN. Nothing like evenhandedness! (23–24)[15]

This satirical episode expresses Frischmuth's displeasure with the Austrian attitude of laissez-faire, of preferring ignorance to disclosure. As she states in 1982, "I enjoy living in this country even if I'm infuriated by the narrow-mindedness — mixed with arrogance — of some of the people" ("Ich lebe gern in diesem Land, auch wenn mich die mit Präpotenz gemischte Borniertheit eines Teils seiner Bewohner . . . in Wut versetzen könnte").[16]

This third section of the novel also relates Vevi Schwarz's upbringing and her childhood experiences as the only daughter of the rather wealthy owners of the "Hotel Seegarten" and the "Pension Seeblick." Her early literary ambitions and her rather unusual, somewhat romanticized view of her childhood are suggested in the title, "Tag- und Nachtstücke in Schwarz'scher Manier I–IV" (Day and Night Pieces in a Schwarzian Manner), recalling E. T. A. Hoffmann or Bonaventura.[17] Vevi's attitude is also embedded in the symbolism of her name, Genoveva, recalling Tieck's "Leben und Tod der heiligen Genoveva" (1800, Life and Death of St. Genevieve). In some detail and with autobiographical overtones, we learn about the stressful existence of a lodging business *(Beherbergungsbetrieb),* about Vevi's less than positive experiences in a convent school, and about her early interest in reading and inventing stories. Through Vevi's eyes, we also get to know her extensive family, among them thirteen aunts, of whom the estranged Trude was "the thirteenth," the unhappy marriage of her parents, bound more by financial and social necessity than love, and her strong, talented, and unusually beautiful mother Regula, the heart and soul of the family and the "Pension Seeblick." In contrast to her mother's physical beauty, Vevi refers continuously to her own ugliness, like that of a gypsy, convinced that she must have been the product of an earlier affair *(Seitensprung)*. This attitude puts Vevi in the position of an outsider, allowing her to make free and uncensored observations and judgments about people and situations around her. As her father commented, "Come, let's toast your freedom! No one expects anything from you, no one kneels before you, no one envies the man who gets you" ("Komm, stoßen wir an auf deine Freiheit! Kein Mensch erwartet etwas von dir, niemand fällt vor dir auf die Knie, keiner mißgönnt dich einem anderen," 45). In the character of Vevi Schwarz with the unique combination of superior intelligence and a good dose of fool's freedom *(Narrenfreiheit)*, Frischmuth dissects the microcosmic world of the village and its inhabitants, as well as the owners and guests of the "Pension Seeblick." This small world encapsulates the author's true notion of *Heimat*. As Frischmuth said in an interview, "But 'the' country? The more seriously I think about it, the more the extent of the word shrivels to Aussee, to the point that only Altaussee remains. To me, the only sensible form of patriotism is local patriotism. . . . Purely emotionally, in other words by wishful thinking, I perceive and feel Austria probably as alpine . . . almost 'Aussee-like' then."[18]

The conclusion of *Einander Kind* entitled "Eleusis," opening with Trude's somewhat bizarre death, is reflective and contemplative. Following the interment of Vevi's mother, the two remaining women gather with friends and close family members in the "Hotel Seegarten." In these familiar surroundings, the ancestral home of the Schwarz family *(Stammhaus der Familie Schwarz)*, they talk about their relationships, their past, and their future, revealing in the process insights into the story's meaning: "To be 'one another's child.' . . . That's what people expect from one another if things are going badly, if they're unhappy or in a crisis. They expect that the other will act like a mother. . . . One should be able to be child as well as mother to each other" (212–213).[19] This sense of the novel is enhanced and projected further with, at the end, the birth of a baby girl, named Regula, assuring the family's continuity and suggesting a strong cyclical progression. This life cycle is also supported by Pröbstl's decision to stay in the village and to work in the "Pension Seeblick": "She doesn't know what she really wants. She wants only for this new life to go on as is" ("Sie weiß nicht, was sie tatsächlich will. Sie möchte nur, daß dieses neue Leben so weitergeht," 219). As Frischmuth states reflectively at the end of the novel, "Nothing ends. No end is final" ("Nichts hört auf. Kein Ende ist endgültig," 223).

The deeper mythological meaning of "Eleusis" in the context of her novel was troubling to Frischmuth. In her fourth Munich lecture on poetics she reflects on that: "For a long time I struggled with what Eleusis really meant for me. . . . What it was about? Was it about regeneration and rebirth rituals which comfort the mystic about life after this one or that there would always be life? . . . Eleusis is also the mystery of an eternally renewed childhood, of the return to the state of being reborn."[20] The theme of "putting 'being a child' in place of 'authority'" ("'Kindschaft' an die Stelle von 'Herrschaft' zu setzen")[21] and the return to one's place of origin emerge as aspects essential to a true understanding of Frischmuth's œuvre, and also the final key to this novel.

In somewhat autobiographical fashion — Frischmuth's parents owned and managed the "Parkhotel" on the lake in Altaussee when she was born — the "Hotel Seegarten" becomes a place of vital significance. It is here where all three women meet, where their fates interconnect, and where a future is engaged. A place of similar importance is the restaurant "Spanferkel" in the previously published novel *Über die Verhältnisse*, which takes place in Vienna. This up-scale eating establishment, owned and managed by the attractive and capable Melanie, called Mela, becomes the unofficial meeting place of Vienna's political and intellectual elite. In the small side room *(Extrazimmer)*, economic decisions, political conflicts, and anticipated high-ranking personnel changes are discussed before being made public. Aspiring politicians as well as the political establishment gather in the discreet surroundings of Mela's realm to plot the future's course. The "Spanferkel" indicating a particularly well-fed pig, but also suggesting political luck and financial gain — "the SPANFERKEL, the SUSTENANCE-PIG for us all, the sow indispensable to hopes of rosier times" ("das SPANFERKEL, unser aller NÄHR-SCHWEIN, die SAU die man haben muß, um noch ROSIGE ZEITEN zu erhoffen")[22] — becomes the place where the political pulse of the country is felt and measured. This life-in-the-big-city novel brings the reader to an entirely different fictional site and context from the provincial setting of the later novel, but the pairing of the country and the city in postwar Austrian life is a phenomenon Barbara Frischmuth considers desirable, and indeed indispensable. Frischmuth, who herself divides her time between Altaussee and Vienna, says in 1982: "For me personally this antagonism, without which I cannot imagine Austria in the future, is expressed between town and country, 'living in the city' and 'being in the country.' Taken separately, each of these conditions is impossible over time; taken together and interacting with each other, they are something like the consciousness of the land in which I live."[23]

The "Spanferkel" reflects indeed the mood of the land: "In terms of the general ambiance, Mela had a daily LIFE-SHOW in the SPANFERKEL. Conflicting opinions intertwine in elaborate forms of the most grotesque kind" (91).[24] From the safe and self-contained vantage point of the small restaurant, the narrator offers a succinct analysis of Austria's past, present, and future. As the following passage from the novel indicates, however, the author is always cognizant that for her any perspective of her homeland *(Heimatbetrachtung)* becomes an observation and an emotional journey:

> Austria is much less a STATE than an ATTITUDE TOWARD LIFE, an OUTLOOK which provides a foot in the door everywhere. It releases everyone from responsibility, but everyone can HAVE A PIECE OF THE PIE. Responsibility is the JOKER in this game and, seen this way, we are more a race of GRAPE-PICKERS than of serfs. The bad ones were always the others, WE brought CULTURE to our former EMPIRE. Had it not been for us . . . . And we all believe that we were the better ones, the MORE PEACEFUL ONES, whom the others treated badly. And if we ever sought REVENGE, then they DESERVED it — the OTHERS of course. And finally, we've suffered enough. How many of our people KILL themselves . . . well, that's why we have our GLORIOUS PAST, which no one can take from us. On the contrary, and we keep stuffing everything into this funnel. (190)[25]

In an essay from 1982 Frischmuth states: "How do I see, how do I feel about Austria? Smalltownish-monarchist, suffering from an excess of history, with arrogance stuck in the lapel like a little piece of ermine, dragging indolence behind their soft slippers."[26] Although the novel's immediate political issue concerns the illegal financial dealings surrounding the election of the Austrian president, the narrator hints at other, deeper and more invasive economic problems in the Austria of the eighties: "This country, busy for forty years establishing its UNIQUENESS, suddenly finds itself forced to take refuge in the GENERAL world situation. We were great at running the country down with our SPECIAL STATUS. . . . For a long time now, this country has lived BEYOND ITS MEANS" (59, 48).[27] The "Spanferkel" becomes "a dry island" ("eine trockene Insel") in "a rampant MORASS" ("dem überhandnehmenden MORAST," 82).

Although a rather serious political climate pervades the "Spanferkel,"[28] the restaurant is also a place where relationships form and human ties are established. Much of the humane, civilized ambiance is created by Mela's feminine sensibilities and intuitions, reinforced by the delights of the Austrian cuisine, because the restaurant is also home to Mela and her daughter Frô. The "Spanferkel" is the symbolic center of both *Heimat* (homeland) and *Heim* (home), where important interactions occur and where past, present, and future converge. It happens that the highest-ranking Austrian politician who is a regular in the restaurant is Frô's father, a fact known only to Mela throughout most of the novel. Politics and private lives finally converge when at the end "the good old side-room . . . for both a highly TRUSTED PLACE, so to speak" ("die gute alte Extrastube . . . sozusagen für beide eine höchst VERTRAUTE UMGEBUNG," 214) becomes the first and final meeting place between daughter and father. Furthermore, Frô meets her future husband, a diplomat of Austrian and Turkish heritage, while serving him dinner, and Mela, at the end of the novel, reflects on the importance of the "Spanferkel" as the one certainty in a life of impending change and approaching age: "Mela sees herself reaching an age when time will be felt only in its FADING, but not because she HAS none. Suddenly her pride welled up. There is after all the SPANFERKEL" (218).[29]

Taken as a whole, Frischmuth's novel is a kind of bildungsroman at the level of national consciousness. As life, politics, food, and time converge in the "Spanferkel" into a harmonious and ultimately positive whole, *Über die Verhältnisse* emerges as a typically Austrian tale in Barbara Frischmuth's œuvre. Like the "Pension Seeblick" and the "Hotel Seegarten," the "Spanferkel" becomes the site of symbolic representation of contemporary Austrian manners and mores, the center that defines the sense of place — *Ich, Heim, Heimat* (I, home, country).

In her most recent work, a collection of short prose pieces entitled

Hexenherz (1994), Frischmuth indulges again her predilection for small village life amidst magnificent natural surroundings. In the somewhat autobiographical tale "Posaune im Ohr" (1994, Trumpet in the Ear), she describes a visit to an old, deaf musician whom she knew in her childhood days. They reminisce about people and events, thus excluding her husband from much of the conversation: "It was more entertaining for me than for my husband because I had known from my childhood on all the people we talked about" ("Für mich war das unterhaltsamer als für meinen Mann, kannte ich doch die meisten, von denen die Rede war, von Jugend an").[30] Beyond individual anecdotes, the narrator offers a detailed description of the musician's remote cabin, the surrounding countryside below the majestic Zinken, a high, pyramid-shaped mountain dominating the area including the small potato field, essential to the livelihood of the local inhabitants. Despite the inherently problematic topic of a musician gone completely deaf, the tale offers a glimpse of a stark but ultimately fulfilling life in the mountains.

A similarly detailed description of a rural village that, typical of Austria, relies on agriculture and tourism for survival, emerges from the tale "Wild-Frau" (1994; "Witch of the Wildwood," 1997).[31] In this story, the sexual desires of a strong-headed woman are skillfully intertwined with the untamed and enticing natural surroundings. The double meaning of the word *Wild* in the title reflects the woman's strong sexual urges and the harsh, uncultivated natural state of the countryside. Moreover, if taken as a noun, it indicates the woman's symbolic symbiosis with the deer population (*Wild* is also the German word for game) roaming freely and uninhibitedly. As in the other tale, Frischmuth shows her talent for uniting human and natural elements, people and animals, into a unifying whole. At the end of the tale, the woman's sexual desires disappear as quickly as a flock of deer observed venturing too close to the house and to civilization.

Perhaps the most striking of the tales in this collection is "Herzsprung" (1994, Skip of Heart — the German here also has the double meaning of "Broken Heart"), in which a woman, following a serious car accident, chooses a place for her recovery with a "view onto a lake with mountains all around and a boat" ("Blick auf einen See mit Bergen rundum und einem Boot"),[32] a fortuitous choice. The close mountain ranges and the rolling meadows, encircling the azure waters of the lake, are filled with beautiful flowers and lush shrubbery, all soothing to her frail physical condition. She regrets not having visited the place earlier: "The town pleased her more and more. She had read about it without attaching special meaning to it and considered all the praise exaggerated. Now she regretted not having discovered it earlier" (113).[33] Her emotional connection to this place deepens as she becomes aware that the inhabitants of the village appear to know her. Several people not only greet her in a routinely friendly manner, but address her by her name, Frau Andergast, becoming another guest *(ein anderer Gast).* Looking for answers, the protagonist reviews her past life. Somewhat reminiscent of the beginning of Anna Seghers's *Der Ausflug der toten Mädchen* (1946, The Excursion of the Dead Girls), she wonders about the effect of her car accident on her memory: "She touched her head where the bump could barely be felt. Was she suffering from memory-loss? One did not lose one's memory from a bump like this. She was absolutely certain that she had never been in this town. Yet what did it mean that people acted as though they knew her?" (115).[34] As past and present, memory and forgetfulness intertwine further, she also meets her ex-husband from whom she had been divorced some fifteen years and who is vacationing with his second wife. In a final rendezvous with her husband, her already weakened heart fails and she dies. Here then, the *Ort* (place/location) takes on existential significance as the present and the past, happiness and sadness, and ultimately, life and death converge. It is finally a place of rebirth and celebration of life, as she is briefly reunited with her former husband, the only man she ever truly loved.

For Frischmuth, the sense of *Heimat* manifests itself in its most basic form as a place one loves, to which one belongs, where one was born, lives, and dies. It emerges in her writing as a place which transcends time and allows her creativity to flow freely. In the essay "Der Ort und die Zeit" (1983, Place and Time), Frischmuth writes: "Not to want to live here any more. To imagine it, write about it, describe it, to go in and out of writing, to create connections between inside and out . . . between here, there, and elsewhere."[35] Inevitably, that special place recalls the novelist's birthplace, Altaussee, and, to a lesser extent, Vienna. The minute descriptions of the beauty of the countryside of southern Austria, of the simple ways of rural life, and of the social and political problems unique to Vienna constitute a fictional representation of *Heimat*. Moreover, her upbringing as the daughter of a hotelier in a long family tradition creates in her fiction the notion of the restaurant, or hotel, as a microcosm of life and society at large: "Born in a tourist area, in Altaussee, deep within Austria. . . . Grown up right there, amidst the cycles of pre-season, high season, low season, and off-season; some five hundred years of restaurant business run through my veins, which apparently still surfaces in my books, but who can jump with impunity over the traces of one's youth?"[36]

If for Frischmuth cultural identity is closely connected to a specific place, linguistic nuances, expressions, and intonations particular to that place add to its uniqueness. Much has been written about Frischmuth's particular penchant for linguistic creativity and playfulness, which, in her own words, stems from her admiration for Lewis Carroll, Jean Paul, E. T. A. Hoffmann, Ferdinand Raimund, and Fritz von Herzmanovsky-Orlando, among others.[37] Her preoccupation with strong imaginative language, a kind of *Bildsprache* (visual language) utilized effectively to encourage reader response and free associations and images, is particularly evident in her earlier works, her children's books and again, to some extent, in her novel *Machtnix* (1993, Don't Bother). Several recent discussions about this "associative nonmethod" *(assoziative Nicht-Methode),* a term Frischmuth herself coined in her lectures on poetics delivered in Munich in 1991, elaborate on that concept.[38] Frischmuth does not, however, use this metaphoric *Bildsprache,* suggesting another, more complex Austrian literary tradition, to express her sense of place. In this context, her use of language is more basic than that: colloquialisms and certain dialect expressions associated with her home-town region and/or with Austria *per se*, scattered throughout the more literary and educated language of her works. This selectively used and carefully integrated vernacular speech, this "color" of her concrete "place" *(Lokalkolorit)*[39] creates a uniquely Austrian feeling and lends substance and conviction to Frischmuth's writings. It creates a hard-to-explain textual intimacy, an innate sense that, much like a childhood experience, cannot be fully explained. When in *Über die Verhältnisse* Mela is finally united with her daughter Frô after a long and frustrating search, their newly found intimacy is expressed and felt through their common language, "a language that exhibits a particular dialect shading, consists of commonly used expressions and speech patterns, and occasionally falls back on KIDS' VOCABULARY that for others can mean something else. A kind of PRIVATE SPEECH, more or less" (193).[40] It is this Austrian private language *(Privatsprache),* in contrast to more commonly accepted High German *(Hochdeutsch),* which contributes to that deep sense of *Heimat* in Frischmuth's works. Words like *Tuchent* (feather blanket), *Erdäpfel* (potatoes), *Fleischhauer* (butcher), and *Bub* (boy) are scattered throughout her works, as are more typically Viennese expressions such as *Schmarrn* (cut-up pancake, an expression used to indicate a worthless object), *wurscht* (don't care), *Badewaschel* (life-guard), and *Mannsbild* (derogatory expression for macho- or rambo-type man) (*Über die Verhältnisse* 93, 151). When in the same novel, the male protagonist calls Mela "a real little Mela" ("ein echtes Melerl," 12), expressing his feelings of endearment through a uniquely Austrian diminutive ending, the language becomes just another means to express the essence of this typically Austrian tale. Gerhard Amanshauser speaks about the importance of a "local color" as a possible answer to an Austrian literary and national identity: "A person who speaks German completely accent-free, for example, would come across to us like a radio announcer reciting someone else's texts." But, he warns, "Clearly, if it's to be striking or pleasant, local color in language should be neither self-conscious nor just stuck on. It must be at once natural and work by subtle effect, and it should animate spontaneous and open gesture."[41] Similarly, Hans Weigel states in his more academic treatise on the same subject: "There is no more an 'Austrian' language than a 'Belgian' language. . . . However, the language in which Austrians dream, think, speak, and write is different from any German outside Austria."[42]

Although not directly involved in the more academic polemics on Austrian cultural and literary identity, Frischmuth's view of *Heimat* as represented in her works and in her language is, in fact, an important contribution to that debate. As Wolfgang Frühwald sees it, Frischmuth's "œuvre is beyond the thematics of language, of intertextuality, of myth studies while being completely devoted to writing a history of Austria, with forms and figures that are close and true to life, experienced and "experienceable"; committed to create the history of her own family, the catastrophes, the guilt, and also — the good fortune of Austria's history as part of the province of mankind."[43] Throughout her long literary career, Barbara Frischmuth has not deviated from the importance of her elemental sense of *Heimat* as a place of identity and spirit; a place of local, anecdotal, and personal significance; a place where colloquial and vernacular speech reflects its uniqueness and singularity. In contrast, nowhere in her works do we detect indications of the more jarring ideological connotation of *Heimat* in the more specifically German sense that reemerged powerfully in Germany during 1933–1945 and which reflected, at least in its extreme manifestations, political and nationalistic tendencies. It is here that at least one of the distinctions between postwar Austrian and German national identities comes through in Barbara Frischmuth's fiction. Reading Frischmuth from this perspective, one is reminded once again of D. H. Lawrence's eloquent statement in his well-known essay from 1923: "Every people is polarized in some particular locality, which is home, the homeland. Different places on the face of the earth have different vital effluence, different vibration, different chemical exhalation, different polarity with different stars: call it what you like. But the spirit of place is a great reality."[44]

Hamilton College

Notes

1. Dagmar C. Lorenz, "Ein Interview: Barbara Frischmuth," *Women in German Yearbook 2* (Lanham, MD: UP of America, 1986) 30.

2. For an excellent discussion of this topic, see Paul Michael Lützeler, "Die österreichische Gegenwartsliteratur im Spannungsfeld zwischen Deutschsprachigkeit und nationaler Autonomie," *Für und wider eine österreichische Literatur*, ed. Kurt Bartsch and Dietmar Goltschnigg (Königstein: Athenäum, 1982) 100–115.

3. Petra Nachbaur and Sigurd Paul Scheichl, eds., *Literatur über Literatur: Eine österreichische Anthologie* (Innsbruck: Haymon, 1995). See among others, Hans Weigel, "Sprache als Schicksal. Vorläufige Bermerkungen über 'Das Österreichische' in der österreichischen Literatur" 127–132; Julian Schutting, "Gibt es eine österreichische Literatur" 25–29; Wendelin Schmidt-Dengler, "Vorwort" 11; Hilde Spiel, "'der österreicher küßt die zerschmetterte hand.' Über eine österreichische Nationalliteratur" 289–296.

4. Barbara Frischmuth, "Zur Identität Österreichs," *Für und wider eine österreichische Literatur* 70.

5. Frischmuth, "Zur Identität Österreichs" 77. Original quote: "Da aber Literatur nicht im luftleeren Raum entsteht, sondern an einem konkreten Ort, ob man nun tatsächlich an ihm lebt oder ihn in der Emigration täglich im Herzen neu erstehen läßt, ob man der gesprochenen Sprache dieses Ortes gestattet, der geschriebenen Sprache des eigenen Werkes etwas von ihrem Kolorit abzugeben oder ob man sich bewußt gegen diese gesprochene Sprache absetzt, ob man ein mehr oder weniger gebrochenes Verhältnis zur österreichischen literarischen Tradition hat oder bewußt eine andere vorzieht, bin ich davon überzeugt, daß sich an

uns allen eine Menge Österreichisches wird finden lassen, wenn man lange genug danach sucht."

6. Frischmuth, "Zur Identität Österreichs" 70.

7. D. H. Lawrence, "The Spirit of Place," *Studies in Classic American Literature* (New York: Viking Press, 1923; repr. 1962) 4.

8. Riki Winter, "Ein Gespräch mit Barbara Frischmuth," *Dossier 4: Barbara Frischmuth,* ed. Kurt Bartsch (Graz: Droschl, 1992) 8, 9. Original quote: "Das ist ein Ort, an dem ich mittlerweile sechs Generationen überschauen kann. Das ist einfach ein so verführerisches Moment, daß man an den Gesichtern das Vergehen der Zeit ablesen kann, aber auch das Wiederkehren, wenn sich durch Generationen hindurch gewisse Züge in den Gesichtern manifestieren, aber auch Verhaltensweisen, Sprechweisen."

9. Barbara Frischmuth, *Die Mystifikationen der Sophie Silber* (Munich: dtv, 1976; repr. 1982) 111. Original quote: "Sie hatte den Begriff Heimat, ja sogar Heimatort immer vermieden und höchstens von ihrem Geburtsort gesprochen. Doch wenn man ihr in diesem Augenblick eine Erklärung des Begriffes vom Heimatlichen abgenötigt hätte, würde sie gesagt haben, daß es mit diesem Einanderkennen zusammenhing."

10. Barbara Frischmuth, "Mein Lieblingsort," *Barbara Frischmuth: Wassermänner,* ed. Hans Haider (Salzburg: Residenz, 1975; repr. 1991) 227. Original quote: "Mein Lieblingsort ist der Ort meiner Träume. Nicht immer der Ort, an dem meine Träume spielen, viel eher der Ort, der in Form eines Bildes in fast alle meine Träume hereinleuchtet, wie ein Zitat aus einem unverkennbaren, längeren Zusammenhang."

11. Barbara Frischmuth, "Von den Langexistierenden," *Traum der Literatur — Literatur des Traums: Münchner Poetik-Vorlesungen* (Salzburg: Residenz, 1991) 68.

12. Barbara Frischmuth, *Einander Kind* (Salzburg: Residenz, 1990) 14, 210–211; subsequent citations from this novel will be followed by the page number in parentheses. Original quote: "Ihre Zwerggranatäpfelbäumchen waren auf der Terrasse so heimisch geworden, daß sie von Juni an bis spät in den Herbst hinein blühten. Gedankenverloren zupfte sie ein paar Nadeln vom Rosmarinstrauch, zerrieb sie und hielt sich die Finger unter die Nase. Düfte, Gerüche, der Gesang der Vögel . . . und vor und unter ihr diese gelbgrüne, südländisch wirkende Stadt, in ihrer Folie aus Dunst und Glast, eine Stadt, die so viel Atem aushauchte, daß man die Schwaden über den Fluß ziehen sah, der sich, aus den Bergen kommend, seinen Weg gemächlich zwischen all den verschnörkelten Fassaden

hindurchbahnte. Das meiste an Gestank drang nicht mehr bis zu ihr herauf, und was heraufkam, wurde gemildert, denn sie hatte ihre Pflanzen auch danach gezogen, wie gut sie dufteten. . . . Ein Garten . . . auf einem Dach, aus dem Felsen herauswuchernd. Sträucher, Bäumchen, Stauden, Blumen, Kräuter, Rasen. Und beim leisesten Lufthauch ein Duften und Summen."

13. Original quote: "Der Weg würde derselbe geblieben sein. Vom Hotel zur Kirche, von der Kirche zum Friedhof. Vorbei am Stallgebäude mit den Kutschpferden . . . . Sie hatte noch den damaligen Fahrplan des Postautobusses im Gedächtnis."

14. Original quote: "Daß die Leute über die Geschehnisse damals wieder nachdenken. Daß sie endlich zugeben können, wie es war. Wenn schon keiner eine Antwort darauf zu geben wüßte, warum es dazu hatte kommen können. Es zugeben. Erinnern, betrauern."

15. Original quote: "Fünfzig Jahre — Zeit genug, um vieles zu vergessen. Dennoch, hüten Sie sich vor einseitigen Schuldzuweisungen. Was hätten Sie auch von zu vielen aktuellen Bezügen in der Provinz? Na also — sehen Sie! Ich meine, wir sind uns doch im klaren darüber, was wir erreichen sollen. Zeigen Sie, was mit all den armen Menschen geschehen ist. Darauf sind sogar in der Provinz die verschiedenen Lager ansprechbar. Sie haben klarerweise völlig freie Hand, aber ich denke, es ist am besten, Sie kehren das allgemein Menschliche hervor. Aufklärung, Aufklärung, und noch einmal Aufklärung! Ein bißchen Kraus, ein bißchen Canetti, ein bißchen Horvath und ein bißchen Grünbaum, ein bißchen Zeitzeugen innerhalb und außerhalb des Widerstandes, ein bißchen MEIN KAMPF und ein bißchen NIE WIEDER. Ausgewogen halt!"

16. Frischmuth, "Zur Identität Österreichs" 70.

17. Paul Michael Lützeler, "Barbara Frischmuths Demeter-Trilogie. Mythologische Finde-Spiele in der postmodernen Literatur," *Dossier 4: Barbara Frischmuth* 92.

18. Frischmuth, "Österreich — versuchsweise betrachtet," *Glückliches Österreich: Literarische Besichtigungen unseres Vaterlandes*, ed. Jochen Jung (Vienna: Tosa, 1978; repr. 1995) 66, 68. Original quote: "Aber 'das' Land? Je ernsthafter ich darüber nachdenke, desto mehr schrumpft der Umfang dessen, worauf das Wort hinzielen soll, auf das Gebiet um Aussee zusammen, bis dann nur mehr Altaussee übrigbleibt. Die einzige Form von Patriotismus, die mir einsichtig ist, ist der Lokalpatriotismus. . . . Rein emotionell, das heißt wunschmäßig, sehe,

empfinde ich Österreich wahrscheinlich als alpin . . . annähernd ausseerisch also."

19. Original quote: "Einander Kind sein. . . . Das erwarten doch die Menschen voneinander, wenn es ihnen schlecht geht, wenn sie unglücklich sind oder in einer Krise. Sie erwarten, daß der andere sich wie eine Mutter verhält. . . . Man sollte einander Kind und Mutter sein können."

20. Frischmuth, "Von den Langexistierenden," 70–71. Original quote: "Ich habe mich lange mit dem Gedanken gequält, was Eleusis eigentlich für mich bedeutet.. . . Worum ging es? Um Regenerierungs-und Wiedergeburtsrituale, die den Mysten damit trösten, daß es nach diesem Leben ein anderes oder daß es immer wieder Leben geben würde? . . . Eleusis ist auch das Mysterium der ständig sich erneuernden Kindschaft, des Zurückkehrens in den Schoß des Wiedergeborenwerdens."

21. Wolfgang Frühwald, "Der Traum 'Einander Kind zu sein.' Über die Erzählerin Barbara Frischmuth," *Traum der Literatur — Literatur des Traums* 119.

22. Frischmuth, *Über die Verhältnisse* (Salzburg: Residenz, 1987) 7; subsequent citations from this novel will be followed by the page number in parentheses.

23. Frischmuth, "Österreich — versuchsweise betrachtet" 70. Original quote: "Darin drückt sich für mich persönlich wiederum dieser Antagonismus aus, ohne den mir Österreich in Zukunft immer unvorstellbarer wäre, nämlich der zwischen Hauptstadt und Landschaft, zwischen 'in der Stadt wohnen' und 'auf dem Land sein.' Jeder dieser Zustände für sich genommen eine Unmöglichkeit auf die Dauer, aufeinander bezogen und in Wechselwirkung miteinander so etwas wie ein Bewußtsein des Landes, in dem ich lebe."

24. Original quote: "Was die allgemeine Stimmung betrifft erlebt Mela eine tägliche LIFE-SHOW im SPANFERKEL! Da verschlingen sich die gegensätzlichsten Meinungen zu ornamentalen Gebilden der groteskesten Art.

25. Original quote: "Österreich ist eben nicht so sehr STAAT als vielmehr LEBENSHALTUNG, und mit dieser THESE kriegt man überall den Fuß in die Tür. Sie entläßt einen aus der Verantwortung, aber man kann überall MITNASCHEN. Sie ist der JOKER in diesem Spiel, und so gesehen, sind wir weniger ein Volk von Phäaken als eines von ROSINENPICKERN. Die Bösen waren immer die anderen, WIR haben KULTUR ermöglicht in UNSEREM ehemaligen IMPERIUM. Wenn wir

nicht gewesen wären. . . . Und wir glauben alle daran, daß wir die BESSEREN, die FRIEDFERTIGEREN waren, denen die anderen übel mitgespielt haben. Und wenn wir uns schon einmal RACHE übten, dann haben sie es auch VERDIENT gehabt, nämlich die ANDEREN. Und gelitten haben wir schließlich genug. Und wie viele Leute sich bei uns UMBRINGEN . . . na, dafür haben wir eben diese GLÄNZENDE VERGANGENHEIT, die uns keiner mehr NEHMEN kann. Ganz im Gegenteil, und wir stopfen weiterhin alles in diesen Trichter."

26. Frischmuth, "Österreich — versuchsweise betrachtet" 67. Original quote: "Wie sehe, wie empfinde ich Österreich? Städtisch-monarchisch, leidend an einem Übermaß an Geschichte, den Hochmut als Stückchen vom Hermelin ins Knopfloch gesteckt, die Trägheit in den Filzpatschen nachziehend."

27. Original quote: "Dieses Land . . . das seit vierzig Jahren damit beschäftigt ist, sich eine EINMALIGKEIT zu bestätigen, ist auf einmal in der Zwangslage, sich ins ALLGEMEINE der Weltlage flüchten zu müssen. Schön haben wir abgewirtschaftet mit unserem SONDER-STATUS. . . . Dieses Land lebt seit jeher ÜBER DIE VERHÄLTNISSE."

28. The political reality behind this novel concerns the scandals involving the Federal Chancellor, Fred Sinowatz.

29. Original quote: "Mela sieht sich in ein ALTER kommen, in dem die Zeit nur mehr spürbar wird, indem sie VERGEHT, aber nicht, indem sie keine HAT. Plötzlich rappelt ihr STOLZ sich hoch. Da ist immerhin das SPANFERKEL."

30. Barbara Frischmuth, "Posaune im Ohr," *Hexenherz* (Salzburg: Residenz, 1994) 57.

31. Barbara Frischmuth, "Wild-Frau," *Hexenherz* 96–104; trans. by Gerald Chapple and James B. Lawson and published as "Witch of the Wildwood," *The Malahat Review* 118 (Spring 1997): 16–22.

32. Barbara Frischmuth, "Herzsprung," *Hexenherz* 106; subsequent citations from this story will be followed by the page number in parentheses.

33. Original quote: "Der Ort gefiel ihr immer besser. Sie hatte schon über ihn gelesen, dem Gelesenen aber keine Bedeutung zugemessen und all das Lob für Übertreibung gehalten. Jetzt bedauerte sie, daß sie ihn nicht schon früher entdeckt hatte."

34. Original quote: "Sie griff sich an den Kopf, wo die Beule gerade noch zu ertasten war. Litt sie an Gedächtnisschwund? Von einer Beule wie diese verlor man doch nicht die Erinnerung. Sie war ganz sicher, daß

sie nie in diesem Ort gewesen war. Was hatte es also zu bedeuten, daß die Leute so taten, als kennten sie sie."

35. Frischmuth, "Der Ort und die Zeit," *Traumgrenze* (Salzburg: Residenz, 1983) 138. Original quote: "Nicht mehr hier leben wollen. Es sich vorstellen, aufschreiben, beschreiben, schreibend ein und aus gehen, Zusammenhänge herstellen zwischen drinnen und draußen . . . zwischen hier und dort und anderswo."

36. Frischmuth, "Ich über mich," *Wassermänner* 200. Original quote: "Geboren in einer Fremdenverkehrsgegend, zu Altaussee, im tiefsten Binnenösterreich. . . . Aufgewachsen ebendort, im Rhythmus von Vorsaison, Hochsaison, Nachsaison und toter Saison; in meinen Adern fließen an die fünfhundert Jahre Wirtshaus, was man meinen Büchern angeblich noch immer ansieht, aber wer springt schon ungestraft über den Schatten der Kindheit?"

37. Frischmuth, "Ich über mich" 201.

38. On this topic, see among others Erika Tunner, "Plädoyer für die Assoziative Nicht-Methode über und zur Literatur zu reden" and Margret Brügmann, "Traumtänzerin mit Fangnetz. Formen Weiblicher Ästhetik bei Barbara Frischmuth," *Dossier 4: Barbara Frischmuth,* 15–21 and 23–39. See also Frischmuth, *Traum der Literatur — Literatur des Traums.*

39. Frischmuth, "Zur Identität Österreichs" 77.

40. Original quote: "Eine Sprache, die eine bestimmte Dialektfärbung aufweist, aus häufig verwendeten Ausdrücken und Redewendungen besteht und von Zeit zu Zeit auf bestimmte KINDERWÖRTER zurückverfällt, die für andere Menschen wohl auch etwas anderes bedeuteten. Eine Art von PRIVATSPRACHE gewissermaßen."

41. Gerhard Amanshauser, "Über Nationalgefühl im allgemeinen und österreichisches Nationalgefühl im besonderen," *Glückliches Österreich* 18. Original quote: "Ein Mensch, der zum Beispiel ein absolut akzentfreies Deutsch spräche, käme uns vor wie ein Radiosprecher, der Texte rezitiert, die andere verfaßt haben. . . . Die lokale Färbung darf offenbar, wenn sie als eindrucksvoll oder angenehm empfunden werden soll, nicht hervorgekehrt oder plakatiert werden. Sie muß gleichsam unbewußt, aus dem Hintergrund wirken, muß Gesten beleben, die spontan und weltoffen sind."

42. Weigel, "Sprache als Schicksal" 127. Original quote: "Es gibt ebensowenig eine österreichische Sprache, als eine belgische . . . wohl aber ist die Sprache, in welcher der Österreicher träumt, denkt, spricht und schreibt, von allem Deutsch außerhalb Österreichs unterschieden."

43. Frühwald, "Der Traum 'Einander Kind zu sein'" 121. Original quote: "Das Werk ist jenseits von Sprachthematik, Intertextualität und Mythenpoesie, ganz dieser Aufgabe hingegeben, eine Geschichte Österreichs zu schreiben, mit lebenswahren und lebensnahen, erfahrenen und erfahrbaren Gestalten, an der Geschichte der eigenen Familie die Katastrophen, die Schuld und — das Glück der Geschichte Österreichs, als Teil der Provinz des Menschen, zu gestalten."

44. Lawrence, "The Spirit of Place" 5–6.

Barbara Frischmuth's *Hörspiele* and the Problematization of Space

Johannes F. Evelein

Introduction

When Barbara Frischmuth attended the 1996 German Studies Association conference in Seattle, she mentioned on several occasions that, though her work has been the subject of numerous studies for quite some time, her *Hörspiele* (radio plays) have not received the critical attention they deserve. To put it more boldly, there is not a single study devoted to her contribution to this genre. This may be surprising, as Frischmuth has produced more than a dozen radio plays since 1970 and was awarded the *Prix Italia* for her piece *Eine Liebe in Erzurum (A Love in Erzurum)* in 1994. Several reasons, however, can be found for the lack of scholarly interest. One reason of practical nature is that most radio plays are generally broadcast only once, in some cases several times, and although they reach a large audience, the fixed broadcast date limits their availability for further study. Because the scripts of radio plays are only rarely published, these works tend to be disregarded once broadcast. But a more serious reason for the frequent obscurity of radio plays is the lack of interest in the genre among literary scholars, many of whom scarcely consider it to be a literary genre at all. As Everett Frost observes: "Serious dialog and criticism that might help foster, encourage, and define the art barely exist. Newspapers do not review radio works, nor do theatre, broadcast, or academic journals regularly discuss it. Partly because radio drama's most publicized history in this country [United States] concerns works produced as popular entertainment, most scholars of literature and drama seem to regard it as a subject unworthy of serious inquiry."[1] However optimistic Klaus Schöning may seem in his assertion that the "*Hörspiel* [radio play], fugitive, managed and upstart *Hörspiel,* is slowly beginning to make an impression on the general cultural awareness,"[2] the radio play has yet to be brought back from the scholarly periphery in which it still resides. Yet, with her many contributions to this "acoustic literature," Barbara Frischmuth is in very good and scarcely peripheral company, especially in the German-speaking countries: After all, as Schöning points out, "There is hardly a German writer who has not written a *Hörspiel*."[3] The list is indeed long and includes Bertolt Brecht, Alfred Döblin, Wolfgang Borchert, Ilse Aichinger, Ingeborg Bachmann,

Heinrich Böll, Max Frisch, Günter Eich, Hans Magnus Enzensberger, and Helmut Heissenbüttel, to name only a few. This fact may not sit well with skeptics of this genre, but it serves as a good illustration of its breadth and as a powerful argument for the study of the radio play to which scholars like Klaus Schöning, Stefan Bodo Würffel, Roland Heger, Rudolf Arnheim, and Mauricio Kagel have made important contributions.

Barbara Frischmuth's first radio play, *Die Mauskoth und die Kuttlerin* (1970, Mauskoth and Kuttlerin), was coproduced by the *Westdeutscher Rundfunk* (West German Broadcasting Corporation) and *Südwestfunk* (Southwest Broadcasting Corporation) in 1970, the same year in which the *Norddeutscher Rundfunk* (North German Broadcasting Corporation) broadcast her play *Die unbekannte Hand* (1970, The Unknown Hand). She continued writing radio plays in the seventies and eighties that were produced by various broadcast corporations including the *Süddeutscher Rundfunk* (South German Broadcasting Corporation), *Österreichischer Rundfunk* (Austrian Broadcasting Corporation), and *Westdeutscher Rundfunk.*[4] In addition, she adapted her drama *Anstandslos* (1992, No Problem) for broadcasting and commissioned Götz Fritsch to adapt *Mister Rosa oder die Schwierigkeit, kein Zwerg zu sein* (1990, Mister Rosa, or The Difficulty Not to Be a Dwarf). Her radio play *Die Mozart hörende Hanako und ihre fünf Kätzchen* (1991, Hanako Listening to Mozart, and Her Five Kittens) was produced in collaboration with Saegusa Kazuko. Frischmuth wrote several radio plays with a children's audience in mind. Of her radio plays only the scripts *Die Mauskoth und die Kuttlerin*, *Ich möchte, ich möchte die Welt* (1977, I Want, I Want the World), and *Eine Liebe in Erzurum* have appeared in print.[5]

This study comprises a discussion of three of Frischmuth's radio plays that are representative of both the genre and her *Hörspiel* œuvre. These three plays span almost three decades and illustrate not only Frischmuth's continued interest in and contribution to this medium, but also her social responsibility as a writer to establish an awareness among her audience about issues ranging from women's rights to the need for intercultural understanding. *Die unbekannte Hand,* the first radio play that I will examine, had appeared in *Der gewöhnliche Schrecken* (The Usual Fright), a volume of horror stories compiled by Peter Handke a year before, and the radio play version conveyed a powerful message about a subject that had started to receive increasing attention: mankind's harmful disrespect for and estrangement from nature. It was broadcast three years later by the *Südwestfunk* and stands as Frischmuth's most critical literary confrontation with society's irresponsible actions, albeit in a humoristic disguise. A turning inward characterizes her 1984 radio play *Binnengespräche* (Inner Conversations) in which a small town and its surroundings set the stage for a meeting between drastically different people whose exchange of experiences in this town creates an intricate multidimensionality of a spatial realm, ranging from memories of a happy childhood to the persecution of local Jewish citizens. This study analyzes *Binnengespräche* as a carefully crafted phenomenology of space, in which space is treated as a perception rather than an external reality. It is argued that in the play — whose very title alludes to the importance of a spatial dimension — Frischmuth brings together characters who share their own perceived realities, thereby creating an intricate poetics of space. It is suggested that the space in the play is presented as a fictitious realm which, as the characters must realize, does not exist anymore, except in their own consciousness — their conscious and willing distortion of the outer reality — and in their subconscious: Only in their dreams can they reconstruct the desired space uninhibitedly. The study concludes with an analysis of Frischmuth's award-winning *Eine Liebe in Erzurum,* which was directed by Fritsch and first broadcast by the *Österreichischer Rundfunk* in 1994. Frischmuth's play is a reconstruction of a relationship between a Turkish doctor and an Austrian female student whose failure is unavoidable because of its violations of culturally defined norms. Frischmuth convincingly denounces these norms, yet it becomes clear that the failure is the result of the partners' mutual sensation of trespassing on each other's cultural space, which excludes the possibility of a reconciliation: A liberated European woman is as much an outcast as a Turkish doctor whose degree is not recognized in Austria. In its analysis of the main theme, *Fremdsein* (alienation), the play skillfully links the main protagonist's personal narrative to the increasing animosity toward Turks in contemporary Germany and Austria and serves as a powerful warning against prevalent xenophobia.

These plays, however different they may be, show an important commonality in the problematized interaction between the characters and their surroundings, a dysfunctionality of the protagonists caused by their disharmonious, dualistic position taken against the space in which they reside, be it their natural environment that strikes back in *Die unbekannte Hand*, the sensation of a paradise lost and the desire to retrace it and redefine its borders in *Binnengespräche*, or the foreigner's cultural alienation and antagonization in *Eine Liebe in Erzurum*.

Since the emergence of the genre of the radio play, or its German equivalent *Hörspiel*, there has been some discussion about what qualifies as such. For this study, *Hörspiel* is understood in light of Gero von Wilpert's definition of the genre's main characteristics:

> Omission of all optical features (set, facial expression, milieu, stage, scenery which is oftentimes replaced by so-called aural scenery) in favor of pure acoustics, in particular the spoken word, background music etc. Acoustics alone give expression to the internal — mental, psychological — and external action, govern the structure, and require — in the interest of the receiver — highly concentrated action, intriguing nexuses between scenes, a small number of protagonists, rich variation, and a short broadcasting time (mostly up to one hour).[6]

Die unbekannte Hand

Frischmuth's 1970 *Hörspiel* gives evidence of an important paradigm shift in the author's œuvre, which indicates a renewed interest in a topic to a large degree neglected by her contemporaries: As Donald Daviau observes, "The evolution evident in the progression of Frischmuth's writings not only involves a shift of perspective from language to character, but also includes a return to an emphasis on nature, a feature that was largely ignored by writers during the phase of linguistic experimentation in the late 1950s and 1960s."[7] Frischmuth feels compelled to establish an awareness about mankind's deteriorating relationship with its natural environment. The social message formulated in her 1976 novel *Die Mystifikationen der Sophie Silber* (The Mystifications of Sophie Silber) finds expression already in this early *Hörspiel*: "The future must be planned differently if the world is not to suffer irreparable damage."[8]

Die unbekannte Hand, set in Vienna, is void of any subtleties. It stages a grotesque apocalyptic cataclysm leaving no room for speculation about what fate awaits a world characterized by sheer disrespect for nature and by an antagonism between man and the animal world, which reduces the latter to exploitable objects. Despite its sobering message, the play is humoristic in its use of the Viennese vernacular, the depiction of the typical coffee house culture, and the use of sound effects that serve both as auditory illustration of occurrences and as a structural adhesive.

The story is simple: During a day at the races, the horses take off without their jockeys and leave the stadium. Simultaneously, dogs start to bark and an occasional goat makes itself heard to the extent that, at times, the dialogues between the various voices — the cast consists of nine male voices, four female voices, and one child's voice — are barely audible. A radio reporter announces that cases of rabies have been reported and that a number of people, among whom are, not surprisingly, an "owner of a butcher's shop and registered member of the Association for Breeding Rottweilers, as well as a head waiter, Mr. Leo L, dealer in saddle, carriage, and race horses, predators, and exotic animals,"[9] have been severely bitten. Meanwhile, by an unidentified person *(von unbekannter Hand),* the locks of animal cages in the Prater zoo have been broken, allowing animals to flee the premises and join the indigenous animals. The Prater is taken over by predators making short work of two prostitutes waiting for clients. To make things worse, as the animals are growing in number, forcing people to remain inside, they appear to be growing in size as well. As "Mr. A" observes, the heavy snow seems to have an additional nutrient: "As if someone had added something to the snow" ("Als wenn wer zum Schnee noch was dazutan hätt"). And his wife remarks: "Especially the dogs, 'cause they keep eatin' snow, they're already as big as garden sheds" ("Vor allem die Hund, weils auch immer Schnee fressen, die sind schon so groß wie Schrebergartenhäusln"). Things are getting out of hand; the Prater proves too small for the increasing numbers of revolting animals, and so will Vienna, Austria, and maybe even the entire world. The play ends with a radio report indicating the global magnitude of this incident: "To everybody's consternation, reports have been received about worldwide snow storms, as well as about ice masses advancing from the poles" ("zur allgemeinen Bestürzung sind Meldungen über weltweite Schneefälle eingetroffen, sowie ein Vordringen der Eismassen von den Polen her"). Upon this, Mr. A can only reply: "Well, there you have it. What did I tell you" ("Na, da hast es ja. Was hab' ich g'sagt").

As mentioned earlier, *Die unbekannte Hand* also appeared as a short story, but the narrative lacks the immediacy of the *Hörspiel*: Whereas the narrator in the short story describes, the various voices in the play act out; Mr. B, the Mother, the Sculptor take the place of a distantly observing narrator. The genre furthermore facilitates this immediacy because of its auditory quality: As the plot thickens, the volume of animal noises increases, impeding communication. And even when the noises at times are reduced to a distant humming, it reminds the listener of the present danger. Taking full advantage of the genre's properties, the play includes frequent radio excerpts as a prominent link between the protagonists and the outside world, craftily adding an interesting metaradio dimension. There are two levels of communication: At the first one are the protagonists whose limited exposure to the imminent threat keeps them from understanding the situation. At the second level, the radio reports provide a framework in which the protagonists' scattered experiences can be placed. Only this radio contextualization makes them aware of the interconnectedness of what appeared to be unrelated events. In fact, the medium of the radio itself becomes the central protagonist, as the other protagonists turn to it when all other means of communication are blocked off. In an authoritative manner, the approaching apocalypse is constructed through a series of reports; their reliability is not questioned, the conclusions drawn are accepted.

The title alludes to a moral institution, an interfering force that stirs up the animal rebellion. In the prose version, *Die unbekannte Hand* becomes a narrative device in that it is used as a leitmotiv that is repeated time and again, reinforcing the metaphysical cause of the catastrophe. Given the title, this metaphysical dimension should have equal importance in the radio play, yet this is hardly the case due to the lack of the leitmotiv reiteration. In this respect, the radio play loses ground against the narrative in its treatment of causality. Yet, language is assigned a crucial role in illustrating the protagonists' contemptuous attitude toward animals, as their speech is permeated with pejorative references to animals such as "someone else should play the monkey" ("Da soll wer anderer den Affen spielen"), "these dirty swine" ("diese Mistviecher"), "the bear is loose" ("der Bär ist los"), and so forth. In addition, their dealings with animals show the exploitative nature of their interest in them. After all, the first scene presents a race course *(Galopprennbahn)* where the audience has just made their bets; the "unknown hand" opens the cages in the zoo, where animals were locked up for the pleasure of people; the first to be bitten is a butcher; and the police officer who is killed by dogs in the Prater only loved his Doberman because it was a thoroughbred, "just like it is in the book" ("wie er im Büchl steht"). But the animals have had enough — Hitchcock's film *The Birds* comes to mind — and mankind's fate seems sealed. There can be little doubt as to what fate this will be, since toward the end of the play, the script reads: "The animal noises resume again. From the various barking, neighing, bleating, croaking, and hissing sounds, it may be possible to compose the melody of a Viennese song (for instance 'Oh, my dear Augustine')."[10] And how does the song go: Oh, my dear Augustine, all is gone . . .

Binnengespräche

Of all the radio plays Frischmuth has written, her 1984 *Binnengespräche* is by far the most philosophical and complex in its treatment of language, the relationship between perception and reality, and the phenomenon for which one of the protagonists coins the term *Gleichortigkeit* (spatial simultaneity). The play could be called a literary phenomenological investigation, its basic premise being that the world around us can only be given meaning through our consciousness and that the world is called into being through our acts of interpretation. Through the eyes of the four main protagonists, *Binnengespräche* creates a mosaic of subjectively perceived landscapes, denouncing the existence of an absolute, fixed reality and illustrating the philosophical proposition that the world does not merely exist, but rather is conceptualized by each individual. In other words, the world becomes visible only through the physiognomy of the protagonists. Frischmuth's choice of the radio play genre seems logical, as its multiperspectivity proves particularly apt to conveying the underlying idea that a neutral object or space that is unaffected by and unrelated to the individual's consciousness does not exist.

To set the stage: Judith and Charles, both living in New York City since 1938, are vacationing in Judith's hometown in Tirol together with their friends Anna and Max, who are both in their forties. In telling each other about their childhood experiences in this village and about the role that the village plays in their lives, they learn that their identity is inextricably bound to this place; although their relationship to their town is highly problematic, they are magnetically drawn back, reevaluating their feelings toward it. The play becomes a reconstruction of a space in which each view, connotation, or memory reveals new dimensions and serves as an illustration of its dynamic nature and shifting boundaries. In other words, the space must be thought for it to exist.

Right at the onset of the radio play, Anna's conversation with Max reflects this anthropocentric, phenomenological view. She tells Max that changes she undergoes translate into transformations of the village. She recalls dreams about the place of her childhood: "And sometimes I am somebody else in my dream. Do you understand? I am someone else, and because of that the place is often a different one, too" ("Und ich bin auch manchmal wer anderer im Traum. Verstehst du? Ich bin wer anderer, und so ist oft auch der Ort ein anderer"). She creates her own subjective reality as the others create theirs: "The images are inside me" ("Die Bilder sind in mir"). Yet, these internal images are not fictitious but rather override any external reality. Anna says: "There are places, though, that transform themselves so drastically that only their former image counts" ("Aber es gibt Örtlichkeiten, die sich so stark verändern, daß nur mehr ihr früheres Bild zählt"). According to phenomenological thought, there can be no world without a "being in the world," the world is subjectively conceived and one's being in it shapes it. Likewise, Anna's being in the village and the landscape surrounding it alters it and leaves traces, making it *her* personal space. Anna uses the metaphor of an imprint of her body to describe this: "There are landscapes that confine you, and when you go, you leave behind your body imprint" ("Es gibt Landschaften, die dich einschliessen, und wenn du gehst, lässt du deinen Körperabdruck in ihnen zurück"). This remark is important in two ways: First, Anna suggests that a space is rarely neutral but becomes part of one's own intimately personal context. Second, once the personal space is created, it is impossible to separate oneself from it. She feels confined by it, because, as she continues to explain, it claims ownership over her language in that it limits the referentiality of her words: The signifiers she uses become linked only to specific signifieds within the personal space. This reduced referentiality sets one apart from other language users and problematizes communication. Anna explains: "Landscapes that occupy your language. When you say 'mountain,' you mean the face of that rock out there, and when you say 'forest,' you're talking especially about those foothills on the lakeside. And when you say 'boat,' you know that actually it's about a very specific rowboat by the name of Mizzi. And before you know it, you have your first secret from the world. Sure, you use the word 'boat' just like the others, but they do not know what you know."[11] Space and language appear to be inextricably connected, and this connection separates the individual from others: As the "secrets" to which Anna refers grow in number, she becomes increasingly alienated from her world.

Anna's *Fremdsein* — the awareness of being different and of speaking a language that appears to be the same yet is drastically different

— becomes a leitmotiv in the play. It also finds expression in her observations of our use of language, which exposes a binary view of the world: "I" as opposed to "the other." Anna points out the fear of people in the village, "of being swamped by strangers" ("überfremdet zu werden"), and shows her sensitivity to a language that perpetuates this dichotomous thinking: "(sarcastically) Don't you know that there still is a tourist center, guest rooms, and tourist guides?" ("[sarkastisch] Weißt du nicht, daß es noch immer einen Fremdenverkehr, Fremdenzimmer und Fremdenführer gibt?") When Judith notes, "Only in this context have I not noticed the strangeness" ("Nur in diesem Zusammenhang ist mir das Fremde noch nicht aufgefallen"), Anna's reply shows her dissatisfaction with her own encapsulated world: "I also wanted to belong to the strangers, to those who come and go again and who don't have to get involved with any of the tragedies that take place here. . . . I envied the foreign lands so familiar to these strangers."[12]

Like Anna, Judith's world also revolves around the village, yet her conceptualization of it deviates from Anna's. To Judith, it is a reminder of her forced departure to the United States, of the sudden interruption of her childhood and her becoming a refugee. She is reminded of her Jewishness, her *Fremdsein*, as she passes the house of Eichmann's brother-in-law, sees Eigruber's daughter, and meets friends whose entire families were gassed. Yet, what fascinates both Judith and Anna are the contradictory feelings of alienation and belonging, of repulsion and attraction that the village evokes in them. As Anna explains, "I fled from this place for years. Nothing could be far enough. Until I realized that this kind of flight doesn't help. A place like this one catches up with you anywhere" ("Ich bin jahrelang vor diesem Ort geflüchtet. Nichts konnte mir weit genug sein. Bis ich eingesehen habe, daß diese Art von Flucht nichts hilft. Ein Ort wie dieser, holt einen überall ein"). Her escaping from the village proves vain, because it equals trying to escape from herself. Judith for her part tries to rationalize the apparent paradox in her own attitude toward her surroundings and hypothesizes about a philosophical concept that embraces the contradictions with which she is struggling:

> JUDITH: The word *Gleichortigkeit* [spatial simultaneity] occurred to me [only now does it become clear that Judith speaks German primarily from memory]. Does a word like that exist in German? Ubiquity in a factual, a spatial sense?

> ANNA: You mean the omnipresence of consolation and horror?
> JUDITH: Maybe. But there is more. Omnipresence in all that is possible. Not only the shapes, but even the divisional lines overlap. Divide the world into murderers and rescuers, into square and round shapes, poor and rich, into those who act and those who are acted upon — each time the world will fall into place differently.[13]

Judith's deliberations about this ubiquity give evidence of her conscious efforts to make her personal space, the village she fled but feels drawn back to, livable. She adopts a holistic view of the world that does not exclude evil but rather reconciles opposites as intrinsic parts of the same system. Likewise, her space becomes an intellectual construct in that she *wants* it to embrace both her parents' love and her neighbors' hatred. The shape reality assumes is the direct result of her intellectual confrontation with it. She is as much the creator of her ubiquitously arranged world as Anna is of her dichotomous world.

Charles, Judith's husband, somewhat ironically questions the holistic world Judith has constructed as autosuggestion, and he plays with the possibility that what is perceived as reality could be mere fiction: "I actually still believe that this place is fiction that turns into reality for only a few short moments. Right now, for instance. A fiction of security that manifests itself suddenly. Or maybe we just make each other believe all this whereas in reality we're sitting in a wasteland and fantasize."[14] According to Max, reality as Judith sees it — a world in which life is still possible — may turn out to be a very fragile product of the imagination, a dreamed up oasis that can easily dissolve and be replaced by a reality we tried to escape, a desert in which life is no longer sustainable.

Binnengespräche, then, is largely a poetics of space, in which each protagonist shapes and adds color to a village that on the surface appears to be a fixed reality. As such, Frischmuth's radio play shows the need for and process of the personalization of space and the conscious effort to establish a modus vivendi where the estranged can reestablish harmony with the past, present, and future. In this context, the medium used is appropriate in that the radio play must be defined by its lack of space since, by its very nature, it is limited to the aural dimension: A space does not already exist, as would be the case in a stage performance, but relies entirely on the creation by the protagonists. Thus, the genre of the radio play proves an adequate vehicle for its content.

Eine Liebe in Erzurum

Frischmuth's 1994 play was directed by Götz Fritsch and translated into English and French the same year it was broadcast by the *Österreichischer Rundfunk.*[15] It is the account of a bicultural relationship that is doomed from the onset. It derives its tragic quality from the fact that both parties, Antonia, a nineteen-year-old Austrian student, and Sinasi, a Turkish ophthalmologist twice her age, are aware of their violation of important codes inscribed in their respective cultures, yet are unable to liberate themselves from them. In documenting the process of estrangement between two partners, the radio play thematizes the obstacles between two cultures and is very critical in its depiction of the breakdown of cross-cultural communication.

Eine Liebe in Erzurum is a reconstruction of the past from the perspective of a fifty-two-year-old, recently divorced woman who engages in a daydreamlike dialogue with a segment of her life whose boundaries are not only defined by the temporal distance, but also, and importantly so, by their spatial dimension. Her memories about her lover Sinasi are intricately entwined with the place where they met, in which they grew closer, and which ultimately caused their separation. It becomes clear that their relationship is determined not only by themselves, but also by Erzurum, a Turkish town in which she is a foreigner and which for Turks themselves is a place of isolation: "the Turkish Siberia," and "something like a penal colony for professors, army officers, and doctors." ("das türkische Sibirien; so etwas wie eine Strafkolonie für Professoren, Militärs und Ärzte"). As in *Binnengespräche*, space assumes a symbolic significance and has properties that transform people and shape their lives.

The strangeness of Erzurum is reiterated throughout the play and affects virtually all domains of Antonia's life. She stands out with her European clothes among women veiled in black, and she quickly realizes that her relationship with Sinasi outside the bond of marriage finds disapproval or at best acceptance "because of the irrefutable certainty that a love like this, between an officer and a foreigner, can only end tragically" ("aus der unumstößlichen Gewißheit, daß eine Liebe wie diese, zwischen einem Offizier und einer Ausländerin, nur tragisch enden könne"). She feels treated like a second-class citizen not only because she is obviously a foreigner, but also because of her gender: "Women weren't greeted openly in the street; that was considered compromising" ("Frauen wurden auf der Straße nicht offen gegrüßt, das galt als kompromittierend"). Her environment has a stifling effect on her, and she begins to see Sinasi, however alienated he may feel himself, as an exponent of the culture that surrounds her. Her love for Sinasi and the environment in which they are become inseparable: "I saw how my love was suffocated by my claustrophobia and rebelled" ("Ich sah meine Liebe zu dir an der Platzangst ersticken und bockte"). Most significantly, her estrangement from the world around her diminishes even her linguistic competence to the extent that, although quite fluent in Turkish, she loses her ability to communicate. Antonia remembers: "The foreign language dissolved on my tongue. I misheard more and more and began to stutter." ("Die fremde Sprache zerlief mir mit einem Mal auf der Zunge. Ich verhörte mich immer öfter, begann zu stottern"). For Antonia, her eagerness to learn Turkish and her ability to communicate in this foreign language served as examples of her appreciation for and eagerness to interact with the culture around her. The sudden loss of her language skills mirrors the defamiliarization with the dominant culture and becomes a metaphor of estrangement: Without understanding the culture inscribed in the language, she is no longer able to speak it. Only through the closeness that she feels to Sinasi can she overcome this inhibition: "I approached the language with Sinasi's tongue. He was my living archive and accepted my efforts like personal gifts" ("Ich näherte mich der Sprache mit Sinasis Zunge. Er war mein lebendes Archiv und nahm meine Bemühungen als persönliche Geschenke entgegen"). Yet, the possibility of cultural integration is denounced as an illusion, as the reasons for her marginalization — her nationality, gender, lifestyle, and finally her linguistic abilities — are too numerous to overcome.

What is disturbing in *Eine Liebe in Erzurum* is the causality of events that seems to be determined by one factor, i.e., the irreconcilability of two different cultures. The piece transcends a failing relationship between two people of different ethnic backgrounds to a dissolution of cross-cultural communication. The structure of Frischmuth's radio play renders this notion of separateness at the personal level in that it consists largely of disconnected monologues or Antonia's faded memories of dialogues. Although she considers making a phone call to Sinasi, which would reestablish contact after thirty-three years, she never does. Her remembered conversations with Sinasi are disjointed flashbacks, and her monologues are characterized by the painful lack of the interlocutor, who leaves questions unanswered: "So you did settle down in Izmir? And got married? Conceived any children? Only two? Given the fact that you were already past forty? Your son is doing national service? No, he is not becoming a regular officer? And he hasn't been posted in the East? Where he shoots at Ahmet's son? Forgive me, my imagination is playing tricks on me again."[16] Also at the level of cross-cultural interaction, *Eine Liebe in Erzurum* signals an estrangement between peoples, a build-up of tension and a distrust to which, according to Antonia, even governmental policies seem to contribute:

> ANTONIA: That was humiliating. The German and Austrian officials wouldn't recognize Sinasi's doctorate. He would have had to do it all over again, would have needed proof of his knowledge of German, and a job at a hospital or citizenship to be able to start his own practice.
>
> ***
>
> SINASI: I doctor, you doctor, he-she-it doctor.[17]

In one of her imaginary dialogues with Sinasi, Antonia informs her former lover about a Europe that he used to be drawn to as a neutral place that fostered cross-cultural contact: "Actually, you had always thought highly of Germany and Austria? You're right, back then nobody could have imagined that, thirty years later, Turks are burned in their houses. Intentionally. In the heart of Europe."[18] The play juxtaposes past and present in that Antonia compares herself, as a stranger in an unfamiliar Turkish city, to foreigners in a country that she calls her own. Her estrangement from the Turkish environment, devastating as it was for her, fades in light of the sheer hatred toward foreigners[19] thirty years later: "I'm living in constant fear that young people, whose classrooms I've gone in and out of, suddenly lay hands on foreigners. At that time, I was a foreigner myself, but never did anybody try to put the house I lived in on fire. Especially not in Erzurum. So you're saying there are too many people in this world? A country, whose population doubles within a generation can't get anywhere? Well, in our country the population has stayed the same, and they're burning those they've asked to come. What's wrong with our world, Sinasi?"[20] The latter question is indicative of the shift of emphasis that has occurred in the course of the play: *Eine Liebe in Erzurum* develops from an account of a personal relationship to a powerful moral statement — without being moralizing — about endangered intercultural relations and the rise of nationalism. It derives its social importance from its forthrightness and ability to place the personal in a larger sociopolitical context. Essentially, *Eine Liebe in Erzurum* is a dramatic treatment of otherness, whereby the other is seen both from the point of view of the other herself, Antonia in Erzurum, and of Antonia as a representative of mainstream culture who reflects on her culture's responsibility in its interaction with the other, i.e., the culturally dissociated. Along with the described shift of emphasis is an increased intensity in the portrayal of cultural differences that ranges from the experience of culture clash to the potential destructiveness it can evoke in people.

Antonia's last monologue metaphorically brings together the two narrative layers and skillfully reiterates the main theme of the radio play. Antonia wonders about her distress that triggered her renewed preoccupation with Erzurum and her love for Sinasi. She remembers a package of photos that she had received from Sinasi: "Out of a cardboard box fell a bundle of letters that Sinasi had written to me while he was still in Erzurum. He had photographed the entire city, especially the streets and alleys that I had gone through the most, and he had sketched me in. With only a few strokes, but nonetheless recognizable."[21] Her memory serves a dual purpose in the play. On the one hand, it shows Sinasi's need to fill the void in his life and his renewed attempt to show Antonia the possibility of her existence in Erzurum. On the other hand, the image supports the underlying moral message of the play in that it urges the listener to do the same: to inscribe the outsider into our existing world.

Conclusion

Frischmuth's radio play *Binnengespräche* begins with a quote from one of Hermann Broch's letters, which shows an affinity with all three plays in its exposure of a moral dimension of space:

> MAX: Everything is packed? The mountains, the lake,
> the whole immoral loveliness?
> ANNA: You're quoting again . . .
> MAX: Hermann Broch, November 21, 1937, in a letter:

> Unfortunately, I don't like this area; it is of an immoral loveliness. I wish I were back in Tirol again.[22]

Broch's oxymoron foreshadows the discussions between the four main protagonists about their perceptions of the space around them, but more importantly, the quote connects the notion of space with ethics and responsibility, i.e., our *being* in space. This connection, as this study has shown, is crucial in all three plays discussed. In *Die unbekannte Hand,* there appears to be a moral entity that passes judgment on a world that has violated the ecological space of which it is a part. Though the play intentionally exaggerates, the message is clear: People who act disrespectfully of their environment ultimately succumb to the consequences for which they themselves are responsible. *Binnengespräche* thematizes the struggle to come to terms with one's surroundings that represent both good and evil. It emphasizes the need for a *terra firma* in a space in which one feels out of place and that seems contaminated by the evils of the past and the potentialities of evil in the future. *Eine Liebe in Erzurum*, finally, presents the difficulties involved with the sharing of space by different ethnic groups, warns against ethnocentricity and a dormant xenophobia, and appeals to our sense of responsibility to include rather than reject the other.

Trinity College

Notes

1. Everett Frost, "Why Sound Art Works and the German *Hörspiel*," *Drama Review* 31 (1987): 110.

2. Klaus Schöning, "On the Development of Acoustic Literature in Radio: The German *Hörspiel*," *Michigan Quarterly Review* 25.1 (1986): 39.

3. Schöning 31.

4. For a list of radio plays by Barbara Frischmuth until 1992, see Maria Renhardt's "Bibliographie Barbara Frischmuth," *Dossier 4: Barbara Frischmuth*, ed. Kurt Bartsch (Graz: Droschl, 1992) 181.

5. Barbara Frischmuth, "Die Mauskoth und die Kuttlerin," *Protokolle* 1 (1971): 108–128; "Ich möchte, ich möchte die Welt," *Protokolle* 2

(1980): 193–209; *Eine Liebe in Erzurum* (Vienna: ORF, 1994).

6. Gero von Wilpert, *Sachwörterbuch der Literatur* (Stuttgart: Alfred Kröner, 1969) 334. Original quote: "Wegfall alles Optischen (Szene, Mimik, Milieu, Schauplatz, Kulisse, oft durch sog. Geräuschkulisse ersetzt) zugunsten des rein Akustischen, bes. des gesprochenen Wortes, untermalender Musik, u.ä., das den alleinigen Ausdruck des seelisch-geistigen und äußeren Geschehens übernimmt, die Gestaltungsgesetze bedingt und im Interesse des Aufnehmenden strengste Konzentration der Handlung, spannenden Zusammenhang der Einzelszenen, geringe Personenzahl, reiche Abwechslung und kurze Sendedauer (meist bis 1 Std.) fordert."

7. Donald Daviau, "Barbara Frischmuth," *Major Figures of Contemporary Austrian Literature,* ed. Donald Daviau (New York: Lang, 1987) 186.

8. Barbara Frischmuth, *Die Mystifikationen der Sophie Silber* (Salzburg: Residenz, 1976) 196.

9. Original quote: "Fleischhauereibesitzerin und eingeschriebenes Mitglied des Zuchtverbandes für Rottweiler, sowie Herr Oberkellner Leo L, Händler in Reit-, Wagen- und Rennpferden, Raubtieren und Exoten."

10. Original quote: "Die Tierlaute setzen wieder ein. Vielleicht ist es möglich, aus den verschiedenen Bell-Wieher-Mecker-Krächz- und Fauchgeräuschen die Melodie eines Wiener Liedes ('O du lieber Augustin' z.B.) zusammenzustellen."

11. Original quote: "Landschaften, die deine Sprache besetzt halten. Wenn du 'Berg' sagst, meinst du die Wand da draußen, und wenn du 'Wald' sagst, meinst du vor allem die Ausläufer am Seeufer. Und wenn du 'Boot' sagt, weisst du, daß es sich eigentlich um ein ganz bestimmtes Ruderboot mit dem Namen Mizzi handelt. Und schon hast du ein erstes Geheimnis vor der Welt. Denn natürlich verwendest du das Wort 'Boot,' wie die anderen es auch verwenden, aber sie wissen nicht, was du weisst."

12. Original quote: "Ich wollte auch zu den Fremden gehören, zu denen, die kommen und wieder gehen und sich auf keine der hier stattfindenden Tragödien einlassen müssen. . . . Ich war neidisch auf die Fremde, die den Fremden vertraut war."

13. Original quote:

JUDITH: Das Wort *Gleichortigkeit* fiel mir ein (erst jetzt wird deutlich, daß Judith das Deutsche hauptsächlich aus der Erinnerung spricht). Gibt es so etwas im Deutschen? Ubiquität in einem tatsächlichen, in einem räumlichen Sinn?

ANNA: Du meinst die Allgegenwart von Trost und Schrecken?

JUDITH: Vielleicht. Aber es ist mehr. Die Allgegenwart in allem, was möglich ist. Nicht nur die Formen, auch die Trennungslinien überlagern sich. Teil die Welt ein in Mörder und Retter, in eckige und runde Formen, in arm und reich, in Tuende und solche, denen getan wird — die Welt zerfällt immer anders.

14. Original quote: "Eigentlich denke ich noch immer, daß dieser Ort eine Fiktion ist, die nur in einigen wenigen Augenblicken Wirklichkeit wird. Jetzt zum Beispiel. Eine Fiktion von Geborgenheit, die sich plötzlich manifestiert. Oder vielleicht suggerieren wir uns das alles nur gegenseitig, und in Wirklichkeit sitzen wir in der Wüste und phantasieren."

15. The English and French translations of this radio play appear in the same volume as cited under note 5.

16. Original quote: "Du hast dich also doch in Izmir niedergelassen? Und geheiratet? Kinder gezeugt? Nur zwei? In Anbetracht dessen, daß du schon über vierzig warst? Dein Sohn leistet gerade seinen Militärdienst ab? Nein, er wird nicht Berufsoffizier? Und ist nicht in den Osten abkommandiert worden? Wo er auf Ahmets Sohn schießt? Oder umgekehrt? Verzeih, meine Phantasie ist wieder einmal mit mir durchgegangen."

17. Original quote:

ANTONIA: Das war beschämend. Die deutschen und die österreichischen Behörden wollten Sinasis Doktorat nicht anerkennen. Er hätte alles noch einmal machen müssen, einen Nachweis seiner Deutschkenntnisse gebraucht und eine Stelle in einem Krankenhaus oder die Staatsbürgerschaft, um eine Praxis aufmachen zu können.

***

SINASI: Ich Doktor, du Doktor, er-sie-es Doktor.

18. Original quote: "In Wirklichkeit hättest du immer von Deutschland und Österreich am meisten gehalten? Du hast recht, damals hat niemand sich vorstellen können, daß man dreißig Jahre später hier Türken in ihren Häusern verbrennt. Absichtlich, im Herzen Europas."

19. Rob Burns and Wilfried van der Will, in *German Cultural Studies,* ed. Rob Burns (Oxford: Orford University Press, 1995) point out that xenophobia in Germany should be understood largely as hatred

directed against Turks: "From the late 1970s onwards animosity towards foreigners in Germany was to all intents and purposes synonymous with hostility to Turks, who constituted roughly one-third of the total number of immigrants in the Federal Republic" (309).

20. Original quote: "Ich lebe in der ständigen Furcht, daß junge Leute, in deren Schulklassen ich ein- und ausgegangen bin, plötzlich Hand an Ausländer legen. Ich war damals auch Ausländerin, aber nie hat jemand versucht, das Haus anzuzünden, in dem ich wohnte. Schon gar nicht in Erzurum. Es sind zu viele Menschen auf dieser Welt, sagst du? Ein Land, dessen Bevölkerungszahl sich innerhalb einer Generation verdoppelt, kann auf keinen grünen Zweig kommen, sagst du? Bei uns ist die Bevölkerungszahl gleich geblieben, und sie verbrennen die, die sie gerufen haben. Was ist los mit unserer Welt, Sinasi?"

21. Original quote: "Da fiel mir aus einem der Kartons das Päckchen mit Sinasis Briefen entgegen, die er mir noch aus Erzurum geschrieben hatte. Er fotografierte die ganze Stadt, vor allem die Straßen und Gassen, durch die ich am öftesten gegangen war, und zeichnete mich ein. Mit ein paar Strichen nur, aber kenntlich."

22. Original quote:

> MAX: Alles eingepackt? Die Berge, den See, die ganze unmoralische Lieblichkeit?
>
> ANNA: Du zitierst schon wieder . . .
>
> MAX: Hermann Broch, am 21. November 1937, in einem Brief: Bedauerlicherweise mag ich die hiesige Gegend nicht; sie ist von einer unmoralischen Lieblichkeit, ich wollte ich wäre schon wieder in Tirol.

On Language, Writing, and Crossing Borders: An Interview with Barbara Frischmuth

Edited and Introduced by Johannes F. Evelein

> People are crossing borders all the time: I think that they are very important for literature. Literature is the medium that can afford to cross these borders more than any other discipline.
>
> — Frischmuth, this interview

In the fall of 1996, Barbara Frischmuth visited Canada and the United States as part of a year-long effort by the Austrian government to commemorate, discuss, and celebrate Austria's 1,000-year jubilee. In this context, she visited a number of universities, gave lectures, and attended conferences, including the German Studies Association Conference in Seattle, where she gave a luncheon address as one of the keynote speakers. The following interview took place on October 4, 1996, toward the end of her travels through the United States, and was conducted in the KUSU-FM Utah Public Radio studio by Lee Austin, radio host for the program "Etcetera" in Logan, Utah. The interview was broadcast on October 30, 1996.

* * *

AUSTIN: Austrian writer Barbara Frischmuth is interested in the borders of language and culture and has researched and written about Islam and Turkish-speaking Germans. One of Austria's best-known writers, Frischmuth traveled through Canada and the United States this fall and spoke on the university campus in Logan, Utah, earlier this month. Barbara Frischmuth studied Turkish and Hungarian and also translates the work of other writers. Her own writing has been translated into more than a dozen languages. Frischmuth's work explores three major themes: the world of children and childhood, multicultural topics, and women's issues.

AUSTIN: How is it that you are visiting the United States and Utah State University?

FRISCHMUTH: It started with the Austrian millennium. The Austrian embassy in Canada tried to do something for literature within the millennium. So I was invited to a trip through Canada together with an Austrian Germanist, and we traveled from Victoria to Vancouver and then to Edmonton, Calgary, and Montreal, where the symposium took place. I was invited to Seattle two weeks afterward — to the German Studies Association Conference. And in between, Jennifer Michaels and Renate Posthofen organized a reading tour through North American colleges and universities.

AUSTIN: A number of your books have been translated. Do you find audiences here who are familiar with your works?

FRISCHMUTH: Within the German-studying community I find them.

AUSTIN: One of your books, *The Convent School,*[1] was written some time ago.

FRISCHMUTH: Yes, it was my first one, published in 1968.

AUSTIN: Does the book have some autobiographical elements to it?

FRISCHMUTH: Elements as far as they are authentic. I lived in a convent school from age ten to fourteen, but this was not the point in writing this text. I was looking for a language that was closed up and ideological, and the language used in the convent school was the one I knew best. But it is not autobiographical in the sense that I talk about my own adventures.

AUSTIN: What kind of language did you say?

FRISCHMUTH: It is a very ideological, closed up language. They have an answer for everything and everything is preformed. Children are exposed to this Catholic ideology, and whenever you have a question, after two years you know the answer that is going to be given to you. This happened to a lot of other jargons within the German language, and when my generation of writers started to write, we were really shocked in finding out how misused the German language was by the Nazis and the Austro-fascists. We realized that we had to take it apart, analyze it, and detect all the phrases that were still used nicely by children, yet had such a terrible background if you took a closer look, so we started to analyze all these types of languages — the language in the shops, the language in school, in sports — and tried to find out what they carried with them that we were not even conscious of. This first process was to get conscious about the language you were going to write in, and so most of us wrote at least one book where we analyzed a language that represented a closed system.

AUSTIN: As the saying goes: "Truth is one of the first casualties of war." Is that the case with language as well?

FRISCHMUTH: There is another saying between the German and the Austrian version of the German language: separated by a common language.

AUSTIN: How do you mean that the German language was abused by the Nazis?

FRISCHMUTH: Even after the war, we all were using phrases that did not exist before the war. There is one dreadful one. When you want to express something you do until you cannot do it any longer, you say: "until gassing." And nobody thinks about the gas chambers when using this phrase. So these were the most obvious things that started to get our attention. And then we went on trying to find out how much Nazism and Austro-fascism had steeped the German language and how many of these thoughts were encrusted into this language we used every day without even knowing what we were saying. That was the big revolution in literature in the 1950s and especially in the 1960s.

AUSTIN: What would be some other examples of writers who were experiencing this?

FRISCHMUTH: Peter Handke started in this way and Wolfgang Bauer and many young Austrians of my generation who now tried to fix the Nazi terminology. But there was so much that Nazism developed out of, so you had to go much further back to make an analysis. We just mixed up language, we broke it into pieces and tried to put it together again in another sense. Of course that never really succeeds, but at least every language, as far as literature is concerned, has to go through these processes of being torn and taken apart, and then young writers start to make it usable again for literature.

AUSTIN: In your books, you pay special attention to feminine issues, but you do not consider yourself to be a feminist.

FRISCHMUTH: I always say that I am a naturally born feminist insofar as I always try to fight for my own rights and my opportunities in this world, but I never joined an organization or never was militant in an ideological way. I do think that we owe theoretical feminism a lot in that it made us think about issues, because until I got married and had a child, I did not think much about me being a woman or a female writer. It just did not concern me. When life came across, it was quite different and I really found out that it does make a difference, especially being a mother. You start to ask other people for favors and you find out that you cannot live on your own having children. That does not work any longer.

AUSTIN: Do you want your writing to prompt your audience to think about certain issues or view gender issues in a different way? Do you have a particular agenda?

FRISCHMUTH: Only in a rather ironic way, because I think that for literature, the phase of complaining about the old issues has come to an end. You cannot write literature with just this. The progress we were able to make was that female writers started to laugh about themselves, which does not mean that they did not forget but rather reached a distance to the problems. That makes literature possible.

AUSTIN: What is your latest published book?

FRISCHMUTH: It is called *Heart of the Witch,*[2] and as you know, witches do not have hearts. My publisher liked this title, which is the title of one of the short stories, so much that he wanted it to be the title for the whole book. For this book I started to write portraits that really exist, so I tried, like a modern painter, to do a piece of literature about a person still living: for example, an old lady, eighty-six or so when she visited me, who wanted to tell me her life's story.[3] At first, I did not want to know about her, but I developed almost an addiction to her story. She showed me her documents. She was a servant in Vienna during the 1920s and 1930s, mostly with Jewish families, and she told me a lot about that — her life, her marriage with a drunken husband. I wrote down her story, but not very realistically, that is, I made a story out of it and I read it to her before I published it so as not to offend her. And she was very happy with it even though I was a little ironic about her too, about her eagerness to be published and so on. She was so vivid and so much alive when she came to me, but the moment the story was published, she never left her house again. This was the last thing she really wanted to happen in her life.

AUSTIN: Can you give us another example?

FRISCHMUTH: I wrote a story about a man in his forties who was drinking, playing the horn, no one I would have otherwise paid attention to.[4] He was doing his duty at the customs, where he turned deaf within a few weeks. This is when he started to learn how to read lips. He had had surgery and had an implantation of a digital hearing device. He started to get so active and now he traveled virtually through the whole world giving conferences about deafness, the implantation, and his character improved in a way that I would have never thought possible. He is the most communicative person I know, and he writes wonderful short articles on the disability in the local newspaper, arranges skiing courses and things like that. I would have never believed that such a change could be possible if I had not experienced it myself. This is another example of a real-life character I used for one of my stories, and I explored this way of writing during the last few years.

AUSTIN: Very different than writing a novel, I suppose.

FRISCHMUTH: Yes. You really have to keep to one person. In a novel, you do a mosaic and you take things from wherever you can use them, and then you steal and do anything to create a figure, a fictitious figure. This is nonfiction and still it is literature. This is very complicated, but I tried to do it and it was very worthwhile doing it.

AUSTIN: You mentioned that you are currently working on a new novel.

FRISCHMUTH: Yes. It deals with the Turkish population in Austria and Germany and the Western way of life. I wrote one novel that deals with this issue, which was published in 1973 and republished as a hardcover edition in 1996, because the problems discussed have become very relevant to the present situation.[5] It will take another year or two to finish the new one. It also deals with Islamic mysticism, which would have been my dissertation topic when I was a student. So I started to learn about Islamic mystic Sufism and dervishes, and I never lost interest in it. But I also was very interested in the old German mystics like Hildegard von Bingen and nuns in the eleventh and twelfth centuries who wrote really impressive texts about their visions. But for me, the issue is rather to combine the computer language, which after all dominates our world, and our everyday-life language with the language of Islamic mysticism that is quite different, and this in the form of a novel.

AUSTIN: Language itself, but also foreign languages, seem to be of special importance to you.

FRISCHMUTH: At the university, I studied Turkish and Hungarian after which I served as a Turcologist with Iranistics as my second field of study, but instead of my thesis, I wrote the novel I mentioned that was published in 1973.

AUSTIN: Generally, we hear more about Islamic fundamentalism than Islamic mysticism.

FRISCHMUTH: Yes, but for me having made Islam a special focus of my studies, I feel obliged to make people aware of other sides of Islamic culture, especially for the German-speaking world, where so many Turks live and where so many young Turks already write in German. They contribute to the German language, but people do not realize it yet. The other thing is that we always talk about fundamentalism and old Islamic culture, calligraphy and the like, but people do not realize that there is a modern Turkish or Algerian literature. Even as far as Iran is concerned, there is a very good poet living in Germany, Said,[6] who is of Iranian descent and left Iran under the Shah as a political emigrant. When Khomeini came to power, he went back for seven months only to find out that he could not live in the Khomeini era either, so he returned to Germany and now writes wonderful poetry in German. These people, crossing borders all the time, are very important for literature. Literature is the medium that can afford to cross these borders even more than any other discipline. I try to make people a little more aware of culture with an Islamic background. I never stress the Islamic religion but rather Islamic culture and civilization.

AUSTIN: Just as the *Convent School* does not deal extensively with religion.

FRISCHMUTH: No, it deals with a Catholic upbringing, Catholic ideology, religious authority, that is, authority in language, how much power it has over language.

Frischmuth concludes the interview by reading her story "I Am Somebody You Can Count On."[7]

Trinity College

Notes

1. Barbara Frischmuth, *Die Klosterschule* (Salzburg: Residenz, 1968); trans. as *The Convent School,* by Gerald Chapple and James B. Lawson (Riverside, CA: Ariadne, 1993).

2. Barbara Frischmuth, *Hexenherz: Erzählungen* (Salzburg: Residenz, 1994).

3. Barbara Frischmuth, "Posaune im Ohr," *Hexenherz* 18–53.

4. Barbara Frischmuth, "Lebensgeschichte," *Hexenherz* 54–59.

5. Barbara Frischmuth, *Das Verschwinden des Schattens in der Sonne* (Frankfurt/Main: Suhrkamp, 1973; trans. as *The Shadow Disappears in the Sun,* by Nicholas Meyerhofer (Riverside, CA: Ariadne, 1998).

6. On November 16, 1996, two weeks after this interview was broadcast, Said received the prestigious Hermann-Kesten Medaille of the PEN-Center in Darmstadt, Germany. Said has lived in the Federal Republic since 1965, where he became well known for supporting authors who are political prisoners.

7. Originally published as "Auf mich kannst du dich verlassen," *Protokolle* 1 (1981): 77–79; repr. in *Traumgrenze: Erzählungen,* by

Barbara Frischmuth (Salzburg: Residenz, 1983) 71–77. The story was then translated by Gerald Chapple and James B. Lawson and published in *Southern Humanities Review* 29.3 (Summer 1995): 267–270.

From a Meeting with Barbara Frischmuth

Gerlinde Ulm Sanford

In December 1996, Barbara Frischmuth had agreed to a meeting and interview[1] in her home in Altaussee. This picturesque village in the Austrian Alps is clustered around and above a crystal clear lake that remains icy cold even during the summer. Two days before Christmas, then, I drove there and, after some vain attempts, finally found Barbara Frischmuth's wonderful house high up on one of the mountains. It blends in well with the other Austrian country houses of the village. This notwithstanding, I felt during the hours with Barbara Frischmuth as if I were in a magnificent castle. My impression was influenced, I am sure, by several distinguished old pieces of furniture in the living room and, furthermore, by the breathtaking view from there to the white rocks of the Loser Mountain.

***

SANFORD: What instigated you to write your first children's book?

FRISCHMUTH: When I was twenty-six or twenty-seven years old, I discovered children's books — English ones, especially Lewis Carroll,[2] George MacDonald,[3] and of course also Tolkien.[4] I read them all in the original English and derived great pleasure from these works. Already when still a child, I was an unusually avid reader. During my childhood,[5] however, there were only a few classics available. Nothing else was obtainable then. — Somehow, I just feel very inclined to write children's books. I do not know though whether I ever pondered the matter very much.

SANFORD: Did your own children play a role in your writing of children's books?

FRISCHMUTH: No, no, my son was born when I was already thirty-two. No, that was never a reason for writing children's books. Quite the opposite: When my son was small, I could not write very much at all for a while. We did invent many stories together then, stories for everyday use, endless series that made reference to our daily life. Still, children's books I wrote before as well as after his birth. I believe that one writes children's books not so much for *other* children, because one does not know those well enough, not even if they are one's own children. Rather, one writes children's books for the child that one was once oneself — for the child that is still cowering inside oneself. Hence, I wrote children's books such as I would have liked to read when I was a child.

SANFORD: Do you consciously use a different kind of language in your children's books? A simpler one perhaps?

FRISCHMUTH: Yes. That happens almost automatically, however. If I talk with the child inside me, or imagine speaking with other children, then it happens almost by itself that the language becomes simpler. Sometimes it is not simple enough though, and then the lector has to interfere. It happens sometimes, therefore, that the professional editor for children's books objects and demands that this or another sentence would have to be unraveled into several simpler sentences.

SANFORD: Yes, I have now and then the impression that your children's books seem to be addressing grown-ups from time to time, or — as you put it — the child in each grown-up.

FRISCHMUTH: Maybe. Indeed, I never saw myself as a professional author of children's books *per se*. I write a children's book when I have an idea that I consider suitable for children. Then I put myself in the child's place and try to write a bit simpler perhaps, but somehow it happens also by itself. When an idea occurs to me as an idea for a children's book, then the first sentence already starts a little differently.

SANFORD: How do you deal with illustrations?

FRISCHMUTH: That is an interesting question. At the very beginning, it was I who discovered illustrators and then initiated, together with Klaus Reichert, the children's books program at the Suhrkamp Insel publishing house. At that time, I was able to propose illustrators for my books. I brought samples by Viennese artists, e.g., Walter Schmögner, Robert Zeppel-Sperl, Robert Doxat. These were actually my discoveries for the children's books. The program, however, was perhaps introduced prematurely and, moreover, came to an end early in time. It was discontinued so soon because it was too involved and costly. In addition,

I left Suhrkamp Insel. At Suhrkamp Insel, I had been able to influence the choice of illustrations or of an illustrator. I could choose then. Later on, with other publishers, that was not the case anymore. That is, in most cases the publisher proposes illustrators. The selection, to be sure, is somewhat limited. Furthermore, with very large publishers, as for example with Sauerländer now, one has no influence on the illustrations at all. Well, in the case of my last book, *Donna & Dario* (1997, Donna & Dario),[6] it was in fact only a matter of the cover illustration.

SANFORD: Do you like that cover of *Donna & Dario*?

FRISCHMUTH: I have yet to become friends with that cover.

SANFORD: Now a specific question. In one of your children's books, you have as the beginning motto a quote by Musäus: "Excellent morals, however, are for youth zeros without numbers" ("Jedoch die treflichen Moralen sind bey die Jugend Nullen ohne Zahlen").[7] I have this volume by Musäus. Were you directly influenced by Musäus?

FRISCHMUTH: No. No, and, moreover, my book *Amoralische Kinderklapper* (1969, Amoral Children's Rattle)[8] is not a children's book. This is a book for grown-ups who play with the *sujet* children's book. This book never was on the market under the rubric children's books.

SANFORD: Well, that is exactly what I thought. The cover, however, might lead one to believe that it is meant to be a children's book.

FRISCHMUTH: Perhaps, but all that is to be put between quotation marks, so to speak. The topic in this book is more "play with language." H. C. Artmann, for instance, published some so-called *Neue schöne Kinderreime* (1978, New Beautiful Children's Songs)[9] that in truth are very mean and cynical. *Amoralische Kinderklapper* was created in my phase of mimicry of language, of experiments with language. Writers at that time experimented with angles and jargons, with special languages.

SANFORD: I find this book very interesting, strictly for the child within the grown-up, however.

FRISCHMUTH: Yes, indeed, it never was intended for children. It really represents only a play with the language.

SANFORD: I heard from Renate Posthofen that you put special efforts into your new children's book, *Donna & Dario.* Could you elaborate on that a little bit, please?

FRISCHMUTH: Well, I had conceived the initial idea for that book a long time ago; i.e., the idea that a cat jumps out of a window and lands on a crow. I could never pursue the idea, however. I carried it around with me yet was unable to incorporate it into anything. Then, February or January two years ago, it happened. We were in our Vienna apartment. It was a Sunday. My husband was dictating his patients' evaluations.[10] My son and I had to go into the kitchen so that we would not disturb him, and there we began to make up a story. I told my son once more about this idea. One word led to another. My son got interested and contributed his inspirations. I got so excited and enthusiastic about the topic that I dropped[11] all other projects and began this book. In addition, that was at a time when my health was not so good. I almost clung to this book and, as it were, told the story to myself. Even in the hospital I wrote. Every day. Not on the day of the operation, of course. Writing this book has indeed helped me a lot. Of course, we embarked on the story by thinking of the two cats belonging to my son.

SANFORD: Did these cats have the names Donna and Dario?

FRISCHMUTH: No, they had different names, yet they looked like the two cats in the book. At any rate, with my son's two cats in mind, we began to imagine a story. During the first phase then, we created the story by talking to each other. That went on until finally one day, my son all of a sudden emphasized: "Mamma, that is your story, not mine!" In other words, this ideal situation that one would write a children's book together with one's own child just cannot be kept up. I had gotten into the habit of asking his opinion for every little detail of the story until, as I said, he stressed one day: "Mamma, that is your story, not mine!"

SANFORD: It really seems to be a great story. A cat landing on the back of a crow! Fantastic. Did the illustrations turn out to your satisfaction?

FRISCHMUTH: Well, the book did not get illustrated at all except for the cover. The thing was, the book had become too long. With illustrations it would have become even longer, and consequently too expensive. One would have had to cut about a hundred pages of text. Yet, cutting would have been impossible; it would have ruined the entire story. Therefore, we decided to limit ourselves to the cover illustration only. It will have to be seen how that works out. The story is more or less the reconstruction of the *contrat social* (social contract)[12] of civilization. The story takes place, however, among different free-roaming animals who decide not to murder anymore and not to permit others to murder anymore either. It is a situation in a city. The animals get their food from the garbage of the restaurants. The garbage collection and the garbage distribution, to be sure, are in need of organization, of registration, of all kinds of bureaucracy without which civilization just cannot exist. In times as ours, the basic ideas of our civilization nearly seem to have been forgotten. Almost nobody seems to think of solidarity, for example. Contemplations of that kind made me even more determined to write about these basic ideas of our civilization. It might be good, so I thought, to discuss these matters in the framework of an animal state.

SANFORD: When you write children's books, do you always include on purpose a certain morality? Do you hide cultural values in the story?

FRISCHMUTH: No, not on purpose. Just the opposite. I am very much against pedagogical strategies in children's books, especially when the pedagogical point is too visible. On the other hand, one has to be very careful — especially when writing for children — to distinguish clearly between good and evil. In children's books, that is absolutely necessary, and there is no way getting around that distinction. When children read, they follow the models presented in the book. Consequently, one has to express the distinction between good and evil much more clearly than one might want to when writing for grown-ups. One has to take a clear position. That makes writing for children sometimes much more difficult than writing for grown-ups. It is absolutely essential to express a very candid opinion. It is impossible to wangle one's way out of a problem with vagueness. Having to make such clear distinctions also affects the manner of telling the story. When writing for children in a simpler kind of language, I cannot afford to be vague. When writing for grown-ups, I have unrestricted possibilities to play with the language. Writing for children reduces my alternatives. As soon as I have simpler sentences, my attitudes, my opinions inevitably become much more closely determined. In an animal story, moreover, I have to observe the natural characters of the animals. I have to allow them to keep their typical attributes in the story. In earlier years, therefore, I was very interested in basic animal research and animal behavioral studies.

SANFORD: Oh, so perhaps you studied Konrad Lorenz?[13]

FRISCHMUTH: Oh, yes indeed. I already read Lorenz as a child: for instance, *Er redete mit dem Vieh, den Vögeln und den Fischen* (1949, He Spoke with the Beasts, the Birds, and the Fishes)[14] and *So kam der Mensch auf den Hund* (1950, Man Meets Dog).[15] My acquaintance with these books goes back to my early childhood, as I had a girlfriend whose father was a veterinarian. She introduced those books into our lives at the convent school. Of course, I read those books not uncritically. However, as far as basic studies are concerned, these books were excellent — I mean books by Lorenz and the people around him. All my animals are very well researched, and I allow them to keep their animal characteristics. That they can speak in my books is almost the animals' concession to me — to me, the writer. I make them speak, and for that I allow them to keep their webbed feet and their animalistic preferences. In other words, these are not human beings, not just human beings that move around in animal disguise. Instead, they are animals who have gained access to human communication through my awarding language to them.

SANFORD: Are these animals often advantaged vis-à-vis the human beings?

FRISCHMUTH: Yes, of course, they have the advantage they always have, namely that they can make do with much less. Moreover, their character is already more or less fixed through their specific animalistic characteristics. A tomcat, for example, can only do certain things — and would like to do only certain things. The same is true for a marten or any other animal. These animals bring along their animal being, a certain character. Hence, animals are most always included in my children's books. These animals have something to offer. It is almost something like a literary principle for me to include animals.

SANFORD: Is that then somewhat in the tradition of the fable?

FRISCHMUTH: No, not exactly. Yet, the animals bring with them their animal being. They bring along their animal being, their environment, a certain character. Just as I did in *Sophie Silber,*[16] where I tied in threads that bring along something from another world, with which I can then deal in my story.

SANFORD: Our world is being enriched that way?

FRISCHMUTH: Yes, the world becomes multilayered, more complex. To be sure, I cannot use in my children's book as complex a language as I do in my other books because the children simply would not understand that. However, by describing so many animals or other creatures in their characteristics, a new kind of complexity comes into being.

SANFORD: When you write your children's books, do you immediately have an idea for which age you want to write?

FRISCHMUTH: No, the writing process is of a totally different nature. At first there are certain ideas. One plays with them and develops them in various possible ways. Only much later, one ponders and decides for whom a text might be suitable. Most of the time, it is actually the publisher who decides that.

SANFORD: Would it be possible at all to rewrite a story with a certain age group in mind?

FRISCHMUTH: That rarely works, I believe. The publisher does that. I have never yet done that.

SANFORD: Any moral aspect of the story you try to hide more or less rather than overtly coming out with a moral message?

FRISCHMUTH: Well, I have no intention to invent a morality. Any morality is already *in* the story, so to speak, and clearly comes out. I certainly do not try to pack some morality into my stories. For instance, there are some spoiled cats who lived in an apartment and ate only lox and caviar. If those cats all of a sudden find themselves in the wilderness, then they learn that this is a totally different situation, and the question of morality immediately poses itself in that case. Thus, one does not at all have to conceive of a morality, since the question of the morality establishes itself. The problem is merely how one — as an individual writer — answers that self-emerging question of morality. Yet, this kind of problem never stands in the foreground. It probably depends on one's own basic attitudes, why one arrives at a certain solution and at no other.

SANFORD: I could imagine that it depends also somewhat on the animals included in the story. A fox, for example steals and kills game.

FRISCHMUTH: Yes, I allow them to keep these characteristics at least partially. However, in *Donna & Dario*, civilization then sets in. The animals still all have particular wishes, yet then, for the benefit of a better or more peaceful life for everyone, they learn to make do without certain things that in a natural environment they might naturally demand. These are the kinds of restrictions with which human beings are constantly confronted. In *Donna & Dario*, such restrictions are imposed upon animals. As it turns out, there exist "evil ones" among the animals too. It becomes rather exciting to see who these evil ones are. For me, this was a difficult decision, and I had to ponder a long time whom to endow with the role of being evil. Finally, I decided to assign this evil role to the martens who keep killing and do not abide by any of the rules of civilization. At the end of the story, nevertheless, they are forced to conform to the rules.

SANFORD: Well then the martens are done a little injustice, so to speak, or not?

FRISCHMUTH: True, but in the real world, the martens in fact commit all kinds of evil acts. For instance, martens are known to kill without eating what they killed.

SANFORD: Aha, indeed?

FRISCHMUTH: Yes, they kill without eating what they killed. Exactly that, however, is the great sin, the great fall from grace — so to speak — in the realm of the animals. Around my house here, I also have martens. It happens, when they get into a chicken coop, that they just bite off the chickens' heads. There exists something like blood intoxication among animals. It is fairly rare, but it occurs. Well, at any rate in my book, it is the martens who suddenly appear in the city, yet they are unwilling to abide by any rules. That is their fault, their crime in my book. They do not at all consider this *contrat social.* They think that they are so superior that they do not have to observe any rules. In the course of the book, the other animals who have joined in the contract — even though they do not always like each other — make the martens understand the city situation and finally pressure them into abiding by at least some of the rules.

SANFORD: Do you plan a new children's book?

FRISCHMUTH: At the moment, I'm not planning anything. At the moment, I'm writing a story for my son, who has asked me to write a story for him. He is a graphic artist, and he would like to illustrate a story. Actually, he drew illustrations for *Donna & Dario*; however, the publisher did not accept them. The publisher, Sauerländer, and for that matter most publishers nowadays have their own illustrators. There are many gifted illustrators around, und under these circumstances, it is very difficult for a young artist to find a position as an illustrator.

SANFORD: Is graphic art your son's chief profession?

FRISCHMUTH: He is a tattoo artist. [She smiles.] With that he earns his money. But he wants to become an artistic book illustrator. He is still very young, and we will have to see how this works out. He is only twenty-three years old.

SANFORD: Please, let us go now to a different group of questions. I heard your presentation on the topic "Austria, What Else?" in Seattle.[17] It was a very well received presentation, I believe. Next year in April, there will be a symposium in Riverside[18] on a related topic: "Austria in Literature." The symposium will examine how Austria is portrayed in literature. I'd like to pose a few questions relevant to that topic. What is *your* opinion about Austria? Or, put differently, when you are in the United States, what do you like about the United States, or what don't you like? What do you like about Austria, and what don't you like about it?

FRISCHMUTH: You know, that kind of question can never be answered objectively.

SANFORD: What you say does not have to be objective.

FRISCHMUTH: It cannot be objective because I have lived in Austria for most of my life. There are probably many things here that do not strike me as special any longer, for they appear normal to me. In America, on the other hand, everything is new to me and strikes me as new. Furthermore, I *like* to live here, despite occasional anger — despite it all.

SANFORD: Hence, you would not take into consideration to move elsewhere, as so many other writers did, such as Felix Mitterer, who moved to Ireland?

FRISCHMUTH: Mitterer did that, I assume, because of tax reasons. The same is true for Christoph Ransmayr, for example. It is their right to move. I cannot do that, first of all, because we have built a house here [in Altaussee]. I feel wonderful here. In this house, I can write better than anywhere else. It would be a disadvantage for me to move somewhere else. Besides, my husband works in Munich. It would not be possible for me to move to another country. It would not be feasible, neither familywise, nor technically. Indeed, it would be very difficult to look for a new place. It might take forever until I'd finally find something in Ireland — something where I could move around with as much ease as here. Therefore, I'd leave Austria only because of political reasons. For that to happen, though, the situation in Austria would have to be quite different from what it is now.

SANFORD: Do you consider yourself a political person?

FRISCHMUTH: Not to an extreme degree. Yet, I live with open eyes and open ears. Yes, there are many things I do not agree with. In addition, however, I think that many charges against Austria, or more precisely against the Austrian government, are being exaggerated.

SANFORD: What for example?

FRISCHMUTH: For instance, if people consider the mere existence of a person such as Jörg Haider to be synonymous with the end of democracy in Austria, or even an indication of the coming of the Fourth Reich. I even think that the intellectuals' hysteria about Haider only worked in his favor. What I miss in Austria is the freedom to really speak about matters; that is, speaking about matters without becoming emotional; without polarizing contiguously. When discussing certain items one promptly risks being branded a fascist or a communist. That means the Austrian culture of discussion is not very far developed at this point — at any rate, not in a democratic way. About many things, one does not talk enough, and often not objectively enough. Instead, one immediately polarizes.

SANFORD: Are the people afraid, or what do you think?

FRISCHMUTH: Yes, on the one hand, surely, they are afraid. Yet, on the other hand, it is also much simpler to see everything just in black and white. — That is now not in reference to children's books! [She laughs.] — It is so much easier just to say yes or no instead of saying, "Well, perhaps it is quite different altogether." People are perhaps afraid to make another wrong decision. Especially among the intellectuals, there seems to exist a subliminal fear of making a wrong decision again, to be on the wrong side once more.

SANFORD: Therefore, one tends to see so easily the emergence of Neo-Nazism everywhere?

FRISCHMUTH: Yes, and that is no help at all. In my opinion, only differentiation and an objective approach can bring about improvements. However, one is here nothing but a voice crying in the wilderness. It is so easy to be branded a fascist or a communist or any kind of -ist. One gets categorized immediately. That is a pity for Austria, to be sure. In America, such categorizing and branding does not happen so easily. In that respect, it is somewhat better there. As far as the quality of life is concerned and the circumstances of life, I think I would not want to change with anybody, though. I believe that here we all are relatively well off compared to the rest of the world. That of course is going to change, and of *that* all are afraid as well.

SANFORD: Why do people think that things will change?

FRISCHMUTH: Because our situation is financially simply not sound anymore. The globalizing, of course, forces the government into re-thinking its structures. At any rate, small countries such as Switzerland and Austria can surely not keep up their high standards by themselves alone.

SANFORD: What do you think about guest workers? What do you think about places like Bad Hall where a good part of the old town section is now inhabited almost exclusively by guest workers, mainly from Turkey?

FRISCHMUTH: In that respect, I am rather positively inclined, at least in the first instance. I have a degree in Turkish studies and, therefore, I am of course interested in that subject matter. However, one should talk much more! Turkish guest workers, as well as those from other countries, who live here are quite reasonable and unemotional when it becomes obvious that regulations have to be found and that matters cannot arbitrarily take over. I continue to think that political asylum has to be secured. Besides, I believe that those people who have been living here for several years and who want to stay here and who work here, that those people have to be accepted and integrated.

SANFORD: Do you think then that these people should learn German, that they should know Austrian customs?

FRISCHMUTH: Well, yes, I do believe that, especially because to speak the language of the country one lives in is indeed very useful. There is now such an ado about that, however. A much criticized bill has been introduced and has been passed already in some of the federal provinces — a bill requiring that immigrants should be able to answer specific questions — just as in the United States — questions about Austrian culture, that a minimum of knowledge in German has to be demonstrated, and that one should be able to expect a certain general knowledge from an immigrant. According to my view, all that is not so bad, because in fact almost everything one knows is useful. Of course, much depends on the tone in which such regulations are enforced. In addition, there is talk that these immigrants should be totally assimilated. That I do not find so desirable because it would mean that they forget totally about their own culture. If one says, my dear people, just forget your own culture, that definitely does not work because there is no true acceptance. Even those who want to assimilate have difficulties. I do believe that one has to grant to all human beings some type of cultural autonomy. That is needed for their self-esteem. Furthermore, it was proven by research that people who are inhibited from being culturally recognizable have an excessive inclination to withdraw again into their original culture, exactly because it has become partially unknown to them. To me, this is indeed a topic of special interest. A study of Turkish juvenile gangs from Frankfurt made evident that the second or third generation of such culturally suppressed groups became Turkish to an especially extreme degree.[19] Culturally suppressed groups easily become victims of radical missionary attempts by fundamentalists, Islamists, nationalists, etc., who operate from Turkey and who operate in Germany, respectively. Thus, many very bad things can come into existence. On the other hand, if one grants to these guest workers some kind of cultural autonomy, if one makes their culture recognizable — and with that I mean that one permits them to have self-respect — then this in turn allows them to be more open-minded in questions of integration.

SANFORD: What is your stand in respect to potential conflict situations, for example, when very conservative parents have to send their children to schools where perhaps one third or more of the pupils in a class might be foreigners?

FRISCHMUTH: That too will be different from situation to situation. I think it is not bad at all for children to be in a class with foreigners. A similar problem is the integration of handicapped people. Of course, it is also a question of the quality of teachers. They have to be able to handle such a situation. If they are not able to handle it, then it becomes a bad situation. If the teachers have a positive attitude, however, then possibly such a situation can be very enriching, very beneficial, and educational. An additional point is this: If parents are so overly conservative and concerned, well, then they ought to seek out private schools and send their children there. A public school for which all taxpayers pay has to be available to the children of all taxpayers, and especially to guest workers, as these pay high taxes. They surely should have the right to send their children to school.

SANFORD: Two more questions. First, what is your attitude toward the European Union (EU)?

FRISCHMUTH: I think it cannot be avoided, and, therefore, I think we should make the best of it. I support the measurements of the EU, while I hope at the same time that the individual countries are not totally at the mercy of globalization. I hope that the individual countries are able to keep up certain standards for which — after all — many generations have fought. This concerns mainly social standards. I hope that those standards do not fall totally overboard.

SANFORD: Have you noticed some changes already?

FRISCHMUTH: [She laughs] In my taxes. They are much higher now.

SANFORD: Oh?

FRISCHMUTH: Yes, of course, the state budget has to be sanitized for the EU. Therefore, the state tries to obtain funds wherever possible. All of us will feel that in one way or another.

SANFORD: Now a somewhat funny question. Do you see a difference between Austrians and Germans?

FRISCHMUTH: Yes, I'm married to a German! Of course, there is a difference, but it is a difference that also exists within Germany. Within Germany, too, there are differences among the people. My husband, for example, comes from Swabia; he has very little in common with someone from Northern Germany. Then again, all that depends also very much on the individual. That notwithstanding, Germany's history is totally different from Austria's history. I do not mean recent history, but rather a long-term view of history. Not the history of the Third Reich. There, Austria and Germany were together, the only difference being that Austria was involved for a shorter period of time. Erich Fried once said that very loudly and clearly. Going further back though, it is quite obvious that the Austro-Hungarian Empire was in character thoroughly different from the German *Kaiserreich* (Empire). If I'm not mistaken, Austria was never a completely German-speaking country. Instead, Austria was the first model — and not such a bad model, as one recognizes now — for the coexistence of different peoples. Why, after all, it did not work out in the end is a different question. Actually, it worked for an astonishingly long time. Moreover, one knows meanwhile that the Austro-Hungarian Empire was indeed absolutely exemplary in some areas — one example being schoolbooks. A friend of mine did research on this and found out that pupils of every, truly every, minority had their own set of schoolbooks during the time of the monarchy. In general, one tried very many things then in a serious attempt at doing everyone justice. Nonetheless, in the end, the Austro-Hungarian Empire failed as the first model of a multi-nation-state — and regrettably so.

SANFORD: Do you think that despite this failure, anything positive was carried over into our times from this very positive attitude toward the minorities as it was found during the monarchy?

FRISCHMUTH: Well, the attitude then was not that positive either. But at any rate, one had to come to terms with one another. A certain section of the population did regard this as very positive. If indeed some of the old monarchy's positive aspects were to be considered for the structuring of the EU, then that could perhaps be beneficial. I think, if the Austrians were only to ponder a little more over their past, then perhaps they could really offer something to the EU — something that other countries would not be able to offer.

SANFORD: To come back for a moment to the question about differences between Austrians and Germans. Do you see a difference in character? It is a cliché, for example, that the Austrians are more warmhearted *(gemütvoll)* and more sociable *(gemütlich)*.

FRISCHMUTH: I'm very careful with such clichés because it is actually always only the individual who embodies these clichés or who does not embody these clichés. A clear difference, however, can be ascertained in the area of language. There is a distinct difference there. Another clear difference lies in typical behavior patterns, in social relationships. The Austrians are not as direct as the Germans in expressing their feelings. They have certain codes for politeness, which even in our modern times have not yet disappeared. These are indeed clear differences. However, as far as character and mentality are concerned, I would not dare say that Austrians are different from Germans. In these respects, all people seem to be pretty similar. Differences then are mainly a form of mere packaging. German spoken by people from Northern Germany sounds indeed more harsh *(schroff)* and abrupt, just as their social manners are more direct. They can sometimes take an Austrian by surprise, or even evoke a negative reaction. Austrians, on the other hand, are said to be complicated *(umständlich),* uncandid, and who knows what else. All these differences are not so important, after all, as they are not true obstacles in communicating with one another.

SANFORD: One specific difference in the language: Earlier you used the Austrian idiom *liegen und stehen lassen* [for "to drop everything"] rather than *stehen und liegen lassen*.[20] I had a long dispute with a Prussian friend who insisted that it has to be *stehen und liegen lassen*

FRISCHMUTH: Yes, it is quite clear that the language is different. There is no doubt that the German spoken in Austria has its peculiarities. What counts is that we can still understand each other and that we can certainly do that very well.

SANFORD: Now, please permit a few general questions to you as a writer and a creator of literature. Do you feel influenced by the classics?

FRISCHMUTH: Hm, influenced. That's an interesting concept.

SANFORD: Goethe, for example. Did he play an important role for you?

FRISCHMUTH: Goethe not so much perhaps. Those people who really interested me were Jean Paul and E. T. A. Hoffmann or Arno Schmidt.[21] If any, then these were the authors who influenced me. Or maybe Lewis Carroll, or James Joyce, or Carson McCullers.[22] There is definitely a good number of writers who had a greater influence on me than Goethe. Then again, in some ways, of course, everyone is influenced by Goethe and the so-called classic writers. They are being taken along into our times as common knowledge, and one might adopt from them without even being aware of it.

SANFORD: Or myths. Did they influence you?

FRISCHMUTH: Yes, I'm now, and always was, very interested in myths. That is a kind of storytelling that in some way united the world, that united society. I find it interesting that myths are topics one can never cease to write about. Topics that are inexhaustible. These are topics that are forever alive, topics that have caused writers to try writing about them in different ways at all times.

SANFORD: What is you attitude toward feminism?

FRISCHMUTH: Very simple. A very pragmatic attitude. I'm a born feminist because I was always worried about my rights and about those of other women. However, I think that some things can just be taken care of logistically. Some aspects of women's rights have already been accomplished; other aspects have yet to be accomplished. Nevertheless, I never was out for taking on an extreme attitude, as this would be nothing but proceeding again according to the old male method. In other words, it would mean exclusions or all too belligerent confrontations. Instead, I try to be realistic and tell myself that women have been oppressed for many thousands of years. Women are developing a totally separate character now — one that cannot be achieved in one or two generations. We will have to work on that for a long time yet. Many generations will have to work on it.

SANFORD: Do you tend to focus more on the differences or the similarities between men and women?

FRISCHMUTH: That depends on my state of mind and my mood. [FRISCHMUTH laughs.] It really depends on that. Therefore, I cannot answer your question clearly. [She laughs cordially.] Yes, with my son, for example, I sometimes have difficulties to see things in an extreme way. As a mother of a son, or sons — I believe — one learns to understand better a good number of male attitudes or male characteristics.

SANFORD: Basically, however, you believe that women are different from men?

FRISCHMUTH: Yes, of course, and that difference was always an important aspect to me.

SANFORD: Yes, I agree, that difference is very important. Some extreme feminists seem to forget that all too easily.

FRISCHMUTH: The questions can only be about balance and about complementing each other, never about being alike. I would not even want that. For instance, I am very happy that women are not forced to join the military.[23]

SANFORD: Goethe was quoted by Eckermann as having said about the creativity of women that it seems to vanish in the wind as soon as a woman has a family.[24] For you that does not seem to be true.

FRISCHMUTH: No, not at all. Children do not harm art.

SANFORD: What do you mean by that?

FRISCHMUTH: I mean that children neither help nor hinder art. An artist will always find ways to create art, regardless of whether there are children or not. For instance, when Paul Rotterdam[25] was kind enough to put us up in his loft for several weeks, I was always afraid that my son would bang against one of his paintings. It was he who then coined the expression: "Children do not harm art." For me that proved to be true also. I was always able to combine my writing and my child. Only in regards to social engagements, I ran into some difficulties. Of course, I had to cut back on some things. For instance, during that time, I could not go to the movies as often as I had been used to. Yet, I went to Oberlin College as writer in residence when my son was only two years and three months old. I just took him along. That was possible. Of course, it is not as simple as it sounds now. With several children, I would not have been able to do that.

SANFORD: Well, I think that Goethe perhaps also wanted to say that women lose their interest in artistic activities as soon as they have a family. Maybe that is wrong.

FRISCHMUTH: Hm, it remains a question. Of course there are collisions.

SANFORD: You mean, if one asks oneself what is more important in life, one's family or one's artistic endeavors?

FRISCHMUTH: During the childrearing period, one does not even have the time to ask such a question. There are two priorities between which one is constantly torn. Certainly, one should not pretend that the situation is easy. That is absolutely not the case. This notwithstanding, I have found that it is possible to have a child and to be a creative writer. Furthermore, I found that this kind of difficult situation can also be very rewarding because by spending time with one's child, one also learns many new things. One gains experience and learns a new kind of entertainment. In other words, the missed movies, the missed theater performances, and the missed parties are compensated for by these new experiences with the child. Of course, that might not be the same for everyone. Moreover, with every additional child, the technical difficulties, the restraints, are increased, and it becomes more difficult to have time for children as well as art.

SANFORD: You have one son only?

FRISCHMUTH: Yes, I have only one son, who is twenty-three now. Ever since he's grown up, more or less, I have been able to return to my field of Oriental studies.

SANFORD: It is wonderful that perhaps now your son can become your illustrator.

FRISCHMUTH: Theoretically, yes. In actuality, it is very difficult. Besides, he does not like the idea that one might be able to say that he owes his job to his mother.

SANFORD: Will you now include your Oriental studies more into your writings again, just as you did in former years?

FRISCHMUTH: Yes, of course.

SANFORD: Do you also travel in the Orient?

FRISCHMUTH: Yes, indeed. For instance, I was in Turkey this year and also during the past years. I am very much occupied with the situation in that country.

SANFORD: When do you like to write best?

FRISCHMUTH: In the afternoon, and perhaps also in the evening, depending on how it works out.

SANFORD: You now write on a PC? Have you been doing that for a long time?

FRISCHMUTH: First, I write everything in longhand, and only afterward do I type it on the PC.

SANFORD: Hm, that is interesting.

FRISCHMUTH: Yes, I cannot change that habit anymore. I have written all of my books in longhand. However, now I write my first draft in longhand, and then I type it on the PC. There I can correct beautifully. I've had this PC only for one and half years. For a long time, I resisted [FRISCHMUTH laughs] — just as I've resisted getting a driver's license. At any rate, with the PC, I get along much better than with a typewriter.

SANFORD: So the actual composing of the story does not take place on the PC?

FRISCHMUTH: No, I have always been unilaterally talented.

SANFORD: Do you have e-mail and Internet connections?

FRISCHMUTH: No, not yet. That is the next step. Right now, I have so many other things that are to be done. Next, I have to go on a reading tour.

SANFORD: Perhaps one more last question. If you write, let's say, a novel, do you start out with a vague idea, or do you have a big concept?

FRISCHMUTH: Most of the time, I have a big concept and know already a lot about my topic. But that too is different from book to book. For instance, I'm completing a novel now on which I have worked for years and about which I know very much.[26] Nonetheless, I do not know what outcome the novel will finally take. That is of course very exciting but also very time consuming.

SANFORD: Do you get your ideas for topics by talking to people?

FRISCHMUTH: That varies very much. I cannot really tell from where I get my ideas. Somehow they are suddenly there. After the first ideas have come up, then one begins to research into a certain direction. It can also happen that an idea disappears again, perhaps because it was not strong enough after all.

SANFORD: Coming back briefly to the image of Austria. Basically, you are positively inclined toward Austria?

FRISCHMUTH: Yes, I like to live here. I am angry about many things, but I am not hysterical as far as Austria is concerned. I think that I have thought about Austria a lot. I especially occupied myself with the so-called coming to terms with the past *(Vergangenheitsbewältigung)*. That did take place and still does take place, although not always in the form that is expected in our days.

SANFORD: Frequently, the Austrians are reproached that they did not go through the postulated process of grieving *(Trauerarbeit)*.

FRISCHMUTH: I believe, however, that many Austrians — namely, all those who are open enough — have gone through that phase a along time ago. I remember, as students the becoming aware of the Holocaust was an enormous shock for all of us. That notwithstanding, one did not want to make a small change with that process of grieving by producing literary outpours. I did a translation, for instance, of a concentration camp diary by Zimra Miko.[27] Still, I would never have dared to treat that topic myself. It could well have been that such a production would not be of high literary quality. One might have had a certain hesitance, a shyness, to take up such a topic. But as far as my memory goes back, in the circles in which I moved, the topic of coming to terms with the past was always present in one way or another.

SANFORD: In your view, is that something that should be taken up in school?

FRISCHMUTH: Yes, of course that should be taken up in school. But in a reasonable way. As it is, in one school, they might leave out that topic altogether; in another, they might present it in such a way that it is not interesting to the children. Indeed, it is very difficult to present that subject matter in a way that children can grasp it and, furthermore, that they can truly comprehend it and mentally reconstruct *(nachvollziehen)* the situation. The problem is that perhaps there are relatively many people in Austria who do not want to think about that topic at all. There seems to be no way to induce them to concern themselves with the Holocaust, regardless of how many publications there are on it. You can find articles on the Holocaust in almost every other issue of most papers and magazines, *Profil* being just one example. Still, some people just do not want to give thought to the horrors of the Holocaust.

SANFORD: True, and some people seem to be tired of it.

FRISCHMUTH: Some just refuse to read anything that might deal with Austria's guilt concerning the Holocaust. In addition, there is another matter that has not yet been examined enough: that so often scorned awareness of having been victimized *(Opferbewusstsein)*. After the war, there was hardly a family that had not lost a family member in the war. The personal loss experienced, therefore, was in the foreground. That, naturally, hurt all those that were affected. However, many people do not go the necessary step further. They do not ponder beyond their personal loss. They do not ask who might have initiated all that, or why all that was enabled to happen. Frankly, I do not know how one could change a people's attitude. I agree that this is a consciousness that perhaps was not supported enough in Austria — a consciousness that one should mourn, however. Yet, one should not only consider a personal loss, but likewise the loss that others may have experienced. Moreover, in my generation, we did not really mourn at all. I, for example, did not know my father, and, therefore, I did not miss him. Very early on, I understood that he had fallen in a war that had been begun by Germans and Austrians. Thus — as a child — I had good reason to block out the entire matter. That again is not especially good. In summary, I think, much has yet to be done in that area. Still, in order to arrive at a constructive understanding, it would be necessary that any such approach does not polarize from the start.

SANFORD: What is your attitude toward Bosnia?

FRISCHMUTH: That is extremely hard to tell. It is so very close. The frictions there will continue, I fear. That goes without question. However, nowadays nothing is sure anymore.

SANFORD: For my next research project, I'd like to examine your children's books, especially your language and then also certain values that you promote there, hidden of course.

FRISCHMUTH: Yes, as we mentioned before. These values almost establish themselves, I have no direct pedagogical intentions.

SANFORD: Then there is the fine humor in your children's books to be considered.

FRISCHMUTH: Yes, laughing is definitely permitted.

Syracuse University

Notes

1. This interview was conducted in German and later translated and edited by Gerlinde Ulm Sanford. Barbara Frischmuth read and approved of the translation and its content.

2. Lewis Carroll (1832–1898).

3. George MacDonald (1824–1905).

4. J. R. R. (John Ronald Reuel) Tolkien (1892–1973).

5. Barbara Frischmuth was born in 1941. Thus, her childhood fell into the years during and after World War II.

6. Barbara Frischmuth, *Donna & Dario* (Frankfurt/Main: Sauerländer, 1997).

7. Johann Carl August Musäus, *Moralische Kinderklapper* (Gotha: Carl Wilhelm Ettinger, 1794) 78.

8. Barbara Frischmuth, *Amoralische Kinderklapper* (Frankfurt/Main: Suhrkamp, 1969).

9. Hans Carl Artmann, *Allerleirausch: Neue schöne Kinderreime* (Erlangen: Renner, 1978).

10. Barbara Frischmuth's husband is a psychiatrist and neurologist.

11. In German "daß ich alles liegen und stehen ließ." Please compare later in this interview the part touching upon language differences between Austrians and Germans.

12. Rousseau, in *Du contrat social* (1762, About the Social Contract), held that in the state of nature, man was unwarlike and somewhat undeveloped in his reasoning powers and sense of morality and responsibility. When, however, people agreed for mutual protection to surrender individual freedom of action and establish laws and government, they then acquired a sense of moral and civic obligation. In order to retain its essentially moral character, government must thus rest on the consent of the governed, the *volonté générale* (general will). — The more perceptive social-contract theorists, including Hobbes, invariably recognized that their concepts of the social contract and the state of nature were unhistorical and that they could be justified only as hypotheses useful for the clarification of timeless political problems. See <http://www.eb.com:180/cgi-bin/g?DocF=micro/554/7.html>.

13. Konrad Lorenz (1903–1997).

14. Konrad Lorenz, *Er redete mit dem Vieh, den Vögeln und den Fischen* (1949; repr. 13th–14th ed., Vienna: Borotha-Schoeler, 1956).

15. Konrad Lorenz, *So kam der Mensch auf den Hund* (1950; repr., 12th–16th ed., Vienna: Borotha-Schoeler, 1958).

16. Barbara Frischmuth, *Die Mystifikationen der Sophie Silber* (Salzburg : Residenz, 1976).

17. At the annual convention of the German Studies Association, in Seattle, August 1996, Barbara Frischmuth spoke on the topic "Österreich, was sonst?" (published in *Reden über Österreich,* ed. Manfred Jochum [Salzburg: Residenz, 1995] 135–145).

18. Annual symposium on "Modern Austrian Literature," Riverside, California, April 1997.

19. Herman Tergilt, *Turkish Power Boys: Ethnographie einer Jugendbande* (Frankfurt/Main: Suhrkamp, 1996).

20. See note 10.

21. Jean Paul (1763–1825); E. T. A. Hoffmann (1776–1822); Arno Schmidt (1914–1979).

22. Lewis Carroll (1832–1898); James Joyce (1882–1941); Carson McCullers, née Lula Carson Smith (1917–1967).

23. All Austrian men over eighteen have to serve in the military for a base period of six months. In addition, ancillary military exercises of up to six months have to be completed to obtain certain ranks. Any male refusing to serve on the basis of being a conscientious objector can instead apply to complete a fixed period of civil service in order to fulfill the basic requirement of serving the republic.

24. See Eckermann, *Gespräche mit Goethe,* from January 18, 1825.

25. Here she refers to a personal friend, a painter residing in New York City.

26. Meanwhile, Barbara Frischmuth completed this novel: Barbara Frischmuth, *Die Schrift des Freundes* (Salzburg: Residenz, 1998).

27. Barbara Frischmuth's translation was published under the name Ana Novac and with a cynical title: *Die schönen Tage meiner Jugend* [The Beautiful Days of My Youth] (Reinbek bei Hamburg: Rowohlt, 1967).

Interview with Barbara Frischmuth on the Topic "Demeter and Persephone"[1]

Gisela M. Roethke

ROETHKE: It seems to me that this Demeter topos goes very far back for you.[2] Did that already start in Turkey, for example? Especially these horse stories that you told me?

FRISCHMUTH: Oh well, I only discovered that a lot later — that that also had something to do with Demeter . . . with this horse-headed Epona, right? Well, the Celts called her Epona. That's essentially an early stage of Demeter in Greece. I was very happy when I found that. It's like this: There is this give and take, back and forth. The figure of Demeter . . . When I read [Hermann] Broch for the first time . . . I was quite a bit over twenty when that appeared for the first time.[3] It was still called *Der Versucher* (1953, The Tempter) then. . . . I only know that I was still a student then — it must have been at the beginning of the sixties. It was then that I read this novel for the first time, and naturally, I always tried to locate it in Altaussee until I found out that it had been written in Tirol; but possibly, it still has something to do with it. Well, the landscape is very similar after all. Somehow, this Demeter figure occupied me a lot. But I wasn't really satisfied with what Broch had done. As much as I liked this book, it moved me immeasurably, but Broch's women figures . . . I always found them unsatisfying.

ROETHKE: Yes, I can understand that.

FRISCHMUTH: And they all have such a dreadful fate, don't they? They either have to commit suicide or . . . I don't know, what his thing was with women; it was quite strange.

ROETHKE: Partially influenced by [Otto] Weininger, I think.

FRISCHMUTH: Well, yes, a bit for sure. And somehow I was also in a quandary, because on the one hand, I regarded Broch very highly, and on the other hand, I felt uncomfortable. This Mother Gisson in his book: on the one hand, she interested me a lot; on the other hand, she was *much* too stylized. Well, I don't know, I suppose the way a man writes this . . .

ROETHKE: Was it clear to you at that time when you read it that he was dealing with a Demeter figure, or not?

FRISCHMUTH: No, not really.

ROETHKE: Because after all, you need to envision the myth to discover this.

FRISCHMUTH: But the book left a deep impression on me. And that was already then something where I thought: Well, I would love to write against it or pick up on this . . .

ROETHKE: Even at that early stage, when you were still so young? That's really interesting!

FRISCHMUTH: But naturally, it wasn't as clear cut, because at that time . . . After all, at that time I was coming more from the experimental side, and I wasn't really interested in novels, at least not in writing them myself. And still, I think that I'm a born prose writer after all, even if I didn't admit it to myself then. In spite of everything, I always had prose in the back of my mind, longer prose, too; therefore such books interested me.

ROETHKE: And when did you get to the Demeter topos itself? That was later, wasn't it?

FRISCHMUTH: Much later. Well, mostly because for a long time, I didn't know what really interested me.

ROETHKE: That's the really interesting part, after all: why someone modern would get turned on by this today — irrespective of the wave that then came about because of the women's movement.[4] Since that has now become a topic in connection with — I want to nearly say — the "adulation" of matriarchy or attempts to revive this or to possibly connect to it in order to make it useful for women today. That is a different matter. Well, what interests me in this is more the psychological side: why just this constellation of all possible ones?

FRISCHMUTH: Yes, that also irritated me for a long time, because I always thought: Why just this story? And then, after all, it was more that I accommodated in this story all sorts of different areas that interested me. Starting with this obsession with horses, which I had for a long time, something like a teenage malady — only that it was delayed with me to a belated kind of puberty — simply because at the appropriate age, I had far too few opportunities — and which then really had to take the detour via a marriage, with a horse ranch and everything, in order to fully experience this. I could not write about this for a long time. These were things about which I really could not write. This business with the horses, that was after all a very fully developed experience over many years. It didn't work. I wrote very little about that.

ROETHKE: So, you think, inhibitions because it maybe hit too close to home, or what?

FRISCHMUTH: No, not inhibitions. There simply was no connection there, no frame. I wrote a few short texts about it, but still more in the manner of this phase of linguistic mimicry, where I tried to imitate the jargon of the race course.[5] But somehow, the great overarching connection was missing. And only when I kept rereading the Demeter myth and thought about it again and again, it suddenly became clear to me: that *is* the connection! There I can accommodate that nearly hermaphroditic horse-woman story. And there I can accommodate my political interests. So, that became the second volume *Über die Verhältnisse* (1987, Beyond One's Means),[6] where I used this foil for a certain kind of history of the conditions in my country. And then this story of Eleusis, for which naturally I needed the longest time, this *Einander Kind* (1990, One Another's Child),[7] which after much back and forth emerged out of this whole pond full of ideas and myths.

ROETHKE: But to this specific myth you then came via an occupation with other myths, or . . . ?

FRISCHMUTH: Well, yes, with Robert von Ranke-Graves and others; that started very early, that I read such things, all of them, and that I was interested in them.[8] But strangely — after all, there are so many goddesses and gods — it was this particular line that always interested me most, with this mother/daughter constellation, and the fact that the mother was never asked by the patriarchal gods. Well, there was always something that interested me about that. Only, it took an awfully long time before I had found the right connection. And without this connection or without this form, it wouldn't have worked. It would have become a one-dimensional story; and I wanted to have several dimensions in it.

ROETHKE: Does it also have an autobiographical dimension in that you grew up as the daughter of a mother, where the father was missing from early on?

FRISCHMUTH: Sure, that is obviously something that I notice much less, since for me it is quite normal to keep using that again and again. But that certainly has to do with the fact that I just grew up that way and that I had a stepfather who did not play a special role in my life — that is for me always something like a basic situation. . . . But what interested me later was not so much my relationship to my mother; after all, I knew that, and that wasn't repressed or hidden. But rather what interested me was the connection, the cultural connection, the cultural context in which all of this is located.

ROETHKE: It is interesting how you kept approaching this material again and again from different vantage points. If, for instance, one takes the archaic vantage point: Why was the archaic so important for you at a certain point in time? Is it nearly experimental that you say, okay, I would like to look at this material from different vantage points, or was it more your interests that changed?

FRISCHMUTH: No, it is simply the following matter: When one begins working on any such idea, in principle, everything is of interest that is connected to it. And only after one has played through all the possibilities . . . for this Demeter, I did a whole series of experiments and preliminary studies, where I actually on paper already turned things around and tried again and again to change them a little bit so that I would find a new way of accessing them. The crowning idea was then simply the one with the three volumes and the three aspects.

ROETHKE: So it was conceived of as a trilogy right from the start?[9]

FRISCHMUTH: Yes, that was clear to me very quickly.

ROETHKE: Did Broch play a role in that? Because after all, Broch's Demeter novel was once originally conceived of as a trilogy, although nothing came of it.

FRISCHMUTH: Well, yes, a little. But later that was not so important. It was simply something where I thought: I would like to push that further.

ROETHKE: Exciting! Well, I have my own theories about how Broch was envisioning that . . .

FRISCHMUTH: Well, I had read all of that in the Lützeler edition.[10] For me, it was not so important anymore from the moment I found my own access to the material, my own model, this connection. Then it was only a question of shaping it. But it took a long time until I found that connection. And also, until I figured out what this meant for me, this myth, or why it interested me. One doesn't know that in the beginning. So, one asks oneself the strangest questions about why.

ROETHKE: So, what was your conclusion then? What did you find out?

FRISCHMUTH: Well, that's what I wrote then. That was it: the three aspects and this mother/daughter story. First the level with the horses . . . There were three steps for me, up to this *Einander Kind*, and that was for me the mystery of Eleusis about which nobody was permitted to talk.

ROETHKE: That's an interesting modern reinterpretation . . .

FRISCHMUTH: Well, myth was interesting for me as a kind of "genealogical research," especially for a female gallery. It was really like that, that it was important for me in regard to this so-called gallery of ancestors. That one can say: Well, okay, if we don't have a history of our own in the usual sense, then we have perhaps a mythical history/story after all. All of this one has to seek out and collect, as much as one might need of it.

ROETHKE: On the other hand, I already saw in your theoretical discussions of this topic that you also distance yourself from such attempts, as for instance those of Heide Göttner-Abendroth, who tries to revive this myth and to make it somehow fertile for today.[11] It appears to me that what you are doing is something else.

FRISCHMUTH: Yes, I don't really believe in that. Naturally, we all live this, but in quite a different form, and that's what's interesting about it. I believe that it is less important that one starts prescribing something again. I always have the feeling with these clear-cut things: here someone wants to explain to me again about my being a woman. I react to such things with a bit of reserve. Because I think: I don't need to have this explained! I posit myself as a woman. So, I don't want to be presented with some ancient models again. I want to know of them, how they reach into my life, but I want to have them understood as a freedom to decide and not as another task I have to fulfill.

I read all of that at certain times, with more or less interest and greater or smaller enthusiasm; but I was more interested in this Demeter story from the aspect of the subconscious, that is, these different possible underworlds. Indeed, originally I had thought that Persephone is a deeply depressive woman and needs to be freed from this underworld. But that turned out way too theoretical for me. At that time, I got something into my hands by a C. G. Jung student who had already sketched this out a little. So then, I immediately rejected that possibility.[12] So I thought: Let's not fall for these cookie-cutter patterns. I think one needs to know all this, and one can rejoice that certain ideas have been around, but one should not let oneself be typified by them. That kind of thing actually scares me off, and I think that literature is much more fruitful in this, because one can always invent something.

ROETHKE: It is interesting that you keep coming back to this myth, but that each time it takes a very different, modern form. This shows that you are, precisely, not fixing the myth but rather keeping it in flux continuously.

FRISCHMUTH: That's the wonderful thing about myth, that it remains open. After all, among the old myths, there are no two tellings that do not vary from each other. So, why should one *now* get fixated on one obligatory form? Each myth — just like fairy tales — has certain elements that are combined ever anew, because the things of this life are limited in number. After all, there aren't so many different basic situations. I mean, everything that is too definitive or too speculative becomes boring for me.

ROETHKE: Now, one can also see all of this in the larger framework of the whole discussion on myth, where one can then ask: How come that in the seventies and eighties of all times, myth, the interest in myth, the interest in "working on myth" has seen such a revival?[13] It is being explained by many as a reaction against modernity. You wouldn't see that in that way, would you?

FRISCHMUTH: No, not at all. I simply think: We enlighten history. In a time where women become conscious of themselves, if one doesn't have any history or none to mention, then one will fetch the other history/story, that of myth. Only, I find that myth for me is at the same time an appeal to the creativity of women, to create themselves, to always create themselves. . . . I also once studied all these things, because it interested me. You know, this never-ending lamentation, even if it wasn't self-pitying, not at all, about the "Not-I" . . . the whole *nouvelle philosophie* ("new philosophy") after all was dealing with that. I don't see it like that at all. I think one has possibilities to overcome this; at least, that's what I claim for myself. If as a woman I don't have a history, well, then I just make one up, I design a new one.

ROETHKE: Do you think that you are finished with this particular myth now, or is this still brewing?

FRISCHMUTH: Oh well, at the moment, the Demeter myth interests me less, because through this *Machtnix* (1993, Don't Bother) story,[14] where I now want to write a second part, I am occupied with quite different things, which actually reach a bit more into philosophy, but another kind of philosophy, or let's say a different presentation of philosophy, as I understand it, because I really don't have a way of approaching canonical philosophy. What's always important to me is to make the world narratable, or speakable. Or to make being a woman narratable/speakable. If that succeeds, then it exists. Then I don't have to worry about my "Not-I" or to just feel myself as the negative impression of the positive male ego. It is all justified that that was said once, but . . . so what?

ROETHKE: Are you distancing yourself especially from Simone de Beauvoir, since you are quoting her?[15]

FRISCHMUTH: Yes, a bit indeed. Naturally, I read her with great enthusiasm; but then, I was actually frustrated by her, as by all women who have spoken against children and family, because I think that's not the way! That most of the time more likely leads to depression. Nobody gains from that. I mean, sure, Simone de Beauvoir was very important and also important for me, in the beginning, in order to start in this direction at all.[16] But, in the end, *all* of that is not binding for me.

ROETHKE: Well, there were after all quite different ways in reflecting on this. On the one hand, some said: Okay, we have no history, so we need to invent one for ourselves or to search for it in literature and myth — the traces that do still exist. Others rolled up their sleeves and tried to scare up the history of women in archives. But this choice, to say: Well, I am more interested in the mythical aspect than in the historical one? . . . I see in your newest stories, in *Machtnix* and also in your story about the skinheads, that apparently you are now bringing these two strands closer together, the politico-historical and the mythical one.[17]

FRISCHMUTH: That was already so in two volumes of the trilogy: *Über die Verhältnisse* and *Einander Kind*; both are also about history and politics.

ROETHKE: It is very well possible that I simply am not so familiar with the political frame of contemporary Austrian politics.

FRISCHMUTH: That had a lot to do with the conditions in Austria.

ROETHKE: In the title you obviously already make this clear. This multivalent title: *Über die Verhältnisse*!

FRISCHMUTH: Oh, jeez! They nearly lynched me when it came out!

ROETHKE: So it was read as a *roman à clef*?

FRISCHMUTH: Yes, yes, unfortunately. I wasn't altogether innocent in this, because I simply had borrowed a few figures . . .

ROETHKE: With the Demeter topos, there are obviously also some connections to Romanticism, because it saw myth as so strong, even as basic. Not only as turned backward nostalgically, of which one has often accused the Romantics, and of which one now also accuses those feminists who occupy themselves with matriarchal theories, namely, that they are proponents of a retrograde utopia. Are there any connections for you between the Demeter myth and Romanticism or not?

FRISCHMUTH: Not consciously.[18]

ROETHKE: So I see that you created this primarily going to the sources available in mythology.

FRISCHMUTH: Yes, von Ranke-Graves and Karl Kerényi and then Hans Peter Dürr and these things. I read *a lot* in those years. After all, it takes a long time until something of one's own takes form and shape.

ROETHKE: I was surprised that you said that the only *literary* connection you had to this topos was via Broch, since there are a whole series of authors . . .

FRISCHMUTH: Well, strangely, I didn't want to read anything anymore that went in this direction, except for the so-called scholarly literature.

ROETHKE: That is probably important in order to be able to develop one's own ideas.

FRISCHMUTH: Oh well, on the other hand, everything has already been dealt with before.

ROETHKE: Another question which interests me in your works is that of continuity from one generation to the next . . .

FRISCHMUTH: Well, I already had similar phantasies in *Die Mystifikationen der Sophie Silber* (1976, The Mystifications of Sophie Silber).[19] There was also always inheritance in the female line, and there was, too, this going back to the cases of death in the "feast of remembrance." So, basically I was already occupied with this in the first trilogy, just not so clearly. And there, the connection to Demeter was not so obvious. In reality, that was already important then.

ROETHKE: In *Einander Kind,* you seem to be going beyond the mother/daughter relationship of the two who are switching their roles; here, the relationship between man and woman also becomes important.

FRISCHMUTH: Yes, this up and down, that the roles are not absolutely fixed, and that this can fluctuate and change. That for me was really the crowning insight.

ROETHKE: That is also cognitively a step further, isn't it? What I mean is a developmental step that this is not limited by gender but rather deals with relationships and mutuality.

FRISCHMUTH: Yes, naturally. And with maternalism and dependency of a childlike nature . . .

ROETHKE: Yes, and learning to accept that one is not always the strong one, but also the weak one. What I mean is to learn to accept the role of weakness.

FRISCHMUTH: In Innsbruck, I was made aware by a female theologian that Jesus once called himself "the Mother" or "the Mother of us all" or some such thing. . . . And today I read in Walker Percy about a doctor who is controlled by someone much younger than him and who is described as being like "a Jewish mother." So, if one sharpens one's ear for this, it occurs much more frequently than one might think; most of the time, one just glosses over it, namely, the fact that this can also be felt between men.

ROETHKE: That is surely very strongly culturally conditioned, more or less fully developed in different cultures. In the United States, this division of gender roles is very strongly developed right from the start. Surely, there are attempts to counteract this, and I see this with my students for example, that there are some — I would say those who are intellectually more open and who love to experiment more — who want to break out of these conventions and who are more ready to accept this ambiguity and maybe even such a thing as the hermaphroditic paradigm, this not wanting to be nailed down to fixed roles. So then this myth is one that acquires a historical dimension after all because the relationship between Demeter and Persephone becomes one that becomes transferable to other relationships, if one wants to make it fruitful for the future.

FRISCHMUTH: But obviously in the most open possible form.

ROETHKE: Yes, that's beautiful. If that would succeed, that would be beautiful!

FRISCHMUTH: That is already the next step . . .

Dickinson College

Notes

1. This interview was held with Barbara Frischmuth by Gisela Roethke at Dickinson College on March 4, 1994. It was translated from German into English by Gisela Roethke.

2. See Barbara Frischmuth, *Traum der Literatur — Literatur des Traums: Münchner Poetik-Vorlesungen* (Salzburg: Residenz, 1991) 64–71.

3. Frischmuth is referring to Hermann Broch's novel *Die Verzauberung* (1976; *The Spell,* 1987), which in its fragmentary form was published under varying titles at different times, among them *Der Versucher* (1953, The Tempter). Frischmuth commented in more detail on her Broch reception in "Lese-Erinnerungen an Hermann Broch," in *Hermann Broch,* ed. Paul Michael Lützeler (Frankfurt/Main: Suhrkamp, 1986) 25–32. In that contribution, she announced her plans to write her own Demeter novel, which later turned into a trilogy (32).

4. Paul Michael Lützeler has provided an interesting discussion of the postmodern aspects of Frischmuth's use of myth in his essay "Barbara Frischmuths Demeter-Trilogie: Mythologische Finde-Spiele in der postmodernen Literatur," in *Barbara Frischmuth,* ed. Kurt Barsch (Graz: Droschl, 1992) 73–97.

5. One of these texts, "Pferdefrau" (Horse Woman), can be found in Frischmuth's volume *Mörderische Märchen und andere Erzählungen* (Munich: dtv, 1992) 82–89.

6. Barbara Frischmuth, *Über die Verhältnisse* (Salzburg: Residenz, 1987).

7. Barbara Frischmuth, *Einander Kind* (1990; repr., Munich: dtv, 1994).

8. Frischmuth is referring to Robert von Ranke-Graves, *Griechische Mythologie: Quellen und Deutung* (1960; repr., Reinbek bei Hamburg: Rowohlt, 1984), originally published as *The Greek Myths* (1955). In *Traum der Literatur*, Frischmuth mentions further sources of her occupation with mythology and this particular myth (65).

9. Here Roethke refers to Frischmuth's Demeter-trilogy: *Herrin der Tiere* (Salzburg/Wien: Residenz, 1986), *Über die Verhältnisse*, and *Einander Kind.*

10. Here Frischmuth refers to the critical edition of Hermann Broch's works in paperback, which was edited and annotated by Paul Michael Lützeler. Hermann Broch, *Kommentierte Werkausgabe,* ed. Paul Michael Lützeler (Frankfurt/Main: Suhrkamp, 1974–1981).

11. See Frischmuth, *Traum der Literatur* 68.

12. Frischmuth is referring here to Ingrid Rieder, *Demeters Suche — Mütter und Töchter* (Zurich: Kreuz, 1986).

13. Roethke is alluding here to Hans Blumenberg's *Arbeit am Mythos*, 4th ed. (Frankfurt/Main: Suhrkamp, 1986).

14. Barbara Frischmuth, *Machtnix oder Der Lauf, den die Welt nahm* (Salzburg: Residenz, 1993).

15. See Frischmuth, *Traum der Literatur* 77.

16. What Frischmuth is referring to with "this direction" is feminism.

17. Roethke is referring to Frischmuth's novel *Machtnix* and to the short story "Das Lachen des Dalai Lama" (The Laughter of the Dalai Lama), in *Hexenherz* (Salzburg: Residenz, 1994) 162–174.

18. This comment must have been a temporary slip of memory on Frischmuth's part, since she had in some detail written about E. T. A. Hoffmann's influence on her own type of creative phantasy. In *Traum der Literatur* 54–59.

19. Barbara Frischmuth, *Die Mystifikationen der Sophie Silber* (1976; repr., Munich: dtv, 1979).

Barbara Frischmuth: Rocking with Rückert, or Crazy like a Fox[1]

Translated by Gerald Chapple and James B. Lawson

The Koran must have a magic power
for it to fascinate the world so.

Let's look more closely, free of magic's spell,
to see whether it be but wicked magic.

Or whether it be in fact a form revealing the
Eternal Spirit, food for our very own spirit.[2]

These verses are taken from Rückert's *Die Weisheit des Brahmanen* (1836–39, Wise Sayings of the Vedic Sages) and are meant as an explanation for his extended labors over the sacred text of the Muslims, which he had in large part translated. (It is, by the way, the only translation of the book into German that preserves something of the widely praised poetry of the original.) Probably best known as the author of *Kindertotenlieder* (1833–34, Songs for Dead Children) and *Geharnischte Sonette* (1812–17, Sonnets in Armor), Rückert was one of those rare people who are absolutely crazy about literature, and he possessed talent and self-discipline to such a degree that he was able to learn foreign languages and bring home to us in German their troves of literary treasures. It takes a large measure of "craziness" indeed to see yourself as a border crosser between two cultures — East and West — without ever setting foot in an Islamic country or ever hearing a word of its language spoken. In spite of this, Rückert took on the translation of the greatest literary works written in Arabic, the Koran and *Die Verwandlungen des Abu Seid von Serug* (1826, The Metamorphoses of Abu Zayd), part of *Die Makamen des Hariri* (The Maqamaat of Hariri) — comic/dramatic anecdotes by the poet, who lived in Basra, Iraq, between 1054 and 1122 — as well as works from the Persian (Farsi), *Die Ghasele des Mewlana Dschelaleddin Rumi* (1838, The Ghazals of Maulana Jelal-uddin Rumi) and *Dreiundsechzig Ghaselen des Hafis* (1866, Thirty-Six Ghazals from the Diwan of Hafiz), to name only the important ones.

Here we must remember that, from the late eighteenth to the beginning of the twentieth centuries, Islamic art and literature stirred up great interest in German-speaking countries. It was because of Hammer-Purgstall's translations of Hafiz that Goethe wrote his *Westöstlicher Divan* (1819, West-Eastern Diwan), that Platen studied Arabic, and that the brothers Friedrich and Georg Rosen translated Omar Khayyam[3] and *Das Papageienbuch von Tuti-Nameh* (1958, The Book of the Parrot), among many other works. This stands in stark contrast to the fact that in our own time, in spite of the presence of two million Turks in Germany and almost 200,000 in Austria, we find barely a trace of Muslim culture in German literature, hardly a mention of it in the younger generation of German-speaking writers.

The poet Zafer Senocak — a "re-constructor" in Rückert's sense of the word, which I will define in a minute — has provided model German translations of the thirteenth- and fourteenth-century Turkish poet Yunis Emre. In one of his essays, "Wann ist der Fremde zu Hause?" (1993, When Does the Stranger Feel at Home?),[4] Senocak deals with the invisibility of Muslim culture in German literature: "If, because of the German constitution, it is blood lines that are blocking the enfranchisement of aliens in Germany, then it's that same blood that is clogging the brains of German intellectuals and blocking intellectual discussion with 'the Alien' within their own country." (The same holds true for Austria, within certain limits, even though Austria has a different tradition in this respect.) This means that, from the standpoint of cultural exchange, we have fallen far below nineteenth-century standards in our literary perception of "Oriental" culture. On the other hand, it seems perfectly natural that authors of Turkish, Persian (Farsi), or Arabic origin have carried over so much from their first, *spoken* language, from their mother tongue (*Mutterzunge* 1990, Mother Tongue is the title of Emine Sevgi Özdamar's first book), and have brought it over into German, their *literary* language, thereby making it accessible to a native German-speaking audience. What they have salvaged in this way gives the German language a new dimension at times, one that is rarely acknowledged.

But back to Rückert, without doubt the most inspired translator of Oriental languages that any German-speaking culture has ever produced. Annemarie Schimmel has rendered yeoman service, but her linguistic imagination cannot be compared with that of a Rückert. And yet, he has so completely slipped into oblivion that we have to ask ourselves what's happened to our ear for poetry all this time, which is otherwise certainly attuned to virtuosity.

Years later I'm still astonished by the fact that the avant-garde, in the

1960s in particular, for all their experiments with language, virtually never went back to Rückert, as far as I can see. And come to think of it, it is Rückert and not Lewis Carroll, an author I admire and love so much, who ought to be honored as the inventor of the portmanteau word. As early as the 1820s, Rückert coined a series of words in his Koran translation such as *Brast* (a contraction of *Brand* and *Brunst*, i.e., of "fire" and "passion"/"rut"), even if he mainly did it for the sake of the rhyme; but the point is, he did do it.

"My work cannot pretend to be a translation but rather a reconstruction," Rückert writes in 1826 in the preface to his brilliant *tour de force* of a translation, *Die Verwandlungen des Abu Seid von Serug*, from *Die Makamen des Hariri;* he also speaks of the German language as "our language, which is receptive to every kind of expansion." And it is precisely this receptivity that he gives evidence of in a most masterful way.

As early as his translation of the Koran, Rückert was inventing words like *Beigeseller* (by-mate), *Schmetterung* (smashness), *Abseyn* (here-be-not), *Gell* (shrill, used as a noun), *Strafpein* (punishpain), *Gnadenvorzug* (advantage *de grâce*), *Schmälerer* (diminutor) and many others, but when translating Hariri he pushed this method to the extreme, guided by the author and the Arabic, a language given to playing on words. Whether *wandersatt* (wandersated) or *Blümliches* (floweries), whether *sieghoffnungtrunken* (victory-hope-besotted) or *nahgestellt* (besided), the "mischievous gloat" *(Schadefroh)* of a poet was "unshyly footing up" *(scheulos auffußen)* his flowers of speech, and the more you take delight in these "bready treats" *(Labebrote)*, the greater your pleasure will be.

Die Verwandlungen des Abu Seid von Serug can best be categorized as a picaresque novel, if the word *novel* doesn't arouse false expectations. Each comic/dramatic anecdote *(maqamaat)* is a separate, self-contained adventure; they are connected only by the appearance of the same characters in each. "One does not see a plot developing [in the book]," Rückert explains, "and yet, in the end, the goal is reached. The arrangement of the stories is therefore like that of the planets, or it can also radiate outward like the leaves of the palm."

In every one of the anecdotes, the narrator, Hareth Ben Hemmam, who only serves as a projection screen, encounters the picaro figure, Abu Zayd, who is not only a trickster and swindler, but a poet and verbal artist of supreme talent as well; he manages to extricate himself from the predicaments he has brought on himself most often by telling clever little tales, riddle-me-rees, and puns that are very close to being experimental. In describing his life experience, he says this about himself:

> I am a sly magician,
> Mr. No- and Everywhere.
> The Persian and the Arab laugh
> When at my pranks they stare.[5]

Others have to put up with monikers like *der Herr vom unverschämten Gesicht* (Lord of the Brazen Face) or *Habegern von Fürchtenichts* (Greedyguts of Fearnaught), even though these are said in jest.

The adventure comprising each *maqamaat* always comes full circle. Hareth Ben Hemman, the narrator, is on a journey, or in the bath, the marketplace, wherever. A man turns up and relieves people of their money, using some kind of pretext, but this is to be understood as something the man thinks is a fair reward to himself for the pleasure others have taken in his improvised poems; he then disappears, often before Hareth Ben Hemmam realizes it was Abu Zayd.

Abu Zayd's excuses for his behavior certainly do not fall on deaf ears, because "Art and reason — are dry in any season. And only the man who grabs for it, gets it — the man who misses, pisses" ("Kunst und Verstand — ist ein trockenes Land. Und nur wer langt, erlangt, — wer säumt, versäumt"). The complaints of an underfed artist from almost a thousand years ago resonate like a distant echo of the complaints heard today in this, the age of budget cuts throughout Europe, except that Abu Zayd's complaints are phrased much more artfully than the more prosaic ones of contemporary scribblers, who lack any feel for art in this regard — they are caught in the grip of the iron principle that "time is money," a phrase which, if I understand correctly, was coined here in the USA. But let him speak for himself, our colleague from Basra, the slyest of foxes, who has seen it all but is still, in spite of his enforced pilgrimages, homesick for his Serug:

> Abu Zayd spoke: "Will anyone here sell lamb — for an epigram? Or some thyme — for a rhyme? Or a piece of meat — for a hymn so sweet? Or a dish of grits — for bits of wit? Or a succulent peach — for a figure of speech? Or a spot of lard — for a thought that's hard? Or dates in a pile — for an elegant style?" And it

> pleased Abu Zayd to keep posing a question — not once did the answer bring on indigestion. [For:] "Wisdom and Art — need money to start — the world gives not a fart."[6]

You can see right away how much these lines must have appealed to Rückert's heart and mind. Rückert languished long as a writer and private scholar until 1826, when, at age thirty-eight, he became a professor of Oriental languages in Erlangen. Finally installed in office, he was now in a position to afford the textbooks, reference works, and dictionaries he so desperately needed.

Shortly before this, he had recomposed two lines from Hariri, most certainly in accord with his own views: "Installed in a stall is better / Than posted to an honorary post," or, more freely, "A place at the table / Beats an honorary label" ("Eine Stell' in dem Stall ist besser / Als Bestallung zur Ehrenstelle"). He hadn't originally intended to end up in an academic career. True enough, when he was twenty, he tried to enroll at the Academy of Oriental Studies in Vienna, but they turned him down because he was too old even then. Since the Academy placed great value on an oral command of Turkish, Persian (Farsi), and Arabic, only very young pupils were accepted, who were then called, appropriately, the *Sprachknaben* (language lads). As a matter of fact, Rückert hoped for a long time that he could live off his poetic works, a hope that has deceived many a budding artist.

According to Annemarie Schimmel in her 1966 edition of Hariri, it wasn't until Rückert was thirty that he finally came to Vienna and met Hammer-Purgstall, the man who introduced him to Persian (Farsi) and Arabic. Rückert was a genius at languages; within the short span of a few weeks, he could commit the basic elements of a foreign language to memory. He is reputed to have performed this amazing feat some fifty times in the course of his life. After his learning-intensive stay in Vienna, he returned to Coburg, where he pursued his Oriental studies for many years. Rückert's awful axiomatic pun about "phi*lo*logists [who] are in reality phi*lie*logists" ("Philologen, die so heißen, weil viele logen") doesn't really apply to Hammer-Purgstall, who was at the time the chief advocate of Oriental studies. Quite the contrary: his translations stuck too closely to the text so that reading them nowadays is an arduous task.

Rückert's translations are completely different. His linguistic powers are the nearest equivalent to the aesthetics being created in recent works by European authors from a Muslim background. According to Zafer Senocak, these writers, "through their use of ironic distance, are managing to reconnect the hidden strands of communication between cultures and are thereby allowing us to experience the many elements of the Other that have been repressed in our own selves." This is precisely the secret of Rückert's reconstructions: to reveal the Other in what is one's own, not in any attempt to appropriate and domesticate it — let alone dominate it — by means of linguistic transfer, but to make it perceptible, to make it into a real experience.

Just how conscious Rückert was of this aspect of his labors is evident in an ironic remark from his preface, "An den Leser" (To the Reader):

> Perhaps a word of apology is in order for what might be called "misguided Oriental taste," for its infinite number of wordplays, for its tinkering with sound, its rhyming prose, its exaggerated images, and the sophistry of its overly artificial mode of expression. But German readers are already used to so many different tastes that I believe I may offer them yet another, in all its pungency, without toning it down or blunting its sharp edge. My task it was to demonstrate that there are both meaning and wit in even this most extravagant of forms, and what is more, meaning and wit that could only be made apparent through this very form. There is not the least reason to fear that the example presented here might corrupt prevailing good taste. It will never occur to our own novelists and writers of novellas to attempt to exchange their present style, which they and their readers find so comfortable, for Hariri's, which offers its own set of difficulties.[7]

But *Die Makamen des Hariri* is filled with such refreshing moral pragmatism that modern-day students of Islam will most definitely not put them on their list of favorite books. It's true that the book's final chapter returns everything to the moral plane, thanks to a spontaneous though not very convincing conversion, but the gloriously articulate Abu Zayd is not just by chance the King of the Beggars, whose gathering place bears the name "Haven for Homeless Hawkers — the Retreat for Reposing Robbers" ("Port der unbehausten Hausierer, — der Ruheort der pausierenden Hantierer"), whereby *Hantierer* is a euphemism for "pickpocket."

Covered with scars from his life experiences, and showing not one iota of respect for the powers that be, Abu Zayd (and we can well imagine his creator in the Basra of a thousand years ago sharing his opinions) paints a picture of the human condition that to us looks very modern and enlightened:

> Whatever you may be, my friend, you're a child
> of the present and not of the past.
> Why do you lust for a noble line,
> Whose great repute your vices revile?
> Whoever may the father be, aristocrat alone is he
> Whose sisters Virtue's daughters be.[8]

Once again Senocak on the matter: "Reality is syncretistic. That is the reality of mulattos, of bastards." And he wonders "whether the Stylites of Identity, on either side of the cultural divide, will ever approve of this diversification of Identity." In my opinion, nothing is workable without a shifting of concepts, especially of the recently created sacred cow, the concept of identity, because its exclusivity has held us all captive for such a long time. In any event, Rückert was *verrückt* (crazy) and *ver-rückt* (relocated) enough to recognize the syncretistic nature of reality and to express it in his writings. In this respect, I count his translations as part and parcel of his literary production. In fact, I should like to go even further and assert that his translations are literature, in the sense of the worldly wisdom he propagated, i.e., "not as the wisdom of the world, but as that wisdom which instructs the world in all the many ways of living in it." He too lived in an age that was becoming more and more prudish, but in spite of that, he wrote his poetry (along with Hafiz and by means of him) with as great a dedication and power of articulation as anyone has ever possessed:

> Scold not the wine-bespotted drunkards, O sanctimonious one!
> No one's blaming you for the sins of another man.
>
> Whether pious I be or godless, go worry about yourself!
> When all has come and gone, we only reap what we have sown.[9]

McMaster University

Notes

1. This is a translation of Barbara Frischmuth's keynote address "Verrückt wie Rückert," given at the annual meeting of the German Studies Association in Seattle, Washington, on October 12, 1996. The speech was then published in German in *neue deutsche literatur* 45.513 (May-June 1997): 195–200. In preparing the translation, we have followed Rückert's spirit and lead in playing rather freely at times with his poetic and punning translations. We wish to thank Klaus Birkenhauer and Maqbool Aziz for their help.

2. Original quote:

> Wohl eine Zauberkraft muß sein in dem, woran
> Bezaubert eine Welt so hängt wie am Koran.
>
> Laß näher treten uns und zusehn zauberfrei,
> Ob es in Wahrheit nur ein böser Zauber sei.
>
> Ob nicht in dieser Form auch eine Offenbarung
> Des ewigen Geistes sei, für unsern Geist zur Nahrung.

3. Frischmuth is referring to *Die Sinnsprüche Omars des Zeltmachers* (1909, The Sayings of Omar the Tentmaker).

4. Zafer Senocak, "Wann ist der Fremde zu Hause?" *Atlas des tropischen Deutschland: Essays* (Berlin: Babel, berliner edition, 1993) 64–76.

5. Original quote:

> Ich bin der alte Wunderreich,
> Der Überall und Nirgendwo.
> Der Araber und Perser ruft
> Ob meinen Streichen ha und ho!

6. Original quote:

> Abu Seid sprach: "Verkauft man hier etwa Rahm — für ein Epigramm? Oder eine Schote — für eine Ode? — Oder ein Fleischgericht — für ein Preisgedicht? — Oder Grütze — für Witze? Oder eine Brotkrume — für eine Redeblume? — Oder einen Topf voll Schmalz — für einen Kopf voll Salz? — Oder einen Dattelstiel — für einen guten Stil?" — Und Abu Seid gefiel sich die Fragen zu mehren, — und ließ sich die Antworten nicht beschweren. [Denn:] "Weisheit und Kunst — ohne Geld ist umsonst — bei der Welt ohne Gunst."

7. Original quote:

Vielleicht aber sollte ich noch ein Wort sagen zur Entschuldigung der unendlichen Wort- und Klangspiele, der gereimten Prosa, der übertriebenen Bilder, des spitzfindigen überkünstlichen Ausdrucks, kurz alles dessen, was man den falschen orientalischen Geschmack nennen kann. Doch deutsche Leser sind schon an so viele Geschmäcke gewöhnt, dass ich ihnen auch diesen bieten zu dürfen glaube, und zwar in seiner ganzen Schärfe, ohne Milderung und Abstumpfung. Die Aufgabe war, zu zeigen, dass auch in dieser ausschweifenden Form ein Geist wohne, und zwar ein solcher, der eben nur in dieser Form sichtbar werden konnte. Am wenigsten ist zu befürchten, dass das hier gegebene Beispiel dem herrschenden guten Geschmack verderblich werde. Unsere Roman- und Novellenschreiber werden sich nicht einfallen lassen, ihre für sie und ihre Leser so bequeme Weise gegen die Harirische, die ihre Schwierigkeiten hat, vertauschen zu wollen.

8. Original quote:

Wer du immer seiest, o Mensch, du bist das Kind
Deines Heut allein, nicht deines Gestern.
Warum bist du lüstern nach erlauchtem Stamm,
Des Verdienst nur deine Laster lästern?
Hochgeboren ist, wer auch sein Vater sei,
Wer der Tugend Töchter hat zu Schwestern.

9. Original quote:

Schilt nicht weinbefleckte Zecher, du mit Reinheit angetan!
Denn es werden fremde Sünden dir ja nicht geschrieben an.

Ob ich fromm sei oder gottlos, geh und sorge für dich selbst!
Weil am Ende jeder nur, was er gesät hat, ernten kann.

The Art at the Heart of Barbara Frischmuth's *Hexenherz*

Gerald Chapple

Right from the start of her career in the late 1960s, Barbara Frischmuth has been a prolific writer. The thorough bibliography Maria Renhardt compiled in 1992 lists over four hundred items in an astonishing variety of genres, which bears eloquent testimony to her impressive œuvre.[1] Her productivity has continued unabated in the last decade. Following upon the publication of a spate of novels from 1986 to 1992, a volume of short prose, *Hexenherz: Erzählungen* (Heart of the Witch: Stories) appeared in 1994.[2] This was her first collection of short, solely creative prose works since the appearance of *Mörderische Märchen* (Deadly Fairy Tales) in 1989.

One of the most fascinating aspects of reading *Hexenherz* is to discover how Frischmuth has, with admirably delicate artistry, created a subtle unity of form and of theme that is not easily or consciously recognized. A versatile author, she is cleverly hiding much of her art. To find the nature of the artistic coherence, the unity at the heart of the volume — its heart, as it were — is the task I have set myself in this article. Oddly enough, there is virtually no examination of this or any other aspect of Frischmuth's craft in this group of stories or, for that matter, in any of her collections of her prose works. This is a fertile field awaiting discovery, for she has shown herself to be a superb artist in a number of forms and styles.

A general comparison of *Hexenherz* to her earlier prose collections will help to establish the literary context within which I will focus on the texts. These collections were almost all miscellaneous ones, composed of many kinds of short prose. The main ones are *Rückkehr zum vorläufigen Ausgangspunkt* (1973, Return to the Preliminary Starting Point); *Traumgrenze* (1986, Borderland of Dream), and *Wassermänner: Lesestücke aus Seen, Wüsten und Wohnzimmern* (1991, Aquarii: Short Pieces about Lakes, Deserts, and Living Rooms), which features essayistic works, poems, and autobiographical sketches. In 1992, the second printing of *Mörderische Märchen* appeared with the subtitle *und andere Erzählungen* (and Other Stories), showing that it too was a loose collection made up either of small groups of related narrative texts or of unrelated stories, many of which had appeared previously. Most closely resembling *Hexenherz* was *Haschen nach Wind* (1974, *Chasing after the Wind*, 1996) because of the tight thematic focus on the similar problems facing the four heroines in each of the four stories.[3] The probing, analytical stories are of medium length, which also gives the book a unity not found in any other prose collection Frischmuth has written up to 1994. Where does *Hexenherz* stand with respect to its artistic skill and unity? Between *Haschen nach Wind* and all the others, although it is nearer to the former in spite of the fact that its stories are not as closely matched as in the earlier book. It differs more radically from the other earlier collections of shorter prose because the arrangement and sequencing of the stories are more structured. But since these formal differences are not readily apparent, I will explore the art of its composition.

If, as yet, no one has evaluated the book's formal artistry, there has also been no study of the book's themes. One critic, in an otherwise positive review, was outspoken about the lack of a theme: "These are simple, often terse stories that in the final analysis have 'searching' as their theme. The search for sense, for love, for recognition — but maybe too the author's search for a real theme."[4] Actually, it was this charge that inspired the purpose of the present article: to present the unifying features in the book — thematic, formal, or otherwise — in order to see if that claim could be refuted. Surely the title was a clue; after all, I could not think of one work of Barbara Frischmuth's where the title did not suit the work, so the question as to whether *Hexenherz* is an egregious case or not had to be investigated and answered. The second issue of theme and title was now coupled with the larger concern of formal structure in order to explore her art and craft in composing the collection as a whole.

How have other reviewers and critics responded to *Hexenherz*? Of the nine further reviews I have consulted, almost all are favorable. Individual stories have received particular praise, especially the concluding story, "Das Lachen des Dalai Lama" (The Laughter of the Dalai Lama), with "Lebensgeschichte" (Life Story) a close second. Many acknowledge, even admire, Frischmuth's skill in portraying women in so great a variety of ages, experiences, and relationships. Others have been attracted to her mastery of oblique, often unsettling narrative techniques or to her humor. With regard to genre, on which critical opinions were mixed, the volume's subtitle, *Erzählungen,* has been seen as not entirely accurate because several texts seem to be brief or undramatic, often "simply" portraits. But stories? Three or four, says Herbert Lodron, the others are off-beat prose sketches *(Prosaskizzen),* an opinion seconded by Reinhold Tauber.[5] Susan L. Cocalis rightly pointed out that there is no great reliance on traditional plot construction,[6] which could support an argument for "Prose Writings," or simply *Prosa*, as a more fitting subtitle.

At this point we should note a curious minor discrepancy regarding the number of stories in the book in case it causes confusion. The dust jacket mentions fourteen, which is one too many.[7] Frischmuth originally wanted to include a fourteenth story but retracted it a short time before publication. A few reviewers were led astray by this error and forgot to count the actual number. Only one, Otto F. Beer, connected the symbolism of the unlucky number with the book's theme.[8] (The 1990 novel *Einander Kind* [One Another's Child] had twelve chapters followed by a long concluding one, but the symbolism of bad luck did not apply in that case.) We will return to this point at the conclusion of this article; for now, it is enough to take Beer's point that the number thirteen is bound to be significant in a book entitled *Hexenherz*.

The emphasis here is on a structural pattern: that the book is divided in two by the seventh story, the one in the center, and most of the twelve stories are linked thematically into pairs, each pair consisting of one story before the central tale and one after it. There is no attempt to make a thorough analysis; rather, I want to present just enough summary, interpretive material, and observations to highlight those features that show parallels, intensifications, variations, echoes among the stories. The thirteen of these will be analyzed in pairs. A Roman numeral has been assigned to each story to identify them quickly without having to repeat titles unduly; the reader is therefore asked to refer back to the following chart frequently. The number of pages is included after the translated title to indicate the relative length of the stories. Following this discussion, the question of the title and thematic unity will be addressed.

A I.	Grundwasserfisch (Groundwater Fish, 13)	**XIII.**	Das Lachen des Dalai Lama (The Laughter of the Dalai Lama, 13)
B II.	Lebensgeschichte (Life Story, 36)	**XII.**	Damenessen (Ladies' Luncheon, 15)
C III.	Posaune im Ohr (Trumpet in the Ear, 6)	**XI.**	Düfte, Nacht (Scents, Nighttime, 12)
D IV.	Schattenspiel (Shadow Play, 12)	**X.**	Mutter, Marina, Marietta . . . (Mother, Marina, . . . , 7)

E V.	Die Kränkung (The Insult, 15)	**IX.**	Hexenherz (Heart of the Witch, 8)
F VI.	Salon Ramona (Salon Ramona, 9)	**VIII.**	Herzsprung (Cracked Heart, 15)
		VII.	Wild-Frau (Witch of the Wildwood, 9)

A.I. "Grundwasserfisch" is a psychological portrayal of a solitary woman, a one-time swindler's moll mysteriously persecuted by unexplained letters coming to her from out of her past. She is looking for a little "Eden" (7), a restored paradise where she can be safe from her shady past, but here, as so often, a lost paradise is a counter for lost innocence and guilt. While taking care of a house and garden for a vacationing family, she seems at first to have regained paradise. But then she experiences two shocks when the house seems to be lifted off its foundations. She immediately wants to escape, to hide in the sub-basement of the house, to go underwater, where she can be silent in a silent world, like a fish, for the woman is not a talker but an almost voiceless writer, a compulsive note-taker constantly registering her psychic state and feelings. The title is a symbol both of the deepest reaches of her self and of her desire to be safe from the fear of betrayal. The desire for security, protection, and shelter is clearly deep-rooted — the other side of her anxiety.

Is an unconscious death wish also feeding that anxiety? The imagery of the fish directs us to a downward pull in her psyche, to a longing for introversion. There is much that is elemental in the story, and it is no wonder that the water imagery predominates. The constant rain, her fear of too much groundwater accumulating, her feeling in the morning that she is like a drowning person struggling through water up to the sun (11) — all this points to water being used here as a traditional symbol of the unconscious. As to the garden image, death is lurking in it in the form of a cat that ominously eats a perky wagtail. All she can do to try to survive is to identify with a fish that is not in a normal body of water but in an underground, sunless world. What Frischmuth seems to be saying is that the woman is trapped inside herself and condemned to live with her ineradicable fear.

A.XIII. In "Dalai Lama," the setting shifts from a suburban house in Vienna to a scene in its subway system, where the vague sense of danger felt in A.I has turned into a brutally real threat that is fatal. It likewise has one central character, also a lone woman, who drifts through memory in one long monologue "as she lay dying," to paraphrase Faulkner. She too is below ground, in the underground, after trying to stop a young Turk from being beaten up by skinheads. She reviews much of her recent life as if viewing a film, as Angelika Griebner observed.[9] Other characters are presented through her flashbacks, until she focuses on the Dalai Lama when death approaches at the end. The play of light and darkness, together with the hallucinatory recollection of the Dalai Lama, introduce a mystic sense of inner illumination as death overtakes her. It is all the more intimate for being narrated in part in the first person, who is for once in the collection *not* a thinly veiled author (which she is in II, III, V, and XII). Doris Metz describes the story — her favorite by a wide margin — as "an unsparing countdown" ("ein schonungsloser Count-Down") that leaves the reader no place to hide.[10] In this moving portrait of the senseless death of a Good Samaritan, Frischmuth's narrative stance is more aggressive than ever before, in what is arguably her best story to date.

This story has the widest horizon of all and is the only one to include a metaphysical theme. It stares the process of dying right in the eye, during which the Viennese lady is guided by Eastern spirituality (by *The Tibetan Book of the Dead* [1400 A.D.; trans. into English, 1927] and the Dalai Lama), most poignantly at the very end when all that her senses can perceive is the laughter of the Dalai Lama. It is also the only story to reach beyond Austria to another culture, but the color symbolism shows how this is in part ironic because the woman's son's Nazi insignia are mirrored in the colors red, white, and black mentioned in one of the quotations from the Tibetan text (171). What began with the brutally physical reality of the narrator's agonized suffering turns toward the comforting, mystical wisdom of the East at the end. A painful, yet hopeful narrative, a powerful curtain closer, and a brilliant choice to end the collection.

This pair of stories is the only one to have stories of equal length, and it forms the "bookends" to *Hexenherz*. Two noteworthy connections: (1) the psychology of dread and the fear of death in the first story become graphically and concretely realized in the second; (2) the heroine of the first story only *wishes* to hide in the sub-basement; in XIII, the story takes place underground involuntarily.

B.II. The first word of Edith "Dittl" Danner's "Life Story" is "she," which virtually sums up in three letters the focus of this text. Since this story is the longest by far in the book, it will receive correspondingly lengthier treatment here.

The story takes its origin from a true event: "Dittl," or whatever her name really was, actually appeared one day at Frischmuth's door wanting to recount her life story (about half of the texts in the book have a decidedly autobiographical origin). Since Dittl was eighty-four and had lived through much of this century, the story not only covers but in great measure takes its life from the reciprocal interaction of personal history with much of the political and social history of twentieth-century Austria (*Zeitgeschichte* is a more useful term, "the history of that period"). Dittl Danner came to bear witness; she was there. The most striking, and violent, instance of this intertwining she reports is her being raped on March 13, 1938. The date is deliberately mentioned: it was the day after the Nazis marched into Austria to "rape" the country, and as if to emphasize her decency, this brutal act took place after she had helped someone escape across the border (41). The story presents the political realities of the time from the humble standpoint of a feisty servant, nanny, cook, mother, and survivor, and she earns our sympathy when we read about her feelings: "I feel dizzy when I look into the gaping jaws of the past" ("Mir schwindelt, wenn ich der Vergangenheit in den Rachen schau," 21). Likewise, we empathize when we hear how cruel Dittl's rich and adventurous personal life has been, the key to it being perhaps the confession about her mother: "She gave me life and often took it away from me" ("Sie hat mir das Leben gegeben und es oftmals genommen," 37).

At the same time, the developing relationship between the writer (in the story) and the narrating heroine gives the story an added dimension. Does the writer — a thinly veiled Barbara Frischmuth — strike us as two-dimensional next to Dittl's full eighty-four years? The criticism may apply at best to the beginning of the story, where she seems to be a mere prop, a foil to the main character, but as the story progresses, the narrator's ambivalence gives way to impatience and fascination, and she goes so far as to dream about their relationship. This is where "witchcraft" enters the story, because, in the narrator-writer's dream, Dittl makes the astonishing claim that she helped complete a novel after its author died.

The author's name is unclear — Schäzler? Witzler? Later on, the narrator is equally unclear as to whether she dreamed about that nameless well-known writer or whether Dittl even mentioned his name beforehand, in real life. Then Dittl says, yes, she knew him and his name was Schnitzler! A fine in-joke, given Schnitzler's knowledge and portrayals of the workings of the unconscious.

Two further aspects of the episode are worth noting. One, the narrator refuses to follow up the mysterious coincidence: "Leave to the dream what belongs to the dream, I said to myself. The business of remembering is a treacherous affair" ("Laß dem Traum, was des Traumes ist, sagte ich mir. Das mit der Erinnerung ist eine trügerische Sache," 48). Two, Dittl may have said she finished a novel in the writer's dream, but, ironically, she does not give the narrator enough material for *her* to finish writing up her story because Dittl disappears from the scene as mysteriously as she had arrived. As the work stands, even without the rounding off of her story, Lodron's categorization of it as a piece of oral history is perfectly accurate.[11]

B.XII. The structure of "Damenessen" is unusual in that it is divided into two halves. The first describes another Frischmuth-style narrator who is visiting Berlin on a reading tour, and the second half takes her back to the Salzkammergut, where she, as the youngest member, attends an annual ladies' luncheon made up entirely of aged widows. The first half may seem lightweight next to all the actors and activity at the luncheon (which spectacularly features a green mamba on the table at the end of the meal). Almost all that happens is that the narrator has to solve a very personal problem: she badly needs a washroom, which she eventually finds, to her great relief. Franz Haas, in an otherwise critical review, comments that this is one of the most exquisitely comic versions of a subject that almost never receives such extensive treatment in good literature (and it is very different from Joyce's Molly Bloom).[12] Others have been puzzled by the split format, wondering what holds the work together. This is not an easy question to answer, but the personality of the author and the essential function of the digestive tract do provide some unity as "Damenessen" moves from the most private to a very public and social setting. The self-ironic author of the first half of the story refrains from satire or caricature in the second, describing the dining scene with humor, combining a good selection of sharply observed physical detail with a fine ear for the characters' significant choice of words.

Instead of one long story about a single unsung hero à la Dittl, we are presented with a whole series of cameo-sized portraits of once-famous ladies now about Dittl's age; altogether, they are the only representatives of that age group in the book. The final irony of the story plays with the theme of the articulate artist: in contrast to Dittl, whose long, but unartfully eloquent story fascinates both listener and reader, the more sophisticated writer in "Damenessen" is chided by her hostess on the way out for not speaking up at all during the luncheon conversation.

C.III. The central figure of "Posaune im Ohr" is a man who is not as old as Dittl or the ladies in XII, but he is a character in his own right. Although he lost his hearing thirteen years earlier, he *can* hear, thanks to an operation and a hearing aid, and he is crusty enough to pick his times to hear to suit himself. The joke at the end is that neither he without his hearing aid, nor the narrator can tell whether he is playing his trumpet in tune.[13] The text sketches a portrait, not a story, and once again, a Frischmuth-like figure is the sketcher, who ceremoniously uses the outhouse at the beginning of the story, thereby setting up the point of the whole first half of XII. The story's point: adversity has made the central figure into a new man, or has "brought to light the man hidden within him" ("den . . . in ihm verborgenen Menschen zum Vorschein gebracht," 57). The book's motif of a person's secret power coming to the surface is the important point in a story that may at first blush seem not to fit. The protagonist is also the wrong sex for a witch, but he certainly has something of the charming old devil in him. If Frischmuth can include a (female) cat (in IV), then why not a male devil too?

Structurally, the unnamed hero is the male counterpart to the heroine of the preceding text who was (self-)portrayed at much greater length; he too is independent, a tough survivor whose unpolished musical art as practiced in the local band can be seen as a rough counterpart to Dittl's cleverly composed bouquets. In a way, "Posaune im Ohr" functions as the missing ending to II.

C.XI. "Düfte, Nacht" is another text that is more of a sketch than a tale, although it is rather long by the book's standards. The low-grade war of irritation that characterizes the life of the married couple generates more tension than in III. The "mixed couple" forms one of Frischmuth's favorite character groupings, a concept that was the subject of a short essay from 1989.[14] The story describes the tensions between the two that result in the subtle struggles and games played out between her, an asthmatic, and him, a person almost blind. At the end, she dreams of two roses she wants him to give her, and although she knows he never will, she insists on waiting instead of simply buying them herself. Her dreams of scented flowers go up in smoke one night, so to speak, when she finds her husband out on the balcony, having a cigarette for the first time in years. He had literally and figuratively stirred up a hornets' nest that afternoon, leading to his being stung, in the hope of helping his eyesight, or so he says. The ironic ending: one night, when she wakes up from a voluptuous dream about a rose, she is confronted by her husband's relapse into smoking after many years, but he stops right away, not because it sets off his wife's asthma, but because his eyes can't stand the smoke. So the story concludes with Frischmuth's delightful twist on Jerome Kern's old hit, "Smoke Gets in Your Eyes."

Once again, nature is a major part of the setting, and gardening — a passion of the author's and the heroine's — is both the chief occupation of the unnamed central figure and a major source of metaphor. On the one hand, the heroine has to breathe in good air as a health measure, which is underlined by the repetition of the first sentence of the text (135, 141). Her desire to breathe, in spite of her condition, is accentuated by the scent of the roses she constantly inhales, in a rhythm that this one-time smoker used to follow when smoking, "except that this scent flowed in right down to her nipples" ("nur daß dieser Duft bis in ihre Brustspitzen drang," 137). It is a sensuous experience, perhaps the last she has left in her now loveless life, which once had more mutual passion (138). He was once ambitious, arrogant, and famous, but he is now a bitter old man. Their marriage has become more of a desert than a rose garden, a place of fighting rather than of the erotic play she now can only dream of. The smoke at the end is the perfect symbolic enemy of the life-giving air that she needs and of the scent of the roses she loves. The concluding irony and the realization that the husband's little rebellion born of frustration has failed are both sad, at best bittersweet. On the whole, a mixed story, more complex than the snapshot of the bachelor in III.

D.IV. "Schattenspiel," the most literary story of the collection, is written in the spirit of E. T. A. Hoffmann, a favorite author of Frischmuth's. The epigraph from Hoffmann's novel *Lebensansichten des Katers Murr* (1820–22; *The Life and Opinions of Kater Murr,* 1969) clearly signals the source and inspiration for a narrating cat, who this time is a pseudo-aristocratic female named Plume. There is a hint of a French pun in that name, and the four or five good puns in the story, along with the cat's topsy-turvy perspective, reinforce the comic mode of the whole story. Plume immediately establishes the atmosphere of the Baroque theater when she asks rhetorically, "What is the world?" ("Was ist die Welt?" 60) and then elaborates her world view in pompous, old-fashioned, self-centered language. The Baroque is everywhere, in the little castle they live in, in the playing out of roles, in Plume's self-inflating portrait of herself, and in her descriptions of the world around her. The title reinforces the sense of a false, theatrical reality because it refers to the shadow theater that Plume's master and mistress stage for their aristocratic hostess in the little Baroque castle where they are guests.

There are two ways that a serious, less playful reality enters Plume's life as she goes about her adventures. The "shadowy" background figures of the cat's mistress and master are lightly sketched in, but we hear just enough about how Plume's mistress was persecuted by the Nazis to be reminded that all is not play or play-acting — the author has once again based some aspects of the human characters on real persons. Second, Plume herself is threatened by the bigger "country" cats of the village, but she uses her wits to avoid an unequal cat fight and ultimately controls them by hitting upon a stratagem: "I was so overwhelmed by my idea that I rolled around in the grass with wild abandon. Only ideas make life worth living" ("Ich war so überwältigt von meiner Idee, daß ich mich hemmungslos im Gras wälzte. Nur Ideen machen das Leben lebenswert," 70). This is typical of Plume's language and provides an example of how Frischmuth exploits the comic discrepancy between animal behavior and human thinking.

The combination of sophisticated and fanciful humor in "Schattenspiel" makes it the most comic story in the book until this point. Here, it's a cat's world, not a dog's. Does it belong in this collection? Yes. After all, every witch must have her cat, and *Hexenherz* has its fair share.

D.X. A different type of comedy informs the tenth story. "Mutter, Marina, Marietta . . ." is another of Frischmuth's prose texts that are so strong on character portraiture that they can afford virtually to ignore the requirements of plot. The realistic text is often ribald in its concern with sex, which is one of its main themes and sources of humor. Luise, the heroine, has reached the boy-crazy stage and is trying to figure out sex and how she can attract her young neighbor Rainer up to her room. Much of the hilarious fun in the opening scene involves confusion about the number of penises on a man she once saw, giving ample opportunity for the occurrence of the word *Schwanz* in its double meaning as "tail" and "prick." Her chief fantasy is to have her pet cats bring her the two "extra" penises, although she can't even remember who the man was. The interest in anatomy and amorous relationships is sustained throughout and is at times almost bawdy (television pornography makes an important appearance). This function is absolutely essential to the story because sex is seen from the perspective of an inquiring young mind. The animal imagery is carried through to a light, comic ending, where Luise and her sisters plop themselves down in front of the television like "a couple of old rhinoceroses" ("die zwei alten Nashörner," 134).

Luise's two companions play the role of mute confidantes, but the real "tomcat" is her father, who divorced her mother because of another woman and has probably had an affair with one of Luise's aunts. Luise finds this to be yet another piece in the puzzle that is sex, eros, and marriage. She does reveal a potentially menacing aspect when she keeps talking, albeit innocently and unrealistically, about castrating the strange man, and if the author is hinting at witchlike qualities here, there are also frequent occurrences of the magic number three: the three *Schwänze*, her father's three lovers, the three women in the story's title, which contains but three words, all beginning with the letter *m*. Less speculative is the fact that Luise is just starting to discover her sexuality and her own identity — she doesn't want to be called "Loisi" anymore (128) and wants her breasts to start growing (131). But the reader smiles when Luise is so intent on watching an episode in a television series starring Rainer's (also divorced) mother (who has huge breasts), because that is not going to teach her what sex really is (or what life is, for that matter) any more than the pornographic movies will.

The cats are the obvious connecting link between the stories in this pair (elsewhere in the book they are mentioned only a few times in passing). A second parallel is the use of humor; in fact, these are the two funniest stories in the book, but the comic effects of the fantastic world of Plume and her theatrical language stand in contrast to the type of comedy inherent in the more earthbound and problematic reality of a prepubescent teenage girl.

E.V. Martha, the woman insulted in "Die Kränkung," is one of the many vulnerable women in the collection. But she gains satisfaction in the end when the vulgar and arrogant man who had publicly humiliated her by mimicking her sexual features gets tartar sauce all over his hand when he tries to pat her behind.

The story's fine psychological portrait of Martha is one of its great strengths (another is the cameo role played by her irrepressibly funny friend Kata Kisch). It is a story of slow and painful self-analysis. Her insecure personality compounds the problem: if she is easy to insult, she is also difficult to compliment. Worrying about the insult leads her to realize that she and her husband, Bruno, have drifted apart (79) and to see that the innocence, the "paradise" she has lost — a key metaphor (86) — has nevertheless brought her some hard-won knowledge of the world's cruelty and cynicism. She has learned to see differently, like the spider, the chief metaphor in the story, who stays on the wall and does nothing but watch, as if it were learning to see. This image expands a major theme of the story, which is indeed related to Robert Burns's oft-reiterated gift of learning to "see yourself as others see you." In short, insult must lead to insight, and it does. And to action: the watching and waiting spider dies just as Martha learns to move from passive watching — her bovine eyes are mentioned four times — to active confrontation when she challenges her antagonist at the end of the story, an unexpected result of his crude behavior.

E.IX. Perhaps surprisingly, one of the briefest stories in *Hexenherz* is the eponymous "Hexenherz," and it is the first of two featuring children. Sabina is the central figure, who, like the much older and married Martha, is just beginning to learn who she is and what powers she has to master life, although she is still almost a child, a young teenager. The rather brief text revolves around the following incident: sibling squabbles give way to the brother's astonished admiration for his sister when she "divines" where his misplaced wallet is. Her incredulous brother asks if she has second sight, then assumes that she simply made a lucky guess. But the reader is told what her brother cannot know: that she has indeed got the power of mind to make an informed guess and that nobody can look into her head, least of all her brother. She has renounced television (unlike the younger and less wise Luise in X) and is learning to do what the motto to E. M. Forster's novel *Howards End* (1921) urged us to do: Only connect! That is why the story's triumphant concluding line tells that her confidence is rising with her knowledge: "And she would soon see considerably more connections than anybody else" ("Und bald schon würde sie wesentlich mehr Zusammenhänge kennen als alle anderen," 127).

Sabina's development from initial feelings of fear and insecurity to new-found confidence and control marks the course of the text's plot line. At the beginning of the story, she feels vulnerable and terrified when, with her heart beating wildly, she goes down into the spooky cellar, needing her hostile brother to help her and give her strength. As Sabina discovers her mysterious powers, Frischmuth combines the themes of heart, sight, and growth in a few short lines: "Something inside her took shape; it was like a strengthening of her heart. She sensed how energy was flowing into her fingers. The most important thing was to pay attention, to see what others didn't see" (125).[15] This is the third and last time the key word "heart" occurs in the story, and this time it is in a central passage.

Even though Sabina is just starting out in life, this is still much more than Martha (in V) would ever see. This, the second, story of the pair, expands on aspects of Martha's earlier problems even though it is shorter. This is confirmed by the more varied animal imagery. Martha identified with the spider, taking on its ability to watch and see. Sabina, at the start, is surrounded by spiders, plus millipedes and slugs, only to have these more primitive forms gradually replaced by a crow in the garden with which she feels a mysterious and silent kinship. A black messenger from a dark, mysterious world? A counterpart to Wotan's raven? As Sabina learns to apply her new-found mysterious power, she becomes the nearest thing to a witch figure in the whole book — Barbara Frischmuth's particular kind of "witch," one without a broomstick, but with a heart, as the text insists.[16] As in Martha's story, "Hexenherz" is also about ways of seeing, but Sabina grows beyond personal insight to possessing a sort of second sight, at the very least metaphorically, but as so often, Frischmuth likes to leave questions about the existence of mysterious powers slightly open. As a result, "Hexenherz" moves *Hexenherz* beyond personal psychology to flirt with parapsychology.

F.VI. What makes "Salon Ramona" something more meaningful than the "hairdresser's quotidian gossip" ("Alltagsgeschwätz einer Frisöse") that Angelika Griebner claimed it was?[17] The short answer is: the ending. But how does Frischmuth get there? The realistic setting in a hair salon is indeed completely ordinary, except for the chaos caused by the owner's children and pets. At the beginning, the female first-person narrator reports this with humor and verisimilitude, but this time "Barbara

Frischmuth" is drawn into the story as one of Frau Ramona's customers, and the chaotic activity she is initially submitted to gives way to an increasing seriousness in the last third of the story. In a barely interrupted monologue, Frau Ramona tells of a holiday in a small village on a lake in the mountains that ended tragically when one of the participants at an evening's drinking party drowns. Or so it seemed; he actually died of a hcart attack. A surprising change of direction in the next and last paragraph gives the text a powerful twist at the end: the narrator once knew the dead man quite well. This upsetting conclusion destroys what should have been an innocuous visit to Salon Ramona: "His death came as a great shock to me" ("Sein Tod empörte mich zutiefst," 95).[18] We can now add the listener in the story to the list of women in the book who experience an unexpected, often life-changing event; mere gossip results in unexpected tragedy for her. Frau Ramona's story is not the sort of hairdresser's chitchat it was made out to be. Perhaps the impact at the end is greater because the length of the text is so short, in fact the shortest in the book.

F.VIII. Marianne Andergast, the heroine of "Herzsprung," is a middle-aged divorcée with cardiac problems, hence the title. The story opens with her being hit by a car, which she manages to survive, but the irony of the ending is that she dies from the consequences of a chance meeting with her husband, whom she had not seen in fifteen years: in spite of her heart problems she insists on an afternoon of love-making, which proves fatal. The whole story is a struggle with fate — the word recurs throughout the story — that starts right with the azure-blue color of the car that knocks her over; does the color suggestively point toward heaven and a higher force? She interprets the accident as a danger sign, reminding herself that "fate doesn't give too many warnings. The next time, it will strike" ("Öfter winkt das Schicksal nicht, beim nächsten Mal schlägt es zu," 117). And strike it does. Frischmuth portrays the psychology of a feisty woman looking back on her life, especially her once very active sex life, which is still alive in her dreams and desires. For although her heart was fatally flawed, she really did have one, was emotionally alive, and had vivid erotic dreams, which made the deadly outcome of the encounter with her husband totally credible. Still, her heart remained a mystery to her in that she never could figure out how she was able simply to pick up and leave her husband fifteen years earlier (113).

Nomen est omen — the proverb alerts us to a significant irony, the name "Ander-gast" (another/second guest), which becomes apparent during the comic penultimate scene in the hair salon when Marianne sees her double in the mirror: her husband's *second* Frau Andergast. At this point, the reader might recall the superstition that if you see your double, your death is imminent; this becomes tragically realized in the story's terse concluding sentence announcing her death. Unlike her first brush with death caused by the azure-blue Volvo, this fateful meeting with her husband and his "duplicate" wife is fatal.

Four obvious similarities connect the two stories in this pair: both involve hair salons and the lake-in-the-mountain scenery of the Salzkammergut, and both end with unexpected heart attacks and strong punch lines. The second of the two stories is more elaborate, more focused on the heroine, whose death is not just simply related by a Frau Ramona-type character in the story.

VII. "Wild-Frau" stands alone, "unpaired," in the book's structural pattern, emphasizing the central role it plays in the disposition of the whole. There might be some difficulty in discerning the story's central function because, for one thing, the title story of the book is in ninth place and, for another, a second potential candidate for the position of key story is "Herzsprung" (number eight), not only because it has the word "heart" in the title. It will take a somewhat longer analysis to build a case for the work's central position and, simultaneously, to throw light on the work as a fine example of Frischmuth's narrative artistry at the heart of the book.

The title provides the main clue: *Wild* in its many associations – *wild* as in "out of control," "uninhibited"; *Wild* as in game (wild animals); and the German phrase for a common-law marriage, *eine wilde Ehe*. Hermann Paul's *Deutsches Wörterbuch* (1992, German Dictionary) has this explanation for *wild*: "Figures in popular belief are called *wilder Mann*, *wildes Weib* because they are thought of as living outside the sphere of human culture."[19] Frischmuth's exact formulation," Wild-Frau," would seem to be original; semantically, she makes use of all the connotations of *wild.*[20] Her twist is that the "witch of the wildwood" stalks the hunter she desires as if he were her prey, so that the motif of "the huntsman hunted" is a major irony of the story, one which the animal imagery appropriately elaborates. Initially, she treats him like a diamond in the rough, mentally constructing a scientist out of a village farmer. But she is hunting him not only to make love to him — the descriptions of which are the most graphic in a book depicting a number of libidinous women —

but even more, to domesticate him (the nuance of *wilde Ehe* surfaces at this point). Early on, it becomes clear that this couple is a case of attracting opposites, another one of Barbara Frischmuth's "mixed pairs."

The third and last section of the story tells of her increasing disillusionment with their lovemaking, and ultimately with the relationship. The climactic questions she asks herself one morning reveal her uncertainty: "She loved her secret huntsman — would she always love him? The real question was, would she be able to love him even more? Or only love him less?" ("Sie liebte den heimlichen Jäger, würde sie ihn immer lieben? Die Frage war vielmehr, würde sie ihn noch mehr lieben können? Oder nur noch weniger?" 21; 103). The irony of their relationship and the growing tension caused by their mutual misunderstanding lead to a seemingly ambiguous ending, although she literally and symbolically closes the door after/on him as a final gesture. The last paragraph focuses on the hunter, not the title figure: "He had loved a will o' the wisp, gone astray and stumbled. Tripped and fallen into the grip of habit. But he still didn't know he'd fallen prey to his fate" ("Er hatte einen Nebelstreif geliebt, war vom Weg abgekommen und gestolpert. Mitten hinein in die Gewohnheit. Er wußte nur noch nicht, daß er abgestürzt war," 22; 104).[21] He was trapped but didn't know it, but a trickier question here is, was she trapped too, and did she know it? Is she, ironically, a victim — the second — of her own dangerous desire?

Three reviewers see the affair as ending but are divided as to the cause. Was it a disenchanting experience once desire was sated, as Lodron says, or was it the result of "erotic sensations turning into pure habit" ("Die erotischen Sensationen [werden] zur reinen Gewohnheit"), as Ingeborg Sperl writes?[22] Beer sees her as an exploitive witch-figure who uses the hunter for her sexual pleasure and then "drops him without giving it a second thought" ("ihn . . . bedenkenlos abhängt").[23] There may be some misreading here, but what is underplayed is a consideration of how myth plays a significant role. The ending might be less ambiguous if we turn to the story's underpinning in legend.

Only one passage gives information about the mythic substratum to the events of the tale:

> And as for her, she could still hear, echoing in her ears, fragments of the tales the villagers told their children about the mysterious huntsmen of legend and about the tree nymphs who, as will o' the wisps, led

> them astray by mixing up the trails. It was surely in those legends that the ancient pattern of their desire could be found: of her desire to overpower him, and of his to let himself be overpowered. (19)[24]

One of the salient features of Frischmuth's style is her fondness for suddenly revealing a text's hidden depth, a deeper layer of reality, in an inserted passage like the one above. On this, the most profound, mythic level, Frischmuth's "Wild-Frau" belongs to a long line of related sirens, Loreleis, and succubuses of which her central figure is the present-day avatar. After all, the hapless hunter was "the first man she'd ever knowingly seduced, with deliberate intent, in fact" ("Der erste Mann, den sie wissentlich, ja geradezu vorsätzlich verführt hatte," 16; 96). Of course, she "leads him astray," as do all the others, but she does not escape unscathed. Both have fallen victim to desire in different ways. The theme of "the hunter hunted" works on a second level: as *Wild*-Frau she is the "wild-game-woman" hunted down by her own desire. The opening words summed up the relationship perfectly: "It had been an insane love affair" ("Es war eine verrückte Liebe gewesen," 16; 96).

There may be some clues in the title, "Wild-Frau." The grammatical form, two nouns connected by a hyphen, points backward in time, suggesting something old-fashioned, ancient. Then, too, the heroine is obviously a *Frau* and has a "wild" passion for her huntsman, but is she also *Wild,* a noun, an animal to be hunted herself, "fair game," as was suggested above? I think so. Whether as legendary will o' the wisp or as woman, she has a heart and follows it, but ultimately into doubt ("would she always love him?"). Beer was right to find erotic witchcraft at work here, but there is more to it. Frischmuth's irony gives a twist to the ancient legends by creating a "witch" who is both contemporary and human, one who suffers precisely because she does have a heart.

A final reinforcing connection: the story's title echoes the title of the volume, and not only as a result of its double-nouned grammatical form. The parallel between book title and central story yields more arguments for the central importance of "Wild-Frau" rather than the story "Hexenherz." The "witch of the wildwood" is an active character, a deliberate seductress; only Marianne (in VIII) is as sexually aggressive. Sabina (in the title story) and Luise (in the following one) are too young to be interesting in the same way, so they are left to speculate and fantasize. "Wild-Frau," the (lucky?) seventh story in the middle of thirteen chapters, is far more substantial than the title story and its plot more developed and deepened through myth. For these reasons, it takes pride of place as the hidden heart of the volume.

To sum up the results of the preceding analysis: it suggests a basic pattern to the linear order of the chapters of 6 + 1 + 6 = 13, with stories in the two groups of six forming pairs related by different degrees of similarity, giving (6 x 2) + 1 = 13.[25] As the stories passed in review, the reader may have noted a general trend: those found in the second half of the book often re-present the same themes and similar characters from the "mated" story in the first half of the book, but now with more complexity, caused either by its theme, its narrative subtleties, or simply by an increase in the number of characters. This pattern is not as pronounced as the one proposed and was therefore not explored, to help keep the argument focused. Thirteen chapters, we might recall from the beginning of this article, was not the number originally foreseen, which was fourteen.[26] The missing story removed just prior to publication — the change that was not reflected on the book's dust jacket — was about a family member. If Frischmuth were to include a story centered around a close personal relationship, then at least one formal and technical difficulty she would face is striking: where would she put it? At the beginning, middle, or end? Then, too, Dittl's disproportionately long oral autobiography would be difficult to balance out, or at least be a hard act to follow, if only by virtue of its sheer mass. But it is difficult to speculate persuasively about rearranging the thirteen stories in order to accommodate a possible addition, which was in any case rejected.

A quick glance at two other works might clarify some minor points regarding the formal structure. At the beginning of this article, we found that the stories and themes in volumes of Frischmuth's shorter prose works are seldom related to each other, sometimes slightly, usually not at all. The exception, *Haschen nach Wind*, is closely centered on women's problems, an economical and focusing effect enhanced by the fact that there are only four medium-length stories in the book. What Frischmuth does in *Hexenherz* is somewhere in the middle. She differentiates many more themes, problems, and characters, which also increased the number of texts and perhaps also played a role in keeping all but one rather short. At the same time, she provides unity by featuring women protagonists almost exclusively and by the ways spelled out above. She chose as well *not* to repeat a highly structured pattern like the one she had invented for her novel *Einander Kind*, written in 1990, just four years earlier. There the chapters followed a system more rigid than in any of her other prose works: a set sequence of three chapters, each with a different focusing figure, was repeated four times, then a much longer chapter tied the novel together. (Hardly any of her novels are given chapter headings, as they were in *Einander Kind*, or are even broken down into numbered chapters.) With regard to degrees of formal order in her prose works, then, we see once again that *Hexenherz* (the book) occupies a middle position on a spectrum moving from works with little or no organizational patterning to those which are highly controlled and therefore usually more tightly unified.

I would like to go back to the question of thematic unity and test the validity of Schild's charge stated earlier that the book lacks a theme. A logical area to examine is the title metaphor, the key element in the volume's imagery. It is quickly evident that almost all of the texts have to do with people's hearts, seen in the usual way as the center of our being, our "heart and soul," the seat of love, and so forth. It is also readily apparent that most texts have to do with *women's* hearts. All kinds of "heart-related" vulnerabilities are displayed, although the heart should be the most protected organ. It is the combination with "witch" that is the crux here because the combination is paradoxical. The book's title metaphor is based on a supposed truth: real witches don't have a heart. If this is so, then should not a heart of a witch be nonsense, an impossibility? Or does it exist in spite of that putative truth? (The reverse is clearly true: real women, i.e., nonwitches, do have hearts, as evidenced too throughout the book.) Of course, a witch's heart can exist in imagination or metaphor, but the title metaphor is admittedly a bit tricky and not immediately transparent. It might help to realize that here we are dealing with a witch of a different kind: Barbara Frischmuth's own type of witch who does not come as an old crone dressed in black and armed with a broomstick. Part of the author's game in the book is to thwart our expectations: these women are not powerful as witches for the simple reason that they *do* have hearts. They can even die from this vulnerability because they are all-too human, which may be one reason that the collection ends with the dying heroine in "Dalai Lama." The major exception is Sabina, in the title story, who indeed has a heart filled first with fear, then with a strengthening, growing confidence in herself. She stands at the positive end of the scale of heroines and their fates. Not even the nameless "witch of the wildwood" is as well off at the end of her story as Sabina is in hers. Other heroines are survivors because they develop coping strategies, like

Martha, or make deals with fate (10, 122); at the other end of the stick, there are two protagonists who do not make it through but die.[27] The question as to whether there is a unifying theme in the book, then, can be answered positively if we understand that "the heart" is very much at the heart of *Hexenherz* and that Frischmuth is talking first about women's hearts and second about the metaphor of witches' hearts.

A final mystery surrounding *Hexenherz* has to do with a void, a story that is not there. In a 1991 interview with Beatrice von Matt, Frischmuth remarked that she was starting to write a cycle of stories that would be connected to a single story, but, strangely enough, that she knew she would *not* be able to write that very story. Since *Hexenherz* is surely the book she meant, and since it is comparatively well organized, this probably means that there is an absent story at the book's heart, one central to the thirteen stories — absent but paradoxically omnipresent. A tantalizing thought, that absent center, a story we do not have, but if we work backward, we can safely surmise that it involved the female heart.

There are other aspects of Frischmuth's craft — intriguing formal features and narrative strategies in the individual stories — that are still there to be profitably examined. What, for example, is the artistic effect of a favorite gambit of hers? The first word in one-third of the stories is the vague, disorienting "She" or "He." Or take the endings: are they weak, as some critics feel, or abruptly powerful, as others claim? Or her narrative voices, especially the masterful, complex use of them in "Dalai Lama." While she has rarely commented on these particular aspects of her craft herself, she has often been forthright about formal matters and compositional techniques in general terms. A statement from an interview with Gisela Ulbrich from 1983 can serve as one instance among many: "Each book and each topic is new, and what interests me most is the formal mastering of it. How I can get at the theme, the problematic, what I can do with language, and how I can construct it."[28] The present article is meant to encourage more analysis and evaluation of the formal and structural artistry of Barbara Frischmuth's works. There are exciting discoveries to be made.

Hexenherz is a compact but multifaceted collection portraying people (and cats) inside and outside families, from children to singles to couples to "mixed pairs" to widows to bachelors and to divorcées. The book's rich variety is shaped, enhanced, and controlled by an artfully composed network of thematic and motivic echoes among stories either unobtrusively joined as pairs or adjacent to each other. Neither rigid nor mechanical, these linkages tell a story of their own about interconnected mysteries hidden within the human heart — not only the female or witchy ones, in spite of the book's title — and between hearts as well.[29]

McMaster University

Notes

1. Maria Renhardt, "Bibliographie Barbara Frischmuth,"*Dossier 4: Barbara Frischmuth,* ed. Karl Bartsch (Graz: Droschl, 1992) 163–221.

2. Barbara Frischmuth, *Hexenherz: Erzählungen* (Salzburg: Residenz, 1994).

3. Barbara Frischmuth, *Haschen nach Wind* (Salzburg: Residenz, 1974); trans. as *Chasing after the Wind: Fours Stories* by Gerald Chapple and James B. Lawson (Riverside, CA: Ariadne, 1996). For a discussion of the volume's themes, see my "Afterword," "'The Vanity of Human Wishes': An Austrian Update," 143–162.

4. S. Schild, "Sinnsuche," *Münchner Merkur,* 8 December 1994. Copies of this review and newspaper reviews below were kindly made available by the *Innsbrucker Zeitungsarchiv.* This clipping service provides all reference information except page numbers.

5. Herbert Lodron, "Leiden und genießen: Manierliche Prosaskizzen von B. Frischmuth," *Die Presse,* 27–28 August 1994, Beilage; Reinhold Tauber, "Vom Leben an den Grenzen," *Oberösterreichische Nachrichten,* 3 August 1994.

6. Susan L. Cocalis, "Barbara Frischmuth, *Hexenherz,*" *World Literature Today* 69.2 (Spring 1995): 346–347.

7. Her only other prose work that might possibly have exploited number symbolism in the chapter count was her first, published in 1968. *Die Klosterschule* (Frankfurt/Main: Suhrkamp, 1968; trans. as *The Convent School,* by Gerald Chapple and James B. Lawson [Riverside, CA: Ariadne, 1993]) had fourteen sections, which might well have echoed the number of stations of the cross in that work.

8. Otto F. Beer, "Die ominöse 13: Hexensabbat und Damenessen — eine Kollektion aus weiblicher Feder," *Der Tagesspiegel,* 4 September 1994.

9. Angelika Griebner, "Schattenspiele am Ende des Sommers," *Neues Deutschland,* 9 December 1994.

10. Doris Metz, "Vor dem Tod: Zwölf Erzählungen und eine," *Süddeutsche Zeitung,* 2 April 1995.

11. Lodron.

12. Frans Haas, "Mary Poppins in der Steiermark: Erzählungen von Barbara Frischmuth," *Neue Zürcher Zeitung,* 4 January 1995, p. 51.

13. His instrument is not a trombone, which a *Posaune* usually is, but another brass instrument, most likely a trumpet. Or might it be a cornet? There is a possible verbal clue here. The nearby mountain referred to in the text is called the "Zinken" and is authentic; but *Zinken*, or *Zinke*, in an older usage was a cornet(to). This link was not made deliberately by Barbara Frischmuth herself.

14. Barbara Frischmuth, "Gemischte Paare," *Paare: Literaturalmanach 1989* (Salzburg: Residenz, 1989); readily available under the same title in *Wassermänner: Lesestücke aus Seen, Wüsten und Wohnzimmern* (Salzburg: Residenz, 1991) 66–69.

15. Original quote: "Etwas in ihrem Inneren nahm Gestalt an, es war wie eine Herzstärkung. Sie spürte, wie Kraft in ihre Finger strömte. Am wichtigsten war die Aufmerksamkeit, sehen, was andere nicht sahen."

16. The story also harks back to "Grundwasserfisch" and turns it around. Sabina symbolically emerges from a cellar, and it was a sub-basement that the heroine in the first story sought to hide in; the crow replaces the little wagtail that a cat ate, and Sabina's confidence is the opposite of the earlier heroine's insecurity.

17. Griebner.

18. Translation mine. The story has been translated in its entirety as "Salon Ramona" by Christiane Seiler and Jeanette Clausen in *Dimension*^{2} 2.1 (Jan. 1995): 68–79.

19. Hermann Paul, *Deutsches Wörterbuch*, 9th ed. (Tübingen: Niemeyer, 1992). Original quote: "Gestalten des Volksglaubens werden als *wilder Mann, wildes Weib* bez[eichnet], weil sie außerhalb des menschlichen Kulturkreises lebend gedacht werden" (1046).

20. English quotations are taken from Barbara Frischmuth, "Witch of the Wildwood," trans. Gerald Chapple and James B. Lawson, *The Malahat Review* 118 (Spring 1997): 16–22. The title presented the translators with their first challenge. To call it baldly "Wild Woman" would be at best misleading, and "Woman of the Wild" was possible but lacked some bite. They turned to the title of the volume and the word "wildwood" to convey the nuance of "primeval," "totally natural." Perhaps the choice was unconsciously influenced by the English version of Franz Lehár's song "Vilja" from *The Merry Widow*, where *Waldmägdelein* becomes "witch of the wood."

21. The translators returned to the hunt imagery to lend more force to the fateful, often fatal, meaning of *abgestürzt.*

22. Lodron; Ingeborg Sperl, "Irrfahrten vor Landkulisse," *Der Standard,* 19 August 1994.

23. Beer.

24. Original quote: "Auch in ihren Ohren klangen noch Bruchstücke jener Sagen nach, die man im Dorf den Kindern erzählte, von den heimlichen Jägern und den Baumfrauen, die als Nebelstreif die Wege durcheinanderbrachten. Darin lag wohl das längst vorgegebene Muster ihrer Lust, ihn zu überwältigen, und seiner, sich überwältigen zu lassen" (100).

25. This may be pure coincidence, but the only other pattern I have found to resemble this was in a book Frischmuth read about witchcraft by Hans Biedermann, where he described ancient groups of witches, or "covens," as being formed of six pairs of witches, headed by a horned shaman figure as the thirteenth member. See Hans Biedermann, *Hexen* (Graz: Verlag für Sammler, 1974) 98.

26. Beatrice von Matt, "Im Land der Amaryllis Sternwieser: Ein Gespräch mit Barbara Frischmuth," *Neue Zürcher Zeitung,* 8 February 1991, p. 41.

27. Angelika Griebner coined the helpful term *Herbstfrauen* (ladies of the autumn) for the great majority of the female protagonists. It is best to beware of overstatement, though, or the word might create a distorted picture as to the variety of characters. We just have to think of the two very young women, Sabina and Luise — apprentice witches, so to speak — not to mention the autobiographical first-person narrator in several stories, and of course Plume the cat. See Griebner.

28. From "Gespräch mit Barbara Frischmuth," *Barbara Frischmuth: "Jahre" "Zeit, Tschechow zu lesen" "Unzeit" "Bleiben lassen": Mit Materialien,* ed. Gisela Ulrich (Stuttgart: Klett, 1983) 107–113. Original quote: "Jedes Buch und jedes Thema ist neu, und was mich am meisten daran interessiert, ist die formale Bewältigung: Wie ich an das Thema, die Problematik herangehen kann, was ich da mit der Sprache mache, und wie ich es aufbaue" (112).

29. I wish to thank the Arts Research Board of McMaster University for their financial support.

On Despotic Mothers and Dethroned Patriarchs: Barbara Frischmuth's *Über die Verhältnisse* and Robert Menasse's *Selige Zeiten, brüchige Welt*

Peter Arnds

I

Gerhard Rühm's visual poem "Wölkchen" (Little Cloud) summarizes very aptly what has been a predominant trend in recent Austrian literature. It depicts on a white page a black cloud in the shape of Austria hovering over a section of the black globe, well detached from it as if the Alpine Republic were not a part of planet Earth. Many contemporary Austrian writers have, in one way or another, been lamenting their country's self-imposed exclusion from the rest of the world. Among these are such authors as Thomas Bernhard, Robert Schindel, Robert Menasse, and Barbara Frischmuth. In their writings, they attempt to break out of patterns they see at work in the minds of the people and in the politics of Austria. They do so by directing the reader's attention beyond the cultural confines of Austria. In his *Auslöschung* (1986, Extinction), as elsewhere in his œuvre, Bernhard makes use of the rhetorical device of exaggeration to contrast the living conditions in the German-speaking countries, particularly in Austria, with those of the Mediterranean countries.[1] Schindel, to give another example, focuses on the cultural differences and tensions between Austrian Catholics and Austrian Jews, but also between Austrians and Germans. To transcend the boundaries of Austria, he locates his novel *Gebürtig* (1992; *Born-Where,* 1995) in a number of settings ranging from North Germany to Venice to places as far away as New York City.

What distinguishes Frischmuth and Menasse from writers like Bernhard and Schindel is their attempt to represent their experience of living abroad in a more objective manner. In doing so, both can rely on a profound knowledge of the respective culture. Although born in Austria, Menasse spent years as a lector in São Paulo,[2] and as a student of Oriental studies Frischmuth lived in Turkey for a year.[3] Both authors' absorption of a foreign culture is reflected in their protagonists' intense immersion in it. In Frischmuth's novel *Das Verschwinden des Schattens in der Sonne* (1973; *The Shadow Disappears in the Sun,* 1998), her year in Turkey finally achieves literary form. Unlike Bernhard, with his technique of exaggeration, which aims to ridicule the conditions at home, Frischmuth and Menasse levy their criticism in a much subtler way. They send their readers on a journey abroad to expose them to foreign cultures and thus open their minds to cultural diversity. Rather than blindly despising anything Austrian and praising what is foreign, like Bernhard in his *Auslöschung*, Frischmuth and Menasse attempt to confront the reader with a more objective presentation of divergent cultures. In this connection, both authors make use of the mirror image to reveal their home country's narcissistic self-involvement. In Menasse's novel *Selige Zeiten, brüchige Welt* (1991, Blissful Times, Fragmentary World), the protagonist's self-reflectiveness, his constant self-mirroring, reflects a phenomenon that Frischmuth also discusses in her novel *Über die Verhältnisse* (1987, this title implies the ambiguity of "About the Conditions" as well as living "Beyond One's Means"): "Formerly all these countries knew that they had a bad relationship with each other. There was, however, not only friction between them, they were also like mirrors to one another. Now they are just mirrors to themselves. That is what is the matter with us, my dear."[4] The Hegelian notion of a recognition and consequently transformation of oneself through contact with the other lies at the root of the œuvre of the two authors and these two novels in particular.

In the following pages, I will discuss these two texts in their relation to each other. What interests me primarily is their shared concern with the notions of matriarchy and patriarchy in regard to Austria and Turkey/ Brazil, and connected to this relationship both authors' adaptation of Greek mythology. It is particularly this three-dimensional relationship underlying the two novels that justifies their comparison. Of particular interest is the nexus between the mother of the protagonist, Austria, and the two foreign countries, Turkey and Brazil. In both texts, the mother plays a ruling part in Austria, where as a matriarchal figure in an otherwise patriarchal society she enjoys a considerable amount of power. Under her rule and due to the absence of the father in Frischmuth's novel and his powerlessness in Menasse's novel, her child does not become exposed to a patriarchal influence until leaving for Turkey and Brazil.

II

Barbara Frischmuth's novel *Über die Verhältnisse* is about the relationship between Mela and her daughter Frô. Mela, the owner of a restaurant specializing in pork dishes, raises her daughter alone, while the father, the Austrian chancellor (the BOSS), for a long time is not aware that he has a daughter. One day, Frô falls in love with a Turkish diplomat, Ayhan Heyn, with whom she runs away to Turkey. Mela and her friend Borisch (as Paul Michael Lützeler has shown, this novel is as much about the relationship between the mother and the daughter as it is about the friendship between women)[5] follow the secretly married couple to Turkey in order to bring Frô home. What follows in the novel is a close analysis of the different impact Turkey has on the three women, from Frô's eager embrace of everything to Borisch's acute interest in Turkish history to Mela's mental and physical refusal to open herself to the foreign culture. Mela gets so sick that Ayhan finally releases Frô, who temporarily returns to Austria with her mother.

Mother and Austria: Mela Rules

In Frischmuth's novel, the male Austrian leaders are ridiculed by the two superwomen Mela and Borisch. The latter ironically labels the male politicians as "rulers of the Alps, . . . grown Lilliputians. In any other country west of Lake Neusiedl, they would at most be allowed to stumble with Snow White's coffin. Only here, under the rule of the Papschis, can they fill their coffin until its bottom falls out."[6] Austrian politics, as a decidedly male domain, is described as "swineries" *(Sauereien),* which are repeatedly juxtaposed with those literally taking place in Mela's pork-based restaurant. Compared to the politics, however, her business is the only swinery that thrives in the midst of this Austrian swamp (82). Paradoxically, Austria is described as the land of the Great Mother — "Mother Austria" ("Mutter Austria," 137) — which is reflected in the mental and, to an extent, also physical strength of both Mela and Borisch. Mela raises her child independently, making sure that the BOSS remains unaware of his fatherhood. Borisch massages many of the rulers and has a weakness for "small frail men" ("kleine zarte Männer," 19). She explains what immense power the two women have: "Consider what possibilities we have. Imagine yourself pouring something into their beer . . . and I break their vertebrae while massaging them" ("Bedenk, welche Möglichkeiten wir haben. Stell dir vor, du schüttest etwas ins Bier . . . und ich breche dem einen oder andern beim Massieren die Rückenwirbel," 54). Mela also has the possibility of directly influencing Austrian politics because her business allows her to support young men who are climbing the career ladder (50–51). She has the function of bestowing strength on those men who sleep with her and consequently emerge "strengthened by her secret power of love" ("gestärkt durch Melas heimliche Liebeskraft,"

41). That Frischmuth identifies Austria with Mela, the Great Mother, is reflected in the fact that both are described as having no sense of history, no rapport with the past or the future, both live only for the present: "Mela lives for the 'now'" ("Mela lebt im Jetzt," 28). This distinguishes her from her Hungarian friend Borisch, who lives almost entirely for the past, for history, as does her native country. The inflexibility of Mela and her country in looking back or forward is seen as a form of paralysis that justifies the presence of the masseuse Borisch. With her acute sense of history, she serves as a balancing weight to the lack of historical vision in Austria and with her hands loosens the Austrian rulers' and also Mela's necks, all of which are stiff from neither turning back nor forward — figuratively speaking that is. Frischmuth makes Austria's inability to look to the past or future responsible for its lack of progress in coming to an understanding with other countries. "Even in school, the future tense is not being taught anymore" ("Selbst in den Schulen wird die Zukunftsform nicht mehr unterrichtet," 136). The population fears any form of change. This becomes obvious when Mela wants to close her restaurant to set out in search of her daughter. Initially, her guests only complain, but when they realize that she cannot be dissuaded from her plans, they start threatening her (155).

Mother and Daughter: Matriarchal Rule Threatened by Patriarchy

The exceptional closeness between Mela and her daughter, Frô, results from the mother's role as sole educator. Mela clings to her daughter a great deal more than Frô clings to her. This unhappy situation is expressed symbolically in the pearl necklace that Mela gives her daughter as a Christmas gift. As Frô looks at herself in the mirror with the pearls around her neck, the mirror reflects the sheen of the *mother* of pearl. She thus figuratively carries her mother around her neck; her mother is holding her by the neck; she is chaining her daughter by means of an expensive gift. How much the mother clings to her daughter also becomes apparent when she visits her in Turkey and falls ill for fear of losing her: "She is ill because of you" ("Sie ist um dich krank," 195), says Ayhan to Frô. Mela's greatest fear is her daughter's independence from her as in the scene when she hears Frô laugh and understands that her laughter is a "fatherly laugh" ("ein väterlicher Lacher," 55). It reminds her of the laugh of Frô's father, whom later on she provokes into laughter merely "to hear it one more time, to compare" ("sie will es noch einmal hören, vergleichsweise," 82).

Mela fails in her attempt to shield her daughter against, as she thinks, the disrupting exposure to men. Frô tears herself away from her mother and from this almost incestuous closeness. She runs off with a patriarch, thus instinctively preferring the traditional gender pattern, in which woman is dominated by man, rather than her mother's domination of her. Frô discards the way of life practiced by her mother, who only unites with men as temporary lovers, and opts for the more conservative alternative of marriage, much to Mela's chagrin:

> Yet, this complete devotion is just too conservative. One does not give oneself up like this anymore nowadays. What is this exclusiveness good for? And whom does she exclude in the first place? If not her next of kin. The old order is no longer valid, Mela tells herself. One just needs to look around. What is really happening in this kind of embrace? . . . And why is it her own daughter who has to embrace the small family life? . . . She might as well have learned how to cook for the restaurant.[7]

Mela's practice of gender separation, her refusal to accept the other as the opposite sex, reflects the dilemma of Austrian conditions lamented by its writers, its almost incestuous homogeneity and closedness to the other as anything foreign. Frô's quest of independence entails her opening to the other not only as the opposite sex but also as what is different and foreign. This first shows itself in the scene where she and Ayhan visit a Turkish restaurant (where she behaves as if she had never eaten outside of her mother's pork restaurant): "Slowly, her tongue got used to the strange taste. . . . Also the smell here was different from her mother's restaurant" ("Langsam gewöhnte sich ihre Zunge an den fremden Geschmack. . . . Auch roch es hier anders als im Spanferkel," 115). Through her contact with Ayhan, Frô is alienated from herself. Wearing a black dress like the Muslim women in Turkey she looks at herself in the mirror (118). She descends from one world into another. Frischmuth uses the two worlds of the Demeter myth, the upper world and the underworld, to discuss the central problematic of opening oneself to another culture. Ayhan corresponds to Hades, the God of the Underworld, and as Frô and Ayhan make love, he "presses her down" (119) into it, into his culture. Their lovemaking binds them together and alienates her from her own culture while at the same time moving her closer to Ayhan's. Their sex is reflected in the mirror. Very much as in the Menasse novel, the mirror image can be interpreted as Hegelian self-reflection. In the mirror Frô recognizes herself, as she looks into it before and after their lovemaking, and she emerges altered through the physical contact with another culture. While earlier in the scene, when her mother gave her the necklace of pearls, Frô was still tied to Mela through this gift, now she realizes, "I am not you" ("ich bin nicht du," 133), thinking about her mother.

Patriarchal Turkey

In Frischmuth's novel, Turkey has, due to the loss of Mela's daughter to a man, the role of the patriarchal underworld. Austria, on the other hand, patriarchal as it may be, represents the realm of the mother, Mela. When she follows Frô to Turkey, she remains irritated throughout her sojourn there. A number of passages indicate the largely patriarchal structure of Turkish society: the latest building boom in Istanbul (171) (which calls to mind the phallic skyscrapers of São Paulo, the Brazilian setting in the Menasse novel), Turkey's trade in weapons (145), but above all the segment that shows Frô and Ayhan in an Eastern Turkish town. Here Frô observes the Muslim women, all dressed in black "or in other muted colors" ("oder sonstige gedeckte Farben," 175) in order not to excite the men. They are all walking in one direction, to the market for their shopping. Frô sees only one woman dressed in a colorful dress and sitting on a horse, "nearly showing her face" ("mit beinah freiem Gesicht") and with a gun, "most likely a Kurd" ("gewiß eine Kurdin," 176). Women's subordinate role becomes visible also in the scene in the restaurant, where Frô is the only woman present and the target of male desire and aggression (177). Even Ayhan becomes aware of it: "A sudden, perturbing vision shows him a woman prepared on a copper platter around which the attentive and voyeuristic men with beards crowd with knives and forks."[8]

The main patriarch in the novel is Ayhan, who runs off to Turkey with Frô, thus breaking into the matriarchal realm of Mela and her daughter. The Austrian BOSS is only a secondary patriarch in that he does not live together with Mela and her daughter, not knowing that he is Frô's father. With Ayhan he only shares his typically male (so the novel tells us) ambition. Ayhan's drive to succeed is noticed by his younger brother and alludes to the Rousseauistic gender pattern that categorizes men as active and women as passive. To his younger brother, Ayhan has never seemed human but more of "a dark, powerful God, whose power [he] has always felt more than that of [their] father" ("ein dunkler, mächtiger Gott . . . dessen Gewalt ich viel stärker zu spüren bekam als die unseres Vaters," 203).

Into this patriarchal world descend Mela and her Hungarian friend Borisch. Mela enters the "underworld" with a feeling of superiority, as a ruler, "as if she were a baroque duchess" ("als sei sie eine barocke Landesfürstin," 164), while Borisch from the beginning remains the more diplomatic one, eager to embrace the foreign culture. This eagerness derives partly from her biculturalness (a Hungarian living in Austria) and partly from her passion for history. While Borisch delves into the history of Istanbul, Mela remains hostile to the new culture throughout her journey until she becomes so ill that she cannot stop vomiting anymore (187).

III

Mother and Son in Austria

Like Mela, Leo's mother in Menasse's novel *Selige Zeiten, brüchige Welt* has difficulties in accepting the foreign culture while living in Brazil. When Leo brings home his first girlfriend, who reaches across the table to help herself to more food, his mother freezes in shock, unable to understand the cultural differences.[9] She is as incapable of leaving her own cultural context as is Leo's girlfriend Elaine. Only Leo seems to be a mediator between the two cultures ("The two would not have understood each other, but he understood both of them" ["Die beiden hätten einander nicht verstanden, aber er habe beide verstanden," 102]), very much like Frô, who readily accepts the Turkish culture.

Let us now look more closely at Menasse's *Selige Zeiten, brüchige Welt* and see where with regard to the role/rule of the mother in Austria and the patriarchal structure in the foreign setting the novel connects with that of Frischmuth. The protagonist Leo Singer is the son of Jewish Austrians who had emigrated to Brazil during Nazi rule and returned to Vienna after the war. Leo spends a part of his childhood in Brazil. The opening of the novel shows him in Vienna as a student of philosophy who does not quite know what to do with his life. He is one of those eternal students enrolled in a liberal arts curriculum who are incapable of finishing their degree. He shares this lability with his father, the boss of a textile company, a weak man who is the mere shadow of himself next to his domineering wife. Leo is full of hatred for his mother, who "as far as he could think back did not have so much as a gesture of tenderness or a kind word for his father, for this soft man . . . who was as correct as he was weak."[10] Much as in the Frischmuth novel, in the midst of such patriarchal elements as fascism in Austria, in Menasse's novel the mother establishes her matriarchal rule over the household. She dominates the father, whose insignificance resembles that of the Austrian "Lilliputians" mentioned in the Frischmuth novel, and she also dominates her child. Her domination is reflected, for example, in two images. As a small child, Leo is always tied to a table leg by his mother so that he will not run away. This reminds us of the way in which Mela tries to chain Frô with a necklace of pearls. Moreover, Leo's mother likes to control ("this brutal contempt of my mother for anything uncontrolled" ["diese brutale Verachtung meiner Mutter für alles Unkontrollierte," 42]) and dictate to Leo what he ought to wear. Periodically, she would give him a Christmas present of woolen gloves and heavy suits from his father's collection. Like Frô, who breaks away from her mother, Leo attempts to liberate himself repeatedly from his mother. He first tries this in Venice as he falls or, as he claims, jumps into a canal, soaks his clothes, and consequently has to buy new ones. In his new clothes, which show him in the most grotesque and clownish colors, he feels as if he were reborn and free.

Leo has a girlfriend, Judith Katz, who reminds him of his mother, and when they first make love in a hotel in Venice, his lovemaking is filled with aggression and violence toward her ("The in out in out in out was accomplished" ["Es war ein es war aus es war ein es war aus es war ein es war aus gestanden," 117]). The poem he writes for her afterward connects the hatred he feels for his mother with his lovemaking to Judith: "His mother. Who lay under him. With a bleeding lap and breasts squeezed dry and her skin torn: And God saw that it was good" ("Seine Mutter. Die unter ihm lag. Mit blutendem Schoß und ausgequetschten Brüsten und zerfetzten Häuten: Und Gott sah, daß es gut war," 119). As he feels threatened by his mother, he feels threatened by Judith, who gives him a postcard of a Giorgione painting showing Giuditta with her foot on the head of a man she has decapitated with her sword.

Patriarchs in Brazil: Löwinger and Hegel

When Leo's father dies, his mother sends him to São Paulo in order to try to sell some of their property. As is the case with Turkey in the Frischmuth novel, in Menasse's text Brazil functions as the patriarchal setting, situated well away from the mother's despotic rule. By giving up his fruitless studies of philosophy and by becoming a businessman, Leo is pushed into the role that has so far been occupied by his father. His mother sends him to Brazil so that he finally may become a real man. Repeatedly, Leo's manliness is questioned. In his new clothes in Venice, he suddenly feels younger and more manly than before (97), and Judith tends to see in him "an aged child" ("ein greises Kind," 130). In Brazil, he initially lives between two factories, one that produces chocolate and one that manufactures ammunition for weapons. Depending on the direction of the wind, on some days he can smell the chocolate, on other days the gunpowder. This detail becomes interesting in light of his view of the women that surround him. He associates the smell of gunpowder with Judith, the smell of chocolate with Regina, a prostitute whom he meets in a bar and who is forever grateful to him for paying for her new teeth: "The smell of chocolate. That was Regina. The smell of gunpowder, that was Judith" ("Schokoladegeruch. Das war Regina. Schießpulvergeruch, das war Judith," 154). Leo fears emancipated, strong women like Judith and his mother, who are almost identical in his eyes. They are like gunpowder to him. On the other hand, he patronizes nonthreatening women like Regina, who is submissive and not very demanding and whose love for him is taken for granted even if he ignores her for weeks on end. In her, however, he soon loses interest. He seems to be in need of the intellectual power struggle with the Austrian women, his mother and Judith, to sustain himself. His relationship with Judith is ambivalent because she both attracts and repulses him: "He loved her. Not. He hated her. Not" ("Er liebte sie. Nicht. Er haßte sie. Nicht," 67). He hates Judith because she reminds him of his mother but loves her because he can intellectually reflect himself in her.

In Brazil, Leo is under the tutelage of Uncle Löwinger, his parents' best friend and a man whom Leo for a long time greatly idealizes. Löwinger is one of the two patriarchs in this novel, and he stands for Brazilian patriarchy as Ayhan stands for that in Turkey. Brazil is more patriarchal than Austria in the sense that aside from the fascist tendencies both countries share in the novel, the Brazilian government is depicted not as democratic but as a dictatorship. The *Herr/Knecht* (master/servant) dichotomy of Hegel's *Phänomenologie* (1807, *Phenomenology*), the novel's central subtext, becomes important in light of this fact, since the masters are the dictators of Brazil: "They are the masters. Today" ("Sie sind die Herren. Heute," 213), and when Uncle Löwinger says that "the masters will soon have to step down" ("die Herren werden bald abtreten müssen," 215), he also refers to himself, since his various businesses thrive largely because the Brazilian government is a dictatorship: "He had his peace, which he needed, committed economic crimes, which this dictatorship facilitated like no other system, and he even played with the inflation produced by the military in Brazil so that there was even an additional profit."[11] Löwinger himself is a master who fires his servants, first his gardener, then the cook, because they do not know how to handle tomatoes (214–15). "An eternal winner" ("ein ewiger Sieger," 156), he is the patriarch because he replaces the dead father for Leo whether Leo wants it or not: "This loved and admired man is not my friend, he is a father, another father, after the weak father the strong father" ("dieser geliebte und bewunderte Mann ist nicht mein Freund, das ist ein Vater, wieder ein Vater, nach dem schwachen Vater der starke Vater," 156). Whereas in Austria Leo is ruled by a strong mother, in Brazil he is ruled by a strong father figure. Löwinger keeps calling him "my son," and the longer Leo remains under his tutelage, the more the two start to look alike: They were "two elderly men who were slightly stooped over" ("zwei leicht nach vorn gebeugte Herren" [note the word "Herren" and its connotation of "patriarch"], 217). Leo sees Löwinger as a mirror image of himself (239), which reminds us of Frô looking into the mirror and coming to the conclusion that she is not like her mother. For Leo and his substitute father, the process is inverted as they become more and more alike. They are even described as Siamese twins as they cling to the salad bowl that Judith has asked for (239). This resemblance is also indicated by their almost identical names: Leo Singer, Löwinger — the "lion" inscribed into the name signals the patriarch that Löwinger is and Leo, while in the older man's company, is becoming. The identity of their names also points to the possibility that Löwinger could actually be Leo's real father. The text toys with the possibility that the strong father may have procreated Leo with the strong mother. When Leo's mother dies, Löwinger weeps and says that he has a secret about her that he wants to give away one day "when the occasion is right" ("bei gegebenem Anlaß," 220). Leo says that he loves him like a father (14), and Löwinger's reaction when he asks Leo whether he has a girlfriend reveals that he could be the real father: "You may speak candidly with me, my son. Grandchil — I mean children play an important part in making life richer" ("Du kannst offen mit mir reden, mein Sohn. Enk — , ich meine, Kinder sind eine wichtige Bereicherung des Lebens," 230). Löwinger's slip of the tongue may, however, merely indicate his own selfishness and the fact that he feels like a father to Leo but is not. The novel plays with this mystery without unraveling it. While it is Löwinger's aim to turn Leo from the milksop that he was in Austria into a patriarch like himself, he initially recognizes their master/servant relationship, and the servant in Leo, whom he believes to be working on his Hegel dissertation: "The servants have to quietly keep on working. Because they are the servants today and because they have to be prepared tomorrow. . . . You must keep on working my son" ("Und die Knechte müssen jetzt still weiterarbeiten. Weil sie heute die Knechte sind und weil sie morgen vorbereitet sein müssen. . . . Du mußt weiterarbeiten, mein Sohn," 213).

The other great patriarch in the novel is Hegel, "the father of the Prussian state" ("de[r] Vater des preußischen Staates," 158), but not only of Prussia since according to Leo "Hegel's category of totality, of the whole, . . . also assigns Brazil its role as a part of the whole" ("Hegels Kategorie der Totalität, des Ganzen, . . . weist auch Brasilien seinen sinnvollen Platz zu, als Teil vom Ganzen," 160). Thus Hegel's philosophy encompasses the whole world as "the world spirit is nowhere at home anymore" ("Heute ist der Weltgeist nirgendwo mehr zu Hause," 160). While in Brazil, Leo repeatedly attempts to write a continuation to Hegel's *Phänomenologie.* He wants to retrace Hegel's evolution of the spirit back to its beginnings, from Hegel, who established himself at the peak position of the Absolute Knowledge, to the present times and their loss of all knowledge (166). Yet, due to procrastination and alcoholism, Leo, the servant, fails in this attempt to dethrone the patriarch, to stand Hegel, the master, on his head. To do so would mean that Leo would install himself as master, as patriarch, by displacing Hegel. Interestingly enough, however, Judith, who follows Leo to Brazil, ultimately succeeds in writing the book Leo has always wanted to write. The result is *Die Phänomenologie der Entgeisterung: Geschichte des verschwindenden Wissens* (1995, The Phenomenology of Despiritualization: The History of the Disappearance of Knowledge), Menasse's very own sequel to his novel. That Judith finally ends up writing this book shows that despite his apparent external transformation into a patriarch, in the end Leo remains as weak as his own father, while Judith, who is as strong as Leo's mother, eventually manages to stand Hegel on his head, i.e., defeat the patriarch. Leo shoots Judith in order to install himself as the author of the book she has written. Thus Leo's association of the smell of gunpowder with Judith acquires a second meaning, as this smell at an early stage in the novel foreshadows the way in which she will come to die.

IV

The Rewriting of Myth in Both Novels

Both texts show that the matriarch cannot survive next to the patriarch in a largely patriarchal society. This is one of the reasons why Leo's mother returns to Austria, why Mela gets sick in Turkey and has to return to Vienna, and why Judith dies. The boundary between women and the patriarch in these texts is, however, not as clearly defined as it is in the original myths that both authors rewrite. If we compare the patriarchs of the original myths, Hades and Oedipus, with their modern versions, Ayhan as the central patriarch of the Frischmuth text and Menasse's Leo as a patriarch in progress, we observe that the power of these figures vis-à-vis women is greatly reduced. As Lützeler has shown, Frischmuth matriarchalizes her version of the Demeter myth. Similarly, Menasse reconstructs the role of women in his rewriting of the Oedipus myth. Both novels use mythological subtexts to develop a connection between the mother, the child, Austria, and a foreign culture.

Contrary to what happens in the original myth, in both novels the child tries to break away from the domineering mother. Frô runs off with the patriarch rather than being robbed by him as Demeter's daughter Kore is by Hades. Leo tries to liberate himself from his mother by changing the clothes that she wants him to wear and by jumping through the mirror surface of two bodies of water, the canal in Venice and a swimming pool in the Brazilian hinterland, in an attempt to reemerge cleansed from her. In the original myth, Oedipus unknowingly slays his father, King Laius of Thebes, and sexually unites with his mother, Jocasta. The movement is away from the father toward the mother. Menasse inverts this process. Leo moves away from the mother toward a father figure, Löwinger and Hegel. Yet, at the same time, he seeks his mother in Judith, as can be seen in the passage quoted above from the poem that follows their lovemaking.

Menasse's incorporation of the oedipal myth reflects the fragility of the patriarchy. The patriarchy shows stability only in the original version in which the son establishes himself as the new patriarch after killing the father and making love to the mother. Menasse deconstructs this patriarchal tradition in his novel, since Leo does not manage to displace the patriarch. Instead, he starts to resemble one of them, Löwinger, more and more closely. Intellectually, he fails to dethrone Hegel, the other patriarch, by writing the sequel, i.e., he does not follow in the footsteps of Hegel in the way that Oedipus follows in the footsteps of his father. Instead Judith, a matriarchal figure herself, since Leo sees in her a projection of his mother, finally dethrones Hegel and "gives birth" (hence matriarchal) to a philosophical construct that stands Hegel on his head. She thus decapitates (compare the Giorgione postcard) the patriarch Hegel, who in his *Phänomenologie* had placed himself at the top, i.e., *caput,* of mankind's evolution of knowledge. By winning the intellectual power struggle with Leo, she also decapitates him as a potential patriarch. To gain power over the other sex, Leo kills Judith. He can only subject woman through male violence rather than, as in the original myth, through his sexuality. This observation is important because the Oedipus myth as told by Sophocles and as later reinterpreted by Sigmund Freud preserves the woman for the sake of her main function as child bearer. Jocasta, the Earth Mother, the mother of all life and of Oedipus, bears him four children.

In the original "patriarchal" myth, the woman is subjected but kept alive until she has conceived children. Freud's Oedipus complex follows this tradition of patriarchy in which the son wants to sleep with his mother. As perverted a thought as this may have seemed to Freud's adversaries, both Sophocles's and Freud's version perpetuate a soundly functioning patriarchy because the love for the mother is linked to the love for woman necessary for the preservation of mankind without which the patriarchy would logically also come to an end. Menasse rewrites the patriarchal Oedipus myth in such a way that its validity is questioned. Leo grows up in an environment in which the traditional roles of father and mother are inverted. His family is determined by a strongly matriarchal structure, which triggers the central conflict of the plot. Because of his domineering mother, Leo has difficulties growing into the patriarchal role that he instinctively wants to fill. He hates his mother because he feels threatened by her in his manliness and because the roles of his weak father and strong mother prevent him from becoming the patriarch that he wants to be. Insecure in his manliness but certain that women need to be subjected, he does not use his sexuality to do so, as in the original myth, but instead uses violence. As we have seen, even his sexual encounter with Judith smacks of this violence. He ends up not only killing his mother (by not going to Vienna when she becomes mortally ill [220]), but also Judith. In this perversion of the myth in which the man has to kill the woman to show his dominance and rid himself of the threat she poses to him, his role as patriarch has become rather unstable.

In Sophocles and Freud, Oedipus's mother, Jocasta, is identical with the Mother of All, the Earth Mother, responsible for the continuation of humankind. Childbirth as part of the patriarchal tradition is thwarted in Menasse's novel as Judith does not bear life, although she is recognized in her function as a potential mother (in Leo's eyes she embodies life ["Sie verkörpert das Leben," 243]). She aborts a child from a man she knew while still in Austria, and Leo is convinced that he must defeat life (Judith) for the sake of his œuvre (243). Their "child," the Hegel book that Judith finally puts together, is a perversion of their warped relationship in which Judith decapitates Leo in an intellectual sense as well as in the figurative sense of a castration. They father/mother an abstract work of philosophy to which Judith gives structure by writing it, i.e., she bears and conceives it, but to which — through repeated oral verbalizations — Leo has provided the content, the intellectual sperm.

In Frischmuth's novel, the patriarchy is destabilized through the matriarchalization of the original Demeter myth. Turkey represents the patriarchal setting that the daughter seeks and into which the mother follows. While his own mother releases Leo from her matriarchal rule and sends him into the patriarchy represented by Löwinger and the Brazilian government (although not all of Brazil may be patriarchal), Frô escapes into the patriarchy from her mother's rule and "Mother Austria" — which it is to her more than anyone else since she was raised by her mother alone (not much in Austria is matriarchal). Although we observe Leo's gradual transformation into a patriarch (resemblance with Löwinger) in the end, I have already mentioned that his position as such is unstable. He can never quite shake off the domination of his mother, which for example shows itself in the scene where he is trying to throw his dead mother's ashes into the wind. The wind blows her ashes back into his direction and they come to stick to his hair, his sweaty forehead, and his clothes (225).

Similarly, the patriarch's position in *Über die Verhältnisse* is not as stable as it is in the original Demeter myth. In her lectures entitled *Traum der Literatur — Literatur des Traums* (Dream of Literature — Literature of the Dream) given at the Ludwig Maximilian University in Munich in the fall of 1990, Frischmuth stresses the importance of her novel's central focus: "The second book, *Über die Verhältnisse,* which I ascribed to the classical aspect, follows most accurately the movements of the characters in the Demeter story. To me, this classical aspect means the mother/daughter story in a patriarchal world, with its special forms of rape and repression. But it also means, based on the society of the Olympians, power, influence, politics, intrigue — the eternal struggle to win."[12] It is this power game that we have observed between the sexes in the Menasse novel and that we also see in Frischmuth's. The power game takes place not only between men in politics, but also between Mela and Ayhan, between the matriarch and the patriarch. In order to win, however, the patriarch in Frischmuth's version can no longer use his male power as ruler of the underworld but has to resort to ruse. When Lützeler writes that "Frischmuth has transformed the patriarchal myth of Hades robbing Kore into a matriarchal one" ("hat Frischmuth den patriarchalischen Mythos von der Entführung des Hades in einen matriarchalischen verändert"),[13] then this cannot only be applied to the detail that Frô is not robbed but runs away with Ayhan for love. As Lützeler points out, Ayhan is not the master of the underworld that Hades is. This becomes clear, for example, in Ayhan's dream in which he envisions Frô as the main ruler in the realm of the dead. She makes him king by placing a crown on his head (142–43).[14] Even within the patriarchal world of the Greek myth there are matriarchal elements. First, the underworld is not exclusively governed by the male principle of death represented by Hades, but also by the female principle of birth.[15] In Frischmuth's novel there appears another Great Mother beside Mela, the female ruler of the underworld, the grandmother of the younger Heyn's wife. She is described as a throning "shadow of a woman" ("ein Schatten von Frau," 205), and everyone, including Ayhan and even Frô, shows her reverence.[16] This reverence for the Great Mother, however, is that of the patriarch for the child bearer, as we have also seen in Sophocles's and Freud's Oedipus myth. The second matriarchal element of the original Demeter myth — Frischmuth has pointed this out — is that Demeter mourns the loss of her daughter Kore and not the loss of a son: "A mother who mourns the loss of her daughter, robbed by a man? One can assume that this moment refers to the ever-expanding patriarchy in which the woman has to follow the man rather than the man, as has so far been common, having to marry into the clan of the woman. . . . What is interesting is that a mother mourns the loss of her daughter, not of her son."[17]

Yet, beyond these matriarchal elements in the original myth, Frischmuth matriarchalizes it even more in that she partly feminizes and ultimately dethrones the patriarch himself. Ayhan is quite different from the other Turkish men populating the novel, and he is certainly different from Hades. What he shares with the ominous Hades, "the Unseen one,"[18] for example, is that he also remains "unseen" for two days after making love to Frô (130). Unlike Hades, Ayhan shows himself ready for compromise when he lets Frô go with her mother, while in the original myth the gods decide this. Ayhan lets her go for psychological reasons because he knows that he will thus win her love sooner than if he did not let her go ("the eternal struggle to win" ["das ewige Ränkespiel ums Gewinnen"]).[19] Diplomat that he is, he understands the necessity that in order to let Frô sever the umbilical cord, he cannot force her to stay. This insight is contrary to all traditional patriarchal myths in which the woman is subjected by man. On the other hand, this sort of psychological insight makes him the true winner in the tug of war with Mela, i.e., in the struggle between the matriarch and the patriarch, who both want Frô. At the end of the novel, Frô indeed does return to him. However, his position as patriarch is weakened after all. He has to resort to a ruse to win Frô, which is a feminization of his figure if we apply to this text the Rousseauistic rule that women's only strength is the art of deception. Even in his relationship with Frô, Ayhan's position as patriarch is destabilized, as it is between Leo and Judith. The younger women in both cases seem to come out as winners at the end, Judith as the author of the Hegel book, which was Leo's greatest concern in life, and Frô in the final pages: "Frô matched him and he would match her until she had reached her full maturity" ("Frô entsprach ihm, und er würde ihr entsprechen, bis sie ihre volle Größe erreicht hatte," 225). Much older than she, he understands that she may one day outgrow him. Now she "was still greedy to be his accomplice, to experience all secrets" ("Noch war sie begierig, seine Komplizin zu sein, alle Geheimnisse zu erfahren," 225), the secrets of his personality and Turkey, that is, an exotic world that would attract her as long as she has not fully fathomed it.

V

The comparison of the two novels has revealed that Robert Menasse and Barbara Frischmuth follow the same pattern in destabilizing patriarchal structures on a fictional level. In rewriting myth, the two authors matriarchalize it. Both disempower the original patriarch while at the same time empowering the mother figure and a matriarchal figure of the next generation, Frô and Judith. Although Frô initially turns away from the matriarchy to embrace the patriarchy, the end of Frischmuth's novel suggests that Mela's daughter will continue the matriarchal tradition of her mother. It is partly due to the mother's rule in the first generation that the patriarchy continues to be destabilized in the second, as Frô's closeness to Mela determines the behavior of Ayhan and as Leo remains a castrated patriarch because of his overpowering mother. Yet, the two younger women follow in the footsteps of the mothers. What the mothers have accomplished in Austria, Frô and Judith do in the patriarchies of Turkey and Brazil, respectively. Frô weakens the patriarchal power of Ayhan, who feels that she will one day even outgrow him; Judith intellectually "decapitates" Leo and dethrones Hegel. While the mother's rule leads to an erosion of the patriarchal structures in Austria, in the superiority of the younger women, the three countries — Austria, Turkey, and Brazil — ultimately come closer together. They unite in a matriarchalization process that transcends the boundaries of Austria. Once again, we hear Leo lecture about Hegel's central category of totality: "The world is becoming smaller. Everything radiates from one place on to all others. So rapidly that soon one will not be able to say any more where precisely something began. . . . The world is a whole. . . . To give an example, what was thought in Vienna yesterday can change Brazil today. . . . Any place is only a small part of the whole. . . . The world spirit has become a conqueror and a discoverer, as once was Cabral. It seeks new continents."[20]

Kansas State University

Notes

1. See for example Thomas Bernhard, *Die Auslöschung* (1986; repr., Frankfurt/Main: Suhrkamp, 1988): "In the Mediterranean countries, everything is completely different, said my Uncle Georg. That was all he said. Back then I was seventeen or eighteen and when I wanted to know what was different from Central Europe in the so-called Mediterranean countries, he said that he would one day explain it to me when I would visit these Mediterranean countries. In the Mediterranean countries, he said, life is worth a hundred times more than here. Naturally, I was eager to know why. The Central Europeans act like puppets, not like human beings, everybody is tense, said Uncle Georg. They never move naturally; everything about them is stiff and ultimately ridiculous. And unbearable. Just like their language, which is the most unbearable. German is most unbearable, he said. I was enthusiastic when he said *The Mediterranean Countries*. It is a shock to come back here, he said. It did not bother him

in the least that with his remarks he had spoiled the appetite of those who listened to him. And what a disgusting cuisine! he exclaimed. There is no cuisine in Germany and Austria and also in the so-called German Switzerland, their food is for the pigs! The much-praised Austrian cuisine is nothing other than an attack on the senses. It is rape of the stomach and of the whole body. When back in Cannes, it takes me weeks to recover from Austrian food. And what is a country without a sea! he exclaimed without finishing the thought. When he drank some Austrian wine, he would turn up his nose. As I could see very clearly, he also disliked the Austrian mineral waters, which are usually considered to be very good, but he made no comment about them" ("In den mediterranen Ländern, so mein Onkel Georg, ist alles ganz anders, sagte er. Näher erklärte er sich nicht. Als ich, damals vielleicht siebzehn oder achtzehn Jahre alt, wissen wollte, was in den sogenannten mediterranen Ländern anders als bei uns in Mitteleuropa sei, sagte er mir, daß er es mir eines Tages klarmachen werde, wenn ich selbst diese mediterranen Länder aufsuchte. In den mediterranen Ländern ist das Leben hundertmal mehr wert als hier, sagte er. Ich war naturgemäß begierig, zu erfahren, warum. Die Mitteleuropäer treten wie Puppen auf, nicht wie Menschen, alles ist verkrampft, sagte mein Onkel Georg. Sie bewegen sich niemals natürlich, alles ist steif an ihnen und letzten Endes lächerlich. Und unerträglich. Wie ihre Sprache, die die unerträglichste ist. Das Deutsche ist das Unerträglichste, sagte er. Ich war begeistert, wenn er *Die mediterranen Länder* sagte. Es ist ein Schock, sagte er, hierher zurückzukommen. Es störte ihn nicht im geringsten, daß er mit seinen Bemerkungen den Zuhörern den Appetit verdorben hatte. Und was für eine abscheuliche Küche! rief er aus. In Deutschland und Österreich und auch in der sogenannten deutschen Schweiz ist es kein Essen, es ist ein Fraß! Die vielgerühmte österreichische Küche ist nichts anderes als eine Zumutung. Eine Vergewaltigung des Magens, wie des ganzen Körpers. Ich brauche Wochen, um mich in Cannes von der österreichischen Küche zu erholen. Und was ist ein Land ohne Meer! rief er aus, ohne den Gedanken weiterzuführen. Wenn er einen Schluck Wein trank, rümpfte er die Nase. Wie ich deutlich sehen konnte, hatte er auch an den österreichischen Mineralwassern etwas auszusetzen, die sonst allgemein als sehr gut bezeichnet werden, aber er gab keinen Kommentar dazu ab," 41–42).

2. Elisabeth Endres, "Hegel hat es Leo Singer angetan," *Süddeutsche Zeitung*, no. 282, suppl., 7/8 December 1991, iv.

3. Ulrike Kindl, "Zur Biographie," *"Jahre,""Zeit Tschechow zu*

lesen," "Unzeit," "Bleiben lassen," mit Materialien, ed. Dietrich Steinbach (Stuttgart: Klett, 1996) 114.

4. Barbara Frischmuth, *Über die Verhältnisse* (Salzburg: Residenz, 1987). Original quote: "Früher haben alle diese Völker gewußt, wie sie zueinander standen, nämlich schlecht, aber sie waren einander nicht nur Reibfläche, sondern auch Spiegel. Jetzt spiegeln sie sich vor allem in sich selbst. Das ist los mit uns, meine Liebe" (99–100). All following quotations from this book are marked with page numbers in parentheses.

5. Paul Michael Lützeler, "Barbara Frischmuth's Demeter-Trilogie: Mythologische Findespiele in der postmodernen Literatur," *Dossier 4: Barbara Frischmuth,* ed. Kurt Bartsch (Graz: Droschl, 1992) 89.

6. Original quote: "Schau Sie dir an, diese Alpin-Potentaten, lauter ausgewachsene Liliputaner. In jedem anderen Land westlich des Neusiedlersees würde man sie höchstens mit Schneewittchens Sarg stolpern lassen. Nur hier, unter der Herrschaft der Papschis, dürfen sie sich so lange den Sarg füllen, bis der Boden durchreißt" (53).

7. Original quote: "Aber diese vollkommene Hinwendung ist einfach altväterisch. Auf diese Weise liefert man sich heute nicht mehr aus. Wozu soll diese Ausschließlichkeit denn gut sein? Und wen schließt sie in erster Linie aus? Die bis dahin am nächsten Stehenden. Die alte Ordnung ist nicht mehr in Kraft, sagt sich Mela. Man braucht sich nur umzuschauen. Was findet denn statt in dieser Art von Umklammerung? . . . Und ausgerechnet ihre eigene Tochter taumelt geradewegs in die Kleinfamilie? . . . Da hätte sie gleich im Spanferkel kochen lernen können" (180–81).

8. Original quote: "Eine momentane, beängstigende Vision zeigte ihm eine auf einer kupfernen Platte angerichtete Frau, um die sich all die hellhörigen, blickwütigen Bartträger mit Messer und Gabel in Händen scharten" (177).

9. Robert Menasse, *Selige Zeiten, brüchige Welt* (Frankfurt/Main: Suhrkamp, 1994) 101–02. All following quotations from this book are marked in the text by including the page number in parentheses.

10. Original quote: "Seine Mutter [hat] kein einziges Mal, soweit er sich zurückerinnern konnte, eine Geste der Zärtlichkeit, ein liebes Wort . . . für seinen Vater übrig gehabt, für diesen weichen . . . Mann, der so korrekt wie schwach . . . war" (37).

11. Original quote: "Er hatte seine Ruhe, die er brauchte, nutzte den Spielraum für Wirtschaftskriminalität, den diese Diktatur wie kein anderes System bot, und spielte noch mit der Inflation, die die Militärs in Brasilien produzierten, so daß sich sogar ein zusätzlicher Profit ergab" (230).

12. Barbara Frischmuth, *Traum der Literatur — Literatur des Traums: Münchner Poetik-Vorlesungen* (Salzburg: Residenz, 1991) 69. Original quote: "Das zweite Buch, *Über die Verhältnisse,* das ich dem klassischen Aspekt zuordnete, habe ich der geläufigen Demeter-Geschichte von den Bewegungen der Figuren her am deutlichsten nachgezeichnet. Dieser klassische Aspekt bedeutet für mich die Mutter-Tochter-Geschichte in einer patristisch orientierten Welt, mit ihren speziellen Formen von Vergewaltigung und Verdrängung. Er bedeutet aber auch, ausgehend von der Gesellschaft der Olympier, Macht, Einfluß, Politik, Intrige — das ewige Ränkespiel ums Gewinnen."

13. Lützeler 87.

14. Cf. Lützeler 87–88.

15. Cf. Richmond Y. Hathorn, *Greek Mythology* (Beirut: American University of Beirut, 1977) 87. He points out that the underworld is the "site of both death and fertility."

16. See also Wolf's description of the underworld in her latest rewriting of the Medea myth: "How my head is aching, Mother, something in me tells me not to descend into these caves again, into the underworld, the Hades, where life comes to an end and is reborn, as always, where from the remains of the dead new life is baked, [I will not go] back to the mothers, to the Goddess of Death" ("Wie mein Kopf mich schmerzt, Mutter, etwas in mir wehrt sich dagegen, noch einmal in diese Höhlen hinunterzusteigen, in die Unterwelt, in den Hades, wo gestorben und wiedergeboren wird seit alters her, wo aus dem Humus der Toten Lebendiges gebacken wird, zu den Müttern also, zur Todesgöttin, zurück," 19) in Christa Wolf, *Medea* (Frankfurt/Main: Luchterhand, 1996).

17. Frischmuth, *Traum der Literatur* 67. Original quote: "Eine Mutter, die um ihre Tochter trauert, um ihre von einem Mann geraubte Tochter? Man nimmt an, daß sich dieses Moment auf das immer mehr um sich greifende Patriarchat bezieht, in dem die Frau dem Mann zu folgen hat, statt daß der Mann, wie bis dahin üblich, in die Sippe der Frau einheiratet. . . . Interessant ist, daß da eine Mutter um ihre Tochter trauert und nicht um ihren Sohn."

18. Hathorn 88.

19. Frischmuth, *Traum der Literatur* 69.

20. Original quote: "Die Welt wird kleiner. Alles strahlt von einem Ort auf alle anderen aus. So schnell, daß man bald nicht mehr sagen wird können, wo genau etwas begonnen hat. . . . Die Welt ist ein Ganzes. . . .

Was gestern in Wien, nur ein Beispiel, gedacht wurde, kann heute schon Brasilien verändern. . . . Ein Ort wäre nur ein kleiner Teil vom Ganzen. . . . Der Weltgeist ist ein Eroberer und Entdecker geworden, wie einst Cabral. Er strebt nach neuen Kontinenten" (159–160).

The Recovering Patriarch: A Literary Type of the 1980s in Novels by Struck, Wolf, and Frischmuth

Ingo R. Stoehr

I

There is an obvious connection, and indeed a surprising one, between two statements by Barbara Frischmuth. First, in Frischmuth's novel *Die Frau im Mond* (1982, The Woman in the Moon), the first-person narrator observes that the relationships between men and women are "the most uncertain of all relationships" ("die unsichersten aller Bindungen").[1] Second, in her poetics lectures *Traum der Literatur — Literatur des Traums* (1991, Dream of Literature — Literature of the Dream), Frischmuth's interest is focused on the female dream of a self-evident presence in literature.[2] On the one hand, it seems obvious that the uncertainty of male-female relationships and the absence of a genuinely female consciousness in literature are causally related; on the other hand, I would like to argue, this causal connection can be understood in terms of addiction.

The connection to addiction is less surprising in the context of the 1980s with its social changes and its literary production. In the mid-1980s some men began to perceive their roles in a different way as a response to the powerful social movements of ecology and of women's liberation in Germany. These men tried to establish new roles for themselves that broke free from the vicious circle of patriarchy. Literature, too, welcomed back such a New Man; however, it was a literature that had been profoundly changed because by then women writers had been successful in establishing a genuine female consciousness as literary subject. Under these changed circumstances, some women writers were also interested in a "detached, ironic, playful" return to man that was based on the women's curiosity of what "can be built together" with men and that was sustained by a "new, egotistical courage, a great security that woman will never be lost again in lack of self and martyrdom."[3] This is the picture of the literary scene as Angela Praesent describes it in her preface to the women's reader *Die Rückkehr zu den Männern* (1987, The Return to Men). She concludes that this is the prerequisite for turning the previous monologues of literary complaints into dialogues between men and women.[4]

Ironically, these dialogues often reach a limit when it becomes clear that it is not so easy for men to break free from the vicious circle of patriarchy because patriarchy exerts a power over them similar to the power that a drug has over an addict. In a sense, similar to the teachings of the self-help programs that became so popular during the 1980s, there are no "New Men" available for these dialogues; at best, there are recovering patriarchs.

The connection of patriarchy and addiction can be illustrated in a comparative approach of three exemplary works, i.e., *Bitteres Wasser* (1988, Bitter Water) by Karin Struck, *Kassandra* (1983, Cassandra) by Christa Wolf, and *Die Frau im Mond* by Barbara Frischmuth. Struck's novel will serve to set the stage for the discussion because its male narrator is literally recovering from alcoholism and because patriarchy is understood as an addictive system. The other two novels reach into opposite realms: the past and the future, respectively. *Kassandra* examines the foundation of patriarchy at a time in the past while *Die Frau im Mond* is oriented toward a utopian model for the future.

II

Even Karin Struck, who once proclaimed the myth of the Great Erotic Mother in *Die Mutter* (1975, The Mother),[5] now enters the new dialogue using the male voice of Franz Leffler, the first-person narrator in *Bitteres Wasser*. He is successfully struggling with alcoholism, not only in being able to return to his job but also by coming to terms with his own sexuality. He, the recovering alcoholic, does not seem to realize that other kind of addiction when he, apparently in a quite positive way, admits: "I am, in regard to eroticism or sex, an animal. . . . I am addicted, I absorb the female body" ("Ich bin, wenn es um Erotik oder Sex geht, ein Tier. . . . Ich bin süchtig, ich sauge den weiblichen Körper in mir auf," 21). While he usually understands this as typical male thinking, he at times questions it because he feels "inside of me man is lurking too much" ("zu sehr lauert der Mann in mir," 23). This is the new side to his thinking: He understands the shallowness of the usual images of masculinity and detests those men for whom women are nothing but sexual objects. As someone caught in the process of gaining these insights, Franz Leffler is a recovering patriarch rather than the prototype of the new man.

This ambivalence locates the narrator and his story in between imagination and truth, which indeed is the premise of Struck's project to the extent that it is stated (or hidden?) on the novel's copyright page: "This novel combines imagination and truth" ("Dieser Roman vereint

Dichtung und Wahrheit," 4). The novel alludes openly to literary traditions from the Romantic's concept of love to Goethe's *Dichtung und Wahrheit* (1833; *The Auto-Biography of Goethe. Truth and Poetry: From My Life)* to confessional literature to the fairy-tale realm with the novel's motto on page 7: "[A tale] about a man who went forth to refuse to be a success, who . . . walked through the valley of hell of our addictive society . . . — and who survived" ("Von einem, der auszog, den Aufstieg zu verweigern, . . . durch das Tal der Hölle unserer Suchtgesellschaft ging . . . — und überlebte"). The fairy-tale character of the motto contributes to the novel in two ways. First, it adds to the novel's ambiguity by creating a realm that makes it easy to avoid answering the question of who has to shoulder the burden of saving the world. Second, it both generalizes and specifies the novel's attack on the world as it is: It is an all-out attack on the addictive patterns that underlie society or, in Struck's own words from the motto, on the *Suchtgesellschaft* (addictive society).

Addictive society can be understood in the context of discussions of dependency and codependency that emerged during the 1980s: Our society is addictive because it is a system that makes its members dependent on it, and it has to do that in order for it to function. One popular American proponent of these discussions is Ann Wilson Schaef, who identifies in her book *When Society Becomes an Addict* (1987) the following three aspects as those that define the Addictive System: dualism, dishonesty, and control (147). The alternative to the destructive addictive society lies for Schaef in what she calls the Living Process System, which she defines by the following three individual processes: sobriety, process, and spirituality (149).

Franz Leffler's story can be described by the six processes that Schaef uses to define the current state of and an alternative to social reality. She demands that we "admit that our society is based on the illusion of control and recognize that the system in which we live is an Addictive System" (50). In Struck's novel, Franz Leffler learns it the hard way. He experiences alienation through a multiple process of dualism. On the one hand, he suffers the basic split within industrial society: "those damn two worlds: home and the workshop" ("Diese verdammten zwei Welten: Zu Hause und Montagewelt").[6] On the other hand, the unbridgeable gulf between the workers and management, into which he falls as a union representative, drives him into desperation: "I needed the alcohol" ("Ich brauchte den Alkohol," 108). He is confronted by his experiences at work with the world of control that he cannot cope with: "I got it: Only money and power mattered; everything else was irrelevant" ("Ich begriff: Nur Geld und Macht waren entscheidend, alles andere war überflüssig," 56).

Addictive society provokes Franz Leffler to react within the limits of its own addictive processes. While he becomes aware of the control mechanisms, he reacts by attempting to control them himself — through the self-deceptive and self-destructive means of substance abuse. Consequently, his entire behavior is a lie, and he struggles to break through his own dishonesty although the latter is encouraged by addictive society. While he is no longer addicted to alcohol at the time he narrates his story, he still is evading through other addictive behaviors, such as smoking and taking tranquilizers. This time, however, he knows that he has to fight it. As far as his previous alcohol abuse is concerned, addictive society did everything to prevent him from knowing — not very subtly but very effectively with the standard stereotypes of advertising.

It is crucial for Franz Leffler to realize that advertising works through stereotypes of masculinity to supply the addictive society with its victims. The White Male System, which is, according to Schaef, the same as the Addictive System,[7] operates in Leffler's experience in three overpowering ways: First, it defines itself as reality by equating with alcohol everything that is beautiful: "bars, whiskey, girls: That's life" ("Bar, Whiskey, Mädchen: Das ist das Leben," 38). Second, it presents itself as inherently superior: "Advertising . . . elevates the drunk to the status of a master in the art of living" ("Die Reklame . . . erhebt den Trinker in den Status des Lebenskünstlers," 38). Third, it pretends to be all-knowing by using "cool slogans" ("saloppen Sprüchen," 38). Unfortunately, it is just now, after alcohol has destroyed his life, that Franz Leffler can see what's behind these stereotypes: Addiction is not the only reality, superior and all-knowing; on the contrary, it is antilife, inferior, and ignorant. In the context of Schaef's observation that "in order to perceive the Addictive System for what it is, one must be *in* it but not *of* it,"[8] the fact that Karin Struck's narrator is a man becomes interesting.

Franz Leffler must struggle so much because as a man he is almost necessarily of the Addictive System. Establishing such a parallel between individual addiction and the depersonalizing infringements of technological mass society suggests an analysis along the lines of Critical Theory. For example, Max Horkheimer and Theodor Adorno argue in their *Dialektik der Aufklärung* (1947, Dialectics of Enlightenment) that any human attempt to control nature will only result in more control over man by nature or by man-made technologies that were designed to control nature.[9] Society, Horkheimer and Adorno conclude, is like a machine that cannot but mutilate human beings even where it sustains them.[10] In other words, only the system benefits, not its members; more specifically, in the White Male System not even the white male individual benefits anymore. Therefore, the destructive powers of addictive society are most effectively unmasked by the suffering of someone who might be expected to benefit from the system.

In a way parallel to the unmasking of the addictive society, *Bitteres Wasser* explores options of an alternative model, which can be described in Schaef's terms of sobriety, process, and spirituality. Indeed, the alternative model in Struck's novel takes on additional force because it is expressed by a male narrator who is quite honest about the connection between his sobriety and his spiritual well-being. In his conscious choice of life without alcohol but full of hard work over a "life of pretense with alcohol addiction as the chairman of the union committee" ("das alkoholabhängige Scheinleben als Betriebsratsvorsitzender," 24), the close interconnection of social and psychological structures is made explicit. Franz Leffler has made his choice to drop out and resist the inhuman pressures of addictive society.

What makes the narrator's account, despite all linguistic awkwardness, so convincing, is that it is embedded in a kind of therapeutic discourse. Here the novel engages a distinctly modern, twentieth-century thought, i.e., the concept of interpersonal relationships as *work*. For example, Niklas Luhmann observes in his *Liebe als Passion* (1982, Love as Passion) that the proper way lovers show their love for each other is by dealing with the problem.[11] What's more, this is in keeping with the "interdependence blueprint" for love, which Francesca Cancian proposes in her study *Love in America: Gender and Self-Development* (1987). One of the aspects of Cancian's model is that it aims at overcoming the "polarized gender roles" of "masculine autonomy" on the one hand and "feminine affection" on the other, which have led to the "false opposition between women's love and men's work."[12] One way of overcoming this false opposition, Cancian argues, involves a therapeutic approach.

In this sense, Franz Leffler does not present himself as the New Man, standing outside the system of male domination and ready for a new kind of relationship that is a true partnership. He presents himself rather as someone who is aiming to become a new man. Similar to his struggle with alcoholism which, due to the nature of addiction as we understand it, will never be over, his attempts to evolve a new consciousness in terms of a

Living Process System will have to be efforts made on a day-to-day basis, and he knows it. The burden of salvation, then, seems to rest on the individual's understanding social structures for what they are: addictive structures. Novels such as *Bitteres Wasser* suggest that this understanding is necessary to make possible a social change from domination to partnership.

A principal difficulty with confessional texts remains unanswered: How reliable is the narrator? In his review article, Matthias Matussek wonders whether the narrator has been brainwashed by the author.[13] Of course, the narrator could also just lay a couple of hurt-puppy lines on his reader and borrow some feminist clichés from his female author to conveniently hide his worst addiction, i.e., his need to move from one relationship to another. But, after all, as a literary construct, he may well represent the recovering patriarch, who is breaking away from the system of patriarchy, which kept him addicted and, thus, a victim himself.

III

Thematically, this is the focal point of social and psychological analysis in Christa Wolf's works: Men are victims, and women are even worse off because the "men, weak, whipped up into victors, need us [i.e., women] as victims in order not to stop feeling altogether" ("Die Männer, schwach, zu Siegern hochgeputscht, brauchen, um sich überhaupt noch zu empfinden, uns als Opfer").[14] Especially the word choice in the German original suggests the vicious circle of addiction: Existence becomes a matter of survival by means of quick fixes. Superficially argued, because they are not *of* but *in* the system of patriarchy, women promise the potential for hope and change. While such an approach always seems to be criticized for placing the burden of saving the world on one of the parties, this issue somewhat misses the point. At least, I believe that literature should not be judged solely by what, if any, answers it offers, but rather by what creative perspectives on reality it offers and, above all, by what questions it raises. And Wolf's texts make the readers question the way things are and why things are this way.

Some questions do not have real answers in Wolf's novels because social reality does not allow it. These are the questions for which Wolf does not use a question mark, just a plain period. Another social reality might yield answers, Wolf seems to suggest. And although Wolf explores other ways of relating and belonging, she also seems to suggest that without men the answer would not be complete. Yet, those men who might be of help are "themselves hopelessly entangled" ("selbst in auswegloser Verstrickung").[15] So even Medea, Wolf's most radical narrator-protagonist yet, ends in the realization of isolation and desperation that makes Wolf's writings so authentic: "Is it possible to conceive of a world, a time that I would fit in. No one there whom I could ask. That's the answer" ("Ist eine Welt zu denken, eine Zeit, in die ich passen würde. Niemand ist da, den ich fragen könnte. Das ist die Antwort").[16]

Wolf's rewriting of classical mythology truly emerges as an archeology of power because the author takes her readers back to what she considers to be the historical intersection of two different ways of life: matriarchal culture and patriarchal culture during that period of time where the first is slowly being replaced by the latter. While it is doubtful that Wolf considers a return to matriarchy desirable or possible, it is quite clear that she considers the patriarchal system to be corrupt and perverted. At the center of this corruption lies power to which men fall prey like addicts to a drug. To understand the social as well as psychological aspects, Wolf investigates the change in terms of power or rather in terms of how power is being exercised. And she has to go deeper under the surface of power relationships because it is there that hidden structures determine what is allowed to be the official truth within a society that has turned addictive, i.e., a society that is based on the processes of dualism, dishonesty, and control.

The truth that is being hidden is, in Wolf's novels, that the female voice is being silenced. However, rather than creating an irrational countermyth, Wolf focuses on a rational analysis. This, then, leads to the evocation of a new female consciousness, which is based on the female narrator-protagonist's understanding of the hidden truth. In Wolf's version of the Medea myth, Medea literally discovers the real truth hidden in the labyrinthine vaults deep beneath the royal palace: the remains of the legitimate, female heir to the throne who was murdered to end the matriarchal line. In Wolf's version of the Trojan War, Kassandra comes to understand the economic and strategic reasons for the war, which lead to Troy's social destruction long before its military end because the city she once knew changes into a totalitarian police state — a change that proceeds with the logic of an addiction.

In *Kassandra*, the readers can witness an entire society becoming an addict. It is an addiction to power, and similar to the strategies of advertising that the narrator in *Bitteres Wasser* discusses, the developing machinery of political propaganda in *Kassandra* glorifies the addict. The most prevalent stereotype in this respect is the image of the hero, which has three major embodiments in Wolf's *Kassandra*: Achilles, Eumelos, and even Aineias.

Achilles — the traditional prototype of the hero, whose wrath is the subject of one of the founding epics of Western literature — is presented in the different light of perversion: Driven from one adrenaline rush to the next by his "naked hideous male lust" ("nackte gräßliche männliche Lust," 88), his appetite for killing and demeaning sex are presented in a repulsive way. Kassandra calls Achilles by a new *epiteton de-formans*,[17] as Christine Maisch refers to it, i.e., "Achilles the brute" ("Achill das Vieh").[18] Not only does Wolf use the same epiteton in *Kindheitsmuster* (1976, Patterns of Childhood)[19] to refer to Nazis, Achilles represents the type of addictive behavior which assigns the roles: Men become heroes; women become objects. Or: Men become dependent; women become codependent.

Wolf's *Kassandra* contains quite a differentiated analysis that shows how the addiction unfolds on several levels. On the one hand, Kassandra is shocked to find out that even women have been turned into this type of hero; Penthesilea is really not any better than Achilles. On the other hand, Kassandra witnesses the remainders of matriarchal structures, e.g., her mother's presence on the royal council, being reduced to insignificance: "Thus out of words, gestures, ceremonies, and silence there arose a second Troy, a ghost town" ("aus Worten, Gesten, Zeremonien und Schweigen ein neues Troja, eine Geisterstadt entstand," 100). Life in this ghost town becomes a nightmare because Kassandra becomes thoroughly isolated from her family and the new type of society as well as from Aineias.

Her alienation from her family goes hand in hand with her alienation from the newly developing social structures because these structures are embodied by the ruling family. Similar to the way her mother, the queen, lost her influence, King Priam, Kassandra's father, is reduced to a puppet ruler while Eumelos emerges as the chief of the increasingly powerful secret police, who really controls the city. Eumelos is a bureaucratic version of Achilles the brute: Eumelos is paradigmatic for what is inherently wrong with patriarchy, e.g., instrumental reason perverting rationality into a totalitarian system, because from the very beginning it contains within itself its own destruction. It is this aspect that makes the analogy with addiction so convincing. It is clear to Kassandra that Eumelos "is presupposing what he had yet to create: war" ("Er setzt voraus, was er erst schaffen mußte: Krieg," 123). This creates new social structures of domination and repression and destroys old forms of belonging; it even destroys personal integrity as Kassandra experiences herself when she censors her own thoughts and actions: "The Eumelos inside me forbade it" ("Der Eumelos in mir verbot es," 81). Eumelos, an invention by Wolf, literally translates as "Good-Song" and prefigures all the Goebbelses of the world as the master of creating reality through language and control. Saying that "wherever we went, he would be there first" ("Wohin wir immer kämen, dieser wär schon da," 158), Kassandra is afraid that the future is his.

While the development of the various versions of the Achilles-type, power-crazed hero produces a rogues' gallery that includes new types such as Eumelos, there are several elements of hope in *Kassandra*, above all the female community at Mount Ida and Kassandra's relationship with Aineias. The latter is central because it represents a brief and very delicate balance between matriarchal and patriarchal patterns that might make possible yet another, new way of relating and belonging in terms of a partnership. Aineias is essential for Kassandra to feel alive; she observes that "when he and I breathed the same air, life flowed back into the husk of my body" ("wenn wir die gleiche Luft atmeten, strömte in die Hülle, die mein Körper war, das Leben wieder ein," 101).

Their love develops in a slow and tender yet almost self-evident way. Kassandra experiences the utterance of the words "Aineias Kassandra. Kassandra Aineias" (398) as a love poem. While this could sound even trivial, it can also be argued following Nicolai's analysis[20] that this chiasm suggests a reciprocal and symmetrical relationship. Their love presents a liberating force because of the context of Kassandra's dreams, which suggest to her that what matters for true love is not a question of domination but indeed a union between male and female aspects. Kassandra's love for Aineias constitutes the major utopian element in the novel; however, it is doomed in the new patriarchal reality of Troy because even Aineias will become a male hero and thus become subject to "the repetition" ("die Wiederholung," 135).

It is clear what Kassandra means by this: Aineias will repeat the behavior the heroes from Achilles to Eumelos have displayed, as indeed he does in the literary tradition of Virgil's *Aeneid*. In this context, it is interesting to observe that Wolf chose to rewrite the traditional myth that usually has Aeneas involved with Creusa, another one of Priam's daughters. According to traditional mythology, Creusa dies during the escape from the destruction of Troy, thus leaving Aeneas free to pursue his career as hero. In contrast, Kassandra in Wolf's version understands that she must part from Aineias because his turning into a hero does not leave room for her to be herself. It would require, as she says, "submission to a role I despise" ("Unterwerfung unter eine Rolle, die mir zuwiderlief," 111) or, in terminology of addiction, submission to the role of the enabler, i.e., the codependent person who often unconsciously and/or unwillingly contributes to the dependency of the addict.

IV

In *Die Frau im Mond*, Barbara Frischmuth expresses the continuing need for utopian thought to find the new human being and to create a better world. The novel presents a society engulfed in the threat of violence, thus suggesting the urgency of a change for the better. However, the utopian model that emerges in the cooperative project of Colombina and Pierrot is ambiguous because it can be seen as limited by the destructive powers of addiction.

The power of imagination is at the heart of utopian thinking, and it is this power that leads Colombina through the city during the night, where she is accompanied and protected by a black panther. Yet, the ambiguities begin with the linguistic presentation of these scenes. The dreamlike scenes possess a linguistic clarity and power of description that the novel's presentation of reality does not have. On the one hand, this could suggest that imagination lets Colombina see the world more clearly; on the other hand, it might mean that it is just an imagined clarity. Since Frischmuth explores elements of fantasy in her novels, the choice concerning the status of these scenes is a genuine one: Either these scenes are indeed a representation of Colombina's dreams, or they are real and can be called dreamlike only to contrast them to what is usually perceived as real.

The black panther is central to these dreamlike scenes, and its meaning may illuminate the issue of dream versus reality. For instance, Ingrid Spörk states that Colombina dreams about roaming the city together with a panther at night.[21] But the scenes could also be placed in the literary tradition of the *commedia dell'arte*, from which the characters of Colombina and Pierrot in Frischmuth's novel are taken. According to William Rose Benét's *Reader's Encyclopedia*, Columbine, a later addition to the ensemble of stock characters of the Italian comedy, "is supposed to be invisible to mortal eyes."[22] Colombina in *Die Frau im Mond* is visible although during her nocturnal quests she is "as good as invisible" ("schon soviel wie unsichtbar," 147). However, the panther is indeed invisible, but he is present because a police dog seems to be able to pick up his scent ("der Streifenhund scheint ihn wenn schon nicht zu sehen, so doch zu riechen," 43). Furthermore, Colombina and the panther become part of the comedic tradition when they "now roam through the new play night after night" ("wandern nun also Nacht für Nacht durch das neue Stück," 81).

In this sense, the panther and the dreamlike scenes present reality at least in terms of the nonrealist literary tradition. Especially in reference to the previous quote, the panther may metaphorically represent the power of imagination. It is what helps Colombina see clearly what is important for her to understand about her world. Yet what she sees also provides an indication of the level of reality of the nocturnal quest. After all, the novel presents Colombina as the witness to a bomb explosion that kills two other characters from an otherwise separate strand of the novel. This intrusion of violence into the act of imaginative understanding of the world (or literally into nocturnal quests with the panther at her side), also shows the vulnerability of imagination (or the panther): This is the one instance in the novel when the panther becomes visible.

Understanding the panther as an embodiment of imagination would actually work regardless of the answer to the question about dream versus reality — perhaps simply because this duality is of no consequence when it comes to creative thinking about solutions to a problem. If the panther is a metaphor for imagination in this novel, it is indeed both dream and reality, panther and imagination, at the same time. This gives rise to a new question concerning the goal of the imagination, or the reason that Colombina goes on these (imaginary or real) nocturnal quests.

While during the day she works on a play about the new human being, Colombina's night quest seems to involve the old human being, i.e., her husband, Pierrot, because his behavior in terms of non-communication suggests old patterns of relating rather than new patterns of belonging, which would instead emphasize cooperation. It is here that the aspect of vulnerability adds further depths to the meaning of the panther. First, the panther seems to be a private symbol for Colombina and Pierrot of their love for each other; therefore, it makes sense to observe the following: "I love you, Pierrot says and sends himself to her as a panther" ("Ich liebe dich, sagt Pierrot und schickt sich ihr selbst als Panther," 17). Second, Cocalis's question concerning whether the panther is to be regarded as Colombina's "husband Pierrot"[23] cannot be positively answered; rather it seems as though the panther represents their imagination, this time specifically the image of Pierrot as Colombina's ideal husband.

It can only be an image because the real husband is out drinking. Yet another question emerges: whether the panther is simply an image of Pierrot or rather a counterimage. The panther might represent what Colombina wishes her husband to be like: "But the panther loves Colombina, and wherever she goes in the night, there he goes too" ("Der Panther aber liebt Colombina, und wo immer sie nachts hingeht, dahin geht er auch," 44). However, Colombina and Pierrot go separate ways at night; her question is: "In which pub is Pierrot?" ("In welchem Wirtshaus sitzt Pierrot?" 42) The panther is her companion on her search for Pierrot, yet at times the panther also appears to be "irritated" ("irritiert," 42) and "unfathomable" ("unberechenbar," 45). On the one hand, this might suggest that the panther indeed is an image of Pierrot, even a quite realistic one. On the other hand, since Colombina has two modes of existence, one during the day and one during the night, one mode involves her husband and the other involves her imagination: Colombina will survive — "be it as day version or as night version, be it with Pierrot or with the panther" ("sei es als Tagversion oder als Nachtversion, sei es mit Pierrot oder mit dem Panther," 137).

This dualism creates a sense of psychological suffering because the relationship with Pierrot that Colombina relies on appears to be precarious. There is a certain amount of feeling that will never be communicated, and this contributes to Colombina's suffering. In an ironic reversal to the traditional role of Pierrot, who, according to Stückemann's introduction to Laforgue's Pierrot poems, has been for centuries the disappointed or deceived lover, this now seems to be Colombina's experience. In one of the dreamlike scenes, she has found Pierrot sitting in a pub, but she does not approach him; she only looks at him through the window. He in turn sees a face in the window but does not recognize that it is Colombina's; however, for the next few days he will remember this face as "the face of his life" ("dem Gesicht seines Lebens," 43). This is a strong expression of how Colombina and Pierrot are attracted to each other yet remain separate. And it is probably no coincidence that Pierrot sits in a pub, playing cards and drinking.

Pierrot's drinking problem runs through his and Colombina's entire story in the novel. Alcohol is a way for Pierrot to deal with his problem that he just cannot "tolerate this rotten world" anymore ("diese verrottende Welt ertragen," 46); e.g., he cannot stand the people's gaping mouths, so he drinks with the people to shut them up. However, the state of the world as it is presented in the novel needs something else: It needs new ideas for a better future, and Pierrot's and Colombina's project as puppet players is to come up with a new play that might initiate such new thinking. At first, however, Pierrot goes out drinking; Colombina wonders "will Pierrot find one [new play] in the pub?" ("Ob Pierrot im Wirtshaus eins findet," 18). It is clear that their lives take place on the social fringes and below the poverty level, or, as the novel states, "on the razor's edge" ("auf des Messers Schneide," 22).

This social marginalization is a continuation of the image of the outsider traditionally evoked by Pierrot, but in *Die Frau im Mond* it is also defined by the subculture of the artistic family and furthermore heightened by Pierrot's drinking, which is exposed as an addiction when Colombina hisses at him that his hands were shaking like an old man's, and not for the first time ("Und dir haben die Hände gezittert wie einem Greis, faucht Colombina, und das nicht zum ersten Mal," 22). As their work on the play progresses, the entire family, Colombina, the children, and also Pierrot pull together. Nevertheless, as they try to change the world through getting their play ready, Pierrot keeps drinking beer, which adds to the general stress of the rehearsals, and finally, Pierrot gets so drunk one time that the opening night of their performance is jeopardized.

Pierrot's addiction underscores how the social and the psychological merge; thus, the meaning of Colombina's nocturnal quests with the black panther as well as the meaning of the new play itself take on additional dimensions. The panther can still be understood as a metaphor for imagination; however, a sense of personal urgency seems added to a more general social imagination that changes Colombina. In contrast to Edith Toegel's analysis that Colombina becomes the protector of all of humankind,[24] Colombina's nocturnal quests leave her much more vulnerable; however, this does not reduce the creative change of Colombina: She sees and understands more clearly, as Toegel points out, issues of knowledge and existence as such, and this alone encompasses an element of hope.[25] As a matter of fact, it is a strong hope because it relies on human imagination rather than giving in to the temptation to use drugs to achieve these moments of clarity, the way Pierrot does, which, according to Marie-Odile Blum, is close at hand in Frischmuth's novels.[26]

The production of the new play never goes on stage in the novel; like the results of Colombina's night quests, its effects are to take place in a future beyond the novel. The novel's world, which is plagued by violence in various forms including terrorist attacks, clearly needs a change, and this change could be brought about by a new show; therefore, "a new play is needed, needed much more than ever" ("Ein neues Stück tut not, ist nötiger denn je," 77). Colombina and Pierrot agree that it should be the play about the new human being, not just the new man or the new woman. They finally decide to develop a show about the Woman in the Moon. It is crucial to distinguish two aspects of the show: the play itself and the stage production.

The message of the play itself is in apparent contradiction to the goal of a play about the new human being because it is actually about the new woman — or, in a sense, it is about the way women once were according to Robert Graves (or, as he is called in the German editions, Robert Ranke-Graves). In her poetics lectures, Frischmuth quotes Graves on the Great Goddess, who is equated to the moon: "The moon's three phases of new, full, and old recalled the matriarch's three phases of maiden, nymph (nubile woman), and crone . . . typified respectively by Selene, Aphrodite, and Hecate."[27] The identity of these deities is fluid because they stand for the same female principle. Ironically, Pierrot, who seems to be entrapped by the male principle in Frischmuth's novel, is traditionally defined by his close association with the moon, i.e., his "lunatic love."[28]

In the play within the novel, the woman in the moon refuses to stay where *man*kind put her: on her pedestal. She leaves it and becomes human, i.e., herself as opposed to someone who is defined by the expectations of others. After initial complaints, people generally ignore her. She becomes pregnant and returns to the moon with her child. When the child becomes bored, they leave again, and this time they find a home on earth when another woman, who once used to be in the moon too, takes them in. In addition to the positive force of the child, the active and compassionate characters in this play are women. Toegel observes that Colombina uses this play as a parable for her own life:[29] to be in opposition to existing reality.

However, the stage production, as it is being discussed and rehearsed, makes clear that Colombina's life is subject to a dualism that allows her to exist in opposition to reality during the night but that also embeds her within reality during the day when she is a wife and a mother. Nevertheless, the stage production points toward the goal of encompassing all human beings because the play does not only express ideas about a new form of human existence, but as a cooperative effort it is the practice of what it preaches: It includes the new human being as woman, man, and child. Such a cooperative inclusiveness anticipates the theme of belonging that Frischmuth explores especially in her Demeter-trilogy, which Margret Brügmann defines as being based on mutual and exchangeable power and trust.[30] This is not simply in opposition to existing reality but rather constitutes a mediation between utopian ideal and destructive reality, and in *Die Frau im Mond* it involves "the comedic family as a reliable unit between cosmic events and earth" ("Die komödiantische Familie als verbindliche Einheit zwischen dem kosmischen Geschehen und der Erde," 108).

A final analysis has to acknowledge all these positive elements that suggest an alternative to the way the novel presents reality, *and* it also has to emphasize the underlying ambiguity in terms of the source of these positive elements, almost to the extent that the utopian dimension of the novel appears as wishful thinking in order to escape ugly reality. Colombina's night quest is also her reaction to her husband's alcoholism, and Pierrot's addiction also threatens the feasibility of the cooperative project in which their entire family is engaged. What is more, the analysis cannot stop here, it needs to relate psychological responses of the individual to the social structures of "male domination"[31] as represented in the novel.

While Struck's *Bitteres Wasser* explicitly discusses individual addiction in terms of addictive society and unveils hidden power structures, Wolf's *Kassandra* can be read as indirectly describing how power renders a whole society an addict and, therefore, hope becomes utopian when patriarchy replaces matriarchy. Frischmuth also assumes patriarchy meant the end to the female principle. However, her novel *Die Frau im Mond* generalizes the utopian model, using elements of fantasy to escape from *and* to subvert a reality that seems less clear than the dreamlike scenes in the novel. It combines the separate stories of three women in an intertwined manner that Cocalis considers to be providing a kind of metalevel to the novel. Only occasionally (and only superficially) do their stories connect, for example, when Colombina witnesses the explosion that kills one of the other women. Of course, speculations concerning their relationship, and possible identity, to each other can be entertained. There is a connection between Colombina and the graphic artist: They both are on a personal quest out in the city. The artist goes to a café, where some of the personnel call her "Bojazzl" (dialectal and affectionate variation of *Bajazz,* meaning "little clown,"

57), and at one point, the artist draws a picture of Pierrot. If Colombina is understood as a projection of the graphic artist, this would also explain why Colombina's story ends at the time of the artist's death in the explosion.

While these are but speculations, they point to the fact that the three women share the basic essence of existence in a way that makes them almost like the three phases of the goddess, representing the female principle. Indeed, these women have at least two specific things in common: They are in opposition to reality, and they are searching for their ideal male partner — or in other words: They feel that they live in a loveless world, and they are looking for love.

The three women in *Die Frau im Mond* experience love in terms of an addiction, or, in Sylvia Adrian's words, they feel that a love relationship is only attainable through the loss of their own identity.[32] Yet Adrian continues to argue that for these women love also includes the promise of overcoming their dependencies. Frischmuth creates the myth of love as an inclusive and cooperative force. "Myths," she quotes Graves, "are always practical."[33] In the form of the novel, the intertwined stories of the three women practice cooperative storytelling; the project of the play within the Colombina and Pierrot section is based on practicing cooperation; the ironic reversals of roles assigned to the Pierrot of the literary tradition suggest another cooperative practice: changing roles of individuals to accommodate social change or to establish one common human existence. Any system that is based on domination introduces dualism to every aspect over which it has control; this is what makes such a system addictive. Therefore, any positive element is likely to acquire a negative, addictive side. But if Western civilization is indeed an addictive society, as is argued in this essay, love's power of imagination represents the ultimate hope for Frischmuth. She asserts that love possesses the force to bring about the necessary changes for a better world because it is forever subversive, or as she writes in *Kai und die Liebe zu den Modellen* (1979, Kai and the Love of Models): "Love cannot be civilized" ("Liebe ist nicht zivilisierbar").[34]

Notes

1. Barbara Frischmuth, *Die Frau im Mond* (1982; repr., Munich: dtv, 1985) 87.

2. Barbara Frischmuth, *Traum der Literatur — Literatur des Traums: Münchner Poetik-Vorlesungen* (Salzburg: Residenz, 1991).

3. Angela Praesent, ed., *Die Rückkehr zu den Männern: Das zweite Lesebuch der neuen frau* (Reinbek: Rowohlt, 1987) 9–10.

4. Praesent, *Die Rückkehr zu den Männern* 11.

5. Karin Struck, *Die Mutter* (1975; repr., Frankfurt/Main: Suhrkamp, 1978).

6. Karin Struck, *Bitteres Wasser* (Munich: Albrecht Knaus, 1988). In the following, page references will be added in the text in parentheses.

7. Anne Wilson Schaef, *When Society Becomes an Addict* (San Francisco: Harper & Row, 1987) 5.

8. Schaef 5.

9. Max Horkheimer and Theodor W. Adorno, *Dialektik der Aufklärung: Philosophische Fragmente* (1944; repr., Frankfurt: Fischer, 1971) 15.

10. Horkheimer and Adorno 37.

11. Niklas Luhmann, *Liebe als Passion: Zur Codierung von Intimität* (Frankfurt/Main: Suhrkamp, 1982) 213.

12. Francesca M. Cancian, *Love in America: Gender and Self-Development* (Cambridge: Cambridge UP, 1987) 27, 29.

13. Matthias Matussek, "In der Freizeit Fragen nach dem Sinn," *Der Spiegel* 18 (1988): 206.

14. Christa Wolf, *Kassandra: Erzählung* (1983; repr., Darmstadt: Luchterhand, 1986) 140.

15. Christa Wolf, *Kein Ort: Nirgends* (1979; repr., Darmstadt: Luchterhand, 1981) 94.

16. Christa Wolf, *Medea: Stimmen* (Munich: Luchterhand, 1996) 236.

17. Christine Maisch, *Ein schmaler Streifen Zukunft: Christa Wolfs Erzählung "Kassandra"* (Würzburg: Könighausen & Neumann, 1986) 22.

18. For example on p. 30 of *Kassandra.*

19. Christa Wolf, *Kindheitsmuster* (1976; Darmstadt: Luchterhand, 1979).

20. Rosemarie Nicolai, *Christa Wolf: "Kassandra"* (Munich: R. Oldenbourg, 1989) 64.

21. Ingrid Spörk, "Vom Imaginären zum Banalen: Über Märchen und Mythen bei Barbara Frischmuth," *Dossier 4: Barbara Frischmuth*, ed. Kurt Bartsch (Graz: Droschl, 1992) 50.

22. William Rose Benét, *The Reader's Encyclopedia,* 2d ed. (New York: Thomas Y. Crowell, 1965) 214.

23. Susan L. Cocalis, review of *Die Frau im Mond*, by Barbara Frischmuth, *World Literature Today* 57.2 (Spring 1983): 276.

24. Edith Toegel, "Suche nach einer weiblichen Identität: Frauengestalten in Barbara Frischmuths neuen Werken," *Seminar* 24.2 (May 1988): 173.

25. Toegel 173.

26. Marie-Odile Blum, "Barbara Frischmuth oder Die Weite der Möglichkeiten, die uns offenstehen," *Frauenliteratur in Österreich von 1945 bis heute*, ed. Carine Kleiber and Erika Tunner (Bern: Peter Lang, 1986) 21.

27. Robert Graves, *The Greek Myths*, vol. 1 (1955; rev. ed., 1960; Harmondsworth: Penguin, 1985) 14.

28. Franz Stückemann, "Lunatische Apotheose: Zum Pierrotzyklus Laforgues," *Sinn und Form* 48.6 (1996): 886.

29. Toegel 172.

30. Margret Brügmann, "Traumtänzerin mit Fangnetz: Formen weiblicher Ästhetik bei Barbara Frischmuth," *Dossier 4: Barbara Frischmuth* 37.

31. Frischmuth, *Traum der Literatur* 81.

32. Sylvia Adrian, review of *Die Frau im Mond*, by Barbara Frischmuth, *Literatur und Kritik* 183/184 (April/Mai 1984): 210.

33. Graves 20; cf. Frischmuth, *Traum der Literatur* 64.

34. Barbara Frischmuth, *Kai und die Liebe zu den Modellen* (Salzburg: Residenz, 1979) 198.

Resident Aliens: Home and Displacement in Barbara Frischmuth's *Das Verschwinden des Schattens in der Sonne* and Waltraud Anna Mitgutsch's *In fremden Städten*

Monika Shafi

The Shadow Disappears in the Sun, Ariadne, 1998
In Foreign Cities, Ariadne, 1995

In the business section of *The News Journal*, a local paper in Delaware, the following advice was given on résumé writing: "Many companies screen résumés by using computers that look for key words. If your résumé's missing those words, it doesn't get read. It's that simple."[1] This recommendation suggests that a certain vocabulary is both crucial for the market discourse, but also — as the computer screening indicates — slightly stereotypical. A similar contradiction marks part of the contemporary critical discourses, whether their heading is post-colonialism, postmodernism, multiculturalism, or cultural studies. The same vocabulary of binary opposition such as self/other, identity/alterity, home/displacement is repeated to the point of often creating highly self-centered and self-generating theories.[2] Yet, like in the résumé example, this language on the one hand is necessary in order to articulate issues of displacement, diversity and integration, issues which after all describe some of the most difficult challenges contemporary societies have to face. On the other hand, without anchoring the terminology in particular stories, one risks standardizing and thereby erasing the specific conditions of displaced human beings. For almost all of us, as Angelika Bammer has pointed out, "to 'be' in the postmodern sense is somehow to be an Other: displaced," but she also warns that the problem "with this notion of displacement is that differences, thus universalized, disappear."[3]

Keeping these theoretical concerns in mind, I would like to examine in the following how the experiences of home and displacement are articulated in two contemporary novels, Barbara Frischmuth's *Das Verschwinden des Schattens in der Sonne* (1973; *The Shadow Disappears in the Sun,* 1998)[4] and [Waltraud] Anna Mitgutsch's *In fremden Städten* (1992; *In Foreign Cities,* 1995).[5] Though these two women writers occupy very different positions in the Austrian literary scene, they share a particular expertise, indeed a first-hand, professional knowledge for this subject matter. Both have been — albeit only temporarily — displaced in other cultures, and both are experienced resident aliens.

In 1960, as a student of Turkish, Frischmuth, born in 1941, won a fellowship to study at the University of Erzurum in Anatolia.[6] The nineteen-year-old Frischmuth spent about nine months in Turkey, to which she frequently returned in the following years. She had planned to write a dissertation on the traces of the dervish order of the Bektashi in Turkey, but by the mid-sixties, after getting a degree as a translator for Turkish and Hungarian, she decided to abandon a scholarly career in favor of writing. Frischmuth based *Das Verschwinden des Schattens in der Sonne* on her own stay in Turkey, but she stresses that the novel is not *her* story.[7] The closest link between fiction and fact is provided by the protagonist, a nameless young Austrian student living in Istanbul, who spends her time researching the same topic Frischmuth had originally pursued for her dissertation.

Like her older colleague Frischmuth, Mitgutsch, born in 1948, studied foreign languages and first prepared for a scholarly profession.[8] Mitgutsch holds a Ph.D. in English literature and has published on twentieth-century American poetry, particularly Sylvia Plath. The author has lived in many different countries (England, Korea, Israel), and one can assume that her six years in the United States provided the background for *In fremden Städten*. The novel describes a young American student, an aspiring poet who marries an Austrian lawyer and settles down in Innsbruck. After fifteen years, she leaves her husband and their two children and returns to the States.

The reasons for comparing these particular narratives are twofold. First, I found it intriguing that the two authors address the dichotomy of home and displacement through a similar setting. Both narratives focus on a female protagonist who lives either temporarily (Frischmuth) or permanently (Mitgutsch) abroad. The tension between home and the absence of it is thus borne out from both ends of the spectrum: The protagonists are residents in the sense that they are part of the daily life of their adopted culture and as such expected to perform according to its norms and rituals. At the same time, they continue to be aliens: distant and different others. Only the extended sojourn offers this possibility of negotiating between being participant and observer, and it thus allows for an in-depth (self-) interrogation of social and cultural conditioning. Having to perform in a different culture also tests, and as the two novels show, tests to the limits, a person's ability to handle otherness, because the encounter with the other is connected to one of the most unsettling fears of all: the fear of losing one's own sense of identity and self. As Jonathan Rutherford explains it: "In the hierarchical language of the West, what is alien represents otherness, the site of difference and the repository of our fears and anxieties."[9]

Frischmuth and Mitgutsch develop the character of the resident alien, and this spells the second reason for the comparison, from opposite perspectives. The strategy Frischmuth employs in her novel is that of becoming an expert of the new culture, for this approach offers proximity as well as protection from the novel playing-field. According to Frischmuth, this position allows for "a sort of 'point of return' that seems suitable for shielding one from an absolute identification with the Other."[10] Mitgutsch, on the other hand, chose for her narrative a diametrically opposed point of view, a "point of *no* return," for the novel's protagonist Lillian has come to stay in her husband's country. In contrast to the expert stance, which requires detachment, objectivity, and distance, the intercultural marriage speaks of fusion, intimacy, and close emotional bonds. Unable to fulfill these demands, Lillian moves back to the United States, where she reaches an ultimate point of no return and commits suicide.

In tracking the intercultural encounters staged in the two texts along these two diverse paths, I am not primarily looking for the protagonists' mastery in overcoming their displacement or erasing their alienness, for such an approach oversimplifies what is at stake in this rapprochement. Though one certainly can identify attitudes and strategies that help cope with alterity, by its very nature alterity will always maintain an elusive, unattainable quality. Also, from an epistemological point of view, understanding "kills" the object of the quest. A foreignness known is no longer foreign, it has lost its ability to mark discontinuity with the self.[11] Dietrich Krusche thus argues for approaching a foreign culture not with the goal of seeking to comprehend. Instead, he advocates the provisional suspension of understanding, in order to create an intercultural experience that "does not (yet) appropriate that which is experienced as 'foreign' with a grasp that penetrates, recognizes, or categorizes; . . . (still) postpones the awarding of validity and competence to one's own categories of recognition; . . . (still) suspends the introduction of a comprehensive pattern of interpretation."[12]

I would thus like to ask what the expert stance and the romance plot each have to contribute to the balancing act between guarding one's own self and exposing it to the demands of different cultural formations? How does each mode help maneuver the tension between the resident and the alien part of the protagonist's identity? Following Dennis Porter's inquiry into the nature of traveling, which he describes as a form of border crossing characterized by both desire and transgression, I also wish to explore whether the two protagonists have been able to combine world- with self-exploration. Have they lived up to the challenge, "if not . . . to make themselves over, then at least to know themselves differently"?[13] Analyzing the dichotomy of home and displacement in these two novels also entails discussing the forms of representation chosen by each author. Representing the world is "a political as well as an aesthetic-cognitive activity"[14] and this duality is nowhere more apparent than in the depiction of cultural alterity. Do the two narratives thus describe the foreign culture more in essentialist terms, as an entity to be known and recorded, or do they follow Krusche's suggestions and suspend the production of knowledge in order to achieve a nonhegemonic view of alterity?

In *Das Verschwinden des Schattens in der Sonne,* Barbara Frischmuth, after a ten-year hiatus, deals with her experiences as a young student in the Turkey of the 1960s. Frischmuth has stressed that the novel offers by no means an autobiographical account, but a way of coming to terms with her sojourn in the other culture. For this purpose the narrative operates on two levels. One level describes the student's wanderings through Istanbul, her circle of friends and acquaintances, as well as her efforts in gaining information about her scholarly project, the dervish order of the Bektashi. Linguistic and historical facts about the order, tales as well as excerpts from their literature form a second narrative, a subplot.[15]

In her scholarly pursuits as well as in her daily life, the protagonist is trying to understand the other culture on its own terms, she tries to understand it from within. The young woman does not want to observe and value the society according to her own personal categories and standards, and she certainly does not want to pass any judgment. She is well aware that any type of assessment or criticism is based on the comparative merit of two ways of life. In that sense, she follows Krusche's suggestion of suspending comprehension in order not to preliminarily fit and fix the other into her own value system. To the extent possible, she is thus attempting to completely mold her behavior according to the rules of her immediate environment and be like the people around her: "I tried to adapt; I tried to live as though I could understand and accept how the system of my various relationships worked. I wanted to make as few mistakes as possible, although I knew that I would always make some" (*Verschwinden* 23).[16]

This approach also explains the almost complete lack of information given about the protagonist and first-person narrator, because she does not want to be known by her origin and native culture, but rather by her presence in the urban student milieu of Istanbul. She is, of course, aware that people initially react to her as a foreigner, but because she is so well versed in the language, the history, and the customs of the country, her alienness quickly disappears. This, however, only applies to her circle of friends and the university locale, which despite its difference is also a familiar social and educational setting. It is important to bear in mind that the novel does not depict the character's encounter with *the* Turkish culture, as it is misleadingly phrased in some reviews,[17] but with a *particular* class and location in Turkey. The young woman encounters the urban, educated, Westernized intelligentsia, which despite its links to the rural, traditional way of life, does not confront her with an orthodox Muslim code, which would have posed a far greater challenge to her integration efforts. At this point, she is somewhat mindful of the surveillance and protection exercised both by her female and male friends, but it does not interfere with her extensive wanderings through the city. It is during these tours that her alienness again becomes most visible. The Turks of chance encounters react to her as if she neither knew the language nor the culture and treat her as the alien she represents to them.[18] By the same token, she is upset by the similarities she "still" (*Verschwinden* 15) shares with the tourists visiting the city.

The protagonist is, however, not trying "to go native," for both she and her friends know that as a resident alien, she is engaged in a temporary cultural switch, in a game of make-believe that will be abandoned once she returns home. Wearing a Şalvar, the baggy trousers of traditional Turkish women's dress, thus turns for her, as her friend Sevim points out, into a symbolic act, a gesture through which she stages her acceptance of Turkish culture and simultaneously marks her own difference, because the Şalvar is being transformed from an ordinary piece of clothing into an exotic garb. Reluctantly the protagonist agrees with the criticism: "I would allow myself to experience, for a moment, a feeling of exoticism, but not only that: I would experience a kind of satisfaction from identifying for a short period of time with a different concept of civilization by wearing one of their visible markers"

(*Verschwinden* 141–142).[19]

This episode demonstrates that her border crossing ultimately lacks authenticity. It is the performance of somebody who will eventually return to her "real" life and locale from where she can then apply her native cultural code in order to objectify and classify the experience with the other. Not only, as Sevim points out, will their time together be reduced to the status of photo memories, it will also become a completely detached experience: "You will calmly sit in your country and do your research and think about how this or that sign can be interpreted, while we here experience war, disease, or revolution. But it doesn't matter, you hear, it doesn't matter; we love you and you love us, and we will live together for a while" (*Verschwinden* 145).[20]

Sevim's emphatic assertion, which is followed by embracing and kissing her Austrian friend, indicates that she is not necessarily blaming her for this situation but only stating its inherent limitations. Sevim knows that in many ways her roommate presents the ideal of a foreign friend. She is not only intrigued and fascinated by the culture but also extremely knowledgeable, as her expertise on the Bektashi reveals. At the same time, it is her scholarship that both provides her with and withholds access to the different environment.

But why does this student, I kept asking myself, seek entrance to another culture through such a particularly difficult subject? Why does she choose an esoteric doctrine riddled with secrets and mysteries that continually thwarts her efforts of comprehension? Mirroring to some extent the student's dilemma, the readers are given some bare-bone facts about the topic but are also confronted with tales and texts that make little sense to the nonexpert.[21] The Bektashi, a Shiite order, was founded in the thirteenth century by Haci Bektas Veli. The order participated in numerous uprisings in Anatolia and was subsequently persecuted, which led to its existence in secrecy (*Verschwinden* 168). It was officially dissolved by the Turkish government in 1928. The Bektashi did not follow the orthodox Islamic code and allowed women, for example, to participate in their ceremonies. Because, as Frischmuth explains, "the order shared the mystical tenets of Shi'ism, it held its literature shrouded in secrecy."[22] Their literature was therefore considered to preserve a "purer" form of Turkish with less influence of Persian and Arabic loanwords. Precisely this linguistic quality led to its rediscovery in the 1960s because the Bektashi texts were considered as the "source for pure Turkish"[23] and, as such, published and promoted by the government. Both

Frischmuth herself and the protagonist are particularly fascinated by the mystic elements of the order.[24] In the subplot, Frischmuth incorporates stories about Haci Bektas Veli as well as elements of *The Conference of the Birds* (ca. 1200 A.D.), an important Persian mystic tale by Farudeddin Attar (ca. 1140–1230). This tale recounts the journey of numerous birds searching for the Simurgh, the divine bird. Only thirty birds survive the ordeal of the quest, which leads in the end to the discovery that they themselves are the Simurgh. The novel's title refers to the mystic idea of the unity of all things, the disappearance of the self in God.[25]

Though the protagonist is constantly scrambling for publications on the subject, she is unsure whether she should indeed pursue it in a standard scholarly fashion. The Bektashi legends told to her by her adviser's wife seem, for example, to be of equal value as any scholarly treatise. The subject matter thus continually seems to slip away from her with any approach she tries to apply, be it standard scholarship, oral history, or folktales. Not surprisingly, she cannot even begin to formulate the exact topic of her project. Occasionally, the protagonist expresses frustration at her lack of progress, yet she has accepted this ambivalent, slippery, and mysterious terrain, where she is searching for a knowledge that those who possess it do not wish to share. Her adviser, a Turkish professor who hardly gives her any concrete suggestions, indicates that the subject itself will ultimately guide her in the right direction. The narrator thus learns that the structures and methods of scholarship, the order she is trained to impose fail in the pursuit of this particular topic so that her inquiry exposes the limits of Western ways of knowledge and logic. In addition, the clandestine activities of the Bektashi mirror the secrecy contemporary political opponents such as her friend Turgut need to practice, and explicit parallels are drawn between current and earlier times of persecution (*Verschwinden* 107). Most important, however, this quest mirrors the protagonist's approach to the city, and in so doing, it mirrors the mystic search leading to self-discovery.

The anonymous student spends many hours wandering, drifting through Istanbul, perceiving of herself as a kind of medium onto which the city could impress itself. She collects images, sights, sounds, and smells but without necessarily explaining or interpreting them for fear of anchoring these impressions in a particular system of knowledge and representation. She is thus able to largely avoid a binary structure of categories and distinctions, for she deliberately withholds comparisons and conclusions. Porter's description of Roland Barthes's book on Japan,

L'Empire des Signes (1970, Empire of Signs), also applies to Frischmuth's narrative set in Istanbul, for both authors reject the "Western representational aesthetic which opposed an Occidental knowing subject to an Oriental object of knowledge."[26] Frischmuth is certainly less radical in her approach than Barthes, but the lack of plot and story, of the data and descriptions one commonly receives from narratives set in different countries, deliberately withholds meaning. In addition, the numerous Islamic mystic tales traversing the text further undermine mimetic traditions and expectations. For the protagonist and for the readers alike, the other location, which in a telling detail of Frischmuth's approach is never explicitly referred to as Turkey, Turkish, or even Istanbul, simply does not make much sense. Yet, it is precisely this lack of clarity, order, and meaning that helps the protagonist avoid the Western modes of objectification. She does not fall for any of the Western hegemonic paradigms; no *Imperial Eyes,*[27] no *Orientalist Discourse,*[28] and no "manichaeism delirium"[29] guide her through the city. Instead, she welcomes the blurring of past and presence, of dreams and reality, and the ensuing loss of self: "My perception of life had changed in a way as if I were almost able to indulge even in the things themselves surrounding me . . . as if there had been a possibility to temporarily erase the boundaries between myself and others" (*Verschwinden* 200–01).[30]

In this regard, this young woman's pursuit of another culture is very productive.[31] She is able to balance the resident and the alien part of her identity in such a way that she is no longer sure which of the two reference systems secures her "true" self.[32] As a result, her view is nonhegemonic, and she comes to know herself differently, thus achieving the twin goals posited in postmodern discourse for a constructive intercultural encounter. At the same time, the refusal to anchor herself in one particular system backfires, and she has to pay a price for not assessing and judging what she sees.

The narrator herself realizes that in trying to read the culture through a historical perspective and in limiting any critique for fear of offending a different way of life, she failed "to get to know things as they really were . . . to see them without regard to their changeable nature" ("die Dinge kennenzulernen, wie sie waren . . . ohne sie auf ihre Veränderbarkeit hin anzusehen," *Verschwinden* 159). She is thus unable to recognize the current challenges the society faces, in particular the mounting political tension to which her friend Turgut, a student activist eventually falls victim. Shortly before his death, she summarizes her stay: "I had subdued my critical ability to conformity and had made experiences that turned out to be failures. I had given in to circumstance, had identified myself too thoughtlessly. I had neglected to obtain accurate information" (*Verschwinden* 219).[33]

It seems to me that this assessment does not so much reveal her failures as the limits and shortcomings inherent in her particular approach. Maybe she had relied too strongly on the alien component of her existence instead of acting more like a resident. Like her friends, she perhaps should have taken a critical stance, speaking out against injustice or underdevelopment. But by the same token, a critic of the poverty, corruption, and brutality of the Turkey of the 1960s, someone who focused on "begging children, mutilated old folks, blood-vending assassins, women hiding their chopped-off noses under their veils, soldiers kissing the hands of their generals" (*Verschwinden* 158)[34] would have judged the country from the outside perspective of a Western observer and would be accused of practicing a hegemonic discourse. In the first days of her stay, this was precisely how the protagonist engaged with the city, but her friends interpreted her critique "as an attack against their way of life" ("als Angriff gegen ihre Art zu leben," *Verschwinden* 159). The novel thus shows the limits intrinsic to each and every perspective; it shows that there is no Archimedean point outside history, culture, and subjectivity. At the same time, it does not advocate what Satya P. Mohanty has called the "relativist view of pure difference,"[35] which does not allow for a critique and value judgment of cultural differences. The protagonist's expertise, her respect for and knowledge of the other culture give her a right, and perhaps also an obligation, to point out injustice and violence, even if this entails the loss of approval.

In contrast to Frischmuth's allegorical style, Mitgutsch takes an almost clinical approach to the protagonist of her latest novel. Though *In fremden Städten* deals with a new topic, the heroine Lillian is a typical Mitgutsch figure. Like in her previous works, the author delivers test cases of a particular condition, considered to be an aberration from the norm, details symptoms, phases, and results, as if her characters were patients whom she has to diagnose but not to heal.[36] Donald Daviau described all of Mitgutsch's main figures as ill-adjusted, estranged, and alienated women who are lacking a sense of self, which makes them either unable or unwilling to accept reality as it is. Daviau concludes: "These characters are all psychologically flawed and carry their problems with them."[37] Maria-Regina Kecht in her interpretation of Mitgutsch's novels draws a similar conclusion. She identifies female alienation, selflessness, and loss of voice as Mitgutsch's central themes.[38] Mitgutsch obviously agrees with this assessment, for she states: "All of my heroines feel alienated and are estranged from their environment. . . . And this difference in experiencing reality can — must — have its effects on language."[39] In this sense, all of Mitgutsch's figures could be characterized as resident aliens, but only in *In fremden Städten* does the author investigate this split within the intercultural realm.

Compared to the challenges and ordeals Barbara Frischmuth devised for her character, Lillian's fate at first glance seems to be relatively easy. A young college student moving from North America to Austria in the 1970s came, after all, to another modern society, which was shaped by a very similar political, socioeconomic, and social system. Despite the differences in history, language, and customs, Lillian was familiar with the social fabric, with its signs and symbols. Her husband and his family thus expect that after an initial period of difficulties and doubts, Lillian will quickly integrate. Yet, like Frischmuth, Mitgutsch shows that the distance between familiarity and alienness is independent of the amount or the extent of differences separating them. The affinity between her former and her current home is of no help to Lillian. Her mental and emotional makeup certainly contribute to her inability to adjust, and the third-person narrator is — a new feature in Mitgutsch's œuvre — highly critical of her behavior. Lillian is described as inflexible (*Städten* 19), impatient (*Städten* 47), or hostile and unapproachable (*Städten* 46), and throughout her fifteen years in Austria, she remains, according to her husband, the archetypal foreigner (*Städten* 30).

Mitgutsch constructs this archetypal foreignness, or "the different facets of foreignness" ("die verschiedenen Facetten des Fremdseins"),[40] as she described the novel's theme, on three separate, but overlapping levels. The first level concerns Lillian's marriage and encounter with Austria; the second tier deals with her return to the United States; and the third stage entails her childhood and adolescence. The novel thus moves from intercultural to intracultural foreignness, arriving finally at Lillian's profound inner alienness. In Lillian's steadfast refusal to follow the norm, be it at home or abroad, Mitgutsch investigates the condition of foreignness. Seen from that perspective, the novel then bears a striking similarity to Alfred Schütz's pioneering analysis of foreignness in his essay "Der Fremde" (1971, The Stranger). Like Schütz, Mitgutsch centers her exploration on the archetypal qualities of foreignness and difference, which she locates primarily in the area of language and memory. Schütz defines the foreigner's condition as follows: "The cultural and civilizational patterns of the group the foreigner approaches offer him no protection but present a field for adventure; they offer no foregone conclusions, but a questionable topic of inquiry; they offer no means for analyzing problematic situations but are a problematic situation in itself, and one that is hard to solve."[41]

Lillian's experiences in Austria certainly confirm this paradigm, and she also shares the foreigner's most common attributes: objectivity and a questionable loyalty to the new society.[42] At the same time, she does not engage in the process of social adaptation, in which the newcomer learns to master the different social patterns, so that in the end the foreigner is no longer a foreigner and his/her particular problems have been solved.[43] Instead, Lillian intentionally arrests herself in a state of permanent foreignness. Her statement, "I belong where I am not!" ("Ich gehöre dahin, wo ich nicht bin!"*Städten* 8) can serve as her life's leitmotiv, because for Lillian it is always the other place that seems to hold the promise for a better, happier existence. Precisely this is what made Austria initially so attractive to the young college student, for its unfamiliarity allowed her to regard it as a stage on which she played out youth, adventure, and the romance with a young Austrian lawyer. This stage quality of the foreign also reappears in Lillian's descriptions of Austria, which are remarkably vague and colorless. Though a precise gift of observation (*Städten* 35) was praised as a particular strength of her poetic writing, this talent fails her abroad. In contrast to the exact topography of Istanbul provided by Frischmuth's character, it appears that Lillian is unable to take notice of her environment, because it only serves as an arbitrary and interchangeable backdrop for her performance as a foreigner. She had hoped, however, that Austria would permanently enable her to lead such a playful, preliminary existence, and she is therefore completely unprepared for the return of the familiar in her marriage with Joseph: "How trivial and suffocating the exotic became as soon as one established oneself in it" ("Wie banal und erstickend das Exotische wurde, sobald man sich darin niederließ," *Städten* 55).

Lillian is equally unprepared for the particular constraints of an intercultural relationship. By marrying Joseph, she had unhinged the American center, and in particular the language center of her life, which, she feels, resulted in the loss of her poetic talent. Though the clash between foreign and familiar structures every aspect of Lillian's life, language becomes the fiercest "battleground" ("Kampfgebiet," *Städten* 47). Since Lillian never completely mastered German, she always loses "the battle for words" ("den Kampf um Worte," *Städten* 25). Unable also to keep her children in the maternal world of English, Lillian feels her motherhood negated and distances herself from her children.

What turns Lillian into the archetypal foreigner is not only her refusal to learn different cultural norms, it is primarily her insistence that difference is indeed insurmountable. In her view, adaptation, assimilation, and integration equal the majority's request to wipe out one's own self and identity. She is acutely aware that in Austria, she will always be, as Schütz phrases it, "a person without a history" ("ein Mensch ohne Geschichte"),[44] for both sides are excluded from the other's past. Lillian also feels that she cannot really share or communicate her Americanness because in so doing, she is only confirming stereotypical images of the United States. She regards, for example, the Thanksgiving dinner party given by her American friend Marlene as a "folklore-show" ("Folklore-abend," *Städten* 59). It parcels out pieces of America and turns them into a Walt Disney-like commodity, providing the Austrian spectators with the comfort of "knowing" the Americans, their openness and hospitality. Lillian wages the same battle when she and her family visit the United States, where she is intent on presenting them with her (former) America, which her Austrian family is of course unable to detect. They experience a contemporary society that, in comparison to Austria, they find primarily lacking so that toward the end, each trip becomes "a ruthless struggle for superiority; they fought over the edibility of food, the beauty of the landscape, the demands of language" ("ein rücksichtsloser Kampf um Überlegenheit, sie stritten um die Eßbarkeit der Lebensmittel, den Reiz der Landschaft, die Zumutbarkeit der Sprache," *Städten* 53). Schütz's statement that "graves and memories can neither be transferred nor conquered" ("Gräber und Erinnerungen können weder übertragen noch erobert werden")[45] describes the core of this dilemma.

Mitgutsch investigates the tension between home and displacement in an absolute way, for, in contrast to Frischmuth, she designed a character who perceives of her situation in strictly binary terms. Lillian sees herself locked in a center-margin dichotomy where she is constantly losing against the dominant majority. Whether it is her language, her past in America, or simply her presence in the country, "everything she encountered spoke to her of her exclusion" ("Alles Vorhandene zeigte ihr, daß sie nicht mitgemeint war," *Städten* 23). Her frustrations thus result not only from personal flaws and problems,[46] but they also spell a deeply political issue, since the binarism on which logocentric thinking rests privileges one term: "Those terms that are pre-eminent and invested with truth, achieve that status by excluding and marginalising what they are not."[47] A permanent resident like Lillian is most aware of the center's material and discursive power to define the minority. It shows her strength, however, that she considers the loss of self, and not the lack of approval, as the worst fate. "It had to be the worst, she thought, to be foreign and not to realize it" ("Das schlimmste, dachte sie, müßte es sein, fremd zu sein und es selber nicht einmal mehr zu merken," *Städten* 61). This logic is also in effect when Lillian returns to America, but it is here, in her (former) home, where her life completely falls apart.

Her lover, a young American performer she had briefly met in Salzburg, is no longer interested in her, and she detests the American way of life embodied in her sister's pragmatic, work-oriented existence. Instead of finding freedom and independence, she is as a native experiencing the same estrangement she had felt while in Europe: "What terrified her was the knowledge that she would never be at home in her own country, while in Europe she would remain a stranger" ("Was sie entsetzte, war das Wissen, daß sie im eigenen Land heimatlos sein würde, während sie in Europa eine Fremde bliebe," *Städten* 141). When she finally meets her father in a dilapidated house on the Atlantic Ocean, she is horrified to detect herself and her own thwarted creative attempts in this utterly miserable old man. Her husband, whom she calls in a last-ditch attempt, refuses to take her back. Recognizing the extent of her isolation and homelessness, recognizing that she has nowhere to go, no goal, no future, she sets her father's house on fire and runs toward the ocean. Her journey has reached an ultimate dead end, resulting in destruction, murder, and suicide.

In trying to establish the reasons for Lillian's estrangement, the narrator probes deeper and deeper into her psyche, peeling away the different layers of cultural foreignness connected to her marriage, to Austria as well as to America. Lillian is thus gradually recognizing the effects of her traumatic childhood on her persona and development. A distant father who could not come to terms with the loss of his wife, and a Bohemian grandmother recounting stories about the glory of prewar Vienna and Europe imbued the child from early on with a deep-felt longing for a location other than the one she occupies: "But ever since childhood she had believed that she would feel better somewhere else" ("Aber immer, schon seit ihrer Kindheit hatte sie geglaubt, daß sie sich irgendwo anders besser fühlen würde," *Städten* 78). One could interpret her restlessness and dissatisfaction with any status quo therefore as the search for the home she never had. Lillian's quest for an elsewhere, however, is always bound to be unsuccessful, for she cannot attain something she is unable to define, since she never possessed it in the first place. She is thus searching to fill a void that, even if attained, would cancel itself out and the search could begin anew. Not surprisingly, Lillian feels most at ease when she is not fixed in any particular location. She likes to literally be in motion: "On board the plane she felt at ease. . . . On the plane she felt safe like in an asylum, caught between two experiences that both lacked grounding" ("Im Flugzeug fühlte sie sich wohl. . . . Im Flugzeug war sie aufgehoben wie im Asyl, zwischen zwei Erfahrungen von Bodenlosigkeit," *Städten* 32).

Daviau has argued that Lillian's main problem is her lack of talent, which she, however, like her father, is apt to blame on outside factors. According to Daviau, Lillian represents "a female version of the pseudo-artist," and he sees her as a postmodern reenactment of the turn-of-the-century "Literat."[48] I agree with the focus on Lillian's artistic side, but I would like to add two other factors to this interpretation.

Throughout her life, Lillian has tried to overcome what in deconstructionist terminology is described as the initial split between self and world. Both in her life as well as in her early poetry, she pursued the dream of an undivided self in which the unity of all things is still intact. The unfamiliarity of life abroad naturally widens the gap between self and object and especially between language and object. The unknown culture makes the split even more painful to bear while simultaneously holding out the promise of finding the lost unity. This inability to perceive of the world and of the self as a comprehensive, intelligible, and distinct unity is, however, the dominant theme of modern poetry, first experienced and articulated by the romantic writers. Seen from this perspective, Lillian is yet another artistic figure who is reenacting the romantic artist's dilemma. Her hope was that she would find a language that would give the world the completeness it had presented to the young child. Instead, she finds herself with a foreign idiom's language tools, with which she cannot even achieve the basic task of communication, let alone transform the world.

Lillian's artistic failure also reveals an important gender component, for the loss of poetic expression coincides with her acceptance of female adulthood centered on marriage and parenthood. Throughout her marriage, she struggles with the conflicting demands of artistic vocation and motherhood, which in the foreign environment are even more difficult to reconcile. In this context, I found it particularly striking that Lillian's story bears traces of Sylvia Plath's life.[49] These allusions concern biographical data as well as poetic themes.[50] Parallels appear, for example, between the New England setting and landscape, in which both the fictitious as well as the actual poet grew up and went to college. Both figures also endured a traumatic childhood marred by a loss that would inspire a lifelong search to fill the void. Furthermore, both gained early recognition, manifest in prizes and awards. One could also name Plath's Fulbright scholarship to study in Cambridge, England, and add as an interesting detail that Plath, after the early death of her father, was raised under the influence of her Austrian maternal grandmother.[51] Most important, however, the central concern of Plath's work is the loss of self, which as Mitgutsch explains, is simultaneously experienced as a threat and as a goal to be attained: "A threat, because the lifting of boundaries effectively means a loss of self and thereby a loss of humanity; a goal, because it is the only way that allows us to cross the threshold to the other, the unknown being, thereby lifting the boundary between one's individuality and the other."[52]

In contrast to Plath, Lillian is unable to express this dichotomy in language; but like Plath, she experiences it as a matter of life and death; and both women represent and resolve it through their suicides.

In conclusion, it seems that both novels ultimately present the ontological dimension of the encounter with the other. The fear and the attraction of "disappearing in the sun," of overstepping the limits of the self, guide both characters in their intercultural encounters, but they travel on different paths and reach different ends. Frischmuth's young student, single and independent, is as knowledgeable as she is fascinated by the Turkish Orient. She has the courage as well as the curiosity to test herself to the limits, searching in scholarship as well as in personal alliances for an *unio mystica* only the foreign can accord. Though able to largely steer clear of instrumentalizing the other, her experiences also teach her the inherent limits of understanding a distant culture.

Mitgutsch's Lillian, on the other hand, takes no interest in the new country she had primarily entered in the hope of overcoming her profound sense of alienness. The *unio mystica* she had attempted early on in her poems cannot be repeated in an environment that constantly reminds her of her linguistic and cultural difference, and keeps her locked in a center-margin dichotomy she is unable to break. Disappointed and frustrated by her middle-class bourgeois life, she recedes into nostalgia and daydreaming, insisting on the insurmountable distinctness of the original cultural code. Though she is rightly criticized as self-centered, unrealistic, and immature, it is precisely through her refusal to accept the majority's opinion that she not only questions its validity but also upholds the utopian dream of an *unio mystica*, of an integration of self and world that is very similar to the one Frischmuth's protagonist is seeking. Lillian, however, is unable to find an appropriate path, since it turns out that neither literature nor romance or motherhood can lead her to this goal, which she can only achieve in death. Ultimately, both stories do explain to us some of the basic elements at stake in negotiating the resident and the alien part of displaced human beings.

University of Delaware

Notes

1. Bob Rosner, "Prince Could Call with Glass Slipper Any Time, So Be Ready," *The News Journal*, 7 July 1997, D7.

2. For a critique of postcolonialism, see Russell Jacoby, "Marginal Returns: The Trouble with Post-Colonial Theory," *Lingua Franca* (Sept./Oct. 1995): 30–37.

3. Angelika Bammer, "Introduction," *Displacements: Cultural Identities in Question* (Bloomington: Indiana UP, 1994) xii.

4. Barbara Frischmuth, *Das Verschwinden des Schattens in der Sonne* (Frankfurt/Main: Suhrkamp, 1973). The translation of this work is, *The Shadow Disappears in the Sun,* trans. Nicholas Meyerhofer (Riverside, CA: Ariadne, 1998). In the following, quotations from that work will be documented by parenthetical citation in the text *(Verschwinden).*

5. [Waltraud] Anna Mitgutsch, *In fremden Städten* (Munich: dtv, 1994). In the following, quotations from that work will be documented by parenthetical citation in the text *(Städten).* The work has been translated into English as *In Foreign Cities,* transl. Michael Mitchell (Riverside, CA:

Ariadne, 1995).

6. For biographical data on Frischmuth, see Hans Haider, "Barbara Frischmuth, eine Biographie," *Dossier 4: Barbara Frischmuth,* ed. Kurt Bartsch (Graz: Droschl, 1992) 151–162.

7. Barbara Frischmuth, "Looking over the Fence," trans. Lisabeth Hock, *Multiculturalism in Contemporary German Literature,* special issue of *World Literature Today* 69.3 (Summer 1995): 460.

8. For biographical data on Mitgutsch, see Petra Ernst, "Waltraud Anna Mitgutsch," *Neues Handbuch der deutschsprachigen Gegenwartsliteratur seit 1945,* ed. Dietz-Rüdiger Moser (Munich: dtv, 1993) 811–812.

9. Jonathan Rutherford, "A Place Called Home: Identity and the Cultural Politics of Difference," *Identity: Community, Culture, Difference,* ed. Jonathan Rutherford (London: Lawrence & Wishart, 1990) 10.

10. Frischmuth, "Looking" 460.

11. Dietrich Krusche, "Utopie und Allotopie: Zur Geschichte des Motivs der außereuropäischen Fremde in der Literatur," *Jahrbuch Deutsch als Fremdsprache* 11 (1985): 132.

12. Krusche 132. Original quote: ". . . das als 'fremd' Erfahrene (noch) nicht im Zugriff des Durchschauens, Erkennens, Einordnens sich aneignet; . . . den Zuspruch der Zuständigkeit und Kompetenz eigener Erkenntniskategorien (noch) zurückstellt; . . . die Einführung eines umfassenden Erklärungsprinzips (noch) suspendiert."

13. Dennis Porter, *Haunted Journeys: Desire and Transgression in European Travel Writing* (Princeton: Princeton UP, 1991) 5.

14. Porter 14.

15. Traces of Frischmuth's original dissertation plan are also visible in the list of works consulted at the end of the novel.

16. Original quote: "Ich versuchte mich anzupassen, so zu leben, als würde ich das Funktionieren des Systems der verschiedenen Beziehungen, in denen ich stand, durchschauen und akzeptieren. Ich wollte so wenige Fehler wie möglich machen, obwohl ich wußte, daß ich immer welche machen würde."

17. See Peter Hertz-Ohmes, "Cultural Complementarities in Frischmuth's Turkish Novel," *The German Mosaic: Cultural and Linguistic Diversity in Society,* ed. Carol Aisha Blackshire-Belay (Westport, CT: Greenwood, 1994) 195–199 and Georg Pichler, "'Seltsam, daß es mir so wenig ausmacht, nicht anzukommen:' Heimat und Fremde bei Barbara Frischmuth," *Dossier 4: Barbara Frischmuth* 57–72.

Hertz-Ohmes calls it "Frischmuth's Turkish Novel" (195), and Pichler argues, "The narrator did not manage to really familiarize herself with Turkey" ("es ist der Erzählerin nicht gelungen, sich wirklich in *der* [emphasis added] Türkei einzuleben," 66).

18. Particularly telling is an episode in the Süleymaniye mosque, in which she meets two Anatolian women. The women do not expect her to have a command of the language and though the protagonist speaks to them, they insist that she cannot understand them (*Verschwinden* 21).

19. Original quote: "Ich würde mir für einen Augenblick ein Gefühl der Exotik gestatten, nicht nur das, ich würde eine Art von Befriedigung erleben, indem ich mich für kurze Zeit durch das Tragen eines ihrer sichtbaren Merkmale mit einer anderen Auffassung von Zivilisation identifizieren könnte."

20. Original quote: "Du wirst mit deiner Wissenschaft ruhig in deinem Land sitzen und darüber nachdenken, wie das eine oder andere Zeichen zu deuten ist, während wir hier Seuchen oder Krieg oder Revolution haben. Aber das macht nichts, hörst du, das macht nichts, wir lieben dich und du liebst uns, und eine Zeitlang leben wir zusammen."

21. The information on the Bektashi order is based on Frischmuth's novel, her essay "Looking over the Fence" 460–461, as well as Nazire Akbulut, *Das Türkenbild in der neueren deutschen Literatur 1970–1990* (Berlin: Köster, 1993) 109–110, and Muhammed Abu Hattab Khaled, "Islamische Mystik in der deutschsprachigen Belletristik: Der Roman *Das Verschwinden des Schattens in der Sonne* von Barbara Frischmuth," *Gottes ist der Orient, Gottes ist der Okzident,* Festschrift für Abdoldjavad Falaturi, ed. Udo Tworuschka (Vienna: Böhlau, 1991) 299–308. John Kingsley Birge, *The Bektashi Order of Dervishes* (London: Luzac, 1965) offers the most comprehensive overview.

22. Frischmuth, "Looking" 460.

23. Frischmuth, "Looking" 460.

24. Particularly in her early works, Frischmuth has shown great interest in the mystic traditions of both Occidental and Oriental origin. See also her essay "Eine Souveräne Posaune Gottes: Gedanken zu Hildegard von Bingen und ihrem Werk," *Women in German Yearbook: Feminist Studies and German Culture,* vol. 2, ed. Marianne Burkhard and Edith Waldstein (Lanham: UP of America, 1986) 11–21, as well as Dagmar Lorenz, "Ein Interview: Barbara Frischmuth," *Women in German Yearbook* 2 (1986): 23–36.

25. Khaled points out that the title is in fact a quote taken from

Hellmut Ritter's work on Attar's *The Conference of Birds* (Khaled 302).

26. Porter 290.

27. See Mary Louise Pratt's study *Imperial Eyes: Travel Writing and Transculturation* (London: Routledge, 1992). Pratt analyzes how "travel and exploration writing *produced* 'the rest of the world' for European readerships" (5).

28. See Edward D. Said, *Orientalism* (New York: Vintage, 1979). In his extremely influential work, he argues for understanding "Orientalism" as a type of discourse, i.e., the Occidental production and representation of the Orient in order to establish and maintain an uncontested Western superiority over its inferior, weaker other (3).

29. Bill Ashcroft, Gareth Griffiths, and Helen Tiffin, *The Empire Writes Back: Theory and Practice in Post-Colonial Literatures* (London: Routledge, 1989). According to Ashcroft, Fanon characterizes the colonizer-colonized relationship as the product of a "'manichaeism delirium' . . . a radical division into paired oppositions such as good-evil; true-false; white-black, in which the primary sign is axiomatically privileged in the discourse of the colonial relationship" (124–125).

30. Original quote: "Mein Lebensgefühl hatte sich geändert, so als wäre ich dazu imstande, mich sogar den Dingen, die um mich waren, hinzugeben. . . . So als gäbe es eine Möglichkeit, die Grenzen von mir zu anderen zeitweise zu verwischen" (200–201).

31. Donald Daviau reads the text as a bildungsroman in which the protagonist learns to come to terms with her losses. Cf. Donald Daviau, "Neuere Entwicklungen in der modernen österreichischen Prosa: Die Werke von Barbara Frischmuth," *Modern Austrian Literature* 13.1 (1980): 190.

32. This blurring of boundaries is already indicated in the opening sections of the novels, in which the protagonist alternates between her original (Austrian) and the current (Istanbul) point of reference without being able to determine which of the two carries the greater validity (*Verschwinden* 7).

33. Original quote: "Ich hatte mein Kritikvermögen hinter die Anpassung gestellt und Erfahrungen gemacht, die sich als Fehlschläge erwiesen hatten. Ich hatte mich den Umständen anheimgestellt, mich zu leichtfertig identifiziert. Ich hatte es verabsäumt, mich genau genug zu informieren."

34. Original quote: ". . . bettelnde Kinder, verstümmelte Greise, meuchelnde Bluträcher, mit dem Schleier ihre abgehackten Nasen

verbergende Frauen, ihren Generälen die Hand küssende Soldaten . . ."

35. Satya P. Mohanty, "Epilogue: Colonial Legacies, Multicultural Futures: Relativism,Objectivity, and the Challenge of Otherness," *PMLA* 110.1 (1995): 112.

36. Daviau considers Mitgutsch's detailed explanation both a major strength and weakness of her narrative style. While providing an in-depth analysis of the character, they also allow "little possibility for the reader to participate" ("Neuere Entwicklungen" 121).

37. Donald G. Daviau, "The Problems of Identity, Reality and Estrangement in the Works of Waltraud Anna Mitgutsch," *Literaturkritik und erzählerische Praxis: Deutschsprachige Erzähler der Gegenwart,* ed. Herbert Herzmann (Tübingen: Stauffenburg, 1993) 109.

38. Maria-Regina Kecht, "Auflehnung gegen die Ordnung von Sprache und Vernunft: Die weibliche Wirklichkeitsgestaltung bei Waltraud Anna Mitgutsch," *Women in German Yearbook: Feminist Studies in German Literature and Culture,* vol. 8, ed. Jeanette Clausen and Sara Friedrichsmeyer (Lincoln: U of Nebraska P, 1993) 113–125.

39. Original quote: "Alle meine Heldinnen fühlen sich fremd und sind von ihrer Umwelt entfremdet. . . . Und dieses Anderssein in der Realitätserfahrung kann sich, muß sich in der Sprache niederschlagen." Qtd. in Maria-Regina Kecht, "Gespräch mit Waltraud Anna Mitgutsch," *Women in German Yearbook* 8 (1993): 136. Konstanze Fliedl stresses that the negativity of Mitgutsch's characters has to be understood within the context of the loss of language, which points to "aporias of communication" ("Aporien der Mitteilbarkeit"), particularly in the novel *In fremden Städten.* See her essay "Anders sprachlos: Zu den Romanen von Waltraud Anna Mitgutsch," *Literaturkritik und erzählerische Praxis* 105.

40. Kecht, "Gespräch" 138.

41. Alfred Schütz, "Der Fremde: Ein sozialpsychologischer Versuch," *Gesammelte Aufsätze* II: *Studien zur soziologischen Theorie,* ed. Arvid Brodersen (Den Haag: Martinus Nijhoff, 1972) 67. Original quote: "Die Kultur- und Zivilisationsmuster der Gruppe welcher sich der Fremde nähert, sind für ihn kein Schutz, sondern ein Feld des Abenteuers, keine Selbstverständlichkeit, sondern ein fragwürdiges Untersuchungsthema, kein Mittel, um problematische Situationen zu analysieren, sondern eine problematische Situation selbst und eine, die hart zu meistern ist."

42. Schütz 68.

43. Schütz 69.

44. Schütz 60.

45. Schütz 59.

46. Herbert Herzmann makes this aspect the dominant focus of his interpretation. See his essay "Das Ich und das Andere: Ichsucht und Ichflucht in Waltraud Anna Mitgutschs Roman *In fremden Städten,*" *Reisen im Diskurs: Modelle der literarischen Fremderfahrung von den Pilgerberichten bis zur Postmoderne,* ed. Anne Fuchs and Theo Harden (Heidelberg: Winter, 1995) 229–240.

47. Rutherford 21.

48. Both quotes from Daviau, "Problems of Identity" 120.

49. Mitgutsch has also published on Plath; see her essay "'Weltverlust' in der zeitgenössischen Lyrik, exemplarisch dargestellt an Paul Celan und Sylvia Plath," *Sprachkunst: Beiträge zur Literaturwissenschaft* 8 (1977): 251–272.

50. For data on Plath's life and poetry, see particularly chapters 1 and 2 of Linda Wagner-Martin, *Sylvia Plath: A Biography* (New York: Simon & Schuster, 1987).

51. Wagner-Martin 31.

52. Mitgutsch, "Weltverlust" 267. Original quote: "Bedrohung, weil die Aufhebung der Grenzen zur Umwelt gleichbedeutend ist mit dem Verlust des Bewußtseins und damit des Menschseins überhaupt, Ziel, weil es der einzige Weg ist, die Schwelle zum ganz Anderen, zum unbekannten Sein zu überschreiten und damit die Kluft zwischen der eigenen Individualität und diesem Anderen aufzuheben."

Dismantling Islam: Orientalism and the Women's Perspective in Barbara Frischmuth's Novel *Das Verschwinden des Schattens in der Sonne*

Dagmar C. G. Lorenz

The Shadow Disappears in the Sun, Ariadne, 1998

In the 1970s, close contacts between Austria and Mediterranean countries, including Turkey, had been firmly established and were expanding rapidly. In Vienna, there was a strong presence of students and migrant workers from the Middle East and Turkey, and Austrians traveled to Turkey in increasing numbers.[1] On the one hand, these developments made the Orient more accessible, while on the other, they activated the xenophobia that continued to linger after World War II. Contacts with increasingly visible and assertive "others" revitalized not only anti-Semitism but also century-old anxieties about Turkey and Islamic culture, notions that in the German-speaking context were largely based on imaginary constructs.[2]

In the postcolonial era, particularly after the 1968 student movement, when a politically correct discourse was emerging concerning gender and minority issues, the traditional Eurocentric approach to otherness came increasingly under scrutiny. Aside from political and theoretical considerations, however, women authors such as Barbara Frischmuth, a student and an aspiring writer, were in no position to assume the stance of a male conqueror vis-à-vis the Orient. The distinct gender roles in Austrian and Turkish culture, expressed, among other things, in terms of space and activities, were bound to produce distinct experiences for an Austrian man and an Austrian woman living in Turkey. Despite these differences, the images of Islamic culture in the works of German-speaking women authors, including those who had traveled in the Middle East, are informed by literary convention rather than empirical observation and the woman writer's own experience of marginalization.[3]

A writer's outlook is affected by the structures of her or his society of origin. Writers approach foreign countries with culture-specific expectations and confront the conditioned responses of members of the culture they want to explore. In Islamic society, speakers of German are perceived first and foremost as non-Muslims and as men or women. Yet, being a woman, Frischmuth might have had a better opportunity to explore the sphere of Turkish women than Christian, or perhaps even Muslim, men. This, however, is not the goal of her narrator in *Das Verschwinden des Schattens in der Sonne* (1973; *The Shadow Disappears in the Sun*, 1998),[4] who focuses on male writers and the male-dominated public sphere, writing about which carries greater promise for her envisioned career as an Austrian scholar. By her own admission, she undertakes her research in view of German-speaking rather than Turkish culture. She considers her stay in Turkey only temporary. "One day I would wake up and all these things would no longer concern me, at least not directly" ("Ich würde eines Tages aufwachen und das alles würde mich nicht mehr betreffen, zumindest nicht unmittelbar," 218).[5]

The narrator's repeated transgressions against the Islamic gender code and general code of conduct, committed naturally, as it were, as her prerogative as a Western woman visitor and an outsider, are not problematized. Nor does the text dwell on the fact that her conduct is not in keeping with the Central European moral code as well. Positioning herself not in between but rather outside of the two cultures leaves the narrator disconnected from the cultural codes and gender codes of both spheres. Nina Berman's examination of Orientalist texts by male and female writers such as Karl May and Else Lasker-Schüler reveals that the experience of gender ambivalence is common among German-speaking authors dealing with Middle Eastern culture. The exposure to different signals and dress-codes as well as the common configuration of the Orient as female initiate experiences carrying overtones of cross-dressing and cross-sexuality.[6]

The lack of interest in the sphere of Turkish women on the part of Frischmuth's narrator goes hand in hand with a predilection for masculine-coded activities and literature written by men. Without further exploration, she seems to dismiss the possibility that the women's sphere, despite its discretion vis-à-vis the outside world and its lack of public visibility, may offer a wide range of activities and roles, and a challenge particularly to her as a Westerner. Yet, having been socialized in Austria, the narrator feels separate from and superior to this sphere. Indeed, her attitude resembles that of a patriarchal male looking down upon women and women's culture. Generally speaking, the narrator comes across as a woman with the intellectual aspirations of an explorer, although these are thwarted by her gender. As a consequence, she interacts, or is forced to interact, predominantly with somewhat eccentric persons who are open to contacts with outsiders and foreigners. Suheyla, the middle-class Turkish woman with whom she used to correspond while she was still in Austria avoids her every time she tries to visit her at her house.

Frischmuth is not a stranger to marginalization. She was the only woman in the *Grazer Autorenkreis* (Graz Group of Authors) and admits that she never enjoyed the same recognition as some of her male colleagues. This experience, one might think, would have inspired greater sensitivity toward a culture that is all too frequently berated and misjudged in the West. "The Oriental is irrational, depraved, fallen, childlike, 'different,' thus the European is rational, virtuous, mature, 'normal,'" Edward Said characterizes the way in which Western writers depict the Middle East.[7] Austrian authors, Otto Weininger, Sigmund Freud, and Adolf Hitler have characterized women in these very terms: as irrational, immature, childlike, different, and depraved.[8] Austrian women writers such as Marlen Haushofer, Ingeborg Bachmann, and Elfriede Jelinek have shown that the prejudices and discrimination against Austrian women continued after World War II. Rationality, virtue, maturity, and normality, appropriated by the male voice, were rarely ascribed to women. Relegated to the position of objects of domination in the discourse of their own culture, Austrian women writers were in no position to reproduce the imperialist/colonialist voice of a male author, although some older women travelers and writers such as Alma Karlin and Bertha Pappenheim had tried.[9]

Although Frischmuth makes use of innovative narrative strategies and deals with women's issues — both suggest self-awareness and sensitivity — her Turkey is a product of traditional Western imagination. Indeed, at one point even her narrator wonders if she has invented her lover Aksu. The latter is a kind of fairy-tale figure, a variation of a character that appears again in *Die Mystifikationen der Sophie Silber* (1976, The Mystifications of Sophie Silber), in the latter work in the guise of a Jew. Hans Haider confirms the fantastic makeup of the Turkish lovers in Frischmuth's novels by characterizing them as *Wassermänner* (aquarii).[10] The figure of the Jew Saul in *Mystifikationen* — he represents a father figure and a love object for the narrator — is as fanciful as Aksu.

Constructed figures such as these are an indication that within her literary universe, Frischmuth proceeds as willfully as a conqueror, or perhaps as turn-of-the century intellectuals did in their texts in an attempt to position themselves as other.[11] None of this has any connection to the actual culture that is used as a framework or point of reference. Similar to the constructs of traditional colonial literature, Frischmuth's Orient also represents a realm of freewheeling fancy, free love, and freedom from responsibility, the privileges of outsiders or clowns. In her representation of Turkey, she follows the Orientalist discourse specific to Habsburg culture, which, according to Berman, is "so ingrained as to blind him [the author] to other histories, other cultures, other aspirations." Orientalist ideology has been thoroughly internalized — it operates on a subconscious level, "without anyone noticing it."[12]

"Three, signifying Allah, Muhammad, and Ali. Or four, signifying Ali, Fatma, Hasan, and Hussein. Five, signifying Muhammad, Ali, Fatma, Hasan, and Hussein. Or six, signifying Allah, Muhammad, Ali, Fatma, Hasan, and Hussein. Or a beehive or a dervish. Whereas Allah, the tulip with the half moon, and Adam and Eve are signified by sixty-six. The Koran, however, consists of six thousand six hundred sixty-six verses" (53–54).[13] This disjointed list of names and images refers to the number of ice cubes to be placed by the Turkish lover of Frischmuth's unnamed Austrian woman protagonist into a Turkish drink, a glass of Raki. It is paradigmatic of the way in which elements of Islamic culture are represented in *Das Verschwinden des Schattens in der Sonne.* The decontextualization of names and dates prevents the Turkish environment and cultural code from becoming manifest. In their fragmentation, the elements mentioned amount to no more than a mere stage setting for Frischmuth's "Turkish novel," as Peter Hertz-Ohmes calls it, causing what is popularly known as the Orient to appear as enigmatic and impenetrable as it does, for example, in the works of Karl May.[14]

In his ground-breaking study *Orientalism* (1978), Edward Said observed that Western authors establish for themselves a "positional superiority that puts them in a whole series of possible relationships with the Orient without ever losing the relative upper hand."[15] Said bases his concept of Orientalism on literature by male authors, who unabashedly posit their point of view as the norm. Regardless as to whether they configure the other as the Orient, as sexual, racial, or species-related difference, it always occupies the narrative position of passivity and inferiority. Animals, women, foreigners, disbelievers signify the unknown and the unknowable that, when cast as uncanny, mobilize both fear and desire, as Julia Kristeva points out.[16] In the same vein, Frischmuth's narrative voice constructs positions of superiority in two ways, vis-à-vis the Orient and the reader, making ample use of the elements of mystery and the uncanny.

The antithesis Orient/Occident can be traced to the religiously biased crusade accounts, in the words of Berman "propaganda literature," as well as to the cultural anti-Turkish prejudices of Martin Luther.[17] Frightening to the pious Christian and far too remote for the average person to verify, the Orient traditionally signified excess, adventure, wealth, sexuality, and danger, mystery and the forbidden fruit. Cast simultaneously as ferocious and decadently luxurious, it represented a realm outside the civilized world, a sphere beyond morality, humanity and, most important, beyond Western law. Out there, the Christian conqueror/traveler could not be held accountable and was free to act on his lust and greed. According to Said, there is nothing mysterious about the trajectory of Orientalist discourses. They are about power, and their "broad imperialist" views are supported by "philology, lexicography, history, biology, political and economic theory, novel-writing and lyric poetry."[18] European cultures derive their intellectual and economic authority over the Orient from these Eurocentric disciplines as well as their literary traditions.[19]

Barbara Frischmuth's *Das Verschwinden des Schattens in der Sonne* was published five years prior to Said's study. Contrary to her other works, the entire novel is set outside Austria, but the narrator is Austrian. Although Georg Pichler does not consider that the narrator's hasty departure may be motivated in part by her having accomplished her mission — she has finalized her dissertation topic — he does reject the notion that she has undergone a growth experience or emerges victorious, as Donald Daviau asserts.[20] Pichler considers the narrator's failure to find a *modus vivendi* (a way of living) in Turkey despite her presumed openness to the central theme: "Clearly, she remained a foreign woman without any political, social, or even revolutionary consciousness" ("Sie ist also nur eine Fremde ohne jedes politische, soziale oder auch revolutionäre Bewußtsein geblieben").[21] However, neither critic addresses the narrator's frequently mentioned frustration, even revulsion and anger, all of which lead to the question as to why the narrator is so upset. The following discussion will show that these strong feelings are caused by the narrator's inability to conceptualize the Orient as long as its people and the physical manifestations of its culture interfere. Unable to hold on to her conventional notions while in Turkey, her victory over the Orient consists of writing about it from a distance, in deconstructing and obliterating its actual characteristics in a text over which she has exclusive control.

Herself a former student of *Orientalistik* (Oriental studies), Frischmuth collected the material for her novel during her studies in Turkey.[22]

The narrator, like the author, has come to Istanbul to conduct research for her dissertation.[23] In the process, she becomes increasingly attracted to and by her mentors steered toward the literature of the Bektashi, a dervish order founded in the thirteenth century by Haci Bektas Veli.[24] At the end of the novel, she chooses the Bektashi poet Pir Sultan Abdal as her dissertation topic and returns to Austria.[25] Similar to Hugo von Hofmannsthal, who, having created literary images of the Orient for many years, failed to take notice of the actual Marrakesh and its inhabitants during his trip to North Africa, relying instead on clichés to portray them, Frischmuth, conditioned by the prejudices inherent in her discipline, also searches for the real Turkey in an imaginary past.

What fascinates Frischmuth's narrator about the Bektashi and brotherhoods such as the Alevi are their presumed deviations from the predominant form of religion in Turkey, the Sunna, orthodox Islam.[26] Throughout the narrative, it is suggested that Islamic mysticism, represented by the Sufi mystics, or dervishes, whom Frischmuth associates with middle-class pan-Islamists such as the Alevi, are in conflict with Sunni Islam. Actually, all pan-Islamic groups are opposed to the secular nation-state, and they exist both in Sunni and Shi'i culture.[27] For example, the Muslim Brothers *(al'Ikhwan al-muslimun)* in Egypt, as well as their radical offshoot, the Gamaa Islamiya, are an integral part of Sunni culture, although they are outlawed.[28] The same is true for the Bektashi and Alevi in Turkey, where the process of Westernization began in the nineteenth century.

After the demise of the Ottoman Empire, it was impossible to revive the Islamic multination-state. Under the Young Turkish leadership, notably Mustafa Kemal, known as *Atatürk,* Father of the Turks, sweeping reforms took place.[29] They involved the closing of the religious courts, which resulted in the destruction of the country's theocratic foundations. The constitution of 1924, the emancipation of women (1925–1935), the introduction of the Roman alphabet (1928), and finally the omission of references to Islam in the constitution of 1928 were landmark victories of the modern nation-state paradigm over Islamic universalism.[30] Some of these events are thematized in Frischmuth's novel, namely, the separation of modern Turks from their cultural roots: the average person has no access to historical texts written with Arabic letters — modern Turkish uses the Roman alphabet. The casual interaction between male and female students may be interpreted as another example of the separation of today's Turks from traditional Islam, but in this case the seemingly

Western patterns are placed into the context of the Bektashi tradition.

Aside from her career goals, the narrator explores ancient Turkish culture with the goal of uncovering structures unknown to her Turkish friends, and thereby gaining the intellectual upper hand. The extensive discussions of her exploits are informed by Frischmuth's own research. However, the scholarly sources mentioned in "Anmerkung" (Annotation, 233) are used so selectively that no consistent image of Turkish history emerges. "The word *abdal* denotes stupid, simple-minded. In the twelfth and thirteenth centuries, there was a sect that called itself *Rum Abdallar,* the Simple-Minded Ones of Anatolia. Its adherents stood out by the fact that they shaved their hair, eyebrows, and beard with a razor and roamed the countryside with drums and kettle-drums" (108).[31] Such passages foreground details that are likely to impress the readers as odd, exotic, even as absurd.

Prioritizing the point of view of a naive first-person narrator is an effective device to create the illusion of authenticity. Predisposed by this narrative strategy, the reader is likely to validate the narrator's perceptions without holding the author accountable — after all, the novel appears to render another person's subjective views. Thus, Frischmuth, the author, safeguards herself against the kind of criticism to which traditional Orientalist writers were vulnerable — it is easy to expose misappropriation and ethnocentrism on the part of an authoritative third-person narrator who assumes a position of objectivity to expound the author's point of view.[32] However, in the case of *Das Verschwinden des Schattens in der Sonne,* the author is concealed by the narrative voice. No claim to objectivity is made as the novel is cast as a personal narrative. Frischmuth's narrative strategy provides the only vantage point from which a contemporary writer can state Orientalist positions with relative impunity, that of anonymity.

Frischmuth's narrator draws her reader into a maze of speculations about occult and secret brotherhoods (i.e., the Bektashi, the Janissaries, the Alevi) and their significance for today's Turkey.[33] Her preoccupation with these intangible groups can be explained by her predicament as a woman and a student. In Turkey, she finds it hard to gain access, and her personal involvements cause her emotional turmoil, thereby interfering with her research.[34] In her aimless wanderings, her lack of progress becomes obvious. Yet, her strolling about is paradigmatic of the way in which she conducts research: As she walks, random impressions, intuitions, and scattered bits of information feed into her paranoid intuitions of being surrounded by a network of secret organizations.[35] The hallucinations of the narrator during an illness reveal the extent to which she has become identified with her object of study and suggest that her scholarship is largely a product of her imagination: "I saw myself kissing the doorstep at the 'Square of the Forty,' then I was 'taken by the hand' and had to pay for the 'sweat of my foot' and the 'girding of the spoons.'" ("Ich sah mich die Schwelle des Platzes der Vierzig küssen, dann wurde ich 'an der Hand genommen,' während ich für den 'Schweiß des Fußes' und für das 'Gürten der Löffel' zu zahlen hatte," 106).[36]

At the opening of the novel, the narrator has already departed into a dream world, as is obvious from her preoccupation with possible links between her friends' mundane activities and secret Bektashi practices. Hertz-Ohmes, drawing from the narrator's hints precisely the conclusions that the text prompts the readers to reach, notes: "By the time she begins to understand the historically elusive Bektashi movement she seeks is truly active under her nose, it is too late, she is on her way home to Austria."[37] Yet, the narrative is not quite so direct: It stops at the suggestion. The same is true for the episodes involving the political events of the 1960s and early 1970s. The social and political issues that prompt outbreaks of violence and government crackdowns are never discussed, although street violence, taken entirely out of context, is depicted. Also here the reader is left to wonder about secret plots and intrigues. In short, the single narrative perspective causes the novel to function like a black box.

Aware that the mystical sects had long been outlawed, Frischmuth's narrator nonetheless holds that "an organization such as that of the Bektashi could not be eliminated by government decree . . . without there remaining groups that continued to exist 'in secret' — an expression used also in conjunction with the twelfth Imam al-Mahdi" (72).[38] Statements such as these validate the narrator's suspicions of a Bektashi presence. On the wall of her lover's apartment, for example, she notices "symbols . . . that had later been painted over" ("Zeichen . . . die später übertüncht worden waren," 54–55). She also hints that there may be correlations between Aksu's almost meditative way of making love, a clandestine drinking party of three women friends, and the secret rites of the Bektashi, in which, she asserts that "women had taken part as well, that they drank alcohol, that they transgressed against the command regarding effigies" ("auch Frauen teilgenommen hatten, daß sie Alkohol tranken, daß sie sich über das Bilderverbot hinweggesetzt hatten," 70).[39] In general, the narrator relishes the transgressions against the orthodox Muslim code, such as the drinking of alcohol by Muslims, because she considers such activities expressions of opposition to the Muslim code.

To come to terms with her Turkish friends' indifference to her discoveries, the narrator introduces the notion that the ties to pre-Islamic shamanism and mysticism were traditionally concealed from the novices of occult orders. She maintains that they were kept unaware of what they were about to become, namely, initiates to "another pre-Islamic tradition that could only survive in secret" ("*vorislamische* Tradition, die ebenfalls nur im verborgenen weiterexistieren konnte," 73). She uses Turgut, her roommate and lover, a politically minded modern student, as a potential case in point.[40] Turgut whistles a medley of revolutionary songs, "consisting of the Marseillaise, the International, and other revolutionary songs . . . and then all of a sudden, all of these turned into a *Gül-benk,* the battle-cry of the Janissaries preceding the attack. It was done with the same commitment to unity that the Bektashi had used in their rituals" (166–67).[41] This passage despecifies even the Bektashi by making the concept Bektashi applicable to any and all revolutionary movements and vice versa. Hertz-Ohmes, aware of the author's technique, and accommodating it in his interpretation, explains: "Part of the narrator's difficulty with her Turkish environment stems from her Austrian (Western) tendency to separate history from present-day experience."[42]

Das Verschwinden des Schattens in der Sonne must be scrutinized precisely where it implies a fundamental difference between Occident and Orient, ascribing to the former historic specificity and denying it to the latter. Why does the novel suggest that Turkey is — and should be — "other," amorphous, ahistorical, emotional, and irrational? In effect, Frischmuth's text, rather than revising traditional Orientalist concepts, relegates the Orient and Islamic culture to the same discursive and conceptual position that Western discourses have traditionally assigned to women, children, non-Europeans, animals, and nature. All of these were denied historical specificity. Except for certain gender role reversals and the reversal of the position of the feminine and the masculine, *Das Verschwinden des Schattens in der Sonne* reproduces the hierarchy established in the Orientalist tradition. Characterizing the Orient as indistinct and ahistorical is, after all, what has always made the Orient Oriental.

The passage mixing revolutionary songs from all over the world sets associations in motion that evoke yet other traditions. In the process

Islamic historicity and Turkish modernity are further dismantled: "Central Asia, the legendary source from which everything is said to have originated, is empty. Wind blows across the dunes and canyons, the sphere of influence of both Iran and China, oasis-mentality, cultural stagnation, superficial adherence to different world religions, farmer or shepherd culture, predominantly shepherds. . . . There is a startling parallel between the Bektashi and the Tibetan lamas: Only through the appropriation of the methods used by the shamans were they able to gain power over the spirit of the nomads. That's the way it is written somewhere" (185).[43] Passages such as these are characteristic of Frischmuth's approach to Islamic culture, whose uniqueness she considers nowhere. Rather, her text undermines and trivializes it by extensive, if not irrelevant, associations.[44]

Even though she makes her pronouncements through an anonymous female voice, Frischmuth, the author, stands at the center of her text, the star and the director of an Austrian one-woman show in a Turkish stage setting. The specifics of Islamic culture, both Sunni and Shi'i, are obliterated while individual elements associated with them are exoticized and universalized. The narrator approaches Istanbul as if it were a museum.[45] She does mention, for example, Islamic monuments, but does so exclusively in terms of their ornamental value or the practical benefit they have for the narrator: "I liked this mosque. It was so big, and yet I could not help but feel that its dome might one day fly away without any effort. . . . It was brighter than all the other mosques, but it was cool nonetheless" (20).[46] The obvious disregard for the sacredness of this architecture corresponds to the way in which most relevant cultural information is obscured. Istanbul, for example, is consistently referred to as "the city." It remains nameless, but the name of one of its neighborhoods, Galata, is mentioned repeatedly. German-speaking readers cannot but associate it with the letters of the Apostle Paul and place it into a Christian context. Altogether, Frischmuth's descriptions do not go beyond stereotypical images of the romantic and dangerous Middle Eastern big city discussed by Berman.[47]

Although the narrator's stated goal is to overcome feeling like an outsider and "to adjust and live as if I had insight as to how the system of the different relationships in which I was involved functioned, as if I accepted it. I wanted to make as few mistakes as possible even though I knew that I would always make mistakes" (23).[48] She makes no serious attempt to this end, except for some superficial play-acting designed to win the trust of the "natives."[49] Her theatrical behavior toward complete strangers on a boat makes a mockery of the local customs. Her attempts to blend in and to function both as a foreigner and as an insider are reminiscent of the cultural maneuvers of Karl May's Kara Ben Nemsi.[50]

The narrator's feelings toward Turkey and her Turkish acquaintances, including her lovers, are ambivalent if not hostile. As a result, she has difficulty expressing herself. Occasionally, she even regresses linguistically. During these phases, she feels revulsion at the smells around her, particularly at the Turkish food, and she comforts herself by placing a piece of pork into her pocket (25). At other times, she articulates her dislikes and aggressions, for example, when she hurls insults against her roommate Turgut, telling him that "he had a head like a bottle, pointed like a Mevlevi hat, so-to-speak, a head, half pear, half pumpkin, with a forehead flat like a board, and the eyes of a male owl, and a face like a fox attached to which were ears the size of a child's slippers. His nose, I said, was red like an unripe grape, and huge, like an eggplant from Morea" (47).[51] Being close to her lover Aksu causes her occasional disgust as well: "Then suddenly any touch by Aksu, regardless how accidental, would cause me revulsion. The latter was so unjustified that I wanted to cry" ("Ich empfand dann plötzlich bei jeder auch nur zufälligen Berührung von Aksu einen Widerwillen, der so ungerechtfertigt war, daß ich hätte weinen können," 84). Finally, the love-hatred she expresses toward Turgut encapsulates the way she feels about everything Turkish: "I love you, just as one would say: I despise you with all my heart" ("Ich liebe dich, so wie man sagen würde, ich verabscheue dich von ganzem Herzen," 210).[52] These statements call to mind with equally ambivalent pronouncements involving a man of partly Turkish (half-Turkish!) background in Frischmuth's later novel *Über die Verhältnisse* (1987, Beyond One's Means). The disarray in the man's bathroom, including a sharp odor emanating from his towel, are told by a third-person narrator and convey an aversion similar to the one experienced by the narrator of *Das Verschwinden des Schattens in der Sonne*.[53]

With her insufficient knowledge of the Turkish language, the narrator can do little more than engage in flights of fantasy as far as her object of study is concerned. She admits: "I still had difficulty reading the old texts. It was impossible for me to trace or guess at the Persian and Arabic loan words" ("Es fiel mir immer noch schwer, die alten Texte zu lesen. Die persischen und arabischen Lehnwörter waren für mich weder ableitbar, noch kombinierbar," 37). Her lack of expertise, however, does not prevent her from speaking with a voice of authority to the reader and to her Turkish roommates, for example, when she holds forth about Turkish lore. At the same time, she refuses to learn from them and is inattentive to their concerns. She justifies her attitude claiming that the Turks do not want her to comment on their way of life and their country's social ills. She suggests that they were offended when she expressed outrage at something that had evoked her disgust, such as stray cats, child beggars, and women whose noses were cut off (158–59).

Yet, rather than discouragement, the narrator's attitude of noninvolvement suggests a dismissal of Turkish reality — ultimately, it would be of no advantage to her in her native Austria. The degree to which she foregrounds her research confirms this impression. Her preoccupation with the past separates her from the world around her. None of this matters, however, as it is not her goal to live in Turkey but to write about it for a German-speaking readership. Her seemingly modern female sensitivities aside, Frischmuth's narrator bears a close resemblance to the traditional male Orientalist: She exploits the foreign culture to conduct research on which she plans to base her career. In the process, she uses some of her contacts as resource persons and others as her casual lovers (219). The narrative obscures these problematic issues by suggesting that there is a radical difference between Turkish culture and the Turkish mind and her Western mentality and intelligence.

The narrator's project involves a quest for hidden archaic structures underlying modern Turkish culture, patterns of which the Turkish population is unaware — the phrase *im verborgenen* (in secret) is used repeatedly. Berman characterizes the rejection of contemporary Oriental art and other phenomena as an expression of a certain antimodernism of many Europeans interested in the Orient.[54] Her observations apply to Frischmuth as well, whose narrator tries to gain an intellectual positional superiority over a foreign culture. She does so by striving for privileged knowledge about Turkish culture and the psyche of its members and by treating their present conditions and concerns as irrelevant. For this reason, she derives satisfaction from contrasting her presumed epiphanies with her friends' apparent oblivion: "What do you intend to do with it?" ("Was willst du damit?") friend Sevim asks her. "I realize that you like the poems of the Bektashi and Alevi, that one can learn something about our contemporary language from them, but all the Velis and Habibullahs, the Hajis and the Pirs, the angels, devils, and demons, what are they good for?"[55] The narrator, in turn, instructs her: "For nothing, I said. They simply are a part of it all" ("Für nichts, sagte ich, sie gehören nur einfach dazu," 141).

Despite occasional hints that the narrator senses that she may be actually out of touch with contemporary Turkey,[56] she makes only one direct statement to this effect: "I had neglected to inform myself well enough. I had reflected only about the appearances and not about the necessities" ("Ich hatte es verabsäumt, mich genau genug zu informieren. Ich hatte nur über Erscheinungen und nicht über Notwendigkeiten nachgedacht," 219). Her insight is immediately eclipsed by her protestations of her love for her friends, an ancient Oriental legend, and Turgut's violent death during a demonstration. The novel's final sentences evoke Turgut's dead body and images of other shooting victims, which the narrator remembers from media reports. The mental collage of dead bodies not only obliterates Turgut's identity, it is paradigmatic of the way in which the narrative dismantles the uniqueness of Turkish culture altogether. Having the memory of the narrator's lover merge with anonymous dead bodies leads the novel to its logical conclusion: On a personal level, it confirms the distinction between the Orient, anonymous and lifeless, and the Occident, cast in the image of the individual survivor, the Austrian woman.[57] These images imply the victory of Western modernity and individuality over the lack of individuality and specificity ascribed to the East.

Partly because the narrator proves unable to gain access to the Turkish mindset, the novel has been commended for its sensitive representation of cultures in contact.[58] The narrator's apparent capitulation before a non-Western world has been viewed as anticolonial. Indeed, Frischmuth's narrative stance does differ from the classical colonial approach of straightforward conquest and control. However, as the previous discussion has shown, conquest is very much at stake nonetheless. Writing from the perspective of a postcolonial woman, Frischmuth is *de facto* precluded from being overtly and traditionally Orientalist. Yet, she retains the notion that there is a categorical difference between East and West, the reason for the presumed inability of the Westerner to comprehend Islamic culture. This assumption is as problematic as the naive posture of power in male Orientalist discourse. Said's caveat must be taken seriously: "How does one *represent* other cultures? What is *another* culture? . . . Do cultural, religious, and racial differences matter more than socio-economic categories?"[59]

Frischmuth's narrator focuses on traditions from which twentieth-century history has separated the majority of the Turkish population while deemphasizing the effects of modernization and the role and content of Islam.[60] Without characterizing either one, Frischmuth foregrounds certain groups that are cast as oppositional and mysterious, including the Bektashi. They remain invisible throughout. Following certain Western writers, Frischmuth mistakenly associates Islamic mysticism primarily with the Shia, the principal form of Islam in Iran, ascribing to the latter, equally mistakenly, liberating, progressive impulses. Thus, her novel not only establishes false oppositions, it mis-represents the conflicts in Turkey and sidesteps economic factors and the country's struggles with a modern dictatorship. Not only are political, economic, and ideological factors excluded from Frischmuth's narrative, her characterization of the Bektashi as a virtually unknown secret sect is misleading. Anyone interested in the Bektashi will today find numerous internet web sites offering more information than Frischmuth's presumed student discovers during her stay in Turkey. While the electronic sources did not exist in the 1960s, a wealth of pertinent literature was available at that time. Only in view of the lack of interest by the Western public can the traditions Frischmuth thematizes be called *verborgen* (secret, or hidden).[61]

Frischmuth's novel problematizes Turkey and Turkish people from the perspective of the narrator whose background is kept obscure. The narrator's voice functions like a spotlight thrown on certain phenomena designated as Turkish. Her culture of origin remains inviolate. The narrator's view of Turkey is the only one allowed to emerge. However, certain concurrences between the author's biographical data and the scant information provided about the narrator suggest that the views of the former and those of the latter are identical. This impression is confirmed by Pichler, who notes that Frischmuth describes her relationship to Istanbul in the same words as the narrator of *Das Verschwinden des Schattens in der Sonne*: the city, the alien realm.[62]

Frischmuth's narrator reproduces the traditional Orient, as a realm replete with magic, legendary creatures, and romance, fantastic and antimodern. The impression arises in *Über die Verhältnisse,* where Turkey is cast as the underworld, Hades, in juxtaposition to Austria, which is associated with Demeter.[63] In other words, Frischmuth follows the patterns of Greek mythology to negotiate Christian and Islamic positions. In accordance with this particular cultural pattern, the underworld status of the Orient evolves in her novel almost naturally.

To enhance the exotic appeal of *Das Verschwinden des Schattens in der Sonne*, certain Turkish names are used repeatedly, while in other cases no names are mentioned at all and the characters are referred to in ethnic terms, as *die Tatarin* (the Tatar woman) or *der Armenier* (the Armenian, 60). Turkish characters are often stereotyped and compared to animals, as, for example, Aksu because of his black, blood-shot eyes (190). The impression of foreignness is also elicited by descriptions of physical traits and body language: "As always when the Tatar woman told me a story, she placed her left hand on my arm while she covered her mouth with her right hand so that only I could understand what she said. She wore green eye shadow and silver earrings with the half moon and the star" (12).[64] The same technique is also used in *Über die Verhältnisse,* where the heavy black eyebrows, the long hooked nose, and the strong black facial hair are mentioned in the case of a "half-Turkish" male (*Verhältnisse* 102). Also dirt, traditionally a mark of foreignness in German and Austrian literature, is thematized in both works. The bathroom of the "half-Turk" in *Über die Verhältnisse* is described as follows: "The tiles above the washbasin were covered with spots of toothpaste, and the tube of shaving foam lay open next to the broken lid" ("Die Fliesen über dem Wasch-becken waren voller Zahnpastaspritzer, und die Tube mit dem Rasier-schaum lag offen da neben dem zerbrochenen Verschluß," 117). In *Das Verschwinden des Schattens in der Sonne,* the frequently mentioned curfews add an air of lawlessness and despotism to the atmosphere in Istanbul.

Finally, Frischmuth's plot lines follow the established Western mode as well. In the violent ending of *Das Verschwinden des Schattens in der Sonne,* the protagonist's exotic love interest is eliminated, the only difference being that Frischmuth's male character dies, whereas in literature by male writers, the victims are usually female. A striking instance occurs in *Die Mystifikationen der Sophie Silber,* where a Jewish male succumbs in the act of love-making, Saul Silber, whose death is already prefigured in Aksu's near-unconsciousness during and after sex.[65]

In conclusion, it can be established that as far as plot line, imagery, positionality within the narrative, and intellectual rigor are concerned, Frischmuth's representation of the Orient, i.e., Turkey, does not break new ground. Since Frischmuth foregrounds contemporary concerns such as the role of women and gender-related conflicts and avails herself of narrative strategies that suggest subjectivity and interactivity, the assumption has been made that her approach of representing and assessing Islamic culture is innovative as well. This, however, is not the case: Only superficial contacts between members of Eastern and Western cultures are discussed; no avenues of negotiating cultural discourses are explored. This may be one of the reasons why Frischmuth's texts are more palatable than those of Esther Dischereit, e.g., *Joemis Tisch* (1988, Joemi's Table), or Jeanette Lander, *Das Jahrhundert der Herren* (1993, The Century of Masters). Although they experiment with certain innovative literary devices, for example, the capitalization of key words, from the point of view of content and outlook, Frischmuth's novels lack the revolutionary spirit they seemingly endorse by validating the dissent of the Bektashi. Upon taking a closer look, neither case involves radical dissent with the mainstream culture.

As far as present-day Turkey and the interactions between German-speaking and Turkish, Christian and Islamic cultures are concerned, Frischmuth's novels neither provide new insights, nor do they provide vistas for change. Instead, they reassure the majority of her readership of the validity of their time-honored clichés: In Frischmuth's novels, East remains East and West, West.

University of Illinois at Chicago

Notes

1. Nina Berman, *Orientalismus, Kolonialismus und Moderne: Zum Bild des Orients in der deutschsprachigen Kultur um 1900* (Stuttgart: M&P Verlag für Wissenschaft und Forschung, 1997) 33, considers this era the fifth phase of contacts between German-speaking and Muslim culture. She points out that the increasing body of literature by minority writers produces a substantially different cultural experience, allowing new vistas into Islamic culture.

2. Berman 17.

3. Berman 295 observes that the Orient portrayed in Else Lasker-Schüler's earlier texts is as mythical, ahistorical, and constructed as that in Martin Buber, Jakob Wassermann, and Hans Kohn's works.

4. Barbara Frischmuth, *Das Verschwinden des Schattens in der Sonne* (Frankfurt/Main: Suhrkamp, 1973). The translations here are mine. A very recent translation of the book is *The Shadow Disappears in the Sun,* trans. Nicholas Meyerhofer (Riverside, CA: Ariadne, 1998).

5. In a similar vein, the narrator states early on: "This city — I am certain to have dreams about this city! I said it often, as if sitting in a train that had pulled out of the station. As if I had already left it behind and could begin telling, telling the many stories I had heard, experienced, and imagined. And no one would be able to make immediate sense of them" ("Diese Stadt, mir wird noch träumen von dieser Stadt! Dies sagte ich oft, so als säße ich in einem Zug, der sie gerade verlassen hat. Als hätte ich sie bereits hinter mir und könnte zu erzählen anfangen. Die vielen Geschichten, die ich gehört, erlebt, mir ausgedacht hatte. Und keiner könnte sich gleich einen Reim darauf machen," 7).

6. Berman 73–76, 332–333.

7. Edward W. Said, *Orientalism* (New York: Pantheon, 1978) 40.

8. Berman characterizes the classification as "masculine Occident, feminine Orient" ("männlicher Okzident, weiblicher Orient," 69).

9. Alma M. Karlin, *Einsame Weltreise: Erlebnisse und Abenteuer einer Frau im Reich der Inkas und im Fernen Osten* (Freiburg i. Br.: Kore, 1995); Bertha Pappenheim, *Zur Lage der jüdischen Bevölkerung in Galizien: Reise: Eindrücke und Vorschläge zur Besserung der Verhältnisse* (Frankfurt/Main: Neuer Frankfurter Verlag, 1904).

10. Hans Haider, "Traummänner und Traumfrauen," in *Wassermänner,* by Barbara Frischmuth (Salzburg: Residenz, 1991) 265.

11. Berman 295.

12. Berman 258.

13. Original quote: "Drei, das sind Allah, Muhammed und Ali. Oder Vier, das sind Ali, Fatma, Hasan und Hüseyn. Fünf, das ist Muhammed, Ali, Fatma, Hasan und Hüseyn. Oder sechs, das sind Allah, Muhammed, Ali, Fatma, Hasan and Hüseyn. Oder eine Bienenwabe oder ein Derwisch. Während Allah, die Tulpe mit dem Halbmond und Adam und Eva sechsundsechzig sind. Der Koran aber besteht aus sechstausendsechshundertsechsundsechzig Versen."

14. Peter Hertz-Ohmes, "Cultural Complementarities in Frischmuth's Turkish Novel," *The Germanic Mosaic: Cultural and Linguistic Diversity in Society* (Westport: Greenwood, 1994) 195–200.

15. Said 7.

16. See Julia Kristeva, "Eine Semiologie des Unheimlichen," *Fremde sind wir uns selbst* (Frankfurt/Main: Suhrkamp, 1990) 202–04.

17. Berman 21, 26.

18. Said 15, 19.

19. Said 19; Berman 99–114 presents an impressive survey of the

extensive literature on the Orient beginning with the twelfth-century translation of the Koran. She lists travelogues, scholarly works, travel opportunity during the nineteenth century, and discusses the activities of the *Deutsch-morgenländische Gesellschaft* (German-Oriental Society).

20. Donald G. Daviau, "Barbara Frischmuth," *Austrian Fiction Writers*, ed. Donald G. Daviau and James Hardin (Detroit: Bruccoli Clark Layman, 1989) 166–172. Daviau states that the narrator, who found herself placed between "the traditional and the revolutionary," has "matured through her experience" (168).

21. Georg Pichler, "'Seltsam, daß es mir so wenig ausmacht, nicht anzukommen.' Heimat und Fremde bei Barbara Frischmuth," *Dossier 4: Barbara Frischmuth*, ed. Kurt Bartsch (Graz: Droschl, 1992) 65–66.

22. Pichler 62–63. Pichler mentions Frischmuth's studies in Hungary and Turkey and characterizes her ensuing relationship to Austria as *kritisch-bejahend* (with approving criticism, 58–59).

23. Judit Györi, "Barbara Frischmuth," *Österreichische Literatur des 20. Jahrhunderts*, ed. Horst Haase and Antal Mädl (Berlin: Volk und Wissen, 1988) 694–715, who considers *Das Verschwinden des Schattens in der Sonne* Frischmuth's most beautiful book to date, notes the autobiographical aspects of the novel (704). Pichler describes the protagonist as a narrator without a name and without history ("namen- und geschichtslose Erzählerin," 63).

24. E. van Donzel, ed., *Islam's Desk Reference* (Leiden: Brill, 1994) 51 defines the "Bektashiyya" as a dervish order in Turkey, whose patron Hajji Bektash Wali came from Khurasan. It is pointed out that the order was associated with popular Shi'a mysticism and its members disregarded Muslim ritual and worship. The term *dervish* refers to members of a religious fraternity who practice Shufiyya. This term, mentioned in the Koran signifies broadly speaking an ascetic outlook on worldly matters. Certain practitioners try to transform the material body by sequences of movements, as do the dervishes by whirling. In Turkish, the term *dervish* refers to mendicants, men and women, who stimulate ecstasy in a whirling dance (*Desk Reference* 83).

25. According to Fahir Iz, "Turkish Literature," *The Cambridge History of Islam*, vol. 2, ed. P. M. Holt, Ann K. S. Lambton, and Bernard Lewis (Cambridge: Cambridge UP, 1970) 682–695. Pir Sultan Abdal was a fifteenth-century representative of the *tekke* poetry, mystical folk literature written in popular language and syllabic meter (688, 691).

26. *Islam's Desk Reference* defines the term Sunna as custom, statute,

i.e., the theory and practice of orthodox Muslims, and the community that adheres to the original dogma (431) in opposition to Shi'a, the "party of Ali," which constitutes a large group of different Muslim sects who recognized the son-in-law of Muhammad, Ali, as the legitimate caliph. Even more important to the Shi'a is Ali's son Husayn. Ali was murdered in 661, Husayn in 681, by government troops. The latter's violent death introduced the motif of passion into Islam and denotes the beginning of the Shi'a (*Desk Reference* 412). However, according to *The Cambridge History of Islam*, mystical movements such as the Sufis "override embattled frontiers between Sunna and Shi'a" (641). The seat of the central authority of the Sunni is Al Ahzar University in Cairo.

27. Telephone interview with Nabil Abdou, November 2, 1997. Hertz-Ohmes 195–200 simplifies matters when he identifies the "hard-line, ultrarational, and dogmatic Sunni administration" and the "more Shi'ite oriented emotional and religious 'others'" as the conflicting forces in Frischmuth's novel, which he ends up characterizing as "complementary" (196), and he observes with regard to the Sufis that they "override the embattled frontiers between Sunna and Shi'a" (*Cambridge History*, vol. 2, 641).

28. The Muslim Brothers were founded in 1928 in Ismailia by Hasan al-Banna, a young teacher. Their program included the following statement: "Islam is a comprehensive system which must regulate all human actions, at the level of the individual as well as society." The Muslim Brothers' idea was pan-Islamic: "Every parcel of land on which the flag of Islam has at one time flown is for all Muslims a fatherland and must be preserved, for which they must work and fight in holy war." From Robert Mantram, ed., *Great Dates in Islamic History* (New York: Facts on File, 1996) 260.

29. They incidentally went hand in hand with this century's first major genocide, the massacres of the Armenians by the Young Turks. These events are usually downplayed or left unmentioned in publication biased toward Turkey. (*Great Dates* 203–204).

30. Kemal H. Karpat, "Modern Turkey," *The Cambridge History* 527–535.

31. Original quote: "Abdal ist ein Wort für dumm, einfältig. Im zwölften und dreizehnten Jahrhundert gab es eine Sekte, die sich Rum Abdallar, die Einfältigen von Anatolien, nannte. Ihre Anhänger waren daran zu erkennen, daß sie ihr Haar, ihre Brauen und ihren Bart mit dem Rasiermesser schoren und mit Trommel und Pauke durchs Land zogen."

32. In an earlier article, I failed to address this problem adequately and asserted: "Convention and imagination of the other language form a part of Frischmuth's literary world, of her expansion of linguistic boundaries. Through the inclusion of Near Eastern culture, she also selectively takes issue with her own German-Austrian conventions; yet, by identifying herself with the latter, she also does not accept the other culture uncritically, as thought it were colorful exoticism, but adopts a critical stance toward it." Dagmar C. G. Lorenz, "Creativity and Imagination in the Work of Barbara Frischmuth," *Women in German Yearbook* 2 (1986) 38.

33. In *Islam's Desk Reference,* the Janissaries, the "New Troops," are defined as regular infantry created by the Ottomans. Their ranks were filled periodically by Christian children. The corps was abolished by Sultan Mahmud II in 1826 because of suspected seditious activities (184).

34. Hertz-Ohmes notes that the Bektashi order was outlawed in Turkey in 1826 because of its seditious activities and its association with the Janissaries.

35. "I cannot say that I paid much attention during my walks. I often did not know through which alleys I had reached a certain place and which streets I had crossed, or if I had noticed anything special. Rather, my walking induced a special kind of reflection and escalated into a dreamlike state. Often I would say something out loud without really talking to myself, but the tone of my voice would startle me and I'd turn around several times. When I stood in front of a certain mosque, any building, or even one of the tea gardens I knew, I tried to find out what had attracted me to this specific place. Often it had been small things, the shape of an archway or the way in which light penetrates through a window at a certain angle" ("Ich kann nicht sagen, daß ich während dieser Wanderungen sehr aufmerksam war. Oft wußte ich selbst nicht genau, durch welche Gassen ich an einen Ort gekommen war und welche Straßen ich überquert hatte oder ob ich dabei etwas Besonderes bemerkt hatte. Es war eher so, daß das Gehen eine bestimmte Art von Nachdenken hervorrief, das sich zu einem traumähnlichen Zustand steigerte. Oft sagte ich dabei etwas laut vor mich hin, ohne wirkliche Selbstgespräche zu führen, doch erschrak ich vor dem Ton meiner Stimme und ich sah mich mehrmals um. Wenn ich vor einer bestimmten Moschee, einem Gebäude oder auch nur einem mir bekannten Teegarten stand, versuchte ich herauszufinden, warum es mich gerade hierher gezogen hatte. Meist waren es Kleinigkeiten, die Form eines Torbogens oder die Art, wie von

einer bestimmten Seite Licht durch ein Fenster fällt," 32–33).

36. Berman notes an often-made association between the Orient and the subconscious, a parallel construction of Europe/the conscious and the Orient/the sub (or un-) conscious ("Europa/das Bewußte — Orient/das Unbewußte," 191). It is not surprising that Frischmuth's narrator receives knowledge about the Orient from subconscious sources, without applying herself rationally.

37. Hertz-Ohmes 197.

38. Original quote: ". . . eine Organisation wie die der Bektaschi durch einen Regierungsbeschluß [nicht] aus der Welt zu schaffen [war], . . . ohne daß es Restgruppen gab, die im verborgenen — ein Ausdruck der auch für den zwölften Imam al-Mahdi angewendet wird — weiterexistierten."

39. The narrator describes her friends' behavior: "Suddenly they began whirling the way the Mevlevi dervishes do . . . and as they whirled faster and faster, they gave off a long drawn-out *huuuu*" ("Plötzlich fingen sie sich in der Art der Mevlevi-Derwische zu drehen an . . . und während sie sich immer schneller drehten, stießen sie ein langgezogenes *huuuu* aus," 69–70).

40. Daviau notes that Turgut was "involved in a radical political group" (168).

41. Original quote: ". . . eine Aneinandereihung von Marseillaise, Internationale und anderen Revolutionsliedern . . . und dann ging mit einemmal alles in einen Gül-benk über, den Schrei der Janitscharen, bevor sie angriffen, mit demselben Bekenntnis der Einheit, wie es auch die Bektaschi bei ihren Riten verwendet hatten."

42. Hertz-Ohmes 197.

43. Original quote: "*Zentralasien, die legendäre Quelle, aus der alles kommen soll, ist leer. Wind, der über Dünen und Schluchten bläst, Einflußgebiet des Irans und Chinas, Oasen-Mentalität, kulturelle Stagnation, oberflächliche Angehörigkeit zu verschiedenen Weltreligionen, Bauern- oder Hirtenkultur, meistens Hirten. . . .* Eine überraschende Parallele zwischen den Bektaschi und den tibetischen Lamas: Nur dadurch, daß sie die Methoden der Schamanen übernahmen, konnten sie Macht über den Geist der Nomaden gewinnen. So steht es irgendwo." These historical contexts are discussed in "Turks and Mongols in the Middle East," in *Great Dates in Islamic History* 77–82. Here, the conflicts between the Sunni under the leadership of Mahmud, who extended the rule of Islam into India and Punjab, and the neighboring

Shi'is is discussed (78).

44. Daviau characterizes her dilemma as being placed "between the traditional and the revolutionary" (168). More correctly, it is a position that the narrator constructs as being traditional outside of Turkish tradition.

45. See Berman 85.

46. Original quote: "Ich mochte diese Moschee. Sie war so groß, und trotzdem wurde ich das Gefühl nicht los, daß ihre Kuppel eines Tages davonfliegen könnte, ohne besondere Anstrengung. . . . Sie war heller als alle anderen Moscheen, aber trotzdem kühl."

47. Berman 166.

48. Original quote: ". . . mich anzupassen, so zu leben, als würde ich das Funktionieren des Systems der verschiedenen Beziehungen, in denen ich stand durchschauen und akzeptieren. Ich wollte so wenige Fehler wie möglich machen, obwohl ich wußte, daß ich immer welche machen würde."

49. "People already reacted to me in an orthodox manner, and I did my part in that regard. If someone praised me, I responded with the formula that was to express my lack of merit, and when I bought a piece of sesame pastry and met a pregnant woman, I asked her if she wanted to take a bite" ("Man reagierte mir gegenüber schon auf orthodoxe Weise und ich tat das meine dazu. Wenn jemand mich lobte, erwiderte ich mit der Formel, die meine Unwürdigkeit zum Ausdruck bringen sollte, und wenn ich mir auf der Fähre ein Sesamkringel kaufte und einer Schwangeren begegnete, fragte ich sie, ob sie abbeißen wollte," 23). Indeed, the narrator's statements are taken seriously by some of Frischmuth's critics. Judit Györi, for example, elaborates that the novel explores being a stranger in multiple contexts: national, linguistic, individual, and social. She does, however, note the narrator's *Realitätsferne* (being out of touch) and recognizes that her intellectual isolation is purposely chosen (705).

50. Berman 87–89.

51. Original quote: "Er [habe] eine Flaschenkopf, spitz wie eine Mevlevi-Mütze, habe, sozusagen, einen Birnenkürbiskopf, mit einer Stirn, flach wie ein Brett, und Uhuaugen in einem Fuchsgesicht, an dem Ohren in der Größe von Kinderpantoffeln hingen. Seine Nase sei rot wie eine unreife Weinbeere und groß wie eine Aubergine aus Morea."

52. Such statements not only validate entrenched stereotypes about relationships between Christians and Muslims; they also add new ones.

Hertz-Ohmes, on the narrator's side all the way, holds that her misunderstandings are "not necessarily" her fault (195).

53. Barbara Frischmuth, *Über die Verhältnisse* (Salzburg: Residenz, 1987) 117. The following love-making scene is reminiscent of the pose in certain Klimt paintings depicting vampirelike males and fragile females: "His face seemed much darker than hers. Yet, it appeared to her as if it had a noticeably arrogant, almost hostile expression when he loosened her hair with one graps of his hand and threw the combs on the sofa. Then he opened her dress. . . . And his hands appeared under her shoulders and grasped her breasts" ("Sein Gesicht wirkte viel dunkler als das ihre, dennoch glaubte sie darin einen überlegenen, beinah feindlichen Ausdruck zu erkennen, wie er mit einem Griff ihr Haar löste und die Kämme aufs Sofa warf. Dann öffnete er ihr Kleid. . . . Und seine Hände kamen unter ihren Achseln hervor und griffen nach ihren Brüsten," 118).

54. Berman 191.

55. Original quote: "Ich verstehe daß dir die Gedichte der Bektaschi und Alevis gefallen, daß man daraus etwas über unsere heutige Sprache erfahren kann, aber all die Velis und Habibullahs, die Hacis und Pirs, die Engel, Teufel und Dämonen, wozu sollen die gut sein?"

56. It parallels Frischmuth's experience, who never wrote a dissertation but rather a novel to process her Turkish experience.

57. Pichler is right in defining the topic as a failure in a strange environment ("Scheitern in fremder Lebenswelt") rather than the difference between two cultures ("Unterschied zwischen zwei Kulturen," 66).

58. See Hertz-Ohmes.

59. Said 325.

60. Sunni Islam. Contrary to Hertz-Ohmes 195–200, the difference between Shi'i and Sunni is theological and does not merely consist of a more "emotional and religious" orientation on the part of the Shi'is. Hence, the assertion that these two forces are "complementary" in Turkey is incorrect.

61. See http://www-leland.stanford.edu/~percin/Bektashi.html; http://www.frosina.org/baba.htm, a site on Baba Rexheb, an Albanian Bektashi leader; http://answering-islam.org/Humor/Bektasi.html, a site on Bektashi humor.

62. Pichler 60.

63. In "Von den Langexistierenden" (Of the Long-Existing Ones), *Der Traum der Literatur — Literatur des Traums* (Salzburg: Residenz,

1991) 69, Frischmuth states: "*Über die Verhältnisse*, which I view under the auspices of the classical tradition, I configured most distinctly according to the popular Demeter story as far as the interaction between the characters is concerned" ("*Über die Verhältnisse*, das ich dem klassischen Aspekt zuordne, habe ich der geläufigen Demeter- Geschichte von den Bewegungen der Figuren her am deutlichsten nachgezeichnet"). The Turkish women are configured as chthonic goddesses: "A seemingly ancient, transparent figure wearing a white muslin scarf around her head and neck. She appeared hardly of this world any longer in terms of her body mass. Only her eyes glowed like pieces of charcoal in a face like that of a melting snowman" ("Eine, wie es scheint, uralte, im Fleisch schon beinah vergangene, durchsichtige Gestalt mit einem weißen Musselinschal um Kopf und Hals, nur die Augen glimmen wie die Kohlestückchen im Gesicht eines schmelzenden Schneemanns," 205); "the ancestress close to being dissolved in smoke" ("die schon beinah *verrauchte* Ahne," 206); "the Fatal Sisters on their throne" ("thronende *Parzen,*" 207). The situation is commented on by the character of the Austrian mother: "Alien, alien, alien — that's what the new family situation is to Mela, everything so unreal" ("*Fremd, Fremd, Fremd* bleibt Mela die neue Familiensituation, alles so unwirklich," 207–08).

64. Original quote: "Wie immer, wenn die Tatarin mir eine Geschichte erzählte, legte sie die linke Hand auf meinen Arm, während sich sich die rechte so vor den Mund hielt, daß nur ich verstand, was sie sagte. Sie trug grüne Lidschatten und silberne Ohrringe mit Halbmond und Stern."

65. Maximilian Aue, "Bewältigung und Einbindung," *Modern Austrian Literature* 27.3 (1994): 69.

Living with the Other: Ecological Aspects of Barbara Frischmuth's Sternwieser Trilogy

Julie Klassen

In her 1983 essay on Hildegard von Bingen, Barbara Frischmuth discusses Hildegard's main work, *Scivias* (1151, Know the Ways), which elsewhere she calls "an apocalyptic book that in fire-breathing images paints impending perdition and urges reform."[1] She quotes the following passage from *Liber Vitae Meritorum* (ca. 1170; *The Book of the Rewards of Life*): "The elements burst out in woeful cries to their creator, because they cannot complete the paths established for them by God and because they cannot fulfill their foreordained functions as they are tossed about by the sins of human beings."[2] Frischmuth comments: "Given the current state of technology, these images gain possibilities of interpretation that one can only too easily imagine" ("Hildegard" 237). For her, Hildegard stands out among mystics because of the totality of her vision, encompassing what the medieval abbess "would have still called the harmony of the cosmos" ("Hildegard" 237). Frischmuth adds that her mind was "alert not only to the expectations for salvation of her own soul, but also to the interconnections between nature and culture," which Frischmuth says today would more likely be associated with ecology ("Hildegard" 237).

Hearing this essay on Hildegard von Bingen as a conference address was my introduction to Frischmuth. Coming back to it after several years, I find it a fitting starting point for examining the interconnections between nature and culture I have found in Frischmuth's own works. Furthermore, Frischmuth's essentially biocentric view invites the insights of ecological literary study. As Cheryll Glotfelty (Burgess) points out, within the broad scope of ecocriticism's inquiry, all types share a focus on the web of relationships which connect human beings to their physical environment.[3] Indeed, ecocriticism confronts an unreflected use of the term "environment" as "anthropocentric and dualistic, implying that we humans are at the center, surrounded by everything that is not us."[4] Since this perceived separateness from nonhuman nature as the "other" functions variously as symptom and/or cause of the exploitation of the physical world, ecocriticism requires female as well as male human beings to consider how they as the dominant species construct the nonhuman other.

Yet, the ecocritical reformulation of self and other must not obscure the problems inherent in the long-standing conflation of women with nature. Ecofeminism addresses this relation of anthropocentrism or speciesism to sexism, racism, and classism as a product of patriarchal dominance, as Karla Armbruster explains:

> While the heterogeneous and dynamic nature of ecofeminism makes it difficult to define, ecofeminist writers do share a general conviction that there are important connections between the oppression of women and the destruction and misuse of nonhuman nature within male-dominated cultures. And whether their work takes the form of theory, cultural analysis, or creative prose or poetry, they all give a sense that it is politically essential to explore and emphasize these connections if the dominations of women and nature are to be substantively challenged.[5]

The potential for successful challenge, as Judith Plant points out, derives support from ecology's insights about adaptation to environment as a constant process:[6] "Since the subjugation of women and nature is a social construction, not a biologically determined fact, [the] position of inferiority can be changed."[7] The various branches of ecofeminist criticism theory participate in this challenge, identifying not only the connections among forms of oppression, but also the inherent potential for transformation on a nonhierarchical basis.

While not nominally an ecofeminist, Barbara Frischmuth's portrayals of women confronting socially constructed dualisms and hierarchies often coindicate abuses of nonhuman nature as an inferior other. Furthermore, she portrays existence as a constant process of transformation for which playful visualization of and experimentation with various permutations is an essential human prerequisite for self-realization. In examining Frischmuth's Sternwieser trilogy, I find it appropriate to adopt Armbruster's combination of poststructuralist feminist and ecofeminist theory "to illuminate ways that an author can create a conception of human and nature intersubjectivity, a relation involving a human identity shaped by an acknowledgment of both connection and difference."[8]

Images of Connection

Of all Frischmuth's works, the first novel of the Sternwieser trilogy, *Die Mystifikationen der Sophie Silber* (1976, The Mystifications of Sophie Silber)[9] presents the most explicit portrayal of interconnectedness among all creatures and things. Here the nonhuman other takes primarily the form of imaginary creatures from tale and myth. Though not eternal, these "long-existing ones" *(die Langexistierenden)* experience intersubjectivity in the ever-changing constellations of identity and existence. At first it would appear that these long-existing ones' longevity and circumscribed magical powers give them sovereignty over their respective elemental domains, which they exercise in their own interest or for the benefit of the hapless human beings, referred to as *die Enterischen*. I suggest this latter term should be translated as "interbeings,"[10] derived from one of the meanings of the Greek root **enter-*, in Latin **inter*, perhaps in the meaning of "between, among" or as "sharing, derived from," to indicate the compound nature of the human being as a creature between, i.e., belonging to, derived from the physical and the nonphysical world.[11]

In their incompetence and folly, the interbeings appear increasingly incapable of using the intuitive/spiritual powers that gave rise to the imaginary beings in the first place. Indeed, the long-existing ones have assembled at the lake resort in Altaussee to ponder strategies for preventing human control of the world from ending in catastrophe. As projections of human fantasy, however, these imaginary creatures have themselves become increasingly endangered by human forgetfulness and unbridled human greed.[12] In contemplating how to counter the peril for human beings from this crisis of imagination, they are thereby struggling to save the basis of their own existence.

Christa Gürtler has linked the importance of rejuvenated imagination and memory in the Sternwieser trilogy to the significance of myth as a repository for forms and values of the prehistoric matriarchal heritage and thereby a source of strength for women's struggle to achieve self-realization in a society of male-dominated institutions and behaviors.[13] Thus, the call to rekindle the powers of imagination represents the effort to re-activate the creative powers of woman in the search for new kinds of relationships and roles for both sexes.[14] Margaret Brügmann and Ingrid Spörk, among others, have also analyzed how Frischmuth thematizes the links between myth, female creativity and development of identity in her works.[15]

While in agreement with these analyses of how female values infuse the three novels of the Sternwieser trilogy, I would like to emphasize how the ecological dimension of women's self-realization expands and gives a more inclusive grounding to the feminist venture. The term "ecology," with its roots in the Greek word *oikos* for house or dwelling place, meant in pre-Socratic thought "the unity of nature and the sciences . . . a state of totality, developing in a cycle in which all things [are] related to and dependent on each other."[16] In the matriarchal age of myth, self and society are still grounded in this state of totality, which Heide Göttner-Abendroth calls a "holistic way of life" *(ganzheitliche Lebensweise).*[17] Indeed, myth makes this experience of interconnectedness with nature possible through its imaginative personifications of natural phenomena.

The factors giving rise to patriarchy in Western culture and thereby subverting the matriarchal myth-making power also estranged human beings from the state of totality, as the growing emphasis on reason increasingly demystified natural objects and the forces of nature; scientific knowledge facilitated the technology for harnessing nature, which human greed focused increasingly on exploitation and expansion of power. As Ynestra King says, "The domination of sex, race, and class, and the domination of nature are mutually reinforcing."[18] Thus, Göttner-Abendroth's concept of the matriarchal aesthetics as an attempt at overcoming the estrangement from this interconnectedness[19] necessarily involves the restoration of respect and responsibility for the nonhuman as well as the human world; ecological abuses must be addressed as coindicative with the oppression of women and dysfunctional human relations.

The long-existing ones, then, in their concern about the threats to their existence, also perform the function of ecological canary in the mine shaft. Indeed, as many of the long-existing ones are personifications of natural phenomena, they address very real perils posed by human assaults on the elements; they speak for the nonhuman others, those elements that in Hildegard's words "burst out in woeful cries to their creator" (qtd. in "Hildegard" 237). Events occurring during the conference, such as the road-builders' detonations on the mountain above the lakeside resort, underscore the urgency of their concerns about human ambition raging out of control (*Mystifikationen* 237).

These apprehensions are also validated by the reaction of Sophie Silber, an actress with a fairy ancestor, and the only human guest invited to the conference. Amaryllis Sternwieser, the narcissus fairy and imaginary being most central to the course of events, has had an age-long connection with Sophie's ancestors — women who have never married but who each pass on the lineage through a single daughter. At one of the early meetings, Sophie Silber is overwhelmed momentarily by an apocalyptic vision of the terrifying consequences of human ecological folly. At first, she sees before her the destruction of all living creatures. Then, in the aftermath, the earth appears covered with a thick layer of debris and decomposing human bodies from which bizarre, new forms of vegetation grow in profusion; garish flowers with faces suspiciously like those of the long-existing ones peer through the leaves (*Mystifikationen* 89). The elemental spirits have at last had their moment of revenge, as in their new metamorphosis, they feed on the substance of their oppressors.

The specter of doom recedes amidst the sociable, if mysterious, festivities of the conference members. Sophie's involvement at the conference with the long-existing ones, whose identity she only gradually begins to intimate, sets in motion a double mystification: Her gradual awakening to the secret powers and significance of the imaginary beings precipitates the reintegration of imaginative energy into her own life; in reconnecting with her past, she is able to face the future with new self-awareness.[20]

Nonetheless, the underlying ecological realities remain. They later spur Amaryllis Sternwieser to consider a return to the elements as a site of resistance: "With our power, we can give things a different character and let them resist the interbeings" ("Wir können mit unserer Kraft den Dingen ein anderes Gepräge geben und sie den Enterischen widerstehen lassen," *Mystifikationen* 248). However, her ultimate choice takes a more conciliatory tack: She urges the other long-existing ones to follow her example and become women and children so that they might thereby attempt to divide up human power in such a way that it no longer represents a danger for the world (*Mystifikationen* 248).

In place of using magical powers, Amaryllis Sternwieser plans, as she says, to teach human beings friendliness, affection, and pleasure in all creatures and things, rooted in recognition of the underlying unity and multiplicity of existence; she hopes thereby to reduce fear, greed, and envy, nurturing instead forms of survival based on mutual support; she wants to awaken the imagination by satisfying curiosity so that human beings can envision better forms of being than those to which they have fallen victim (*Mystifikationen* 248). Indeed, at this final meeting of the long-existing ones that conjures up a sort of harmonic convergence, Sophie Silber's vision of the future already anticipates these benefits: She views her "new life before her, with all its hidden possibilities . . . until she [sees] herself as an old woman, who, surrounded by other people with whom she [stands] in relationship, . . . [forgets] her ailments, or at least endure[s] them more easily" (*Mystifikationen* 249).[21]

To be sure, Amaryllis Sternwieser's formidable transformation to human form will cost her the magical capacity to merge with nature and necessitate forgetting the previous life forms. At the long-existing ones' festival of memory, she had recapitulated in a trance her previous incarnations as moon goddess and earth goddess, even back to the preindividuation stage of primordial unity with plant and animal life. As Amaryllis Sternwieser had explained after the memory festival, however, forgetting past lives and the experience of unity is not viewed as a loss but also has its function: "For this night concerns the origin and everything that came forth from it, everything that has been and the transformation, the multiplicity of forms, and their unity in which we gather together again as beings in the passage of all holy times so that we can once more disperse, happy about the oblivion, in order to live the many lives which the change of things and forms brings with it" (*Mystifikationen* 105).[22] Within the dynamics of interconnectedness, then, forgetting is the vital complement to memory that facilitates living fully in one's present existence, the challenge which will dominate her efforts at self-realization as a human being.

Images of Difference

More specifically, if connection predominates in *Die Mystifikationen der Sophie Silber*, the role of difference as an essential part of identity formation prevails in the second novel, *Amy oder Die Metamorphose* (1978, Amy, or The Metamorphosis).[23] Having awakened as the mortal Amy Stern, the former Amaryllis Sternwieser must now concentrate on retrieving a memory of her current life up to this point. Without the magical power to take on other forms, her metamorphosis means embodying herself, in the root sense, in the world as an individuated mortal with ethical choices.

In the first hours of existence, Amy still has access to residual magical senses that make her privy to the unseen currents of human desire and the ubiquitous, silent language of things — the wares in the store displays called out, "Buy me, buy me" ("Will mich haben!" *Amy* 12). A close encounter with a car shocks her consciousness into identification with her body, but even then, reminders of her past life linger for a while, sometimes in encounters with people who seem comfortingly familiar (they are the new permutations of the long-existing ones); sometimes they come as disturbing dreams or as traces of a memory she cannot recall (*Amy* 70).

Even as Amy's life increasingly depends on her mortal abilities, she retains a certainty about the possibility of entering into a relationship with everything and everyone ("die Möglichkeit, in allem und jedem miteinander in Beziehung zu treten," *Amy* 62), which facilitates an unusual awareness of human and nonhuman interdependency. For example, as she reflects on the simple acts of getting clear, cold water from the tap and lighting a flame on the stove, it dawns on her how utterly city dwellers depend upon the proper functioning of technological systems for their basic needs: water supply and sewer system, fuel, electricity, garbage removal, transportation, in short, one big process of devouring, digesting, and eliminating (*Amy* 68). As she thinks about the implied degree of solidarity and compromise, as well as the impossibility of fail-safe human oversight and humans' own dislike of being controlled, she wonders: "What, however, if the world were a unity? What if even consciousness is not a one-time leap of mutation, which only concerns human beings, but is rather a gradual, evolutionary increase with all possible variants? What if it were possible that even things start to want to withdraw themselves from control?" (*Amy* 70)[24] Reminiscent of Sophie Silber's vision of carrion-eating plants, awareness of urban complexities could render the notion of essential interdependency more a threat than a comfort.

However, Amy's apprehensions reveal at least three further aspects. First, Amy's awareness of the potential rebellion of mute objects shifts the emphasis from the environmental consequences themselves to the underlying illusion of control and its ethical implications: Whether based on overestimation of ability or presumptiveness about sovereignty, urban management takes for granted the prerogative to impose human hierarchy on the elements and what Hildegard von Bingen calls their "foreordained functions" to human will. Whereas the necessities of urban life require planned operations, its illusion of control is a form of hubris that risks urban chaos. Rebellion as an expression of the elements' cry of woe would prove itself not just a philosophical postulation, or a mystical or poetic vision of unity, but part of the very real dynamics of entropy, whose consequences human beings accelerate or ignore at their peril.

Second, although this portrayal of city contrasts with the bucolic image in the back of Amy's mind (what the reader recognizes as the Sternwieser cabin and well at Altaussee), Amy realizes that a retreat to a simpler existence would not alleviate the question of dependency, as rural survival also relies on propitious natural and human conditions (*Amy*

68–69).[25] More directly, Amy is reminded later in the novel by a voice in the park (representing the realm of nature): "Your way leads into the houses. You can't go back . . . Amy Stern, Amy Stern . . . you were the one who took the path into the city (*Amy* 157)."[26] After all, in choosing metamorphosis as the human Amy Stern, Amaryllis Sternwieser had tacitly accepted the urban Viennese setting. perhaps as the ultimate ethical challenge to the goal of influencing human society and, with it, the fate of the earth.

Third, Amy's acknowledgment of the elements' urge to escape control and misuse indicates an empathetic recognition of what she has in common with nonhuman nature. As she says, somehow she sees everything with different eyes ("Irgendwie sieht sie alles mit anderen Augen," *Amy* 70). Significantly, here Amy draws a parallel to the dependence of her own process of self-realization on the immanent, physical awareness of herself in the world. Rather than any rational process or magical perception, it is the "vegetative mechanisms" ("vegetative Mechanismen," *Amy* 70) of her body that help her build a bridge to her own history; she relies on external stimuli such as a person or place to trigger her own conscious recollections. Amy finds the value of bodily knowledge confirmed by her friend Pola, an actress who strives to engage her full substance on stage "to let it speak with the archaic tongue of the body" ("mit der archaischen Zunge des Leibes," *Amy* 71).

Both Brügmann and Spörk identify Amy's experience of the body and the skin in particular as the central experience in her development of self-identity and human relationships.[27] I will not try to summarize their detailed observations but rather emphasize the significance of the body as the site where human beings can experience nature as both part of themselves and part of a larger whole. Leslie Adelson confirms this essential liminality of the body when she stresses the "complex specificity of human bodies — socialized, engendered, historically signified and, at the same time, real, that is, not merely products of discourse or objects of institutionalized power."[28] Amy experiences her body, to borrow ecofeminist Stacy Alaimo's wording, as "not only a place that has been inscribed by cultural forces, . . . but a threshold where nature and culture dissolve."[29] Amy's encounters affirm the capacity to reach out to other human beings through their common rootedness in the physical world. Whereas she initially feels somewhat at the mercy of her vegetative mechanisms, she gradually learns to value them as a valid and valuable source of knowledge. For example, although she cannot recall her past relationship to Wolfgang, Amy is certain that they have not had sex, since otherwise his skin would speak to her (*Amy* 95).

Amy's developing sense of self as rooted in bodily intelligence also proves essential when she begins with some trepidation to recognize the cost of the intuitive sense of interconnectedness she feels toward her circle of women friends. She is pleased to realize that they value her presence as an empathetic listener and counselor. Indeed, Amy is beginning to fulfill Amaryllis Sternwieser's goal of helping human beings envision better ways of being. Yet, Amy also understands the danger of being simply a vessel for others' problems and begins to ponder the questions, "Who am I, and what are my problems?" ("Wer bin ich und was sind meine Probleme?" *Amy* 75) As she searches for an alternative to dependency on human and nonhuman others, she begins to assert herself against what Val Plumwood has called "the Ocean of Continuity," which "can collapse the self/other dualism into an undifferentiated whole."[30]

Nonetheless, Amy does not flee to the opposite extreme of false autonomy, Plumwood's "Desert of Difference," where identity politics lead to isolation of people in groups based on gender, race, class, and so forth. Amy's ongoing metamorphosis reflects the conviction that personality is not immutable but is constantly undergoing changes in response to a myriad of factors. In this experimentation with the components of identity, Frischmuth models how feminist theorist Teresa de Lauretis conceptualizes the subject as "shifting and multiply organized across variable axes of difference."[31] To quote Armbruster, such a view of the subject "acknowledges the socially constituted and changing nature of the subject, and thus . . . the differences among us, without inevitably isolating us from each other."[32] Thus, humans' hybrid status as interbeings *(die Enterischen),* an apparent deficit in the first novel, proves its advantage for grounding individuation within structures of interdependence that invite responsibility for and participation in new models.

As a consequence of her insights, Amy decides to give up her medical studies to become a writer; she sees in this engagement of her energies and imagination the possibility of helping people understand themselves, while participating herself in the many voices of life (*Amy* 160–167). The ensuing entanglement in the world of her own relationships brings complications, but also new possibilities. As she decides whether to bear the child she has conceived, she writes her first texts, which she calls "excerpts from a dolphin literature" (*Aus[züge] aus einer Literatur der Delphine*) (*Amy* 238ff) . These three fragments commence when the youngest female of the clan is about to give birth for the first time. In her labor, she is supported by the storytelling dolphins, both male and female, whose songs about dolphin evolutionary history recount the time when dolphins had lived on land and had had contact with people; they inform her about the principles of dolphin childraising.

Amy chooses this format, she tells a friend, to get another perspective on human relations, one that prevents too easy an identification with daily life (*Amy* 242). Thus, the thrust of the dolphin excerpts could be interpreted as motivated chiefly by the desire to improve human existence. However, the fragments not only contrasts dysfunctional human relationships with the dolphins' peaceful society. Amy also wants to satisfy her urge to seek alternative models for living together (*Amy* 246). Significantly, the story-telling dolphins also link the onset of humans' greedy abuse of each other with the violence toward other creatures as the factor that sent the dolphins back to the sea where pollution still threatens their existence (*Amy* 265–266).

The dolphins perceive as their only defense the invention of a common language in which they can impart to humans the dolphins' nature and their insights about fostering mutually nurturing relationships and the value of diversity (*Amy* 266). The elements' cry of woe to their creator gives way to creatures who want to remedy their own situation by influencing human perceptions and behavior. As Gürtler points out, the dolphins' goal recalls the long-existing ones' abandonment of their isolation to teach human beings another way of existence. She demonstrates how this goal has been taken on in human society by the women's movement, which seeks to develop a new language that can subvert the patriarchical order[33] by changing the map of reality. In linking the mythological past with the plight of the dolphins in the present world, Amy's fragments also convey the ecological imperative to implement models that respect the diversity of life as a value in itself.

Indeed, even telling others about her dolphin literature initiates aspects of Amy's confrontation with the institutional and societal subordination of women and nature. The various reactions she encounters verify the potential power of her voice. Whereas Klemens, the father of Amy's unborn child, feels threatened by Amy's literary aspirations, the somewhat mysterious Herwater obviously understands her dolphin excerpts and supplements them with his own interpretations of these creatures' return to the sea. Once Herr von Wasserthal, sovereign of the water spirits and compatriot of Amaryllis Sternwieser in his previous life, this eccentric environmental activist now patrols the city canals, watching for failures in the system, and tries to win participants like Amy for his battle to counteract the abuses humans inflict on nature and each other. He praises dolphin society because it represents a conscious consensus to abide as a group by the most optimal among livable models, a goal he is trying to achieve for human society (*Amy* 267–68).

Although Amy does not refer to or add to her fragments from dolphin literature again in the third part of the trilogy, *Kai und die Liebe zu den Modellen* (1979, Kai and the Love of Models),[34] its paradigmatic character hovers in the reader's consciousness as the backdrop for Amy's efforts to find new solutions to old patterns of male dominance and female submission.[35] Raising her son, Kai, essentially in the absence of his father, she experiments in her life and in her writing with the kinds of community-creating behavior that might achieve the necessary breakthrough in human relations. In the process, she develops an empathetic connection to the various parts of society that suffer from their treatment as "other" by the male-dominated perspective: women, foreigners, children, and old people, as well as outsiders like Herwater, whose views cast them as eccentrics.

Amy's conscious attempt to assume responsibility for her own web of relationships makes her keenly sensitive to other patterns of dependency, and how they might be changed into mutually supportive behavior. Here Frischmuth's concept of mutual parenting as an ethical and practical alternative to hierarchical forms of association emerges in distinct contours well in advance of its embodiment in the 1990 novel *Einander Kind* (One Another's Child),[36] or in Frischmuth's formulation of the concept in her 1990 Munich lectures on poetics, *Traum der Literatur — Literatur des Traums* (Dream of Literature — Literature of the Dream 70).

Brügmann and Spörk emphasize how Amy's efforts to achieve the envisioned models in the Sternwieser trilogy cannot yet bear fruit for her generation as seen in her failure to achieve this new model of relationship with Klemens; the intentional community she imagines for Kai cannot solve all the problems of the real, everyday challenges of mothering. However, it is significant that the final three scenes of the novel relate, respectively, an inner monologue, a dream, and a discussion with a friend about Herwater, all of which point to new possibilities that do not need to be postponed.

The inner monologue gives voice to the pros and cons Amy sees for moving into a cooperate apartment. Even with the best of like-minded intentions, a group of diverse people will experience frustrations when common ideals cannot be fully realized. Yet, the cost of not trying is high: "What if," Amy thinks, "I become bitter and bitterer in thinking about all the possible models of life, whereby simply no one wants to play along in the manner demanded by the model?" (*Kai* 200)[37] She resolves to let things happen and to be open for everything and all feelings, yet without putting up with any emotional blackmail.

The dream that immediately follows these deliberations shows on a fantastic level what exhilarating fulfillment such an opening of self could mean. In it, she finds herself falling out of the clouds into a body of water and moving effortlessly (dolphinlike?) through green and gray currents into the depths. She becomes aware of the balloonlike forms anchored to the bottom, containing crouched forms whose eyes follow her and beseech her to free them. When she eventually succeeds in biting through one of the membranes, she starts a chain reaction of liberation that ends with a flowing together of all the bodies in a happy entanglement of limbs and hair (*Kai* 201–03).

As the dream ends, Amy notes, "My entire self perceived this profusion of touching, and I saw the smile that appeared on every mouth" ("Mein ganzes Ich empfand diese vielen Berührungen, und ich sah das Lächeln, das sich auf die Münder legte," *Kai* 203). Unlike her vision of urban chaos, Amy's dream, replete with parallels to both birthing and her dolphin excerpts (as well as images reminiscent of Herr Wasserthal's underwater realm [*Mystifikationen* 65–66]), mediates a nonthreatening experience of unity in which she has broken through the barriers to liberate co-creatures. Amy awakes to find her little boy crawling into bed with her; before she falls asleep again, she thinks about how she and Kai are dependent on each other and how much they have yet to try out; she hopes they can hang on until they have found the manner of living they need to invent (*Kai* 204).

In the final scene, Amy tells her friend and editor Helene about an evening with Herwater, about his ecological concerns and the enjoyment of walking through the city with him. Yet, for all the affinity she feels for him and his ideals, she fears the possible emotional entanglement. Although the end is left open, her answers to Helene's questions, especially against the backdrop of her thoughts about living arrangements and the dream, indicate that Amy is ready to risk intimacy with a partner who already embodies some of the values her models envision; she feels as if she has known Herwater much longer than Klemens and can imagine that his friendship would mean a lot (*Kai* 207). Thinking about the inevitable complications, she admits that pain at least heightens one's attentiveness ("Schmerz erhöht zumindest die Aufmerksamkeit," *Kai* 206–07). More importantly, as she had earlier told Pola, the future cannot help, unless "we invent a way to make life not only bearable, but also enjoyable to live" (*Kai* 104).[38] She will presumably not settle for living vicariously through the next generation's potential but will engage in the next stage of her own transformation.

One ecocritic has noted that "human beings are the earth's only literary creatures" and asserts if creating literature is so important, its influence on human behavior and the natural environment should be examined carefully, with the question in mind: "From the unforgiving perspective of evolution and natural selection, does literature contribute more to our survival than it does to our extinction?"[39] The biocentric imperative for partnership that emerges in the Sternwieser trilogy indeed envisions patterns that contribute to our survival, if we will give them a chance.

Frischmuth, like Hildegard von Bingen, is aware of herself in this endeavor as an instrument, not in the sectarian religious sense or as the representative of those in power, but as a present-day agent to communicate insights that might help save the world: "I mean an instrument for the preservation of that which we have not created, an instrument for the preservation of such a great multiplicity of models that we have not even yet comprehended most of them and can look forward to their discovery, whether we imagine them as organized by evolutionary laws or called into existence by God. And in any case, we have no right to the apocalypse, not even on a small scale" ("Hildegard" 246).[40] While not shrinking from the portrayal of apocalyptic possibilities, Frischmuth is also mindful of Amy's initial aversion to what she calls Herwater's bent to proselytizing (*Kai* 207). Instead of ecological invective, Frischmuth pursues Amaryllis Sternwieser's ploy of awakening the imagination so that we as readers might envision in the multiplicity of models better forms of being than those to which we have fallen victim and which victimize the nonhuman world around us. She exhorts us to find ways not only to bear life in the meantime, but also to enjoy living it.

Carleton College

Notes

1. Original quote: "Es handelt sich dabei um ein apokalyptisches Buch, das in gluthauchenden Bildern das drohende Verderben malt und zur Umkehr mahnt." This characterization of *Scivias* is from Frischmuth's Munich lectures on poetics, *Traum der Literatur — Literatur des Traums: Münchner Poetik-Vorlesungen* (Salzburg: Residenz, 1991) 15, hereafter referred to as *Traum*.

2. Barbara Frischmuth, "Eine souveräne Posaune Gottes. Gedanken zu Hildegard von Bingen und ihrem Werk," *Die Presse* (Vienna), 15/16 October 1983; rpt. in *Wassermänner. Lesestücke aus Seen, Wüsten und Wohnzimmern* (Salzburg: Residenz, 1991) 237. This essay was originally delivered as a paper at the annual Women in German conference, held on Thompson Island (Boston), October 1983; hereafter referred to as "Hildegard." Original quote: "Die Elemente brechen zu ihrem Schöpfer in Wehgeschrei aus, weil sie die ihnen von Gott bestimmten Wege nicht zu Ende gehen und die ihnen auferlegten Dienste nicht vollenden können, denn sie werden herumgewälzt durch die Sünden der Menschen." Due to discrepancies in the separate English and German translations from the Latin, I have translated Frischmuth's quotation directly rather than using the published English translation (see Hildegard of Bingen, *The Book of the Rewards of Life [Liber Vitae Meritorum],* trans. Bruce W. Hozeski [New York: Garland, 1994] 125).

3. Cheryll Glotfelty (Burgess), "Introduction," *The Ecocriticism Reader: Landmarks in Literary Ecology*, ed. Cheryll Glotfelty and Harold Fromm (Athens: U of Georgia P, 1996) xix.

4. Glotfelty xx. Compare the German term *Umwelt* (environment) and Carl Amery's similar critique as the underlying premise in *Die ökologische Chance* (Munich: Süddeutscher Verlag, 1985).

5. Karla Armbruster, "Buffalo Gals, Won't You Come Out Tonight," *Interdisciplinary Studies in Literature and Environment* 3.1 (1996): 17.

6. Judith Plant, "Searching for Common Ground: Ecofeminism and Bioregionalism," rpt. in *Learning to Listen to the Land,* ed. Bill Willers (Washington, DC: Island, 1991) 213; originally published in *The New Catalyst* (Winter 1987/88).

7. Plant 215.

8. This wording is a paraphrase of Karla Armbruster from Greta Gaard, "Introduction," *Interdisciplinary Studies in Literature and Environment* 3.1 (1996): v.

9. Barbara Frischmuth, *Die Mystifikationen der Sophie Silber* (1976; repr., Munich: dtv, 1979), hereafter referred to as *Mystifikationen.*

10. Since my translation, I have found a reference to "interbeing" by the Vietnamese Buddhist monk Thich Nhat Hanh, who explains this Buddhist concept as the coexisting of all creatures and things (Peter Levitt, ed., *The Heart of Understanding: Commentaries on the Prajnaparamita Heart Sutra* [Berkeley: Parallax P, 1988] 3–5). He is quoted by Deborah Janson, "A Symphony of Voices: Ecofeminist Dialogics in *Die Lehrlinge zu Sais*" (unpublished manuscript, October 1997) 14–15. (Quoted here with Janson's permission.)

11. *The American Heritage Dictionary of the English Language*, 1976 ed. Although Christa Gürtler, *Schreiben Frauen anders? Untersuchungen zu Ingeborg Bachmann und Barbara Frischmuth* (Stuttgart: Akademischer Verlag, 1983) implies that the term *Enterische* (interbeings), with the meaning *Unheimliche* (sinister ones), belongs to other archaic expressions from folktales and sagas, she gives no corroborating sources (297). A humorous etymological derivation would emphasize human reliance on the digestive system, as **enter* gives rise to the word "enteron," meaning "intestine," "the alimentary canal or system," with the accompanying English adjective "enteric."

12. Frischmuth comments that the vitality of the imaginary creatures is tied to their survival in human consciousness ("Was sie zu 'Langexistierenden' macht, ist ihr Überleben im Bewußtsein der Menschen," *Traum der Literatur* 53).

13. Gürtler 294. She cites Robert von Ranke-Graves's assessment that the age of true myth was the age of the matriarchy, which ended with the establishment of patriarchy ("Die Errichtung des Patriarchats beendete die Periode des echten Mythos," in Robert von Ranke-Graves, *Griechische Mythologie,* vol. 1 [Reinbek: Rowohlt, 1960] 18). She also quotes Heide Göttner-Abendroth, adopting her sociohistorical approach to myth as an expression of complex social practices in archaic matriarchal societies, which thereby serves as a source of information about their structures and mentality. Cf. Heide Göttner- Abendroth, *Die Göttin und ihr Heros* (Munich: Frauenoffensive, 1980) 16.

14. Gürtler 303.

15. Margaret Brügmann, "Traumtänzerin mit Fangnetz: Formen weiblicher Ästhetik bei Barbara Frischmuth," *Dossier 4: Barbara Frischmuth*, ed. Kurt Bartsch (Graz: Droschl, 1992) 23–40. Ingrid Spörk, "Vom Imaginären zum Realen: Über Märchen und Mythen bei Barbara

Frischmuth," *Dossier 4: Barbara Frischmuth* 41–56.

16. Peter Morris-Keitel, "ecology," *A Dictionary of Cultural and Critical Thought*, ed. Michael Payne (London: Blackwell, 1995) 153.

17. Heide Göttner-Abendroth, "Kunst als Ghetto: Eine kritische Betrachtung der Geschichte der Kunstöffentlichkeit," *Manuskripte* 66 (1979): 49; qtd. in Gürtler 47.

18. Ynestra King, "The Ecology of Feminism and the Feminism of Ecology," *Healing the Wounds: The Promise of Ecofeminism*, ed. Judith Plant (Philadelphia: New Society, 1989) 20.

19. Gürtler 294–295.

20. Sophie Silber's insight that the pleasure of acting relates to the art of transformation (*Mystifikationen* 175ff.) is a recurring theme in the other two novels that are part of the Sternwieser trilogy.

21. Original quote: "Und sie sah dieses neue Leben vor sich, mit all seinen verborgenen Möglichkeiten . . . bis sie sich als alte Frau sah, die, umgeben von anderen Menschen, mit denen sie in Beziehung stand . . . die eigenen Beschwerden vergaß oder zumindest leichter ertrug."

22. Original quote: "Denn diese Nacht gilt dem Ursprung und allem daraus Entsprungenen, dem Gewesenen und der Veränderung, der Vielfalt der Formen und ihrer Einheit, in der wir uns als Wesen im Ablauf aller heiligen Zeiten wieder sammeln, auf daß wir von neuem auseinandergehen können, um, glücklich vor Vergessen, die vielen Leben zu leben, die der Wandel der Dinge und Gestalten mit sich bringt."

23. Barbara Frischmuth, *Amy oder Die Metamorphose* (1978; repr., Munich: dtv, 1980), hereafter referred to as *Amy*.

24. Original quote: "Wie aber, wenn die Welt eine Einheit ist? Wenn auch das Bewußtsein kein einmaliger Mutationssprung ist, der nur den Menschen angeht, sondern eine graduelle, evolutionäre Steigerung mit allen möglichen Varianten? Wie, wenn es möglich wäre, daß auch die Dinge anfangen, sich der Kontrolle entziehen zu wollen?"

25. My interpretation thereby counters Gürtler's comment that Frischmuth does not always escape the polarization of nature and civilization characteristic for the ecological and the alternative movements (Gürtler 305–306).

26. Original quote: "Dein Weg führt in die Häuser. Du kannst nicht zurück . . . Amy Stern, Amy Stern . . . du warst diejenige, die den Weg in die Städte genommen hat."

27. Brügmann 36; Spörk 41.

28. Leslie Adelson, *Making Bodies, Making History: Feminism and*

German Identity (Lincoln: University of Nebraska Press, 1993) 3. Adelson examines in detail the ongoing debate over materiality among various critical schools.

29. Stacy Alaimo, "Displacing Darwin and Descartes: The Bodily Transgression of Fielding Burke, Octavia Butler, and Linda Hogan," *Interdisciplinary Studies in Literature and Environment* 3.1 (1996): 63. She refers to Judith Butler, *Gender Trouble: Feminism and the Subversion of Identity* (New York: Rutledge, 1990) as the source for regarding the body as a location of cultural inscription.

30. Val Plumwood, *Feminism and the Mastery of Nature* (London: Routledge, 1993) 3; qtd. in Armbruster 18.

31. Teresa de Lauretis, "Eccentric Subjects: Feminist Theory and Historical Consciousness," *Feminist Studies* 16 (Spring 1990): 116; qtd. in Armbruster 22.

32. Armbruster 22–23.

33. Gürtler 331–332.

34. Barbara Frischmuth, *Kai und die Liebe zu den Modellen* (1979; repr., Munich: dtv, 1981), hereafter referred to as *Kai.*

35. Gürtler also points to this programmatic character of the fragments, if with a slightly different focus (292).

36. Barbara Frischmuth, *Einander Kind* (1990; repr., Munich: dtv, 1994).

37. Original quote: "Wenn ich bitter und bitterer werde im Gedanken an all die möglichen Lebensmuster, bei denen bloß niemand mitspielt auf die von dem Muster geforderte Art?"

38. Original quote: "Und wenn wir uns jetzt nicht um unser Leben kümmern und etwas erfinden, das es nicht nur erträglich, sondern so macht, daß wir es gern leben, dann kann uns auch die Zukunft nicht helfen."

39. Joseph Meeker, *The Comedy of Survival: Studies in Literary Ecology* (New York: Scribner's, 1974) 4; qtd. in Glen A. Love, "Revaluing Nature," *The Ecocriticism Reader* 228.

40. Original quote: "Ich meine Werkzeug zur Erhaltung dessen, was wir nicht gemacht haben, Werkzeug zur Erhaltung einer so großen Vielfalt von Mustern, daß wir die meisten von ihnen noch gar nicht begriffen haben und uns noch freuen können an ihrer Entdeckung, ob wir sie uns nun als von der Natur und ihren evolutionären Gesetzen veranstaltet oder dennoch als von einem Gott ins Dasein gerufen vorstellen. Uns jedenfalls steht die Apokalypse nicht zu, auch nicht im kleinen."

Challenging the Silence: Barbara Frischmuth's Lectures on Poetics and *Mörderische Märchen*

Rhonda Duffaut

Despite Barbara Frischmuth's emphatic rejection of a politically conscious feminist agenda in her work, much of it centers around social issues of women. Moreover, although she concedes to differences between men and women, she does not believe these to be innate. Consequently, a feminine aesthetic, insofar as this exists for her, would be generated by a woman's position and cannot be thought to be a universal quality. Because the presence of female voices is very much connected with the situation of women, it is not surprising that Frischmuth concerns herself in her lectures on poetics with the issues of motherhood and writing. While motherhood and writing have been primarily considered mutually exclusive, Frischmuth's literary texts and lectures show three significant aspects, namely, how the presence of women in literature combats the silence brought on by motherhood, the recognition of fantasy and imagination of women and not necessarily as woman, and the deadly threat of silence to both women and imagination. She further demonstrates in the volume *Mörderische Märchen und andere Erzählungen* (1992, Deadly Fairy Tales and Other Stories), including "Geschichten für Stanek" (Stories for Stanek), that all these are possible only when one takes up the position of writer or narrator through the act of writing or narrating.[1]

Although her novels and later short stories portray this kind of feminine aesthetic most strikingly, an investigation of her lectures on poetics in conjunction with "Geschichten für Stanek," an early set of stories, reveals how her "feminine dream"[2] of the self-evident quality of women's voices in the literary milieu has informed her work early on. After all, she shows that women have in fact been very active writers and narrators.

In all five chapters, Frischmuth presents numerous examples of "women's presence" in literature. Her most significant model, however, is the female narrator, Scheherazade, in *Tausend und eine Nacht (A Thousand and One Nights),* since Scheherazade narrates "against death" ("wider den Tod," *Traum* 11). Scheherazade must take up the position of narrator in order to entertain the king, or she will be killed. Thus, the act of narrating keeps her alive. Over the course of her narration of stories filled with magic and fairies, she becomes the mother of four children. Consequently, Scheherazade literally incorporates the three aspects of motherhood, imagination, and challenging silence that constitute Frischmuth's feminine dream.

Just as silence would result in Scheherazade's death, so also Frischmuth regards the absence of women writers and characters to be a type of death. Thus, like German-speaking writers such as Ingeborg Bachmann and Nelly Sachs, she equates silence with death. In contrast to these writers who depict masculine language as silencing women and to Virginia Woolf's thematization of the silence of women as a result of the lack of creative and quiet space, Frischmuth stresses the effect motherhood in Western culture has had in effectively keeping women from producing literature.[3] As she asserts, "throughout the centuries, being a mother appeared to be *the* impediment that prevented women from participating in art and science" ("Das Muttersein schien durch die Jahrtausende als der Hemmschuh, der die Frauen an Kunst und Wissenschaft hinderte," *Traum* 74). Consequently, motherhood silenced women by hindering their active participation as writers. And their inability to take up the position of writer or storyteller meant ignoring or, more drastically, killing an integral part of themselves.

Moreover, literary mother figures have been omitted or restricted to limited models. For example, the mother figure in the *bürgerliche Trauerspiel* (bourgeois tragedy) was either absent or played such an insignificant role as to be virtually absent.[4] In addition, portrayals of mother figures have been restricted to Christian models of women. As Frischmuth contends, "Mary, the mother, is the sole form of femininity that next to Eve, the sinner, has remained in the Christian *Abendland*" (Occident) ("Maria, die Mutter, das ist die einzige Form von Weiblichkeit, die neben Eva, der Sünde, dem christlichen Abendland verblieben ist" *Traum* 74). For Frischmuth, then, women have not only been silenced by their absence, but they have also been silenced by means of restrictive models.

In "Der weibliche Traum" (The Feminine Dream), the fifth chapter of her lectures on poetics, Frischmuth underscores the fact that women have been forced to choose between what have become two mutually exclusive activities, i.e., writing and motherhood. Although children might distract one from writing, Frischmuth finds the choice between writing or motherhood both restrictive and deadly. As we have seen, to choose to write at the cost of motherhood is to silence an integral part of being female. Referring to the violence of this choice, Frischmuth indicates how women "must un-female, un-mother themselves, to be suitable for literature" ("[müssen] sich ent-frauen, ent-muttern, um als literaturfähig zu gelten," *Traum* 88). Additionally, to be silent, that is, not to write, as a result of motherhood absentes mothers from literature in a way that is also deadly to women writers.

Given the confinement to motherhood, to writing, or to restrictive models, it is not surprising that many women consider and are portrayed as considering silence to be a type of death. As a consequence of this history of silencing, any moments of silence in and between narration gain an ominous quality. To the female narrator, Scheherazade, the silence between her stories reminds her of her own mortality.[5] By contrast, the philosopher Jacques Derrida associates the silence or absence of *différance* with a kind of deconstructive liberation.[6] Since *différance* is a constituent of presence (i.e., signifiers in a significatory system) and simultaneously is responsible for the destabilization of that system, it undermines any notion of a rigid, eternal presence. This deconstruction of rigid structures might free up notions and models of signification, but it has yet to strongly impact the practice of alternative models of signification. And for Frischmuth, who is invested in women's practice of writing, alternative models can motivate other women to challenge the silence impressed by traditional models of mother or writer.

Ironically, this deadly silence in fact drives narration. As the pause in narration functions to underscore the presence of the signifiers, theorists such as Jean-François Lyotard, for instance, maintain that every pause can be considered as much a "phrase" as any other signifying complex.[7] Thus, using the terms of Lyotard, we might understand Frischmuth's perspective on the relationship between death and narration to be that death is a *phrase* in a series of long narrations that are life. As in Christa Wolf's *Kassandra* (1983, Cassandra) and in *Malina* (1971; *Malina,* 1990) by Ingeborg Bachmann, death provokes the narrative. In reference to narrative as fending off one's own death, Frischmuth asserts that narration can be viewed as a practice against death of the past. Since history in general and a person's own history constitutes that person, remembering the past helps one move into the future.[8] Further, Frischmuth considers the silence of fantasy a type of death.[9] Since fairies, for example, not only stand for fantasy but are contained in our past childhood fantasies, stories of fairies once again bring into focus our own history. Therefore, taking up the position of storyteller is ultimately motivated by the silence of death.

Whereas narration in Frischmuth's example of *Tausend und eine Nacht* appears to flow ceaselessly to prevent moments of silence, the narrator in Frischmuth's "Geschichten für Stanek" interrupts her stories or is interrupted. Consequently, the narrator in the former, though no less significant, moves to the background, and the narrator and her imagination in the latter are brought into focus. Through her narration, the narrator in "Geschichten für Stanek" acquires a subject position (a presence) and a voice. Crucially, then, her subject position challenges the objectification of female figures that often occurs by male authors.[10] In "Der weibliche Traum," Frischmuth articulates her concern that women acquire a subject position when she imagines her comment to men: "You cannot speak about us forever, you must speak with us" ("Ihr [Männer] könnt nicht ewig über uns reden, ihr müßt mit uns reden," *Traum* 72). Similarly, Frischmuth's narrator demands recognition. As she tells Stanek, she must narrate: "When I've thought everything through, I have to tell the story to someone in order to hear it myself. . . . If I don't tell someone, the story won't let me rest, and the words creep into my ears again and again. Then I can't sleep, and finally, I even lose my appetite" (44).[11] Since withholding her stories prevents her from eating and sleeping, her storytelling is another way in which she remains alive.

The interruptions of the stories, moreover, indicate a relationship, which the narrator might initially construct, between the listener and the narrator, but which she cannot manipulate completely. The narrator's initial compunction, for example, may be to tell the first story as a distraction. She and Stanek's sister, Karoline, or Kari, are traveling in a train to find Stanek, whom they hope to find at the horse races, and in telling a story, "at least it makes them think of other things" ("so kommen [sie] wenigstens auf andere Gedanken," 41). Thus, we have a narrator and a listener.

And yet, while the title, "Geschichten für Stanek," clearly underscores the listener, the female narrator gains presence by means of her storytelling. In the first story, for instance, Stanek, for whom, as the narrator says, the story was conceived, is not even present. Instead, Kari takes his place. "Well, she is Stanek's sister" ("Sie ist ja Staneks Schwester," 38), thinks the narrator. The status of the receiver in this case is slightly diminished. Reception of the story is further minimized in that Kari shows little interest in the story being told, as she is tired and dozes off. While the narrator needs an audience in order to take up that position, the first story ironically shows how the listener functions mainly as a motivating factor for narration. The need to narrate thus supersedes the function of narration, which is thematized in the stories as distraction, entertainment, or education.

The narrator not only presents female characters in her stories, but she also makes them a complementary part of the narrative. After all, each story the narrator tells offers a picture of cooperation between the sexes. In this way, Frischmuth's text calls into question patriarchal norms of unequal gender roles by "presencing" women not merely as "supplementary"[12] but as a self-evident constituent of the world. In "Die Nonne und das Pferd" (The Nun and the Horse), the nun and the horse reciprocate tasks. The nun aids Esmeraldo, the horse, and in return, he teaches her about the world. This act of sharing and coexisting does not detract from the fact that Esmeraldo is a horse and she is a nun, hence very different. If, as Dagmar Lorenz asserts in reference to Frischmuth's text *Die Frau im Mond* (1982, *The Woman in the Moon*) that "men and women do not form homogeneous groups,"[13] we see here that Frischmuth's characters also retain their differences. Nevertheless, their relationship enhances their different genders and dissimilar social positions. Thus, despite their difference, the male and female figures coexist. Like Frischmuth's characterization of Clarice Lispector's work, Frischmuth's stories do not necessarily portray a "feminine world" ("weibliche Welt," *Traum* 84), but they do present "the world as cofounded" ("die Welt [als] Mitbegründendes," *Traum* 84). And this, in Frischmuth's opinion, constitutes the feminine quality.

This feminine quality can further be seen in "Die Pfändung" (The Retribution) and "Eine Bären-Geschichte" (A Bear Story), both of which depict the interaction between a female and a male. In the former, the animal, this time a fox, is female, and the human is male. In the latter, the animal/human relationship reflects that of "Die Nonne und das Pferd." In both these stories, the characters are thrown together by circumstances but choose to remain together. Even the woman in "Eine Bären- Geschichte," who is forced by the bear to stay, soon loses any desire to flee because the bear allows her to live out her dream (58) of cooperation and mutual respect with a male. Contrasting with what had long been considered innate gender roles, Frischmuth's stories introduce an element of choice into the male/female relationships that demystify "given" gender roles precisely by their fantastic nature.

However, this mutual respect and cooperation only functions outside of the norm — hence, the fantastic world of talking animals. The nun, the bailman, and the woman all leave their societal roles, which dictate their professional and ultimately their gendered behavior. The nun's relationship with Esmeraldo temporarily frees her from war and her passive role in the *Betorden* (order of prayer); the bailman is likewise momentarily liberated from the guilt of his crime of embezzlement; and "Eine Bären-Geschichte" illustrates the temporary freedom of the woman from her abusive husband.

It is only in "Eine Bären-Geschichte," the narrator's last story, that the woman survives the dream that took her out of her restrictive role as wife. Whereas the other characters die because they venture from the correct social path, the woman remains alive despite her transgression. In reference to this element of punishment, Jack Zipes shows that historically one of the social functions of fairy tales and fables was to instruct children to become respectable members of society.[14] Consequently, those characters in traditional fairy tales who veer from the correct path are reprimanded with temporary death, as in the Grimms' tales. By contrast, in Frischmuth's stories, it is precisely when the characters venture from the respectable, yet restrictive, path that they are able to experience difference and their dream of cooperation.

Returning to Frischmuth's notion of a "feminine dream," we see that women are not merely present in these stories, but more significantly, a female figure embodies the dream. Although the woman's dream is destroyed as her husband kills the bear, she retains a memory of it. Indeed, she has literally incorporated the experience since her body has been physically altered from the bear's last hug. Does Frischmuth equate femininity with fantasy as Freud did by labeling women "the dark continent"? I would contend that like the woman in "Eine Bären-Geschichte," Frischmuth shows how all individuals must allow themselves to experience difference in order to acquire difference.[15]

Just as the volume commences with Stanek, so it concludes with "Was Stanek dazu sagt . . ." (What Stanek Says to This . . .). In this story, Stanek discusses the role of the listener. If, as we saw, the main focus was on the narrator and the act of narration in the first story, so too this last story, although in Stanek's words, is about what the female narrator says. The topic of storytelling and imagination remains the impetus for narration.

In order to counteract the narrative silence forced on women, Frischmuth claims that women must begin to write.[16] And one of the consequences of assuming a narrating position is that one reuses already existing signifying complexes. Illustrating the utilization of existing complexes in her lectures, Frischmuth discusses intertextuality and how authors have admitted to borrowing characters as well as patterns. With the appropriation of certain models inevitably comes the possibility of altering those models. In his analysis of fairy tales, Zipes refers to this alteration as "re-utilization," whereby authors consciously change the tales in order to critique social conditions.[17] Alteration is also important for Frischmuth, for it aids her in counteracting the deadly threat of silence to imagination and women. Without change, there would be no chance to reverse the silence.

Her *Mörderische Märchen*, which until now have received very little critical attention, not only have to do with the death of her characters, but they are also about the death or silence of imagination and female voices. Thus, they are "deadly" insofar as they are critical. Just as Frischmuth re-utilized stories in *Amoralische Kinderklapper* (1969, Amoral Children's Rattle) to illustrate how children can alter language, so her *Mörderische Märchen* reuse tales and themes that call into question existing views of gender power relations and bourgeois methods of progress. In doing so, she brings into focus her own female presence as well as the broader importance of fantasy and female voices. To illustrate this thoroughly, I will focus mainly on the tales "Lizzi Lampe zum Tee" (Lizzi Lampe for Tea) and "Das Wasser der Liebe" ("The Waters of Love").[18]

The most obvious assumption of a feminine presence or voice is Frischmuth's "re-utilization" of two well-known Grimms' fairy tales, namely *Little Red Riding Hood* (1812) and *Hansel and Gretel* (1812) for her story "Lizzi Lampe zum Tee," the second story in the volume of tales. By combining the two Grimms' fairy tales, which reinforce strict social mores and values, Frischmuth alters both the social function of these original tales and contemporary gender and sexuality roles. Moreover, her texts expose the process of socialization in traditional fairy tales and criticizes normed gender roles that are depicted in tales that are common cultural icons.[19]

Analogies of the two Grimms' tales abound in Frischmuth's tale. Frischmuth situates Lizzi around the same age as Red Riding Hood. *Blutjung* (very young) as Lizzi is, she cannot yet imagine what dangers lie ahead for her despite the fact that she has heard much "about the dangers and risks of her approaching sex-life" ("über die Gefahren und Risiken des ihr bevorstehenden Geschlechtslebens," 15). Further, the house in the woods that draws her with the scent of food is similar to the house in *Hansel and Gretel.* Like the siblings in the well-known fairy tale, Lizzi exuberantly partakes of the carrots in Mother Wolf's garden, and like the wolf in *Little Red Riding Hood,* Mother Wolf partakes of Lizzi. Additionally, with her uncle aging, Lizzi, like the female characters in the Grimms' tales, is to create a home away from home by abiding by gender roles of passivity and obedience.

In his analysis of literary fairy tales, Zipes identifies certain common characteristics of fairy tales that aid in interpreting how Frischmuth modifies these in her own tale. Contrary to the Grimms' tales, Lizzi Lampe is not sent from home on a task to help the family. In fact, she views her visit to her uncle to be a recreational repose from her parents. Thus, in contrast to Hansel and Gretel and Red Riding Hood, Lizzi has the luxury of spending the summer away from home. Moreover, although Lizzi is familiar with the house she encounters in the woods (a humorous allusion to the readers' inevitable recollection of *Hansel and Gretel*), she cannot recall the information. Frischmuth updates the tale, for Lizzi in fact knows the house "from the commercial about Mother Wolf's sweet, juicy field-grown carrots" ("aus dem Werbespot über Mutter Wolfs süße, saftige Freilandkarotten," 16). The addition of advertisements to her tale suggests how capitalism preys on desires. Advertisements feed on, as Jacques Lacan terms it, a "lack" in the individual.[20] As a result of this emptiness, individual desire can never be satiated. Therefore, advertisements merely function as a promise of fulfillment but can never satisfy an individual completely. The empty promise of the advertisement is indicated by Mother Wolf's consumption of Lizzi, leaving only her hair ribbon behind. Whereas the Grimms' wolf consumes the grandmother and young girl — and they are saved in the end — in Frischmuth's tale, Lizzi is killed.

Moreover, instead of reinforcing and thereby restricting gender definition, Frischmuth's tale "queers"[21] sexual definition. Whereas the wolf in the Grimms' tale plays the role of the grandmother in order to entice the young girl closer to him, Mother Wolf is female. The female personification of the wolf generates tension with her desire. Insofar as Mother Wolf's desire for Lizzi transgresses dictated boundaries of heterosexual desire, her character calls the very nature of gender into question. Complaining to Lizzi that her sons never think of her, Mother Wolf tells Lizzi, "But that they would even once bring home such a charming creature so that I might amuse myself? . . . You know, what I'd like most of all would be to take you into my care indefinitely; it would surely do me good" ("Aber daß sie mir einmal so ein reizendes Geschöpf nach Hause brächten, damit ich mich auch amüsiere? . . . Weißt du, am liebsten würde ich dich zu mir nehmen, für immer, es würde mir sicher guttun," 17). These passages lend themselves to two very different interpretations. While on the one hand, Mother Wolf's comparison of her own amusement to that of her sons' refers to their equal desire to eat her, as the expression *zu mir nehmen* implies, on the other hand, the comparison also suggests sexual desire. Just as her sons desire young girls, so Mother Wolf seems to desire the young girl for herself. Her implied sexual desire for Lizzi shows that desires might be directed to particular objects, but never fixed.

The danger to Lizzi is not only out in the woods, but it also exists right at home. Alluding to the Grimms' wolf, Frischmuth's uncle figure uses all his senses, i.e., sight, hearing, touch, and taste, to recognize Lizzi; however, he cannot control his senses. Thus, Lizzi is not even safe at the home of her uncle. Although her parents show concern by referring to his growing lack of control, they allow her to visit him alone for the summer.

In contrast to the emphasis placed on the uncle's overflowing sensuousness, Frischmuth stresses the restriction of Lizzi's imagination as a result of the prescription of certain sexual roles. She has heard much about the dangers to women, but she is too young to understand the information. Her parents have even warned her to beware of her own uncle. She is constantly receiving sexual input. Therefore, it is only in a dream-state that Lizzi can indulge herself: "Lizzi Lampe felt as if she were in a dream — and lost in that dream" ("Lizzi Lampe kam es vor wie ein Traum, und traumverloren," 15). But Lizzi does not abide by prescribed gender roles. As Mother Wolf says, Lizzi is "not doing [her] sex any honor" ("[macht ihrem] Geschlecht keine Ehre," 18). She has not learned to be passive or obedient.

It, therefore, becomes evident that Lizzi must negotiate her way through many dangers. The danger for Lizzi not only lies in her relationship with men or in her transgression of the correct path, but also in her own indulgence, on the one hand, as a result of her youth and, on the other hand, as a result of the media's elaboration of the vegetables. These two causes of her indulgence are in tension. Lizzi might be young and imaginative, but the text implies that, as a result of the advertisements, her dreams are, to a certain extent, already defined. Lizzi's situation can then be compared to religious indoctrination in *Die Klosterschule* (1968; *The Convent School,* 1993). Mother Wolf will continue to sell her vegetables and prey on the desires of the public by means of the media. Although Mother Wolf's advertisements generate the desire to overindulge, Lizzi's application of this proves deadly, for she transgresses her prescribed gender roles. Frischmuth's revision of the Grimms' tales, then, shows how Lizzi's socialization restricts her imagination and the gender possibilities of femininity.

While not direct revisions of existing tales, the other tales in the volume also stress the need for imagination and female voices. Like the Stanek stories, these concern themselves with the interaction between the sexes. Moreover, like "Lizzi Lampe," "Das Wasser der Liebe," the first tale in this volume, calls attention to the restriction of imagination and of femininity. But whereas the former does this in its revision of existing tales, the latter makes this evident by employing models of sexuality and identity.

With the personification of the fish as female and the mouse as male, Frischmuth not only thematizes gender difference, but also fundamental differences of identity. Thus, what might normally be thought of as animal instinct of a preying-fish and a gerbil is formulated into identity. From the opening of the tale, we gather that the fish has preyed on all the other fish in the tank and longs for another. Her longing to consume another fish is associated with love. Therefore, the fish perceives herself to be engaging in a kind of seduction in order to lure males to her. Through her seduction of the male gerbil, it becomes apparent that the fish objectifies herself to attract the attention of males. She adopts what Silvia Bovenschen calls the "male gaze."[22] In this "game of love" ("Spiel der Liebe," 9), the fish believes the gaze of a male, and her eventual internalization of this gaze by eating him, will give her an identity. However, her belief in the "security within the body" ("Geborgenheit im Leib," 9) misleads her, for "although she had literally incorporated so much, she hardly knew who she was" ("obwohl sie sich so vieles einverleibt hatte, wußte sie kaum, wer sie war," 9). It is her very identification with and incorporation of predominant male images of women that prevent her from gaining insight into herself.

Whereas the identity of the fish corresponds to the gaze of another, the gerbil's identity is attached to a place. He longs for the landscape of his home. His most painful memories originate from this yearning. A distinction is created between *Trennungsschmerz* (pain of separation) and

Sehnsuchtsschmerz (pain of longing) (10). He wishes to return to his origins from which he obtained his identity: "It was the desert in his mind, the desert that establishes views, which triggered the longing for his old homeland — the one that gives names" ("Es war die Wüste in seinem Kopf, die Sinnesart stiftende Wüste, die das Weh nach der älteren Heimat, der namengebenden, auslöste," 10). Driven by the memory of his homeland, the gerbil is unable to curb the feelings of yearning for his old identity. In his homeland, he and objects had names, had meaning. In his present situation, he feels alienated. The hairless skin of the boy, who the animals refer to as "the higher being" ("das höhere Wesen," 10), disgusts him. Sometimes he is allowed brief moments of freedom to run around, but this now makes him afraid, having grown accustomed to running within the small tunnels attached to his cage.

Although it is precisely their imagination that enables the fish and the gerbil to enter into these deadly circumstances in the fish tank, the tale also illustrates how they limit themselves to certain images. For instance, the gerbil "saw the original image from his mind" ("erblickte das Urbild aus seinem Kopf," 11) and ignores all the inconsistencies and warnings that would save his life. Similarly, the fish ignores the difference of the gerbil: "His eyes were small, and sometimes something spilled out, but their gaze was directed at her. That was enough to excite her no end" ("Seine Augen waren zwar klein, und manchmal schwappte etwas darüber hin, jedoch war ihr Blick auf sie gerichtet. Schon das erregte sie maßlos," *Mörderische Märchen* 11). Since his gaze is directed toward her, as she thinks, she believes him to be the one for whom she has longed. This neglect of difference is also seen in "Das Gebrechen der Eule" (The Owl's Affliction).

Because of their insistence on the familiar images of their desire, which makes it impossible for them to see the obvious difference in the situation, they succeed in killing one another. The fish is interested only in drawing him to her and eating him as she has the rest of the fish in her world. The gerbil, on the other hand, is only interested in setting foot on the sand that he sees at the bottom of the tank and which he believes to be the same as his homeland. "It was not enough for him to see this promise of his homeland; he wanted to feel it" ("Es genügte ihm nicht, diese Verheißung von Urheimat zu sehen, er wollte sie fühlen," 12). Consequently, he jumps into the fish tank. And ironically, her desire to have him admire her form also implies eating her. She imagines allowing him "to admire/taste the full length of her" ("von der ganzen Länge zu kosten," 13). Like the figure of Mother Wolf, the fish combines sexuality with consumption. The story leaves readers, like the boy introduced at the end, unclear as to why the fish is bitten, that is, why the gerbil would bite the fish as he is drowning, but we do know that the animals' longings have led to their death.

Similar to her earlier works in which Frischmuth portrays silence as deadly to her female figures, these fairy tales depict how the limitation of imagination threatens the very life of the characters. Therefore, the integration of Frischmuth's earlier "Geschichten für Stanek" with her later work in the *Mörderische Märchen* volume brings into focus consistencies in her work. Although she might not follow a program, we see how Frischmuth continues to pursue sociocultural aspects that underscore the socialization of gender roles, especially those of women. Thus, her claim for a self-evident feminine presence in literature challenges existing roles while simultaneously offering a model to other women writers.

Pennsylvania State University

Notes

1. Barbara Frischmuth, *Mörderische Märchen und andere Erzählungen* (Salzburg: Residenz, 1989; repr., Munich: dtv, 1992). All citations from "Geschichten für Stanek" are from this volume. However, *Geschichten für Stanek* (Berlin: Literarisches Colloquium, 1969) was initially published as its own volume.

2. Frischmuth titles her fifth lecture on poetics "Der weibliche Traum." In order to capture the implications of sociocultural influences, I have chosen to translate the title as "The Feminine Dream." It was published in *Traum der Literatur — Literatur des Traums: Münchner Poetik-Vorlesungen* (Salzburg: Residenz, 1991) 72–89. All German/ English citations from this text will appear marked as *Traum*.

3. In several instances, Frischmuth stresses the pressure placed on women to focus on raising children and not to pursue a career in writing, but for a woman to do both is frowned upon even more (*Traum* 75–77).

4. In her paper "Die vergessenen Mütter: Zur Asymmetrie der Herzen" (The Forgotten Mothers: Of the Asymmetry of Hearts), Renate Möhrmann explores the possible reasons and implications for the absence

of mothers. Presented at a special symposium in honor of Ruth Klüger, UC Irvine, October 21, 1996.

5. For Jacques Derrida, the presence of signifiers reminds one of one's own mortality. See *The Postcard,* trans. Alan Bass (Chicago: U of Chicago P, 1987) 270, 338–368. In Scheherazade's case, the opposite is true. Thus, the absence of signifiers for the female character while necessary for signification also proves ominous.

6. As Derrida asserts, "*Différance* is the non-full, non-simple, structured and differentiating origin of differences. Thus, the name 'origin' no longer suits it." Since origins are eliminated, the dichotomies of inside/outside and presence/absence must be reconceptualized. Through this process of reconceptualization, meanings are freed up from master narratives ("Différance," *Margins of Philosophy,* trans. Alan Bass [Chicago: U of Chicago P, 1982] 11).

7. Jean-François Lyotard, *The Differend: Phrases in Dispute* (Minnesota: U of Minnesota P, 1988) 9.

8. As Frischmuth says, "With tongues hanging out from nightmares of the past, of history, driven into the unknown desert of the future?" ("Mit hängender Zunge, von den Alpträumen der Vergangenheit, der Geschichte, in die unbekannten Wüsten der Zukunft getrieben?" "Vom Genuß der Literatur," *Traum* 11).

9. In "Von den Langexistierenden" (Of the Long-Existing Ones), Frischmuth quotes E. T. A. Hoffmann's fairy tale "Klein Zaches genannt Zinnober" (Little Zaches, Called Zinnober), in which the fairies Isabel and Rosabel observe that if they recede from the consciousness of humans, they will die (*Traum* 56).

10. Ortrud Gutjahr, in "Ironischer Mythos?" *Sehnsucht und Sirene,* ed. Irmgard Roebling (Pfaffenweiler: Centaurus, 1992), observes that the silence of the character of Undine is a consequence of her objectification.

11. Original quote: "Wenn ich mir alles ausgedacht hab', muß ich es wem erzählen, um es selber zu hören. . . . Wenn ich es niemandem erzähle, läßt es mir keine Ruhe, und die Worte kriechen mir wieder ins Ohr und wieder und wieder. Dann kann ich nicht schlafen, und zum Schluß verlier' ich auch noch den Appetit."

12. See Jacques Derrida, *Of Grammatology* (Baltimore: Johns Hopkins UP, 1976) 144.

13. Dagmar Lorenz, "Creativity and Imagination in the Work of Barbara Frischmuth," *Women in German Yearbook* 2, ed. Jeanette Clausen and Sara Friedrichsmeyer (Lincoln: U of Nebraska P, 1986) 43.

14. Jack Zipes, *Fairy Tales and the Art of Subversion* (New York: Routledge, 1983) 9.

15. Frischmuth grapples specifically with the acceptance of difference in *Das Verschwinden des Schattens in der Sonne* (Frankfurt/Main: Suhrkamp, 1973). A translation of this volume is *The Shadow Disappears in the Sun,* trans. Nicholas Meyerhofer (Riverside, CA: Ariadne, 1998).

16. Frischmuth explains that women must simply begin to write ("einfach anfangen, ans Werk gehen!" *Traum* 72).

17. Zipes 64.

18. "Das Wasser der Liebe" was translated as "The Waters of Love" by Gerald Chapple and James B. Lawson in *Dimension*^{2} 4.2 (May 1997): 244–251.

19. While Zipes observes that the Grimms' literary fairy tales dictated specific roles to both boys and girls, Frischmuth concerns herself with the process of restriction of Lizzi's particular gender role.

20. Lacan argues that desire is caused by a wish to fill a lack left as a result of the separation from the other. See Jacques Lacan, *The Four Fundamental Concepts of Psycho-Analysis* (New York: W.W. Norton, 1981) 29.

21. Judith Butler employs this term to characterize practices and terms that remain never fully owned, continually calling into question seemingly fixed, given practices. See Judith Butler, *Bodies That Matter* (New York: Routledge, 1993) 230.

22. Silvia Bovenschen, *Die imaginierte Weiblichkeit* (Frankfurt/Main: Suhrkamp, 1979) 11.

Of Female and Other Dreams: Barbara Frischmuth's *Traum der Literatur — Literatur des Traums*

Robert Weigel

I

In the 1990s, it was the task of the literary critics to put Barbara Frischmuth's work in a broader postmodern context. Thus, her lectures on poetics[1] were analyzed and regarded in terms of postmodern discourse. Following Linda Hutcheon's *A Poetics of Postmodernism* (1988),[2] Paul Michael Lützeler stood at the forefront in examining and underlining these postmodern features with his insightful studies about Frischmuth's lectures on poetics and her Demeter trilogy. In the introduction to his volume *Poetik der Autoren* (1994, Poetics of Authors),[3] he emphasizes the increasing autobiographical character of most poetics in the postmodern condition;[4] contrary to traditional poetics in literary history, which attempted "objectively" to determine aesthetic categories, postmodern poetics are characterized by an intentional subjective orientation.

Aesthetics, however, is also not Barbara Frischmuth's main concern in her lectures on poetics. In her first chapter, entitled "Vom Genuß der Literatur" (About the Enjoyment of Literature), she begins with a report about the joy of reading, which for her is the most important aspect but has been forgotten by many of today's critics. The impressions she delivers are both an invitation and a request for us, the readers, to recall the value of our enjoyment of literature; and Frischmuth illustrates this value with her subjective description of, in a nutshell, her "adventures of reading and writing" *(Lese- und Schreibabenteuer).*[5] Her direct and straightforward style equally invite us to enjoy both reading literature in general and her poetics in particular, i.e., to look forward to and indulge in her *Traum der Literatur — Literatur des Traums* (1991, Dream of Literature — Literature of the Dream). There she touches upon topics such as "intertextuality, dream, mythology, history, femininity,"[6] which can easily be identified as part of postmodern thought.

It may therefore appear as if Frischmuth in many ways were giving up Broch's demand for totality for decentralization, diversification, multiple codification; at the same time, we must not, however, neglect her demand for universality, which, according to Margret Brügmann, is subjectively colored "with emphasis on female experience" ("mit einem Akzent auf weiblicher Erlebniswelt").[7] If literary postmodernism is characterized by skepticism toward utopia — envisioned, for example, by Broch's strive for totality — then Frischmuth distances herself from this antiutopian postmodern approach with her emphasis on the female experience, which is rooted in feminism. Although the latter's questioning of traditional value systems is representative of the postmodern,[8] Frischmuth, both in her last great literary work, the Demeter trilogy, and her follow-up lectures on poetics, stresses her ethics of *Einander-Kind-Sein* (being a child for one another); it is remarkable that she arrives at this conclusion despite (or because) of all uncertainties pointed out by postmodern thought. In this feminine-based ethics, Frischmuth may see a necessity for humanity — similar to Broch's conviction that democracy, threatened by fascism and communism, had to return to politics based on decency; in Margret Brügmann, however, the postulational-ethical character[9] of her ethics causes an unpleasant feeling[10] that, in addition, she is unable to get rid of.

Even if utopias are based on and strive for a more human world, hardly anybody today takes interest in them, despite the fact that the disintegration of values diagnosed by Broch is at an advanced stage; both utopias and their values are, rather, ridiculed and considered naive. Frischmuth's approach might appear naive, since she attempts to replace the decrepit patriarchal society and its power structure, because, as she holds, "interhuman relations have also to be seen in the light of non-biological childhood" ("die Beziehungen zwischen Menschen auch im Sinne von nichtbiologischer Kindschaft zu sehen sind," *Traum* 71). The question arises if it is not her attempt to illustrate ethics through aesthetics, i.e., her combining history, myth, and the present as well as nonsense, reason, and morals, which make her the outstanding author some believe her to be because of her affinity to feminism and the postmodern literary scene in general.

For Frischmuth's ethics to be able to be mother and child for each other at the same time *(Einander-Mutter-und-Kind-sein-dürfen)* does not pursue an ideologically motivated, narrow-minded replacement of the encrusted patriarchal system through matriarchy, which could end in similar conditions. Rather, what she has in mind is coexistence of the two, based upon dialogue. This coincides with her multicultural basic position, also expressed in her essay "Der Blick über den Zaun" (1996; "Looking over the Fence," 1995). There Frischmuth does not go into multicultural discourse per se but rather defines multiculturalism as "suggesting, as far as possible, a trouble-free and peaceful coexistence of as many nations speaking different languages as possible" ("ein möglichst reibungsloses und friedliches Miteinander möglichst vieler Sprachvölker suggeriert werden [soll]")[11] — although, as the Austro-Hungarian example illustrates, reality and history might not always have proven it. But according to Frischmuth, it is language that plays an extraordinary role in exploring the other to understand it; in this context, she refers to her early years of studies in Turkey. (Postmodern) doubts or at least skepticism toward language as the medium for meaningful communication are legitimate and interesting but, as Frischmuth maintains, "if you want to write a novel, you will have to act for a while as if this language you produce is capable of carrying meaning because otherwise you cannot write a novel at all" ("wenn man einen Roman schreiben will, dann muß man für eine gewisse Zeit auch so tun, als ob diese Sprache, die man da entwickelt hat, tragfähig sei, sonst kann man den Roman nicht schreiben").[12]

To her, the novel — or literature in general — seems the most appropriate medium for multicultural exploration and approximation of the other, or the foreign. The above-mentioned look over the fence separating cultures *(Blick über den Kulturzaun)* therefore is an absolute necessity. And the first to risk it[13] can be literature, which for her is a carpet from Tibet with manifold woven stitches *(maschentausend-abertausendweit)* whose threads, however, can be loosened at any time, implying openness, and whose threads like fabric can be drawn in many directions but, it must be noted, not in just any direction because it is about connecting links (*Anknüpfungspunkte, Traum* 8). Frischmuth almost playfully asks the reader to play along with her rather open usage of the term literature; as a reward, she will unroll that carpet from Tibet with its host of patterns and demonstrate that everything is connected and how (*Traum* 7). This includes, on the one hand, its (postmodern) recognition of the important role of intertextuality: Literature develops from literature. Yet, it implies a broader context that transcends the fragmentary post-modern condition. Understanding and, ideally, penetrating different worlds and imaginations can be achieved by looking across cultural fences and grasping the "other" literature, as Frischmuth has exemplified with her novel *Das Verschwinden des Schattens in der Sonne* (1973; *The Shadow Disappears in the Sun*, 1998).[14] "The main mystic idea, the unity of all, is tied to people's inner lives, which, although varying, are the same in all cultures" ("Der Hauptgedanke der Mystik, die All-Einheit, ist an Seelenlagen gebunden, die sich bei Menschen aller Kulturen finden, wenn auch die Formen entsprechend variieren").[15] It represents a human element that transcends all cultural differences, and to grasp it through language is less a task of literature than one of its inherent qualities. This comprehensive humanitarian foundation is representative of Frischmuth's above-mentioned ethics, which, indeed, both desires and demands the same: "the assertion that we should all be able to be children for each other" ("die Vorstellung vom Einander-Kind- Sein-Dürfen," *Traum* 71). By reverting to mythologies or interpreting them anew from a different, feminine perspective, Frischmuth sets out to demonstrate the literary "depiction of possible worlds,"[16] or rather to illustrate her postulate "to identify things possible as doable" ("mögliches als machbar auszuweisen") as she demanded in her essay "Europa, das ich meine" (1996, Europe As I See It).[17]

It becomes obvious that Frischmuth's work cannot easily be classified. Despite apparent affinities to feminism and certain postmodern tendencies, classifying her as either one would be reducing her insistence on her own, personal views. Borges's dictum that "any great and lasting book must be ambiguous"[18] might also hold true in a postmodern context because of its interest in diversification, multiple codifications, as well as irony and parody — elements that also characterize Frischmuth's work; but the ambiguity implied also suggests the ethical, which is made transparent through the aesthetical — the ethical, as we have seen, also being one of Frischmuth's main concerns. Let us therefore have a closer look at some of her chief arguments in her lectures on poetics.

II

The very title of Frischmuth's discourse, *Traum der Literatur — Literatur des Traums*, hints, according to Tunner, at her "asssociative nonmethod" *(assoziative Nicht-Methode)*[19] and appears to be following the idea of "life as a dream," or "dream as life," which in the world of literature was used by Pedro Calderón and Franz Grillparzer (for the German-speaking world). Thus, we are *in medias res.* Frischmuth deals with the influence of the world of dreams on literature and its "style when it is based on dreams" ("Machart, wenn sie aus dem Traum kommt," *Traum* 80); in short, the interdependence and interrelationship of dreams and literary creation. She illustrates the "interwovenness" *(Gestrick)* by exposing us to her personal readings of her favorite authors;[20] for German literature, it is the Romantics Jean Paul and E. T. A. Hoffmann whose sense of humor, the humorous, and the comical do not only relate them to

Lewis Carroll, whom she esteems highly, but also to the dreamlike elements in literature per se: besides pure enjoyment, nonsense, like the dream, represents "something like the spontaneous onslaught of the subconscious . . . and triggers the child in us" ("etwas vom Einbruch des Unbewußten . . . und bedient das Kind in uns," *Traum* 16). In this context, Frischmuth refers to Jean Paul's *Rede des todten Christus vom Weltgebäude herab dass kein Gott sei* (1796, Sermon of the Dead Christ from the Top of the World That There Was No God) and the idea of childhood, which the latter demonstrated "convincingly" as hope "in contrast to power" ("Kindschaft . . . im Gegensatz zu Herrschaft"); she also emphasizes, however, that our overpowering desire "to be somebody's child, a superior's child" ("jemandes Kind zu sein, eines Übermächtigen Kind," *Traum* 23) today can only be countered by attempting "to be a child for one another" ("Einander-Kind-Sein," *Traum* 23), her ethics that she illustrated in her Demeter trilogy. Here and now, Frischmuth, referring to Peter Handke's *Wiederholung* (1986, Repetition), says it is "language and scripture that more and more occupy the position of god, as this place is called in postmetaphysical terminology" ("die Sprache, die Schrift besetzen immer mehr das Gott-Feld, wie der Ort des Erscheinens postmetaphysisch genannt wird," *Traum* 31). This also marks the change from the nineteenth to the twentieth century: with the character of the jolly teacher Wuz (in *Schulmeisterlein Wuz,* 1793) — one of the few literary characters in German literature with the ability to be happy — literature fulfilled its dream of the "coproducing reader" ("vom mitschöpferischen Leser," *Traum* 35). Frischmuth explains that in Handke's *Nachmittag eines Schriftstellers* (1987, Afternoon of a Writer), literature is also perceived as dreaming, but on a different level: "The topic is literature itself" ("Der Gegenstand ist nur mehr sie selbst," *Traum* 35). But these are the dreams of literature per se, and they belong to the complexity of questions (raised by Handke) asking why, what for, and what is literature, which are related to the self-reflexive aspect of today's discussions on literature. Frischmuth points out that it was a female, literary character who gave the most decisive answer to this question: Scheherazade, who tells stories to save her life. Before we discuss female writers and the female dream, I would like to make some general remarks on the issue of the dream and literature, without including the topic "the dream of literature" mentioned above.

Literature's fascination with the world of dreams stems from its mysteriousness and, according to Frischmuth, its blurring of appearance and reality, its distortions and combinations of pictures that do not exist as such in reality but because of their interconnection and interwovenness offer several layers of meaning. In this context, she indirectly puts in relative terms Freud's achievement to bring to public attention both the relationship of dream, childhood, and literature (which many were aware of in the first place) and the verification of the importance of the subconscious for an understanding of matters of the human soul — the meaning of the subconscious coming from the "nonmeaning of the conscious," or its insufficient grasp of reality. Not only do we find an increase in the value of dreams as an independent expression of the subconscious, of the soul — with its "surplus in meaning" — but dreams are also seen as a kind of sign language, the "dream script from which we can decipher the thoughts and ideas of the dream" ("Traumschrift, aus der die Traumgedanken entziffert werden," *Traum* 37). Frischmuth does not go into detail but rather refers to Elisabeth Lenk's criticism of psychoanalysis. The interpretation of dreams does not recognize the dream as an art form with its own, autonomous meaning; thus, it negates the imaginary, the very dimension which Frischmuth is enthusiastic about and inspired by as a model for literary transformation; for her, it symbolizes "a more uninhibited stringing together of the most different ideas while trusting in the interconnection of all things," ("ein unbefangeneres Aneinanderreihen unterschiedlichster Einfälle im Vertrauen darauf, daß alles zusammenhängt" *Traum* 41) like the tapestry of a big carpet. It also means possible "crashes in time and shattering of people" ("Zeitenstürze und Personenzersplitterung," *Traum* 42) as reality today captures it in the handy formula of the loss of identity; and linguistically, it makes possible the word-intensifications *(Wortverdichtungen)* that are derived from the world of dreams and are not only used in the literature of nonsense *(Unsinns-Literatur),* e.g., Lewis Carroll's compounds, which he called *portmanteaus* and which, be it consciously or subconsciously, were also used by James Joyce. If dreams provide this kind of unlimited possibilities, why then, Frischmuth concludes, "shouldn't everything be possible in literature" ("sollte es also nicht auch in der Literatur alles geben können," *Traum* 42–43). She illustrates her point with an example from her own writing and refers to a text that remained fragmented but was added as an appendix to her lectures on poetics. As implied in its title, "Turf-Turkey" (1970, Turf-Turkey),[21] she attempted to amalgamate her real life experiences with both the equestrian sport and its jargon and her academic interest in Turkish culture and language in an associative and dreamlike way, which is characteristic for a literature of the dream.

The most important chapter by far, according to Frischmuth, is, however, the one dealing with the female dream, which she now links with the so-called long-existing ones *(Langexistierenden)* from the fourth chapter; these long-existing elements and figures are often derived from myths and are those characters that survived in people's (literary) subconscious for more than a lifetime. They are Frischmuth's own fairies and kings of the Alps from her novel *Die Mystifikationen der Sophie Silber* (1976, The Mystifications of Sophie Silber) as well as those mythical figures that are the background for her Demeter trilogy mentioned before. In her introduction, Frischmuth talked, as we have seen, about the role of the female narrator in *A Thousand and One Nights* — Scheherazade — about Murasaki Shikibu, who was writing in eleventh-century Japan, and about Hildegard von Bingen. In Shikibu's *Geschichte vom Prinzen Genji* (1000–1010, The Tale of the Prince of Genji), the author creates a kind of "dream man" *(Traummann)* for herself; and although this Japanese author treats her topic ironically at times, Frischmuth considers it "the first great, fulfilled female dream in literature" ("den ersten großen in der Literatur verwirklichten Traum," *Traum* 13).

For Frischmuth, this female dream means "that it must simply be completely natural to be present in literature, not only as a reader but also as an author" ("einfach die Selbstverständlichkeit, in der Literatur anwesend zu sein, nicht nur als Leserin, sondern auch als Schreibende"). The female dream therefore is nothing but "the dream that it must be completely natural" ("der Traum von der Selbstverständlichkeit") to forget history and centuries of male dominance, and to "simply do, to set oneself and therefore set the female" ("einfach tun, einfach sich setzen und somit das Weibliche setzen").[22] In the same context, she inten-tionally distances herself from postmodern discourses about the female, which in most cases simply conclude "that the female does not exist or that it will always be 'the other' or the 'dark continent'" ("daß es das Weibliche nicht gibt oder daß es immer 'das Andere' ist oder der 'dark continent'"); Frischmuth responds with a simple "why" and pleads for self-determination: "What I do as a woman, as an author, that is female."[23]

Without bitterness and ideological inflexibility, Frischmuth attempts to set (anew) the female within the confines of today's possibilities, however not only for the present but also for the future — "a wild future" ("eine wilde Zukunft"), which she is excited about "because everything will be possible" ("in der alles möglich ist," *Traum* 73). Again, we find her trying to realize ideas that from a rational point of view would seem impossible, but that both dream and a literature taking its form and structure from dreaming can put into action, or rather, language. Although she would generally agree with the non-normative judgment that literature is neither male nor female, she likes to put emphasis on differentiating who is writing, because "the way a man or a woman perceives the world is not only influenced by gender but might even be determined by his or her social upbringing" ("die Art, wie einer oder eine die Welt wahrnimmt ist nicht nur sexuell, sondern auch sozial beeinflußt, wenn nicht bestimmt," *Traum* 73). This is followed by a sideswipe against academic feminism and its often obscure position concerning the thousand-year-old prejudice that motherhood and being a mother restrict the creative development of female artists, writers, and scholars. In this context, she also turns against the interdependent adoration of geniuses *(Genie-Kult),* which she identifies as a male pose: the idea of having to sacrifice one's self and give up all mundane "inferior duties" ("niedrige Verpflichtungen," *Traum* 77) — as she claims about Joyce's Stephen Dedalus in *A Portrait of the Artist as a Young Man* (1916) — for something superior, the arts. On the other hand, she is neither categorically for nor against having children; but from a literary point of view, she considers it an enhancement because as a topic, motherhood is as interesting as anything else "because it is part of being human just like dealing with violence, war, and power" ("weil zum Menschsein gehörig, wie die Auseinandersetzung mit Gewalt, Krieg und Herrschaft"); beyond that, motherhood "possibly can set something against power, and that is childhood" ("der Herrschaft möglicherweise sogar etwas entgegensetzen, nämlich Kindschaft," *Traum* 77).

All of this is related to the female dream that it must be completely natural to be part of literature. For Frischmuth, it was Clarice Lispector who was serious about fulfilling this dream: In her writings, the feminine in the world becomes transparent, "transparent in a way that has to be recognized as something that cofounded this world" ("sichtbar in einer Weise, die es als diese Welt *Mit*begründendes erkennen läßt," *Traum* 84) because she includes her circumstances (i.e., motherhood and childhood) in her literary work. Frischmuth thus concludes that "in the last instance, literature is a matter of writing, of finding form, of expressiveness in an existential sense, and its topic is important in so far as it can be dealt with in respect to truth. . . . To do that, however, everything concerning human beings — men, women, and children — must be admitted, equally admitted" (*Traum* 83).[24] Taking this into account, it is much easier to understand Frischmuth's fascination with myth, because, as she points out referring to Robert Ranke-Graves, "the first mystery was motherhood" ("das Urmysterium war die Mutterschaft," *Traum* 64). Her obviously intensive studies of myths made it even clearer to her that myths can hardly ever be interpreted in just one definitive way. Rather, they allow different answers that contribute to the fact that they do carry meaning even today although we have to look for it by ourselves (*Traum* 68). For Frischmuth, however, it is an invitation to continue writing the stories of the myths or to (re)write them anew for the here and now; and a closer examination and analysis of Demeter's story did thus not only reveal its "freshness and literary innocence,"[25] but also the fact that a mother is mourning for her daughter and not her son. Thus, her reworking of this myth in the Demeter trilogy almost automatically leads to the question as to what the meaning of the Eleusinian mysteries, a heavily discussed issue among scholars, is for her. In her trilogy *Herrin der Tiere* (1986, Mistress of the Animals), *Über die Verhältnisse* (1987, Beyond One's Means), *Einander Kind* (1990, One Another's Child), she therefore attempted "to translate for today's world" ("ins Heutige zu übersetzen," *Traum* 68) both the archaic and classical as well as mystical components of the myth.

Here we return to our starting point, Frischmuth's ethical approach: Eleusis for her is also "the mystery of childhood, which perpetually renews itself, the mystery of returning to the womb, of being born again" ("auch das Mysterium der ständig sich erneuernden Kindschaft, des Zurückkehrens in den Schoß, des Wiedergeborenwerdens" *Traum* 71). "Eleusis as the idea of being able to alternately be a child for one another . . . because if we do not alternate in being children and mothers for one another, this mystery will ossify to a symbiosis that will reverse to something pathological" ("Eleusis als die Vorstellung vom Einander-Kind-Sein-Dürfen, abwechselnd . . . wenn wir uns nämlich nicht abwechseln im Einander-Kind-, Einander-Mutter-Sein, erstarrt dieses Geheimnis zur Symbiose, die sich ins Pathologische verkehrt," *Traum* 71) — as it is illustrated by the present time. Frischmuth admits that she arrived at this insight only by contemplating these mysteries. Naturally, names such as Demeter, Kore, etc. only play a rather unimportant "historical-realistical role" ("historisch-realistische Rolle," *Traum* 71); thus, in her construct, Demeter is merely an image, "an intellectual rule of the game, . . . impetus to talk, and borrowing place for characters" ("gedankliche Spielregel, . . . Sprechanstoß und Figurenanleihe," *Traum*

69) and therefore reflects the "state of suspense between dream and reality, between imagination and experience," which, as we may conclude, is also characteristic for the "conditions *[Weltzustand]* of Barbara Frischmuth's characters in general."[26]

Auburn University

Notes

1. Barbara Frischmuth, *Traum der Literatur — Literatur des Traums: Münchner Poetik-Vorlesungen* (Salzburg: Residenz, 1991). In the following cited as *Traum*.

2. Linda Hutcheon, *A Poetics of Postmodernism: History, Theory, Fiction* (New York: Routledge, 1988).

3. Paul Michael Lützeler, ed., *Poetik der Autoren: Beiträge zur deutschsprachigen Gegenwartsliteratur* (Frankfurt/Main: Fischer, 1994).

4. Jean François Lyotard, *The Postmodern Condition: A Report on Knowledge* (Minneapolis: U of Minnesota P, 1984).

5. Erika Tunner, "Plädoyer für die assoziative Nicht-Methode über und zur Literatur zu reden," *Dossier 4: Barbara Frischmuth*, ed. Kurt Bartsch (Graz: Droschl, 1992) 21.

6. Paul Michael Lützeler, "Ethik, Traum und Lust: Barbara Frischmuth, 'Traum der Literatur — Literatur des Traums,'" *Poetik der Autoren* 295.

7. Margret Brügmann, "Traumtänzerin mit Fangnetz: Formen weiblicher Ästhetik bei Barbara Frischmuth," *Dossier 4: Barbara Frischmuth* 24.

8. See Toril Moi, *Sexual/Textual Politics: Feminist Literary Theory* (London: Routledge, 1985). "The principal objective of feminist criticism has always been political: it seeks to expose, not to perpetuate, patriarchal practices" (xiv).

9. Lützeler, "Ethik, Traum und Lust" 295.

10. Brügmann 38.

11. Barbara Frischmuth, "Der Blick über den Zaun," *Schreiben zwischen den Kulturen: Beiträge zur deutschsprachigen Gegenwartsliteratur*, ed. Paul Michael Lützeler (Frankfurt/Main: Fischer, 1996) 23. The translation here is mine. "Der Blick über den Zaun" was translated

into English as "Looking over the Fence" by Lisabeth Hock and published in *Multiculturalism in Contemporary German Literature*, special issue of *World Literature Today* 69.3 (Summer 1995): 459–462.

12. Riki Winter, "Gespräch mit Barbara Frischmuth," *Dossier 4: Barbara Frischmuth* 23.

13. Frischmuth, "Blick" 27.

14. Barbara Frischmuth, *Das Verschwinden des Schattens in der Sonne* (Salzburg: Residenz, 1996). The translation is *The Shadow Disappears in the Sun,* trans. Nicholas Meyerhofer (Riverside, CA: Ariadne, 1998).

15. Frischmuth, "Blick" 22.

16. On this question in general see Arpad Bernath, "Ein Dichter wider Willen? Das Verhältnis von Philosophie und Literatur bei Hermann Broch. Eine Einführung in die Problematik," *Romanstruktur und Menschenrecht bei Hermann Broch*, ed. Hartmut Steinecke und Joseph Strelka (Bern: Lang, 1990) 91.

17. Barbara Frischmuth, "Europa, das ich meine," *Literatur und Kritik* 305/306 (Juli 1996): 55.

18. Jorge Luis Borges, *Labyrinths: Selected Stories & Other Writings* (New York: New Directions, 1964) x.

19. Tunner 19. She also makes clear though that "nonmethod does not imply without method" ("wenn auch Nicht-Methode, so durchaus nicht ohne Methode").

20. Although Frischmuth emphasizes these personal aspects and it was not her intention to compose a scholarly, stringent discourse, I would also like to point out that she is more than familiar with a variety of scientific studies on the subject, e.g., Elisabeth Lenk, *Die unbewußte Gesellschaft* or Jens Heise, *Traumdiskurse*.

21. Barbara Frischmuth, "Turf-Turkey," *manuskripte* 10.29/30 (1970): 55–58; repr. in *Traum der Literatur — Literatur des Traums* 90–114.

22. Qtd. in Winter 11.

23. Qtd. in Winter 11.

24. Original quote: "Literatur ist letztlich eine Sache des Schreibens, der Formfindung, der Ausdrucksfähigkeit im existentiellen Sinn, und ihr Thema ist insofern wichtig, als es sich im Hinblick auf Wahrheit bearbeiten läßt. . . . Dazu muß aber alles, was die Menschen, Männer, Frauen und Kinder betrifft, zugelassen sein, gleichrangig zugelassen sein."

25. Except for Hermann Broch's novel *Der Versucher* (later renamed

Die Verzauberung [1976; *The Spell,* 1987]), which was originally conceived as a Demeter story (and is mentioned by Frischmuth), there is no other literary attempt of relevance.

26. Wolfgang Frühwald, "Der Traum, 'Einander Kind zu sein.' Über die Erzählerin Barbara Frischmuth," afterword to *Traum der Literatur — Literatur des Traums* 118.

Contributors

Peter Arnds has been Assistant Professor of German and Italian at Kansas State University in Manhattan, Kansas, since 1995. He earned his M.A. from Ludwig-Maximilians University in Munich, Germany, in 1990 and his Ph.D. from the University of Toronto in 1995. His teaching and research interests include nineteenth- and twentieth-century German literature. His research focuses on comparative and interdisciplinary issues, specifically on links between literature and philosophy as well as psychology, contemporary German and Austrian literature, and Wilhelm Raabe and his nexus with Victorian writers. Recently, he has published *Wilhelm Raabe's "Der Hungerpastor" and Charles Dickens's "David Copperfield": Intertextuality of Two Bildungsromane* (1997). He is currently working on a project entitled "The Carnivalization of Contemporary Austrian Literature: Venice in Novels by Gerhard Roth, Robert Menasse, and Robert Schindel" and on a book focusing on the conflicting tendencies of unification versus fragmentation in German and Austrian novels after 1989.

Gerald Chapple is Associate Professor of German at McMaster University in Hamilton, Ontario, where he has been teaching German and comparative literature since 1966. He was awarded his Ph.D. in German by Harvard University in 1967. His interests lie in modern German and Austrian literature, translation criticism, and the practice of literary translation. Apart from recent articles on Heinrich Zimmer and Barbara Frischmuth, he has coedited *The Romantic Tradition: German Literature and Music in the Nineteenth Century* (1992) and cotranslated Barbara Frischmuth's *Haschen nach Wind* (1974; *Chasing after the Wind*, 1996), for which he was awarded the Austrian Government Translation Prize. Currently, he is editing a collection of essays, *Towards the Millennium: The Austrian Novel 1971–96* (1998), and he is translating Frischmuth's novel *Hexenherz* together with James B. Lawson.

Rhonda Duffaut has been Assistant Professor of German at The Pennsylvania State University since 1998. She received her M.A. in German literature in 1990 from the University of California at Irvine. After studying at the Albert-Ludwigs University in Freiburg im Breisgau and the University in Göttingen, Germany, she earned her Ph.D. in German from the University of California at Irvine in 1997. Her main teaching and research interests focus on postwar German and Austrian literature with a particular interest in Austrian literature and culture. In addition to an article entitled "Ingeborg Bachmann's Alternative "States": Re-thinking Nationhood in Malina" (1996), she published another essay about "Ingeborg Bachmann's Malina" in 1997. Her other publications include several entries in the *Feminist Encyclopedia of German Literature* about women writers such as Hrotsvit von Gandersheim, Frau Ava, Friederike Mayröcker, Ingeborg Drewitz, Anna Seghers, and Ilse Aichinger. Currently, she is completing a book entitled *Language Games: Discourse, Gender, and Nationality in Ingeborg Bachmann's Prose,* and she is working on a project dealing with constructions of identity in postwar German literature.

Johannes F. Evelein is Assistant Professor of German at Trinity College in Hartford, Connecticut, which he joined in 1997. From 1993 until 1997, he taught German and Dutch language and literature at Brigham Young University. He received his M.A. in German and Scandinavian languages from the University in Groningen, Netherlands, in 1988. His Ph.D. in German was granted in 1993 by the University at Albany (SUNY) in New York. His teaching and research interests involve expressionism, German exile literature, language and identity, literary criticism, and computer-assisted language learning. His publications comprise a book on expressionist drama entitled *August Strindberg und das expressionistische Stationendrama: Eine Formstudie* (1996) and several articles, including "Drama Turning Inward: Strindberg's Station Play and Its Expressionist Continuum" (1998), "Hermann Kesser: Ein Vergessener" (1999 forthcoming), and "Männergedanken? Anna Seghers's Transit and the Portrayal of Gender" (forthcoming). His current projects center on the creative act of writing and an article about Lion Feuchtwanger.

Julie Klassen is Professor of German at Carleton College in Northfield, Minnesota, where she has taught since 1978. She earned both her M.A. in 1967 and her Ph.D. in German in 1973 from Stanford University. Her teaching and research interests include nineteenth- and twentieth-century literature, with an emphasis on drama, realism, literature of the German Democratic Republic, and, most recently, links between literature and ecology. In 1995, she received a prize in the *DAAD/Monatshefte* syllabus contest for her course on the forest in German literature and culture. Her publications include articles on "Reviving Brecht: Transformations, or The Reciprocity of Outward Signs and Inward States" (1994) and "The Rebellion of the Body against the Effect of Ideas: Heiner Müller's

Concept of Tragedy" (1986). A contribution to the Festschrift for Ursula Mahlendorf, "Absent Fathers and Prodigal Sons in Ulrich Plenzdorf's *Die neuen Leiden des jungen W.*" is awaiting publication, and '"Natur als Politik': Carl Amery's Ecological Philosophy" is forthcoming in a 1999 issue of *Colloquia Germanica* devoted to literature and ecology. Her next projects will be a continuation of her work on Frischmuth and Amery.

James B. Lawson is a retired Associate Professor of German at McMaster University in Hamilton, Ontario, where he began teaching in 1955. He received his M.A. degree in German from Johns Hopkins University the same year. His main interests have been in German literature of the nineteenth and twentieth centuries, the German novel, and literary translation. Apart from his translations of Heinrich Zimmer, he has most recently published two translations, together with Gerald Chapple, of prose works by Barbara Frischmuth: *Die Klosterschule* (1968; *The Convent School*, 1993) and *Haschen nach Wind* (1974; *Chasing after the Wind*, 1996). The latter won an Austrian Government Translation Prize. He is currently cotranslating Frischmuth's newest novel, *Die Schrift des Freundes* (1998, The Script of the Friend).

Dagmar C. G. Lorenz is Professor of German at the University of Illinois at Chicago, which she joined in 1998, after having taught at The Ohio State University in Columbus since 1975. After studying at the University of Göttingen in Germany, she received her master's degrees in German and English from the University of Cincinnati in 1971 and 1975, respectively, and her Ph.D. in German from the same institution in 1974. She is the author of *Ilse Aichinger* (1981); *Franz Grillparzer, Dichter des sozialen Konflikts* (1986); *Verfolgung bis zum Massenmord, Diskurse zum Holocaust in deutscher Sprache* (1992); *Insiders and Outsiders, Jewish and Gentile Culture in Germany and Austria* (1994); and *Keepers of the Motherland, German Texts by Jewish Women Writers* (1997). She is coeditor of *Transforming the Center, Eroding the Margins: Essays on Ethnic and Cultural Boundaries in German-Speaking Countries* (1998). Currently, she is preparing an anthology on contemporary Jewish writing in Austria, to be published in 1998.

Jennifer E. Michaels has been teaching at Grinnell College since 1975. She is presently Professor of German and Samuel R. and Marie-Louise Rosenthal Professor of Humanities. She earned an M.A. in German from Edinburgh University in Scotland in 1967 and an M.A. (1971) and Ph.D.

(1975) in German from McGill University in Montreal. Her main teaching and research interests are in twentieth-century German and Austrian literature and culture. Her most recent books are entitled *Franz Jung: Expressionist, Dadaist, Revolutionary, and Outsider* (1988) and *Franz Werfel and the Critics* (1994). In addition, she has published a number of articles on German and Austrian writers, including Theodor Plievier (1992), Felix Mitterer (1995), Elisabeth Reichart (1996), Franz Werfel (1997), and one entitled "Confronting the Past in East and West Germany" (1997). She is currently working on the contemporary Austrian writer Doron Rabinovici.

Renate S. Posthofen is Associate Professor of German in the Department of Languages and Philosophy at Utah State University in Logan, Utah, which she joined in 1995. She studied at the Albert-Ludwigs University in Freiburg im Breisgau, Germany, until 1987 and received her M.A. in German from the University of Pittsburgh in 1984. Her Ph.D. in German was granted in 1993 by the University at Albany (SUNY) in New York. She is the author of *Treibgut: Das vergessene Werk George Saikos* (1995) and a number of articles dealing with contemporary Austrian literature and culture, including such authors as Robert Schindel, Robert Menasse, Ruth Beckermann, Claire Goll, and György Sebestyén. Together with Dagmar C. G. Lorenz, she is the coeditor of *Transforming the Center, Eroding the Margins: Essays on Ethnic and Cultural Boundaries in German-Speaking Countries* (1998). Currently, she is working on a project dealing with issues of gender and identity in texts by contemporary Austrian women writers.

Gisela M. Roethke is Associate Professor and Chair of the German Department at Dickinson College in Carlisle, Pennsylvania, where she started teaching in 1985. After starting her studies at the University of Bonn, Germany, she received her M.A. in foreign languages from Washington State University in 1970 and her Ph.D. in German literature from Harvard University in 1988. Her teaching interests center on German cultural history and women's studies issues. She has been active in the women's studies program at Dickinson College and in the consortium between Dickinson College, Franklin and Marshall, and Gettysburg College. Her most recent book is entitled *Zur Symbolik in Hermann Brochs Werken: Platons Höhlengleichnis als Subtext* (1992). Her publications include articles on Broch, Mathilde Franziska Anneke, and Christa Wolf. She is presently working on a book-length study on the uses of the myth of Demeter and Persephone in twentieth-century German novels.

Monika Shafi is Professor of German at the University of Delaware in the Department of Foreign Languages and Literatures, which she joined in 1986. She studied at the Universities of Aachen and Freiburg, Germany, where she received her M.A. in German and political science in 1979. Upon the completion of her studies at the University of Maryland, she received her Ph.D. in German in 1986. She is the author of *Utopische Entwürfe in der Literatur von Frauen* (1989) and of *Gertrud Kolmar: Eine Einführung in das Werk* (1995). Her publications also include articles on various nineteenth- and twentieth-century German authors, among them Annette von Droste-Hülshoff, Theodor Fontane, Irmgard Keun, Christa Wolf, Ingeborg Drewitz, Jeannette Lander, and Günter Grass. Currently she is working on a book manuscript entitled *Germans as Foreigners — Foreigners as Germans.*

Edith Toegel is Associate Professor of German at Hamilton College in Clinton, New York, which she joined in 1992. After studying in Vienna, Austria, she received her M.A. in English and American literature from Tufts University in 1974. Her Ph.D. in comparative literature was granted by the University of Washington, Seattle in 1980. Her research interests focus on comparative topics as well as American, Austrian, and German literature and culture of the nineteenth and twentieth centuries. She is the author of *Emily Dickinson and Annette von Droste-Hülshoff: Poets as Women* (1982) and *Marie von Ebner-Eschenbach: Leben und Werk* (1997). She also published articles on Margaret Fuller, Bettina von Arnim, George Saiko, Klaus Schlesinger, and Barbara Frischmuth. Currently she is working on the American poet May Sarton.

Gerlinde Ulm Sanford has been at Syracuse University since 1967, where she is Associate Professor of German. She received her Ph.D. in German and French studies from the University of Vienna in 1962. Her current teaching and research interests focus on Goethe and modern Austrian literature. Her publications include *Wörterbuch von Berufsbezeichnungen* (1975), *Konkordanz zu Schillers aesthetischen und philosophischen Schriften* (1977), and an annotated edition of *Andreas Gryphius' Aemilius Paulus Papinianus* (1978) as well as articles on Alois Brandstetter, Felix Mitterer, Werner Schwab, Robert Schindel, and Peter Turrini. By the end of 1998, she will have completed a book that examines Goethe's *West-östlicher Divan* as guide to old age and aging and a longer article on the social conditions of old age depicted in selected plays by Felix Mitterer.

Ingo R. Stoehr has been Instructor of English and German at Kilgore College, Texas, since 1991. He earned his *Erstes Staatsexamen* (equiv. M.A.) in English and German from Johannes-Gutenberg University in Mainz, Germany, and, after having taught at the Odenwaldschule from 1981 to 1983, his *Zweites Staatsexamen* (equiv. M.T.A.). He continued his studies at the University of Illinois at Urbana-Champaign and then at the University of Texas at Austin, where he received his Ph.D. in 1989 from the Department of Germanic Languages. He is the author of *Beyond the Zeus Principle: Two Hundred Years of Love and Politics in the Novel* (1993). He has coedited *Dimensions: A. Leslie Willson & Contemporary German Arts and Letters* (with Peter Pabisch, 1993) and edited *The Ethics of Popular Culture: From Frankenstein to Cyberculture* (1995). In addition, he has published articles in linguistics, translation theory, and twentieth-century German literature as well as literary translations. Since 1994, he has been the editor of *Dimension²: Contemporary German-Language Literature*, a bilingual literary magazine. His next book project will be titled *History of Twentieth-Century German Literature.*

Robert Weigel has been Associate Professor of German in the Department of Foreign Languages and Literatures at Auburn University since 1993. After having studied at the Bavarian Julius-Maximilians University in Würzburg, Germany, he pursued his graduate education at the University at Albany (SUNY) in New York, where he received his M.A. in history. Upon completion of his doctoral studies, he was granted his Ph.D. in German in 1992 by the University at Albany (SUNY) in New York. His general research interests involve Austrian and Jewish aspects in literature, the experience of exile, and contemporary Austrian literature and culture. His publications include a book on Hermann Broch's ideas on mass psychology entitled *Zur geistigen Einheit von Hermann Brochs Werk* (1994) and articles relating to the works of Elias Canetti, Stefan Zweig, Franz Werfel, Arthur Schnitzler, Franz Grillparzer, and contemporary Austrian authors such as György Sebestyén, Karl Lubomirski, and Matthias Mander.

Index

Titles by
Barbara Frischmuth
published by
ARIADNE PRESS

http://ariadnepress.com

Chasing after the Wind
Four Stories
Translated by Gerald Chapple
and James B. Lawson
Afterword by Gerald Chapple
Contents:
Let It Be
Tree of the Forgotten Dog
Chasing after the Wind
Bad Timing
ISBN 0-929497-039-6
1996

The Convent School
Translated by Gerald Chapple
and James B. Lawson
Introduction by Gerald Chapple
ISBN 0-929497-75-9
1994

The Shadow Disappears in the Sun
Translated and with an Afterword
by Nicholas J. Meyerhofer
ISBN 1-57241-059-0
1998